A CONCISE ENCYCLOPEDIA *of* ISLAM

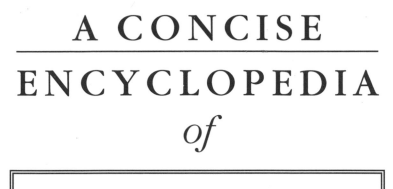

OTHER BOOKS IN THE SAME SERIES

A Concise Encyclopedia of Judaism, Dan Cohn-Sherbok, ISBN 1–85168–176–0
A Concise Encyclopedia of Hinduism, Klaus K. Klostermaier, ISBN 1–85168–175–2
A Concise Encyclopedia of Christianity, Geoffrey Parrinder, ISBN 1–85168–174–4
A Concise Encyclopedia of Buddhism, John Powers, ISBN 1–85168–233–3
A Concise Encyclopedia of the Bahá'í Faith, Peter Smith, ISBN 1–85168–184–1

OTHER BOOKS ON ISLAM PUBLISHED BY ONEWORLD

Approaches to Islam in Religious Studies, Richard C. Martin, ISBN 1–85168–268–6
Averroes: His Life, Works and Influence, Majid Fakhry, ISBN 1–85168–269–4
The Faith and Practice of Al-Ghazálí, William Montgomery Watt, ISBN 1–85168–062–4
Faith and Reason in Islam: Averroes' Exposition of Religious Arguments, translated by Ibrahim Najjar, ISBN 1–85168–263–5
Islam and the West, Norman Daniel, ISBN 1–85168–129–9
Islam: A Short History, William Montgomery Watt, ISBN 1–85168–205–8
Islam: A Short Introduction, Abdulkader Tayob, ISBN 1–85168–192–2
Islamic Philosophy, Theology and Mysticism: A Short Introduction, Majid Fakhry, ISBN 1–85168–252–X
The Legacy of Arab-Islam in Africa: A Quest for Inter-religious Dialogue, John Alembillah Azumah, ISBN 1–85168–273–2
The Mantle of the Prophet, Roy Mottahedeh, ISBN 1–85168–234–1
Muhammad: A Short Biography, Martin Forward, ISBN 1–85168–131–0
Muslim Women Mystics: The Life and Work of Rabiᶜa and other Women Mystics in Islam, Margaret Smith, ISBN 1–85168–250–3
On Being a Muslim: Finding a Religious Path in the World Today, Farid Esack, ISBN 1–85168–146–9
The Qur'an and its Exegesis, Helmut Gätje, ISBN 1–85168–118–3
Revival and Reform in Islam, Fazlur Rahman, ISBN 1–85168–204–X
Speaking in God's Name: Islamic Law, Authority and Women, Khaled Abou El-Fadl, ISBN 1–85168–262–7
What Muslims Believe, John Bowker, ISBN 1–85168–169–8

A CONCISE ENCYCLOPEDIA *of* ISLAM

GORDON D. NEWBY

ONEWORLD
OXFORD

A CONCISE ENCYCLOPEDIA OF ISLAM

Oneworld Publications
(Sales and Editorial)
185 Banbury Road
Oxford OX2 7AR
England
www.oneworld-publications.com

Reprinted 2004

A CIP record for this title is available
from the British Library

ISBN 1-85168-295-3

Cover design by Design Deluxe
Typeset by LaserScript, Mitcham, UK
Printed and bound in India by Thomson Press Ltd

Contents

Preface and acknowledgments

Writing about Islam in a single volume is a daunting task, but it is one that I happily took on because of my longstanding desire to help more people in the English-speaking world understand and appreciate this religion. Islam is not only a world religion, claiming about a fifth of the world's population, it is also a system of culture and politics. Muslims are found in most countries of the world, speaking most of the world's languages. There is no central authority that can speak for all Muslims, and there is no single way to be a Muslim. It is, like the other great religions of the world, diverse, dynamic, and difficult to define in only a few words, terms, and entries.

This *Concise Encyclopedia of Islam* is meant to represent Islam's diversity and offer the reader a short definition of major terms and introduce major figures. In writing this *Encyclopedia*, I have chosen to use the distinction that was made by the late M.G.S. Hodgson in his *Venture of Islam*, between those subjects that are "Islamic" and those that are, in his word, "Islamicate." By "Islamic," he meant those subjects that have to do with the religion, and by "Islamicate," he meant those subjects that are products of the culture that Muslims, and Jews, Christians, Zoroastrians, Hindus, and others living under Islam, have produced. We speak of "Islamic science," meaning the scientific advances during the time of the Western Middle Ages, but those scientific advances were a product of the interaction of Jews and Christians as well as Muslims living in Islamic countries. The religion of Islam contributed to the development of that and other branches of learning, because Muslim rulers chose to sponsor learning as part of their vision of themselves as Muslims. I have chosen to leave the political and cultural material to others. This volume contains terms that are related to Islam as a religious system.

As I mentioned, Islam is a diverse and dynamic religion. No Muslim will accept everything that I have presented in this volume as Islamic. In attempting to represent Islam's diversity, I have tried to include material that tells the story of the major groups within Islam. This means that the views of the Shîʿî as well as the Sunnî are included. My choice to do this is, in part, a corrective. Works of this kind have often been heavily weighted toward the Sunnî perspective. The reasons for this are complicated, but it had much to do with the history of how the West came to learn about Islam and the desire of Western Orientalist writers to essentialize Islam and not acknowledge the nuances and differences that they did in Western Christianity. Recognizing complexity in someone else or in another religious system is an important step toward understanding that religion as well as one's own.

This single volume is not intended to be the end and the answer to questions about Islam, but, rather, a beginning. At the end of the volume, the reader will find a bibliography listing additional English-language reference works, monographs, and introductory texts. I strongly urge readers to seek out as many of those texts as possible. Many of the references should be available in local libraries. There is also a wealth of information about Islam on the Internet. Many basic Islamic texts are available in English translation on line. I have listed a few of the gateway URLs that should serve as a start into the rapidly growing world of the Islamic Internet. One caution, however, is that the Internet is rapidly changing, with many varied opinions expressed in the sites. Remember that the many different opinions reflect the great diversity within the religion called Islam. There is also a time-line of major dates and events in Islamic history to assist the reader in placing the information in the *Encyclopedia* in historical perspective.

The terms in the *Encyclopedia* are transliterated from their appropriate Islamic languages. The diacritic marks on the terms represent the consonants and vowels in the original language. This is meant to be an aid to the student of those languages in locating the term in an appropriate language dictionary or encyclopedia. Without the diacritics, it is difficult, particularly for the beginner in the language, to distinguish what appear to be homonyms. For the reader who doesn't know the Islamic languages, the pronunciation guide that follows this preface will assist in a reasonable approximation of the sound of the terms to be able to talk with those who do know how to pronounce them.

The information for this volume has been drawn from many different sources. In the bibliography, I have left out the many specialty monographs and other works for lack of space. Additionally, I have been aided by many individuals who have patiently read my drafts and offered helpful suggestions. I would like to thank my colleagues at Emory University in particular. Profs. Mahmoud Al-Batal, Kristen Brustad, Shalom Goldman, Frank Lewis, Richard Martin, Laurie Patton, Devin Stewart, and Vernon Robbins have each strengthened my efforts. The best parts of this volume are to their credit, and the deficiencies are mine. I would also like to thank the editors of Oneworld Publications for the opportunity to write this volume. It has provided me a wonderfully concentrated time to review the Islamic religious scene and the years of study I have devoted to Islam, and the opportunity has been personally enriching. Finally, I wish to express my thanks to my wife, Wendy. Her support, encouragement, and forbearance have kept me well and happily throughout this project.

The publisher and author would like to thank the following organizations and individuals for providing the pictures reproduced in this volume.

Pages 46, 47, 48, 54, 61, 66, 76, 134, 138, 141, 154, 189, 208 © Peter Sanders Photography Ltd. Pages 19, 32, 104, 127, 188, 201 © D.P. Brookshaw. Pages 72, 99, 101, 144, 171, 178, 210 © Aga Khan Trust for Culture. Page 170 from the collection of Prince and Princess Sadruddin Aga Khan. Map, page xii, by Jillian Luff, Mapgrafix. Cover photograph (far right) of children, Jakarta, Istiqlal Mosque – Religious Education; Mock Hajj © Mark Henley/Impact. Cover photograph (center) interior of the prayer hall, Islamic Cultural Center, New York © Omar Khalidi.

Transliteration and pronunciation

Many of the terms in this *Concise Encyclopedia* are transliterated from their original scripts in the Islamic languages of Arabic, Persian, Turkish, or Urdu. The system listed below will assist those who wish to identify the correct term in the original language. The pronunciation guide will assist in approximating the sound of the words. The system of transliteration is that used in many scholarly publications on Islam. The order of the list is the order of the Arabic alphabet.

Consonants

Arabic letter	Symbol	Approximate pronunciation
أ	ᵓ	glottal stop
ب	b	English b
ت	t	English t
ث	th	English th as in thin
ج	j	English j
ح	ḥ	guttural or pharyngeal h
خ	kh	German ch
د	d	English d
ذ	dh	English th as in this
ر	r	rolled or trilled r
ز	z	English z
س	s	unvoiced s as in sit, this
ش	sh	English sh
ص	ṣ	velar or emphatic s
ض	ḍ	velar or emphatic d
ط	ṭ	velar or emphatic t
ظ	ẓ	velar or emphatic voiced th as in this
ع	ᶜ	pharyngeal scrape; often pronounced like glottal stop

Arabic letter	Symbol	Approximate pronunciation
غ	gh	voiced kh
ف	f	English f
ق	q	uvular or guttural k
ل	l	English l as in list
م	m	English m
ن	n	English n
ه	h	English h
و	w	English w
ى	y	English y as in yes

Vowels

ـَ	a	short a as in bat, sat
ـِ	i	short i as in sit
ـُ	u	short u as in full
ـَا	â	long a as in father but held longer
ـِي	î	long i as in machine but held longer
ـُو	û	long u as in rule but held longer
ـَوْ	aw	diphthong as in English cow
ـَيْ	ay	diphthong as in aisle

The final feminine singular ending in Arabic, -at, is transliterated as -ah unless the word is in a compound with a following Arabic word, when it is transliterated as -at. The definite article al- is normally not capitalized, even at the beginning of a sentence and its consonant, l, assimilates to the letters t, th, d, dh, r, z, s, sh, ṣ, ḍ, ṭ, ẓ, n, as in the example *ash-Shams* (Arabic: the sun). This system of transliterating the definite article replicates the pronunciation rather than the system of writing to help the reader communicate the term orally.

Terms transliterated from Persian, Turkish, and Urdu generally follow the Arabic pattern, although the pronunciation might not be fully represented. For a full discussion of various systems of transliteration and the benefits of each system, see M.G.S. Hodgson, *The Venture of Islam*, vol. 1, Chicago: University of Chicago Press, 1974, pp. 8–16.

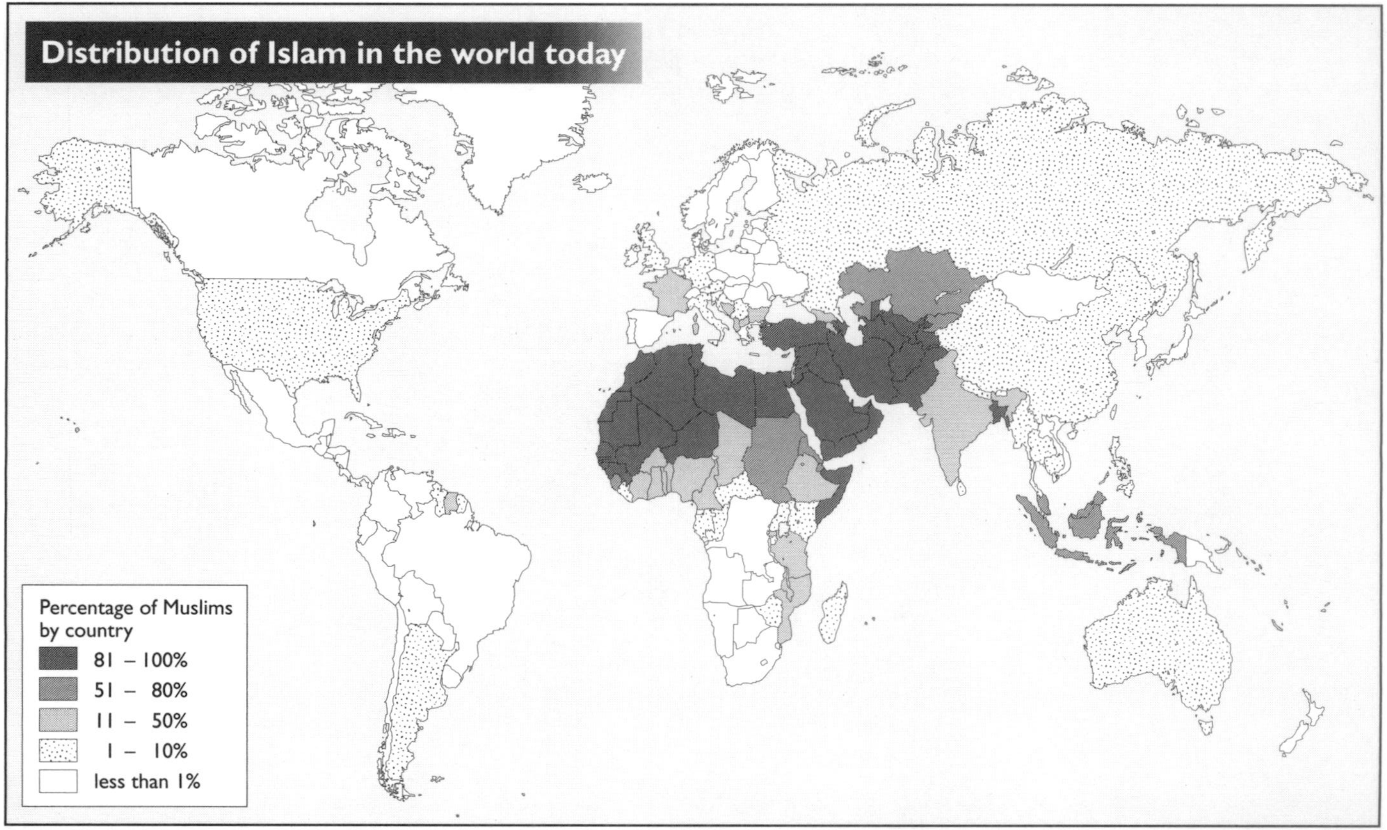
Distribution of Islam in the world today
Percentage of Muslims by country
81 – 100%
51 – 80%
11 – 50%
1 – 10%
less than 1%

Introduction

Seek Knowledge as far as China
(*ḥadîth* of the Prophet)

Geography

Islam is a world religion, by which we usually mean that it is found in most major places and among most peoples throughout the world. Like other world religions, Islam has its own particular geography. When we speak of the geography of a world religion like Islam, we often mean two things. First, we mean, where do we find the religion's followers? Where did the religion start, and how has it spread? These are historical and physical questions. Second, we mean, how is the world divided on the spiritual map of the religion's believers? What land is sacred and what is not? These are questions of sacred geography. Since the physical and sacred realms interact, we need to ask both sets of questions.

Islam, like Judaism and Christianity, began in the Middle East. Today, it ranks behind only Buddhism and Christianity as the most populous religion in the world, with one-fifth of all humanity professing the faith. A common impression is that Islam is an Arab religion, but less than twenty percent of all Muslims are Arabs. The largest Muslim country in the world is Indonesia, and there are more Muslims in South Asia (India, Pakistan, and Bangladesh) than there are in the Arab Middle East. There are Muslims throughout Europe, Asia, Africa, and the Americas. It is often thought to be a religion of nomads, but well over half of all Muslims live in cities. It is a religion that continues to attract more members. In North America, Islam is the fastest-growing religion, with more members than either Judaism or the Episcopalians. The classical division between the *dâr al-islâm*, the "abode of Islam," and the rest of the world is no longer a useful geographic distinction. While Islam's spiritual borders remain, Muslims live side by side with Jews, Christians, Buddhists, Hindus, and others throughout the world. Muslims live in most countries, whether there is an Islamic government or not.

Since Islam's earliest expansion out of Arabia, it has been a religion of many ethnic, racial, and linguistic groups. The majority of Muslims in the world speak a native language other than Arabic, but the Arabic language and some aspects of Arab culture bind Muslims together. The spiritual center of Islamic sacred geography is Mecca, with the Kaʿbah and other shrines holy to all the world's Muslims. Ibrâhîm (Abraham) and Adam allegedly prayed there to Allâh (God). Muḥammad reestablished God's worship there, so many Muslims face Mecca five times a day in prayer and, if they can, journey to this center of the earth once in their lives for *ḥajj* (pilgrimage). The sacred scripture of Islam, the Qurʾân, is written in Arabic, and is recited daily in Arabic by Muslims in prayer. Arabia looms large in the spiritual imaginations of Muslims around the world.

Another important center of the Islamic sacred world is al-Quds (Jerusalem). Muslims believe that Muḥammad made his *isrâʾ* (night journey) from Mecca to Jerusalem and went from there to heaven. In Islamic cosmology, just as in Judaism and Christianity, Jerusalem is the place closest to heaven. Jerusalem is regarded by many Muslims as one of the three cities to which one can make pilgrimage, the others being Mecca and Madînah. Islamic worship was established at the *qubbat aṣ-ṣakhrah*, the Dome of the Rock, as soon as Muslims entered the city in the seventh century, and Muslims have included the city as a place of visitation and as a place to live ever since.

Mosques feature in Islam's sacred landscape, and wherever Muslims live, they build places of worship that are pointed toward the sacred center of Mecca. Schools, fountains, hospitals, and other public works are also products of the Islamic impulse to improve this world through pious constructions, and in these the sacred and profane realms are blended. Tombs of saints, *walî*s, are also found throughout the world where Muslims live. Some are small and plain; others are elaborate and decorated with the finest examples of Islamic art, but all mark out important points on the Islamic sacred map of the world.

An important feature of the world of Islam is that in the daily lives of Muslims, sacred space is portable. A Muslim should perform *ṣalât*, pray, five times during the day, and it can be anywhere. Classrooms, offices, and factories, as well as mosques, are places for *ṣalât*. Indeed, anyplace that can be made ritually pure, often by a prayer carpet, can serve as a location for *ṣalât*. With the potential for nearly a billion Muslims around the world to face Mecca in prayer each day, there is a web of sacred Muslim space that encompasses the earth.

Islam and Other Religions

Islam is the youngest of the three monotheistic world religions, with Muḥammad coming after the prophets of Judaism and Christianity. For Muslims, Islam is the completion and perfection of a process of revelation that started with Adam, the first human, and ends with Muḥammad, the "Seal of the Prophets." History is divided into two periods: the time of God's active revelation through His prophets, and the time from the revelation of the Qur'ân to the time when the world will be judged, the *yawm ad-dîn* (Day of Judgment). Judaism and Christianity have a special place in Islam. Jews and Christians are "People of Scripture," *ahl al-kitâb*, and have a special legal standing in Islamic law, or *sharî'ah*. Other religions, such as the Sabaeans and sometimes Hindus, have been included in this category, and in various historical periods they have been partners in shaping and developing Islamic civilization. Islam is a proselytizing religion. Muslims are commanded to bring God's message to all the peoples of the earth and to make the world a better, more moral place. Muslim missionaries are found throughout the world working on the twin goals of converting others to Islam and promoting Islamic values.

Muslim Scripture

According to the *sîrah*, the biography of Muḥammad, God sent the first revelation to His Prophet when Muḥammad was forty years of age. From then until his death in 632 C.E., some twenty-two years later, the Qur'ân, as the revelation is called, came to the Prophet in bits and pieces through the intermediary of the angel Jibrîl (Gabriel). Today, it exists as a book with 114 *sûrahs*, chapters, a little shorter in length than the Christian New Testament. The chapters and verses, *'âyahs*, are not in the order of revelation, and to many outside Islam, the juxtaposition seems to be disjointed and difficult to understand at first reading. The Qur'ân differs from Jewish and Christian scripture in that it is not a narrative history, a series of letters, or a biography of Muḥammad. It contains admonitions, rules, promises, references to past revelations, prayers, and warnings about the coming *yawm ad-dîn*. For those who know Arabic, for whom the Qur'ân is part of their daily prayers, who live surrounded by the sights and sounds of its words, the revelation has a rich texture of meanings interwoven with Muslim life and history. The revelation is the foundation of Islam's aesthetic and daily life, and is part of the everyday speech of Muslims in many languages around the world. Points are made and wisdom is expressed by reference to passages from the Qur'ân. For many Muslims, the ideal is to memorize the Qur'ân, thus internalizing the Word of God.

An axiom among Muslims is that the Qur'ân cannot be translated into another language and remain the Qur'ân, nor can it be imitated. A large part of it is written in *saj*ʿ (rhymed prose), and it is rich with rhetorical devices, like alliteration and paronomasia, which cannot be replicated in other languages and carry the same meaning and tone. All translations are commentaries (*tafsîr*). There is a rich, living tradition of commenting on the Qur'ân, and reading just a few of them shows the reader the multiple levels of meaning contained even in a single Qur'ânic verse. The Qur'ân in Arabic is the carrier of Islamic culture.

In addition to the Qur'ân, the life of the Prophet Muḥammad is regarded by some Muslims as almost sacred, and by many more as an important source of how to live. The *sunnah* of the Prophet, Muḥammad's life as exemplar, is a model that Muslims try to follow. His life and actions guided the formation of some aspects of *sharîʿah* and Islamic practices of personal piety. Muslims may, for example, eat honey or cleanse their teeth, because the Prophet did so. They will go on *ḥajj*, performing the rite in a way similar to the way he did it in his Farewell Pilgrimage at the end of his life. And they will strive to govern their communities in imitation of the society that Muḥammad and his Companions (*ṣaḥâbah*) founded at Madînah. The Qur'ân and the *sunnah* together form the basis for a complete Muslim life.

Pillars of Islam

Early in the history of Islam, scholars and Qur'ânic commentators distilled five basic activities and beliefs that are fundamental to all Muslims. These are known as the *arkân al-islâm*, the Pillars of Islam. Each of these five actions requires an internal spiritual commitment and an external sign of the intent (*niyyah*) as well as the faithful completion of the action, showing Islam's medial position between the extremes of orthodoxy and orthopraxy. Fundamental to this list is the balance between faith and action. A Muslim starts with the belief in one God, called Allâh in Arabic. God is the source of all there is in the universe, and so all activity, spiritual and physical, is in relationship to God. Muslims are asked to be thankful to God, praise Him, and obey His commands. Additionally, since all humans and other creatures are part of God's creation, each Muslim has an obligation to help take care of that creation. To be a Muslim is to have an individual responsibility to God and a social responsibility to Muslims and other human beings in the world.

The first on the list is the declaration of faith, the *shahâdah*, which also means witnessing. The declaration that there is no deity except Allâh, and that Muḥammad is the Prophet of Allâh is part of each of the five daily prayers and is heard from minarets in the call to prayer. Pronouncing the *shahâdah* with the intent to convert and in front of witnesses is sufficient to make one a Muslim in the eyes of most Islamic communities.

When one has become a Muslim, one is obligated to perform five ritual prayers (*ṣalât*) a day: the dawn prayer, the noon prayer, the afternoon prayer, the sunset prayer, and the night prayer. These prayers are in addition to any individual supplications, *du'â'*, that the believer may wish to make at any time.

The third duty is to give charity, *zakât*. Social welfare is one of the hallmarks of Islam, and Muslims are obligated to take care of those less fortunate than themselves. In some Muslim countries, the collection and distribution of alms is a function of the state.

Once each year, many Muslims perform a fast, *ṣawm*, each day for the month of Ramaḍân, during the daylight hours only. It is a total abstinence fast, and, when it is broken, Muslims are enjoined to eat the good things that God has given. Muslims should not fast if their health will be injured, if they are pregnant, or if they are traveling. Islam encourages Muslims to care for their bodies as well as their souls.

Once during a Muslim's lifetime, if physically and financially able, the *ḥajj* should be performed. This ritual brings Muslims from all over the world together in Mecca for rites around the Ka'bah, and binds all Muslims, whether on *ḥajj* or not, in celebration of acts performed by Muḥammad and Ibrâhîm before him.

Over time, some groups have added to or modified this list, with *jihâd* as the most common addition. *Jihâd* means "striving" or "making an effort," and each of the actions listed above requires such personal effort. In cases when *jihâd* is applied to political and military situations, usually called "holy war," it is a community obligation and not an individual one, and it is limited by complex rules and regulations, just as "holy war" is limited in Judaism and Christianity.

History

Just as with the geography of Islam, the history of Islam may be viewed from several vantage points. In traditional world history, Islam begins with the revelation to Muḥammad in 610 C.E., when he was forty years of age. The official Muslim era begins in 622 C.E. with the *hijrah*, the establishment of the community in the Arabian city of Madînah. This is the beginning of the Muslim calendar, and all preceding is counted as the period of the *jâhiliyyah*, the age of "ignorance." Another way to talk about the beginning of Islam is to chart it from God's first revelation to humankind, to the prophet Adam. From this perspective, Islam is the oldest of all the religions of the world.

When Muḥammad was born in Mecca in 570 C.E., Arabia was on the edge of the great Mediterranean and Middle Eastern cultures, but it was in the center of a competition between the Roman and Persian empires. This brought soldiers into Arabia who were also missionaries for Judaism and several varieties of Christianity. As a result, most Arabs had a sophisticated knowledge of the two monotheistic religions available to them. Some had converted to either Judaism or Christianity. They also had their own elaborate variety of polytheism and worshiped hundreds of deities, often in the form of stone idols that they carried with them or that were placed in Arabia's central shrine, the Kaʿbah in Mecca.

Muḥammad was born into the Hâshimites, a poor clan of Mecca's dominant tribe, the Quraysh. He was orphaned early, with his father dying before he was born, and his mother afterwards. From humble beginnings, he soon distinguished himself as an honest, trustworthy businessman engaged in the town's trade, international commerce. When he married a wealthy widow, Khadîjah, for whom he had worked as a trade agent, he had enough resources to be able to take time to contemplate his rise in fortune. We are told that he went every year into the mountains above Mecca for a spiritual retreat, gave charity to the poor, and practiced devotional exercises. During one of these retreats, when Muḥammad was forty years of age, during the month of Ramaḍân, the angel Jibrîl visited him and brought him the first five verses of the ninety-sixth chapter of the Qurʾân as the first of a series of revelations from Allâh.

For the next two years, Muḥammad kept his mission within his family, receiving support from Khadîjah. He continued to receive revelations, and he came to understand that they were part of God's Scripture and that he had been selected by God as a prophet. When he made his mission public, calling on his fellow Meccans to turn toward Allâh, only a few joined him. Many others felt threatened by his message of reforming the ills of society and were hostile to his attacks on polytheism. Mecca was an important polytheistic religious center, and the city's religious practices were tightly connected to its economy. In the ten years that comprised the first part of his mission, many staunch followers joined him, but the leaders in Mecca plotted to kill him.

In 622 C.E., Muḥammad sent a band of his followers from Mecca to the town of Madînah, where they were welcomed by some of the prominent members of the tribes of the ʾAws and the Khazraj, the tribes that were to be known as the *anṣâr* (allies). Muḥammad, accompanied by his Companion Abû Bakr, made their way to Madînah, pursued by hostile Meccans. When they arrived, Muḥammad negotiated a treaty with all the inhabitants of the city, both Jews and polytheistic Arabs, that put him in the center of resolving all disputes. This so-called "Constitution of Madînah" gave Muslims and Jews alike a formal membership in the nascent Muslim community, and would serve as a model for future relations between Muslims and the *ahl al-kitâb*. In the next few years, most of the basic elements of Islam were established publicly. Prayer was instituted, fasting was regulated, and the basic rules for individual and communal behavior were set forth, both in the ongoing revelations of the Qur'ân and in the words and deeds of the Prophet.

From the very beginning of the *hijrah*, the polytheistic Meccans tried to stop Muḥammad and his new religion. They pursued Muḥammad and Abû Bakr as they left Mecca. They sent military expeditions against the community in Madînah, and they tried to build a political and military coalition of the tribes in the Ḥijâz against the Muslims. The Muslims fought back, winning a first victory at the battle of Badr, a draw at the battle of Uḥud, and another series of victories that culminated in a negotiated defeat of the Meccan coalition and the triumphal entrance of the Muslims into Mecca for a cleansing of the Kaʿbah of the polytheistic images and the establishment of Muslim worship. When Muḥammad died in 10/632, most of the tribes in Arabia are reported to have submitted to Islam.

With the death of Muḥammad, we are presented with two different ways of relating Islamic history. Since Muḥammad was the last of the line of God's prophets, the issue of who was to lead the Muslim community arose. There were those who had expected that the world would end before Muḥammad's death and were surprised that it had not. There were those who expected that the community would be led by someone chosen from among those that had the "best" genealogy. Shî'î Muslims contend that Muḥammad appointed his cousin and son-in-law, 'Alî b. Abî Ṭâlib, as his successor at Ghadîr Khumm and that 'Alî was to be both a spiritual and political leader of the community. From 'Alî and Muḥammad's daughter, Fâṭimah, a line of *Imâms* carried on the leadership of the Shî'î community as members of the *ahl al-bayt*, the household of the Prophet, giving them absolute legitimacy in Shî'î eyes.

The Sunnî view of succession differs from the Shî'î view. From this perspective, Muḥammad was the last of the prophets and had no successor to his spiritual mission. As for the political leadership of the community, they chose Muḥammad's closest advisor and companion, his father-in-law, Abû Bakr, as the caliph. According to this view, the Arab Muslims swore allegiance to Abû Bakr in much the same way that leaders were chosen among some bedouin tribes in the pre-Islamic period. Abû Bakr ruled for two years, meeting the challenges of those tribes in Arabia that left the Muslim community with the death of Muḥammad. The military organization that the first caliph constructed carried Islam outside Arabia, following the explicit intentions of Muḥammad himself. Abû Bakr, in part following the model of the Prophet, appointed no successor, and another close companion and father-in-law of Muḥammad was chosen, 'Umar b. al-Khaṭṭâb, who ruled from 13/634 to 24/644. He called himself *'Amîr al-Mu'minîn*, the Commander of the Faithful. He built a rudimentary state bureaucracy and expanded Islam into Syria–Palestine and Egypt.

At the death of 'Umar, a council chose 'Uthmân from the 'Umayyad clan, the leading clan of the Quraysh, and he is credited with tending to the religious side of the caliphate. He commissioned a panel to collect all the different versions of the Qur'ân and to make an official recension. This was meant to replace all other collections, including one made by 'Alî b. Abî Ṭâlib. He then distributed that recension to all the metropolitan centers with the instructions to eliminate other extant versions. While he was not successful in making only one version – Sunnî Islam allows seven canonical readings of the Qur'ân – his effort went a long way in making a standard text and strengthened the claims of the caliphs to a role in governing the religious life of the community. He is also noted for appointing many of his family members to positions of leadership, which produced great resentment in some quarters. As a result, he was assassinated in 36/656.

The head of the ʾUmayyads, Muʿâwiyah, claimed the right of revenge for the murder of his relative, and he accused ʿAlî b. Abî Ṭâlib, who had just been sworn in as the new caliph, of complicity in the assassination. Muʿâwiyah challenged ʿAlî's right to rule, and the conflict that ensued spread out of Arabia into Syria and Mesopotamia. ʿAlî took his armies into southern Iraq, capturing the cities of Baṣrah and Kûfah, defeating opposition armies at the Battle of the Camel in 36/656. That left only Syria outside his control, and he launched a campaign against Muʿâwiyah's forces. At a crucial point in their fight, Muʿâwiyah's forces proposed a negotiation and ʿAlî accepted. From the start, they conducted the negotiations on different terms and with differing expectations, and the parleys failed to lead to a satisfactory end. Some of ʿAlî's forces, frustrated with the lack of satisfactory outcome and disillusioned with his leadership, seceded and began to attack both ʿAlî's troops, who would become known as Shîʿî, and Muʿâwiyah's forces, the ʾUmayyads. They became known as the Khârijites, and were eventually hunted down by both sides and reduced in number, but not before severely weakening the Shîʿî cause. When ʿAlî was assassinated by a Khârijite in 41/661, he was succeeded by his son, Ḥasan, who abdicated, and Muʿâwiyah became the sole caliph and the first of the ʾUmayyad dynasty.

In the retrospect of this early conflict over succession, the Sunnîs, who became the majority and claimed orthodoxy, called the first four caliphs – Abû Bakr, ʿUmar, ʿUthmân, and ʿAlî – the "Rightly Guided Caliphs" in an attempt to diffuse the Shîʿî and Khârijite claims to legitimacy. Shîʿî Islam evolved from a political movement into a strong theological stance about the nature of Islam itself and continued to resist being absorbed into the Sunnî sphere, even when the two communities lived side by side. Shîʿis developed a system of laws and religious practices that are, with minor differences, parallel to the Sunnî rites and practices. In some periods, both Shîʿis and Sunnîs shared the same institutions of higher learning for religious instruction. Even with their differences, most Muslims come together in rites like the *ḥajj*.

As the different versions of Islamic practice spread first throughout the Mediterranean world and then beyond, to South Asia, to Africa, and to Southeast Asia, they brought a new model for living grounded both in the Qur'ân and the *sunnah* of Muḥammad. Based on *sharî'ah*, the religion provided behavioral models for every aspect of life from how to eat and sleep to how to pray. It brought a worldwide network of trade in commodities and ideas that made the Islamic life attractive wherever it went. Even in the earliest period, when Muslims were conquering the ancient empires, Islam's success at conversion was through attraction rather than coercion. By the end of the century after Muḥammad's death, Islam had spread from southern France in the West to the borders of India in the East. When Islam was a half a millennium old, it was established in China and Southeast Asia, and now Islam is the fastest-growing religion in North America.

Divisions and Unities

Islam, like the other major religions of the word, is divided by geography, language, ethnicity, and beliefs. Within Sunnî Islam, Muslims in different areas will often belong to different schools, *madhhab*s, of Islamic law. Rules of inheritance, codes of conduct, and manner of dress will vary slightly from one school to another, but the differences will be less than the differences between denominations in Protestant Christianity. Ethnicity and language are markers of difference among Muslims, but divisions are outweighed by the unities as one looks across the Muslim world. The annual pilgrimage, the *ḥajj*, often acts as a force to unify Muslims from around the world, as each pilgrim comes to Mecca dressed in identical pieces of white cloth. All Muslims share the Pillars of Islam, read the same Qur'ân, and pray in the same language, Arabic, even if they are otherwise unfamiliar with that language. Divisions like the Sunnî–Shî'î split, and the sectarian splits within each of those major divisions, are made more pronounced when politics and territorial claims are involved, but over the long history of the religion have not produced great chasms of difference.

Mysticism and Spirituality

A major strain of spiritual expression in Islam is mysticism, often called Ṣûfism from the habit of early mystics of wearing woolen robes. As with mystical traditions in other world religions, Ṣûfism tends to cross all geographic and doctrinal borders, so that one can be a Sunnî or a Shî'î and still be a Ṣûfî. In keeping with other aspects of the religion, Islamic mysticism is both personal and communal. Early mystics like al-Ḥasan al-Baṣrî and al-Ḥallâj are examples of men whose individual mystic lives had great impact on the history of this spiritual quest. Al-Ḥasan al-Baṣrî is an example of someone who was both a respected transmitter of *ḥadîth* and a mystic, while al-Ḥallâj was someone whose mystic journey carried him beyond the bounds of the community in the eyes of some who misunderstood his esoteric teachings, and earned him a heretic's death.

The most common form of Islamic mystic expression is through the Ṣûfî orders, *ṭarîqah*s, which were prominent from the middle of the fourth/tenth century until modern times. Muslims were often deeply involved in the aspects of the religion dominated by *sharî'ah*, and still members of a Ṣûfî order. These orders were often centered on shrine-mosques that contained the tombs of the founders of the order, or special places of mystic worship, called *dhikr.* They were the community center, and the shaykh or *pîr*, served the same function as the *'âlim*, and was often the same person; he led the community in worship and regulated the daily lives of the individuals under his care. In the Ottoman Empire, the lives of the majority of the non-elite Muslims were governed in part through the *ṭarîqah*s rather than solely through the *sharî'ah* courts. Nevertheless, in the history of Islamic mysticism, the mystic impulse has come in large part from the Qur'ân and the *ḥadîth* and has remained grounded in the precepts found there, even while taking flights of the mystic journeys.

Linked to all forms of mysticism and spirituality in Islam are the practices of asceticism, the use of spiritual guides or masters, and an aversion to contamination. Asceticism, even though condemned as "monkhood" in early *ḥadîth*s, surfaces regularly as part of spiritual exercises along the mystic path. Even though Islam has been characterized as a religion of individual responsibility, Muslims often choose a wise master as a guide along the mystic and spiritual path. Such a person, often but not necessarily the head of a *ṭarîqah*, would lead the initiate into the exercises, rules, and mores of the mystic community. This might also include an introduction to the esoteric, *bâṭin*, mysteries of Islam.

An additional mode of expressing spirituality, both within the mystic tradition and without it is the avoidance of contamination. This can be both spiritual and physical, but physical purity is a concern within Islam. Maintaining cleanliness in person, food, and mind is a recurring theme in Islamic discussions of daily life as well as in mystical circles.

In recent times, particularly in the West, Ṣûfism has become a popular part of "New-Age" religion. Often this form of Islamic mysticism is divorced from a complete Islamic life and retains only the outward trappings of the mystic tradition. In such cases, some regard this form of mysticism as non-Islamic.

Islam and the Modern World

Most Muslims in countries with large Islamic populations are living in societies that were former colonies of Western nations. In these countries, the politics of resistance and liberation became mixed with a religious ideology of Islam. As in many other cases of religious opposition to modernism, this form of Islam has been termed "fundamentalist." This is the most visible form of Islam in the Western media today. It is characterized as violent, retrograde, and repressive. This is, however, a mischaracterization of Islam and Muslims in the modern world.

Throughout the history of Islam, Muslims have lived in and dealt with their "modern" world. In the second/ninth century, when the Islamic Empire embraced large numbers of Hellenized peoples, Muslim clerics and theologians debated the role of Greek science in a religious society. In the thirteenth/eighteenth century, the debate, sparked by Napoleon's invasion of the Middle East, included the rights of individuals. In the late thirteenth/nineteenth and early fourteenth/twentieth centuries, Muslim intellectuals were occupied by the concepts of modernity and the coexistence of science and religion.

A survey of the Internet or a visit to any country where Muslims live will show that there are Muslims who live fully in the technological age. They use computers, automobiles, cell-phones, and television, just as people do elsewhere. But Muslims are also a large part of the developing world, living as farmers and pastoralists. Their religious practices often seem more old-fashioned or traditional, and there are those who romanticize that version of Islam as more authentic. The person on the cell-phone may be a traditionalist, and the shepherd may be avant-garde in his religious thinking. And, as is the case with other religious groups, any Muslim may have a greater or lesser engagement with the tradition and its practices at various times during life.

A

Aaron

See HÂRÛN.

ʿabâʾah

An outer wrap or cloak, sometimes striped.

ʿAbbâsids

The SUNNÎ dynasty that ruled from 133/750 to 657/1258, succeeding the ʾUMAYYAD dynasty. The hereditary caliphs of this dynasty claimed legitimacy through descent from al-ʿAbbâs, the uncle of MUḤAMMAD, making them part of the family of the Prophet (AHL AL-BAYT). The city of BAGHDÂD was built as their capital. Under their rule, and often as a direct result of their patronage, the earliest major works of Islamic law (SHARÎʿAH), QURʾÂN commentary, (TAFSÎR), and history (*taʾrîkh*) were written. Under the patronage of ʿAbbâsid rulers and their courts, all of the intellectual and artistic fields of Islamic civilization developed and flourished. Because most histories of early Islam were written under their control and for their aggrandizement, negative views of the ʾUmayyads and the SHÎʿÎ were often a part of their polemical picture of early Islam. Such views have often been incorporated into Western scholarship about Islam to the detriment of a more balanced view of the character of all the early groups. Modern attempts to revive the caliphate have often looked to reviving the legitimacy of the ʿAbbâsid dynasty. (*See also* KHILÂFAT MOVEMENT.)

ʿabd (Arabic: servant, slave)

This is used frequently in compound names, where the second element is a name or epithet of God, such as ʿAbd Allâh (also written as ʿAbdullâh), Servant of God, ʿAbd ar-Raḥmân, Servant of the Merciful, etc. Muslims consider being a "slave" of God to be a high honor and the highest form of piety. While Islamic religious texts do not condemn slavery, it is not fully condoned as an institution either. A slave who is a Muslim should be manumitted, even if he converts while a slave, and the ḤADÎTH contains numerous statements that recommend freeing slaves or ameliorating their lives through good treatment.

Abdalîs

See DURRÂNÎS.

ʿAbd Allâh b. al-ʿAbbâs

See IBN ʿABBÂS.

ʿAbd al-ʿAzîz, Shâh (1746–1824)

A prominent Indian ṢÛFÎ religious reformer and SUNNÎ polemicist against SHÎʿÎ beliefs and practices, his *Tuḥfah-i isnâ ʿashariyyah* should be singled out among his writings for lasting impact, influencing religious discussions in PAKISTAN.

Abdel Rahman, Omar (born 1938)

Egyptian fundamentalist and spiritual leader of AL-JAMÂʿAT AL-ISLÂMIYYAH, he was convicted of heading the plot to bomb the World Trade Center in New York City in 1993, and is serving a life sentence in a maximum security prison.

ʿAbd al-Muṭṭalib b. Ḥâshim

The Prophet MUḤAMMAD's grandfather, who became his guardian after the death of his father, ʿABDULLÂH. He is featured prominently in the pre-Islamic history of the KAʿBAH and the well of ZAMZAM, the water of which was his right to distribute to pilgrims bound for MECCA. In the Year of the Elephant, the year of the Prophet's birth, he is said to have been involved in repelling the attack of the forces of the Ethiopian general ABRAHA, who attacked Mecca.

ʿAbd al-Qâdir b. ʿAlî b. Yûsuf al-Fâsî (1007/1598–1091/1680)

He was the chief member of the ṢÛFÎ establishment in Morocco in the eleventh/seventeenth century. He is primarily noted as the progenitor of a line of religious scholars and aristocrats in the city of FÂS.

ʿAbd al-Raḥmân, ʿÂʾishah (born 1913)

Prominent Egyptian author who wrote under the name Bint al-Shâtiʿ. Her *al-Tafsîr al-bayânî lil-Qurʾân al-Karîm* argues for including the study of QURʾÂN in literary studies. Her writings about women and Arabic literature can be regarded as religiously conservative. She has argued against historical influence on the Qurʾân and against multiple interpretations of Qurʾânic words and verses.

ʿAbd ar-Râziq, ʿAlî (1888–1966)

Egyptian intellectual whose *al-Islâm wa-ʾusûl al-ḥukm* (Islam and the bases of political authority), published in 1925, argued against the notion that Islam is a political as well as spiritual system and is still the subject of debate today.

ʿAbduh, Muḥammad (1849–1905)

Egyptian theologian, reformer, and architect of Islamic modernism, his aim was to restore Islam to its original condition through the elimination of TAQLÎD (adherence to tradition). He considered revelation and reason to be compatible and thought that sound reasoning would lead to a belief in God. For him, science and religion were compatible, and he asserted that one could find the basis for nuclear physics in the QURʾÂN. His most popular work, *The Theology of Unity*, has influenced many subsequent modernists, such as RASHÎD RIḌÂ.

ʿAbdullâh b. ʿAbd al-Muṭṭalib (died *c.* 570)

Father of the Prophet MUḤAMMAD by ÂMINAH BT. WAHB, he was of the HÂSHIMITE clan, and died before Muḥammad's birth. According to the SÎRAH, he possessed the light (NÛR), which he implanted in Âminah, from which came the Prophet.

Abdurrahman Wahid (born 1940)

Known as Gus Dur, he is a prominent Indonesian modernist, reformist, and theologian, leader of the NAHDATUL ULAMA, an association of traditionalist religious leaders. He became the president of Indonesia in 1420/1999 in the aftermath of scandals that had rocked the country, but became caught up in scandals of his own, and, as this is being written, is about to be impeached by the legislature.

ABIM

Angkatan Belia Islam Malaysia, a Malaysian Islamic youth movement founded by Anwar Ibrahim. The organization has widespread influence in Malaysian society.

ablution

Ritual cleansing to remove impurities, ablutions are of two sorts, major, GHUSL, and minor, WUḌÛ'. *Ghusl*, the complete washing of the body, is required after sexual intercourse, masturbation and involuntary sexual emissions before a worshiper can perform a valid prayer, recite verses from the QUR'ÂN or touch a copy of it. In order for the *ghusl* to be valid, the worshiper must recite the declaration of intent (NIYYAH). *Wuḍû'*, the washing of the head, face, hands and forearms to the elbows, and the washing of the feet three times, is required before prayer. *Wudû'* is normally performed with ritually pure water, but, under some circumstances, sand or dust may be used accompanying the washing gestures. This is known as TAYAMMUM. SUNNÎ and SHÎ'Î differ about some aspects of this practice, Shî'î insisting that the feet be washed, while some Sunnî allow the shoes to be rubbed if the feet have been placed in clean shoes at the place of *wuḍû'*. Mosques generally provide facilities for *wuḍû'*, and the traditional bathhouse, the *ḥammâm*, was a place for *ghusl*. As a result of this religious requirement, when Muslims expanded into what had been the ancient Roman world, they incorporated Roman waterworks and improved on them. In the Middle Ages, Islamic cities were among the cleanest in the world, and Muslims were leaders in this branch of civil engineering.

abortion

Abortion, when understood as the intentional expulsion of the fetus to terminate a pregnancy prior to full gestation, is regarded by most Muslim jurists as contrary to Islamic law (SHARÎ'AH) and, therefore, blameworthy. Following the principles of the sanctity of human life, abortion may not be used to terminate an unwanted or unplanned pregnancy. Some schools of law, such as the ḤANAFÎ school (MADHHAB), allow therapeutic abortion prior to the 120th day of the pregnancy, the day of ENSOULMENT, but only for valid concerns for the health of the mother. After ensoulment, the fetus is regarded as having legal rights that can compete with the rights of the mother.

Abraha

An Abyssinian general who ruled Yemen and, according to legend, tried to capture MECCA in the year of MUḤAMMAD's birth. His use of a war elephant and his defeat are referred to in Q. 105, known as the "chapter of the elephant." (*See also* FÎL.)

abrogation (Arabic *naskh*)

The doctrine, based on Q. 2:106; 13:39; 16:101; 17:86; 87:6–7, that God rescinded some previous revelation to the Prophet. Later jurists applied the doctrine to argue that the QUR'ÂN superseded Jewish and Christian scripture. Jurists also used the doctrine to harmonize apparent contradictions in the Qur'ânic text. (*See also* NÂSIKH WA MANSÛKH.)

Abû Bakr (573–13/634)

Close Companion of MUḤAMMAD, father of Muḥammad's wife 'Â'ISHAH, and first caliph of Islam, he accompanied Muḥammad on the HIJRAH. When he assumed the caliphate, the nature of the office had not been defined, and Abû

Bakr decided to follow the "example" of Muhammad. One of his first acts was to send Muslim forces north into Byzantine territory, thus starting the expansion of Islam out of Arabia. Attacks by Arab tribes, challenging the new caliph and fledgling Muslim state, forced him to change the job from part-time administrator to full-time general and leader of a growing community. In the two years that he ruled, he set a pattern of strong, pious governance.

Abû Dâ'ûd, Sulaymân b. al-Ash'ath (202/817–275/889)

One of the six highly ranked compilers of ḤADÎTH in the SUNNÎ tradition. He wrote most of his major works in the city of BAṢRAH, but is said to have traveled widely to collect the materials for his major work, the *Kitâb as-sunan*. He is credited with being the first to give detailed notes about his estimation of the soundness or weakness of traditions, providing a basis for later *ḥadîth* criticism. While he does not rank as high as AL-BUKHÂRÎ and MUSLIM, his collection contains a number of citations not contained in the works of those two.

Abû Dharr al-Ghifârî (born 32/652)

An early Companion of MUḤAMMAD who advocated, during the reign of the caliph 'UTHMÂN, that more wealth be given to the poor. Some accounts of his life say that he was the fifth person to believe in Muḥammad. He is held as a model of proper Islamic social justice by some modern Islamic socialists. (*See also* ṢAḤÂBAH.)

Abû al-Futûḥ ar-Râzî (died *c.* 525/1131)

The author of one of the earliest SHÎ'Î commentaries on the QUR'ÂN. He wrote in Persian because Arabic was little understood by the majority around him. He claimed to have been influenced by AṬ-ṬABARÎ and AZ-ZAMAKHSHARÎ.

Abû Ḥanîfah (81/700–150/767)

Founder of the ḤANAFÎ school of SUNNÎ law, which is characterized by the use of RA'Y (individual legal opinion). Little is known about his life. He lived in KÛFAH as a cloth merchant, and collected a great number of traditions, which he passed on to his students. He never held any official post or worked as a judge, (QÂḌÎ).

Abû Ḥâtim ar-Râzî, Aḥmad b. Ḥamdân (died *c.* 322/934)

An early ISMÂ'ÎLÎ DÂ'Î, who operated in the region of Rayy (Tehran) and Daylam. His best-known work is a dictionary of theological terms.

Abû al-Hudhayl al-'Allâf (*c.* 131/749–235/849)

Mu'tazilite theologian who helped develop KALÂM. His theology served to counter the foreign influences of his time, such as dualism, Greek philosophy, and the anthropomorphists within the Muslim traditionalists. (*See also* MU'TAZILAH.)

Abû Hurayrah (600–58/678)

A close Companion of the Prophet from the battle of Khaybar (7/629), he was reputed to have a phenomenal memory, transmitting over 3,000 Prophetic traditions. He is known as Abû Hurayrah because when he worked as a goatherd he kept a small kitten to play with. Biographies attribute a number of uncertain names to him, including 'Abd Allâh and 'Abd ar-Raḥmân, names he took when he converted to Islam. He was suspected by his contemporaries of fabrication, and modern scholarship assumes that some of the traditions were ascribed to him at a later time, but Western scholarship has probably been too harsh in attributing to him the fabrication of those ḤADÎTHS that are not genuine. (*See also* ṢAḤÂBAH.)

Abû Lahab, ʻAbd al-ʻUzzâ b. ʻAbd al-Muṭṭalib

An uncle and violent opponent of MUḤAMMAD, mentioned in Q. 111 as condemned to Hell along with his wife for their opposition.

Abû al-Layth as-Samarqandî, Naṣr b. Muḥammad b. Ibrâhîm (died *c.* 393/1002)

A ḤANAFÎ theologian and jurist, his works have become popular throughout the Islamic world, particularly in Southeast Asia. He wrote a TAFSÎR, and several other works, including a theological tract in question-and-answer form, titled *ʻAqîdah*, which has been printed in Malaysia and Indonesia with interlinear translations.

Abû al-Qâsim

One of the nicknames of the Prophet. (*See also* MUḤAMMAD.)

Abû Sufyân (563–31/651)

The aristocratic general of the MECCA-based opposition to MUḤAMMAD at the battles of BADR and Uḥud. At the battle of KHANDAQ (the battle of the Trench) he withdrew his troops, realizing the futility of the cause. He later accompanied Muḥammad on one of his campaigns. He became one of Muḥammad's fathers-in-law when the Prophet married one of his daughters, ʼUMM ḤABÎBAH.

Abû Ṭâlibʼ ʻAbd Manâf b. ʻAbd al-Muṭṭalib

Uncle of MUḤAMMAD and father of ʻALÎ. He provided support for Muḥammad after the death of his grandfather, ʻABD AL-MUṬṬALIB, and protected Muḥammad from attack by the pagan Meccans. According to tradition he died three years before the HIJRAH, unconverted to Islam. Later Muslims have speculated about his fate, since he died before the establishment of Islam but had aided Muḥammad and the Muslims so importantly.

Abû ʻUbaydah (died 18/639)

One of ten believers promised Paradise by MUḤAMMAD, he was a distinguished warrior for Islam and was active in the formation of the early Islamic state.

Abyssinia

Known in Arabic as Ḥabash, Abyssinia, now called Ethiopia, played an important part in the early development of Islam. It was to there that MUḤAMMAD sent the first HIJRAH, a small band of Muslims who were, according to tradition, well received in the court of the Christian ruler, who is said to have remarked on the similarity between Christianity and Islam. In the pre-Islamic period, there were active trade relations between Abyssinia and MECCA, and it was from there that ABRAHA came. Islam penetrated only slowly into the interior of Ethiopia, but the development of an active slave-trade helped promote conversion to Islam along the coast. In modern times, although Muslims comprise a large minority of the population, the country is so thoroughly identified as Christian that Islam has little influence on the social and political fabric of the country.

ʻÂd

The people of the prophet HÛD mentioned frequently in the QURʼÂN (Q. 7:65ff., 11:50ff., 26:123ff., *et passim.*) Their failure to heed Hûd's warnings resulted in their destruction. The people of ʻÂd, along with the people of THAMÛD are mentioned in the Qurʼân in the ranks of those destroyed by God for disobeying Him, as exemplars of bad behavior.

adab

(Arabic: knowledge, politeness, and education)

This term parallels the Arabic word ʿILM, meaning "knowledge of the non-religious sciences." Knowledge of the two combine to form a complete Muslim.

Adam

The first human created by God, and known as Abû Bashar, the Father of Humans, he was created out of clay and allowed to dry, after which God breathed into him His spirit. He is said in the QURʾÂN to be God's viceroy, and to have been taught all the names of things in the universe, which set him above the angels. All the angels prostrated themselves before Adam except the rebellious IBLÎS. The figure of Adam is prominent in many extra-Qurʾânic legends and stories. According to one of these, he built the foundations of the KAʿBAH and performed the first worship there. In another story, an eagle and a fish discussed their sighting of the first human and remarked that, because of his upright walk and his hands, they would not be left alone in the depths of the sea or the heights of the air. He is held to be the first prophet. (*See also* NABÎ.)

adat or adat law

Customary law in Southeast Asian Islamic communities regarded as harmonious with Islamic law and holding a status close to natural law. *Adat* law, or its equivalent, has developed alongside SHARÎʿAH and complementary to it to provide regulation of those areas that *sharîʿah* does not cover. There has been much discussion among legal scholars about the role and legitimacy of *adat* law, but most allow its function on the principle that what is not expressly forbidden by the *sharîʿah* is permissible. (*See also* ʿURF.)

aḍḥâ

See ʿÎD AL-AḌḤÂ.

adhân

The call or announcement to prayer preceding each of the five canonical prayers. In a mosque, it is made by a muezzin (Arabic MUʾADHDHIN), but each Muslim can also pronounce the call. SUNNÎ and SHÎʿÎ practices vary slightly in their wording, and the tunes vary slightly from place to place in the Islamic world. The first person to be appointed by MUḤAMMAD to call the Muslims to prayer was BILÂL, whose stentorian voice could be heard throughout MADÎNAH. The Sunnî call consists of seven elements:

1. *Allâhu akbâr*: ALLÂH is most great.
2. *Ashhadu ʾan lâ ilâha illa-llâh*: I testify that there is no deity but Allâh.
3. *Ashhadu ʾanna Muḥammadan rasûlullâh*: I testify that Muḥammad is the prophet of God.
4. *Ḥayya ʿalâ ṣ-ṣalât*: Come to prayer.
5. *Ḥayya ʿala l-falâḥ*: Come to salvation.
6. *Allâhu akbar*: Allâh is most great.
7. *Lâ ilâha illa-llâh*: There is no deity but Allâh.

These elements are repeated a varying number of times in each call, depending on the region and the school of Islamic law. In many mosques, electronic recordings on timers have replaced the human call. Shîʿîs will add *Ashhadu ʾanna ʿAliyyan wâlîyyu-llâh* (I testify that ʿAlî is protected by God), between 3 and 4 above, and *Ḥayya ʿalâ khayri-l-ʿamal* (Come to the best deed) between 5 and 6 above.

adoption

Adoption has no standing in SHARÎʿAH in spite of MUḤAMMAD's adoption of Zayd

b. Ḥârithah. The adopted child retains both the biological family name and inheritance status. Muslims have resorted to using such devices as the WAQF TO PROVIDE INHERITANCE OUTSIDE THE *sharî'ah*'S STRICTURES.

al-Afghânî, Jamâl al-Dîn
(1839–97)

Islamic modernist, pan-Islamist, and anti-imperialist, who influenced Muḥammad 'ABDUH and RASHÎD RIḌÂ among others. His diverse ideas have become popular with many different modernist groups.

Afghanistan

Situated in Central Asia, and historically part of Persia, or Greater Iran, this Muslim country has been a buffer in the post-World War II period between Pakistan, Iran, and a number of former Soviet Islamic republics. The official languages are Pashtu and PERSIAN (Dârî), and a minority of the population speaks Uzbek, Turkmen, Balochi, and Pashi. Bilingualism is common. Its diverse inhabitants are predominantly SUNNÎ, with about fifteen percent SHÎ'Î. Having achieved independence from the Soviet occupation in 1409/1989, until recently it was under the rule of the ṬÂLIBÂN, an Islamist group whose aim is to rule Afghanistan according to their strict interpretation of the SHARÎ'AH. The estimated population in 2000 was 24.8 million.

Shrine complex of Ali, Mazar-i Sharif, Afghanistan.

Afsharids

The dynasty that ruled Iran from 1736 to 1796 and was named after its founder, Nâdir Shâh Afshâr.

afterlife

The QUR'ÂN is filled with passages that indicate that all souls will have an afterlife, either in Heaven or in Hell, depending on each person's faith and actions in this life, and that every soul will be judged at the Day of Judgment (YAWM AD-DÎN). Muslims differ about whether torment or reward starts immediately or is deferred until the Day of Judgment and whether believers will actually behold the face of God in Paradise. (*See also* JAHANNAM; AL-JANNAH; MUNKAR WA-NAKÎR)

Aghâ Khân

Title of the IMÂM of the NIZÂRÎ ISMÂ'ÎLÎ leader since the nineteenth century. The current *Imâm*, Prince Karim al-Husayni, Aghâ Khân IV, is held to be the forty-ninth hereditary *Imâm* directly descended from 'ALÎ and MUḤAMMAD's daughter, FÂṬIMAH. In addition to his role as a spiritual and intellectual leader of the community, the current Aghâ Khân has founded the Aghâ Khân Foundation, a recognized leader in international development.

'ahd (Arabic: command, covenant)

This term is used in the QUR'ÂN to mean, among other things, God's covenant with humans and the commands in that covenant. It also means a religious pledge or vow, such as to fast under certain circumstances. By extension, it has also come to mean a political or civil agreement or contract, which is often pledged with religious reference or sanctions.

ahl al-ahwâ' (Arabic: people of inclination)

Derived from a term in the QUR'ÂN meaning "predilection," it is applied in the SUNNÎ tradition to people who deviate from the accepted general norm of beliefs and practices, without, however, becoming heretics or apostates.

ahl al-bayt (Arabic: people of the house)

This term occurs twice in the QUR'ÂN (Q. 11:73, 33:33). In Q. 11:73 it refers to the "house" or family of the prophet IBRÂHÎM, while in Q. 33:33 it has a more general sense. In its pre-Islamic usage, the term was applied to the ruling family of a clan or tribe, and thus it implies a certain nobility and right to rule. In post-Qur'ânic usage, particularly among the SHÎ'Î, it has come to mean the people or family of the household of the Prophet, in particular Muḥammad's cousin and son-in-law, 'ALÎ b. Abî Ṭâlib, his wife, the Prophet's daughter, FÂṬIMAH, their sons Ḥasan b. 'Alî and Ḥusayn b. 'Alî and their descendants (IMÂMS), revered especially by the ITHNÂ 'ASHARIYYAH Shî'î. One of the main differences between Shî'î and SUNNÎ beliefs is the strong reverence held among the Shî'îs for the family of the Prophet. In popular belief, this is sometimes raised to a cosmological level, with the belief that the family of the Prophet holds the world together, and that it was for the family that the world was created.

ahl al-dhimmah

See DHIMMÎ.

ahl al-ḥadîth (Arabic: supporters of tradition)

The term generally refers to those in the second Islamic century who advocated the centrality of ḤADÎTH from the Prophet in the formation of the Islamic state. While there was considerable debate about how to apply the *ḥadîth*, and which were valid, the traditionists also came to mean those who, in subsequent centuries, stood in opposition to making speculative theology, KALÂM, central to religious understanding.

ahl-i ḥadîth (Persian/Urdu from Arabic: people of tradition)

Those members of a sect of Muslims in India and Pakistan who claim to follow only the traditions of the Prophet. They reject the necessity to follow any school (MADHHAB) of Islamic law or any other form of TAQLÎD. They attempt to identify and eliminate any innovative practice (BID'AH) from any source. As a result, their opponents call them WAHHÂBÎ, after the movement in Arabia, but they deny this, since they hold that even the Wahhâbî are practitioners of *taqlîd*, since they accept the legal pronouncements of AḤMAD B. ḤANBAL. The movement, which originated in the nineteenth century, has an active training network, with its own schools and publications, the most prominent of which is *Ahl al-ḥadîth*, a weekly publication.

ahl al-ḥall wa-al-'aqd (Arabic: people of influence)

The person or persons qualified to elect a caliph (KHALÎFAH) in Islamic political theory. The number varies from one person, usually a caliph designating a successor, to a body of persons representing all Muslims and acting as a SHÛRÂ, which body would have power over any ruler.

ahl-i ḥaqq (Persian: people of truth)

An esoteric syncretistic offshoot of Islam based on additional chapters of the QUR'ÂN, they are found primarily in Iran. They are a secret group, whose writings are difficult for the uninitiated to understand because of their use of secret and technical terms. They believe in successive ages in which the Divine is made manifest and in metempsychosis and a series of reincarnations of humans in which the actions of previous incarnations are rewarded or punished. They are led by PÎRS and worship in assemblies that often involve animal sacrifice.

ahl al-kitâb (Arabic: people of the book)

A concept that originated in the QUR'ÂN, these people were originally Jews and Christians who had received revelations from God. The term was extended to others as Islam spread into India and China. Membership in the group entitled a person to preferred status in Islamic law as DHIMMÎ.

ahl al-ṣuffa (Arabic: people of the row)

The name of a group of poor and pious Muslims who made the HIJRAH with MUḤAMMAD and were wards of the community. Much legendary material surrounds the history of this group, whose numbers range from slightly above thirty to over a hundred.

Aḥmad al-Badawî (*c.* 596/1200–675/1276)

The most popular of the saints (*walîs*), in Egypt. At the age of thirty, he underwent a mystic transformation that involved reading the QUR'ÂN in its seven readings, refusing to speak and only communicating by signs, renouncing sexual relations, and making journeys to the tombs of famous holy persons, mainly in Iraq. He is said to have induced a famous woman, Fâṭimah bt. Barrî, to propose marriage to him, but then rejected her offer. This story has produced a popular Arabic romance. After a vision, he journeyed to Ṭanṭâ, in Egypt, and stood on the roof of a private house gazing at the sun until his eyes turned red, all the while fasting for forty days. He is credited with a miraculous cure of a boy with diseased eyes. After his death, a mosque was built over his grave, which has become the site of veneration and of miracles. He appears to have become the patron saint of prisoners and the finder of lost articles.

Ahmad Barelwi, Sayyid

See BARELWÎ, SAYYID AḤMAD.

Aḥmad b. Ḥanbal (164/780–241/855)

MUḤADDITH, theologian, and founder of the ḤANBALÎ MADHHAB, he was persecuted by the 'ABBÂSIDS during their inquisition (MIḤNAH) because he refused to say that the QUR'ÂN was created. This persecution, involving beatings and imprisonment, earned him great status among the opponents of the *miḥnah* and of the beliefs of the MU'TAZILAH. His most famous work, the *Musnad*, was only partly completed by him and was finished by his son, 'Abd Allâh. It is organized by the name of the first member in the ISNÂD and not by subject, as with the other major collections. The collection reflects his intellectual strength as more than a mere collector of tradition, and the MADHHAB that follows him is based on his subtlety of thought and his reliance on ḤADÎTH rather than personal judgment (RA'Y). His school has the reputation of being stringent among the four SUNNÎ schools of Islamic law. Through IBN TAYMIYYAH, Ibn Ḥanbal has influenced the WAHHÂBÎ movement and the SALAFIYYAH.

Ahmadiyah, or Aḥmadiyyah

A proselytizing messianic reform movement in Islam, started in India and based on the teachings of Mirzâ Ghulâm Aḥmad (d. 1908), who regarded himself as the MAHDÎ and appointed by God to reform and restore Islam. He also claimed to be an *avatar* of the Hindu deity Krishna and the incarnation of JESUS. When he died, his followers elected a successor (*khalîfah*), and began to operate as an independent religious group. The group split into two, with the more modernist one moving to Lahore. The Ahmadiyah Movement in Islam has congregations around the world and its members contribute monthly sums to the central organization. It is strongly committed to missionary work, (DAʿWAH), and publishes editions of the QUR'ÂN and numerous religious tracts. They believe that their reformed version of Islam represents the true religion, and they include the mention of Mirzâ Ghulâm Aḥmad in their creed. In 1984, the government of Pakistan declared the movement to be un-Islamic for its claim that there were non-legislative prophets after Muḥammad, and the worldwide movement moved to London. The term is also used as the name of a major ṢÛFÎ order in Egypt, also known as the Badawiyya.

Aḥmad Khân, Sir Sayyid (1817–98)

An Indian Islamic modernist who promoted modern education, ecumenism, and social reform. He came from a noble but impoverished Islamic family and, through hard work, became a judge at the court of justice in Delhi under the rule of the East India Company. After the Indian Mutiny of 1857, he decided to work toward the betterment of Indian Muslims and in conjunction with the British government. After visiting England, he started a journal, *Tahdhîb al-akhlâq*, with the aim of removing prejudice and ignorance among his fellow Muslims. He drew inspiration from SHÂH WALÎ ALLÂH, and founded the Mohammedan Anglo-Oriental College, later Aligarh Muslim University. He saw the essential harmony between science and religion, contending that "the work of God (nature) was identical with the word of God (the QUR'ÂN). He was attacked as a *nečarî*, a naturist, by his opponents for demythologizing the Qur'ân, but this opposition was overcome by his vision of a strengthened Islamic community in the subcontinent. Some see him as a spiritual forerunner of the idea of PAKISTAN. He was knighted by the British, thus earning the honorific "Sir" as well as "SAYYID."

Ahmad Sirhindi

See SIRHINDÎ, AḤMAD.

ʿÂ'ishah (614–58/678)

The daughter of ABÛ BAKR, she was the Prophet's third and favorite wife, whom he married after the death of KHADÎJAH, his first wife. Extensive biographical traditions describe her as playful, witty, intelligent, well educated, and, in later life, a potent political force. She was betrothed to MUḤAMMAD when she was still a child, and it is said that she brought her dolls with her when she went to live with him. Her playfulness clearly attracted the Prophet, who is said to have enjoyed playing games and running races with her. A well-known incident occurred that threatened her marriage while she was on a raid with Muḥammad. She left her camel-litter (Arabic, *ḥawdah*) shortly before the troop broke camp, dropped a necklace, and spent some time looking for it.

Assuming that she was still asleep, the warriors loaded the litter on the camel and went off, leaving her in the desert. She was discovered by an attractive young man, who escorted her back to MADÎNAH, where gossip implied that there had been an improper relationship. A number of Muḥammad's close advisors suggested that he return her to her father's house. Among those who advocated her return was ʿALÎ B. ABÎ ṬÂLIB, thus provoking a lasting enmity between the two. Her playful spirit is probably best illustrated by the story of the joke she played on Muḥammad. Honey was one of the Prophet's favorite foods, and his wives liked to treat him with it. One day, when he was returning from one of his wives, ʿÂ'ishah pretended that he had bad breath. He was almost on the point of renouncing honey when she told him that it was a joke. In her later years, she assumed the role of leading matriarch of the community and a source of information about the Prophet. Particularly among the SUNNÎ, she was known as the "Mother of the Believers," the *'Umm al-Mu'minîn*. As with the other wives of the Prophet, she was forbidden to remarry after Muḥammad's death, and was left a childless widow. Her political activity surrounding the caliph ʿUTHMÂN is the subject of some controversy. She opposed his rule, but also opposed his assassination. At a critical juncture, she joined a ḤAJJ to MECCA and abandoned her leadership in the succession controversy. About four months after the assassination of ʿUthmân, she took a force of about one thousand, among the leaders of which were Ṭalḥah and az-Zubayr. After taking the city of BAṢRAH, they met ʿAlî b. Abî Ṭâlib in a battle known as the battle of the Camel, because most of the fighting was around the camel bearing ʿÂ'ishah's standard. ʿAlî won, and both Ṭalḥah and az-Zubayr were killed. ʿÂ'ishah was treated with respect and honor, and she spent the next two decades in seclusion from the politics of the Islamic state. She eventually became reconciled with ʿAlî, and her opinion was sought about every major event in the life of the community. She is regarded as an important transmitter of traditions about Muḥammad and to have possessed a codex of the QUR'ÂN.

ajal (Arabic: fixed term)

The word refers to the fixed term of a person's life, which is held in the QUR'ÂN to be neither prolonged nor shortened except as it is written in the book of God's decrees. The notion of a fixed term to life has been the subject of much discussion and speculation, some holding that if a person dies, whether young or old, it is a decree from God, and if that person had not died in the manner he did, then he would have died in some other manner. In modern times, this same argument is used to counter those who argue that one should not try to use modern medical means to save a person's life. It is argued that it is by God's will that life-prolonging means are available to humans.

akdariyyah

The name of a well-known difficult law case of inheritance involving a woman who dies leaving a husband, her mother, her grandfather, and her full sister. Different schools of law interpret this in different manners: only the HANAFÎ interpret the distribution to exclude the sister; the rest include all the heirs named in the QUR'ÂN.

akhbâr (Arabic: report; sg. *khabar*)

In early Islamic usage, this term was synonymous with ḤADÎTH. In later usage, it has come to mean those traditions that are secular and used for history (TA'RÎKH). They have the same literary form, with an ISNÂD and a MATN, but are usually not subject to the same rigorous critique, and often the chains of transmission are incomplete.

al-Akhḍar (North African Arabic)

A dialect variant from North Africa for AL-KHAḌIR.

al-âkhirah (Arabic: the last, the final)

In Islamic ESCHATOLOGY it refers to both the final resting place of the soul and the end-time itself – after judgment, as opposed to this world. Over time, there has been considerable speculation about whether this is a spiritual or a physical realm and whether the delights and/or punishments described in the QUR'ÂN are to be taken literally or metaphorically. (*See also* YAWM AD-DÎN.)

akhlâq (Arabic: innate disposition)

This refers to ethics. Speculation about moral behavior in Islam has, for the most part, been within the confines of proper religious behavior, but the introduction of Hellenized notions of ethics caused many to treat this subject as separate from the religious codes of behavior. Among the philosophers and Hellenized speculative theologians, the introduction of the works of Aristotle chiefly led them to discuss issues of the innate goodness or evil in humans and the nature of natural law. These speculations influenced ADAB literature, which, in turn, influenced the theologian AL-GHAZÂLÎ. In modern Islamic thought, particularly in the colonial and post-colonial phase, Muslims speculating about ethics have been concerned with the ethical implications of activism, holding that moral behavior involves improving the lot of the community.

âkhûnd

Persian term for a religious leader. (*See also* MAWLÂ.)

ʿâlam (Arabic: world)

Usually found in the plural, *ʿâlamîn*, in the phrase, *rabb al-ʿâlamîn*, "Lord of the Worlds," it reflects the view of the QUR'ÂN that the universe consists of (probably) seven worlds and seven heavens, *samâwât*.

Alamut

The fortress of Alamut, situated on the summit of a nearly inaccessible peak in the Alburz mountains in Iran, was the headquarters of the ISMÂʿÎLÎ SHÎʿÎ from the fifth/tenth century through the seventh/thirteenth century. In the SAFAVID period it was used as a prison and called the "castle of oblivion."

ʿAlawids

The SHARÎFÎ royal family of Morocco, who have ruled since the seventeenth century.

ʿAlawiyyah

Also known as the Nuṣayriyyah, this is the only sect of the SHÎʿÎ "extremists" the GHULÂT, known to exist today. The term is derived from their veneration of ʿALÎ B. ABÎ ṬÂLIB, and can refer to Shîʿî in general. They are found mostly in western Syria. In their doctrine, they regard ʿAlî as divine. They also believe that they started as lights that were imprisoned in human forms and condemned to cycles of reincarnation, out of which only the elect can escape. In each epoch there is a trio of divine beings, ʿAlî, MUḤAMMAD, and SALMÂN AL-FÂRISÎ being this epoch's trio. They appear, however, hidden, and it is the duty of the believer to recognize the trio and escape the cycle of reincarnation. Because JESUS was an earlier manifestation, some ʿAlawiyyah celebrate Christmas. President Assad of Syria is of this group.

Albania

A European country on the Adriatic sea, Albania, once a part of the Ottoman Empire, has a Muslim majority and is the birthplace of the BEKTÂSHÎ ṢÛFÎ order.

Alexander the Great

See DHÛ-L-QARNAYN.

Alf laylah wa-laylah (Arabic: *Thousand and One Nights*)

The title of an eclectic collection of tales from different periods and cultures set in a frame story. This set of stories, primarily meant as light entertainment, became popular in the West through the collections of the stories and the translations made by Orientalist travelers. The eighteenth-century French translation by Jean Antione Galland, and the nineteenth-century English translations by Sir Richard Burton and William Lane helped implant fantastic notions about Arab and Islamic peoples in the minds of Westerners.

Algeria

The second largest African country, it is located in North Africa, the MAGHRIB, between MOROCCO and Libya and TUNISIA. During OTTOMAN times it was part of the empire, and then came under French influence and colonization in the nineteenth century. After a bitter war of independence from 1954 to 1961, Algeria became independent in 1962. The current government is besieged by radical Islamist groups, who are engaged in terrorist and guerrilla actions to force their acceptance in the electoral process from which they were excluded. The country is made up primarily of Arabic speakers of Berber origin, although only about thirty percent of the population speaks Berber. The country has a majority SUNNÎ population, is mostly rural and home to a variety of ṢÛFÎ orders. A once-thriving Jewish population is now estimated to be around one hundred thirty thousand.

'Alî b. Abî Ṭâlib (*c.* 597–41/661)

Son-in-law and cousin of MUḤAMMAD, he was the fourth caliph (KHALÎFAH) of the SUNNÎ and the first IMÂM of the SHÎ'Î. He was either the second to believe in Islam, after KHADÎJAH, or third, after ABÛ Bakr, a point much debated in Sunnî–Shî'î polemics. His blood relation to Muḥammad, his appointment by the Prophet at GHADÎR KHUMM, and his marriage to Muḥammad's daughter, FÂṬIMAH made him the first *Imâm* among the Shî'î. They had two sons, Ḥasan and Ḥusayn, and two daughters, 'Umm Kulthûm and Zaynab. 'Alî assumed the caliphate in 656, after the death of 'UTHMÂN. Stories implicating 'Alî in 'Uthmân's murder are without foundation and reflect an anti-'Alid bias. He was, nevertheless, the most respected leader among those who opposed 'Uthmân, and they looked to him to stop the innovations (BID'AH) that the caliph had introduced. 'Uthmân's closest relative, MU'ÂWIYAH, demanded the right of blood vengeance, and accused 'Alî of harboring the murderers and of complicity in the killing. The underlying cause was, however, one of politics and the vision of the direction of the community, and the two soon left Arabia for their support strongholds in Iraq and Syria. In the ensuing civil strife, the two armies fought until the 'UMAYYAD forces under Mu'âwiyah appeared to be losing. 'AMR B. AL-'ÂṢ advised, according to legend, that Mu'âwiyah have his men place copies of the QUR'ÂN on their lances as a signal to invite the two sides to decide by means of the holy Scripture. The QURRÂ' among 'Alî's troops at first supported his participation in the arbitration. However, its terms ultimately proved harmful to his cause, at which point many of them turned against him and seceded, blaming ʿAlî for submitting to the arbitration rather than relying on God. At the battle of NAHRAWÂN, ʿAlî attacked those of the secessionists who refused his amnesty and slaughtered many in a move that was roundly condemned at the time. The result was that ʿAlî was forced to retreat to Kûfah and abandon his fight with Muʿâwiyah, after which ʿAlî's influence declined. He was killed by a separatist (Khârijite) assassin, IBN MULJAM, in 661. The Shîʿî festival of Ghadîr, 18 Dhû-l-Ḥijjah, is celebrated to commemorate what they regard as his appointment as Muḥammad's successor. (*See also* KHAWÂRIJ.)

Aligarh

A town in Uttar Pradesh, India, associated with the reformist movement of Sayyid Aḥmad Khân, who started a boys' school around 1871. By 1875, the school was operating on English models, and eventually developed into the Mohammedan Anglo-Oriental College. The main language of instruction was English, except for Islamic religious subjects. In 1920, the college became Aligarh Muslim University, absorbed a school of medicine, and became the institution that produced many Indian Muslim leaders in the first half of the twentieth century.

ʿAlî ilâhî (Arabic: ʿAlî is my god)

A popular designation and term of opprobrium for those SHÎʿÎ who are said to regard ʿALÎ as divine.

ʿālim

See ʿULAMÂʾ.

ʿâlimah (Arabic: learned woman; pl. *ʿawâlim*)

In Egypt this term refers to female performers of poems and songs associated with the MAWLID and recited at births, weddings, and during RAMAḌÂN.

Aljamia (Spanish, from Arabic *al-ʿajamiyyah*: non-Arabic)

The Spanish Romance rendering of the Arabic term for non-Arab, it refers to the dialect that developed among the northern Iberian inhabitants under Muslim rule, in which proto-Spanish and Arabic mixed. The literature, Aljamiada, is a mixture of Spanish and Arabic, usually written in Arabic characters and generally concerning religious or legal topics, although there are striking examples of SÎRAH literature, both in poetry and prose, and some important letters. This literature continued to be produced after 1492 until the expulsion of the Muslims from Spain in 1609 by King Philip III, and afterward by the MOORS in Tunisia.

Allâh

The Arabic name for God. The name Allâh was known in pre-Islamic Arabia as the head of the pantheon among polytheists and as the name for God among Arabic-speaking Christians and Jews. With the advent of Islam, Allâh is defined as the One, eternal, neither born nor bearing and not having an equal (see Q. 112). Allâh is the creator of the universe and its judge, is merciful, compassionate, all-knowing, all-seeing, rewarding good and punishing evil. Muslims have developed numerous theologies to attempt to define Allâh, but there is no single theology or creed that embodies a universally accepted full definition. In general, Allâh is considered completely transcendent, and only communicates with humans through the intermediary of an angel, such as JIBRÎL, as in the case of the revelation to MUḤAMMAD. The Islamic mystical (ṢÛFÎ) tradition admits the possibility of apprehending the divine through a beatific vision, and many Muslims hold that all humankind will see Allâh on the Day of Judgment, YAWM AD-DÎN. The QURʾÂN presents a few views of Allâh, but is not a theological tract nor a treatise on His nature, except as it affects the human capacity to repent of sins and comply with divine regulations. Western scholarship has tried to demonstrate an evolution of the idea of Allâh through the chronological arrangement of the *sûrah*s of the Qur'ân, but most Muslim scholars see the revelation as a totality, and will admit only that humans may come to understand Him in a progressive fashion. Muslim exegetes of the Qur'ân know of ninety-nine "names" of Allâh, the so-called "beautiful names," AL-'ASMÂ' AL-ḤUSNÂ. Some of these seem to be characteristics, like merciful or all-knowing, but others, along with other passages from the Qur'ân, imply that Allâh has human attributes. For some Muslims, the fact that He is described as a hearer or one who sees means that He has ears and eyes like humans. The anthropomorphists have been opposed from an early date by those who understand such terminology in a metaphoric or abstract manner (such as, for example, the MU'TAZILAH). The introduction of Greek philosophy (FALSAFAH) into the theological debates in Islam complicated the discussion of the nature of Allâh just as it did in Western theology, since such a philosophical system strives to resolve all contradictions. At the core of Islamic understanding of Allâh, however, is the fact that God is a mystery, approachable but ultimately unknowable by humans.

Allâhu 'akbar

See TAKBÎR.

Allâhummah (Arabic: O Allâh!)

An invocation of ALLÂH found in old Arabic texts.

All-India Muslim League

A movement derived from the modernist Aligarh movement in 1906, it developed into the movement that resulted in the creation of PAKISTAN under the leadership of MUḤAMMAD 'ALÎ JINNAH. After the creation of the state in 1947, it became one of several political parties in Pakistan.

Almohads

See AL-MUWAḤḤIDÛN.

Almoravids

See AL-MURÂBIṬÛN.

Almsgiving

See ZAKÂT.

Amal (Arabic: hope)

A popular militant SHÎ'Î movement among Lebanese Muslims. Started in 1975, it has maintained ties with Iran since the Revolution of 1979. (*See also* AṢ-ṢADR, MÛSÂ.)

Ameer Ali, Syed (1849–1928)

Indian jurist, historian, and modernist, best known for two influential books: *A Short History of the Saracens* and *The Spirit of Islam*. He came from an Indian ISMÂ'ÎLÎ SHÎ'Î family that was in service to the East India Company. He was educated in English and Islamic subjects and took particularly to the study of English law. At the age of twenty, he went to England, where he was called to the Bar. He served on the Bengal High Court and returned to England with his English wife in 1904. In 1883 he became the only Muslim on the Viceroy's Council, and he was active in the British Red Crescent Society. He was active politically in both England and South Asia in promoting reform and developing the interests of Muslims. He was a supporter of the KHILÂFAT MOVEMENT along with the AGHÂ KHÂN. His book *The Spirit of Islam* was a liberal interpretation of Islam based on Western modernist models. It became popular throughout the Islamic world and had great influence in the West, as did his *A Short History of the Saracens*. His irenic views did much to promote a better understanding of Islam among Western readers.

âmîn (Arabic: safe, secure)

This term is used much like the English "Amen." Cognate to similar terms in Christian Syriac and Jewish Hebrew, it is used as a response to a prayer or the recitation of the first SÛRAH of the QUR'ÂN. According to tradition, it has particular power when said in proximity to the KA'BAH.

amîn (Arabic: trustworthy)

In the sense of "trustworthy," this term became an epithet applied to MUḤAMMAD because of his trustworthiness, as *al-Amîn*. It also is a term applied to Muslims who hold positions of financial or legal trust.

Amînah

The name in the legendary TAFSÎR of one of the wives of SULAYMÂN (Solomon). She is the one to whom he is reported to have given his signet ring; she, in turn, gave it to a demon who took Sulaymân's place. It was only after many adventures and much repentance, according to the story, that Sulaymân was able to get his ring and his kingdom back.

Âminah bt. Wahb (died 576)

The mother of the Prophet MUḤAMMAD, she belonged to the Zuhra clan of the QURAYSH, and is reported to have been of very noble lineage. She was married to 'ABD ALLÂH B. 'ABD AL-MUṬṬALIB, but the marriage seems to have been one in which she remained with her family, receiving visits from her husband. Her pregnancy with the Prophet is represented in miraculous terms in the SÎRAH. She is said to have been visited by the angel JIBRÎL and told of Muḥammad's impending birth and mission, and, during the pregnancy, a light is said to have shown from her womb bright enough to illumine the castles in Syria. She died when Muḥammad was six. Up to that time, Muḥammad was in her and her family's care, except when he was sent to a wet-nurse among the bedouin tribe of the Banû Bakr b. Sa'd, a common practice among the Meccan elite. She is described in the *sîrah* as the most beautiful and noble woman in Arabia.

amîr (Arabic: commander)

The term has been applied as a title to generals, princes, governors, and even caliphs.

Amîr al-Mu'minîn (Arabic: Commander of the Faithful)

A title applied to caliphs, generally indicating their temporal power, whereas the term KHALÎFAH, (caliph), refers to their deputyship, and IMÂM to their role as a religious leader.

amr (Arabic: command)

The usual Qur'ânic word for "command," generally the divine command.

'Amr b. al-'Âṣ (died *c.* 42/663)

A Companion of MUḤAMMAD, he was one of the most astute politicians of his generation. After the siege of MADÎNAH by the people of MECCA in 8/630, he converted to Islam and was sent out as a missionary. The caliph ABÛ BAKR sent him at the head of an army into Palestine, and he commanded the army that captured Egypt. He also set up the system of administration of the country. He was replaced by the caliph 'UTHMÂN, and retired from active life in disgust and consternation at his removal. In the arbitration between 'ALÎ and MU'Â-

WIYAH, he seems to have had a large part in maneuvering the process in favor of Muʿâwiyah. In the assassination plot that killed ʿAlî, he seems to have escaped only because he was not feeling well that day and did not appear in public.

Âmû Daryâ (Persian)

The river Oxus. Some Arab geographers also called this river *Jayḥûn* after the biblical river Gihon, one of the rivers on the boundary of Paradise.

ʿânâniyyah

One of many Jewish sects that flourished in the turbulent period at the end of the ʾUMAYYAD and beginning of the ʿABBÂSID periods. Named after ʿÂnân b. David, who flourished in the mid-eighth century, this sect was identified by Muslim heresiographers with the Karaites, and was granted equal status along with the Rabbinic Jews, *rabbâniyyah*, in the newly emerging ʿAbbâsid caliphate.

ʿAnâq (Arabic)

In the ISRÂʾÎLIYYÂT TAFSÎR tradition, she was a daughter of ADAM, the twin of Shîth (Seth), the wife of QÂBÎL (Cain), and the mother of the giant ʿÛj. In the stories that mention her name, the commentators hold that all of the early births after the expulsion from Paradise were male–female twins to provide enough pairs to populate the earth. In one of the traditions, Qâbîl killed his brother Hâbîl (Abel) out of jealousy, because Qâbîl wanted to mate either with his own sister or his mother.

ʾAnas b. Mâlik (died *c.* 91/709)

Early Companion of MUḤAMMAD and prolific traditionist. He participated in the wars of conquest and in the FITNAH wars on the side of ʿAbd Allâh b. az-Zubayr, the rival caliph. This earned him some political trouble, but his reputation as a traditionist did not suffer, and his heritage is found in the major *sunan* collections.

al-Andalus

The term derived from the Germanic Vandals and used by Muslims in the medieval period to refer to the Iberian peninsula or to that portion of the peninsula held by Muslims. It is the preferred form for Arab writers to the name Ishbâniyah, Spain. The Latin-speaking supporters of the Reconquista, which ended with the expulsion of most of the Muslims in 897/1492, preferred the terms "Hispania, Spania, and Iberia."

angels (Arabic *malâʾikah*, sing. *malak*: messengers)

Supernatural, created beings mentioned in the QURʾÂN as individuals and groups. Their functions include that of messengers, intercessors, recorders of deeds, and agents of divine punishment. IBLÎS is sometimes thought to be an angel as well as a JINN. JIBRÎL (Gabriel) was of the highest rank of angels and the bringer of revelation to MUḤAMMAD. At the time of the creation of the first human, ADAM, God instructed all the angels to bow to him. Iblîs refused and was cast out of the ranks of the angels along with some rebellious demons, to rule Hell and try to tempt humankind to evil. Islamic angelology owes much to the speculations by Jews and Christians, with which Muslim commentators became familiar at an early date. Just as in Jewish and Christian texts, angels are divided into two general groups, regular angels and archangels, the latter being capable of more important tasks and multiple assignments from God. In the TAFSÎR tradition, angels are grouped into tribes as well. In astrological speculation, an angel was supposed to be in charge of each star in each constellation, often lending a name to the star. (*See also* MUNKAR WA-NAKÎR.)

Angkatan Belia Islam Malaysia

See ABIM.

Anglo-Muhammadan Law

The laws of personal status founded on British colonial interpretations of Islamic law and applied to Muslims in British colonial courts.

ʿankabût (Arabic: spider)

Spiders have a special place in Islamic lore, because a spider is supposed to have saved the lives of MUḤAMMAD and ABÛ BAKR. While the two were fleeing the Meccans during the HIJRAH, they hid in a cave. A spider, presumably by God's command, quickly spun a web over the entrance, so that the Meccans would think the cave to be empty, since they did not think a spider could spin so quickly.

anṣâr (Arabic: helpers, allies)

They were the Medinese who welcomed MUḤAMMAD and his companions after the HIJRAH from MECCA. Members of the two major tribes in MADÎNAH, the Banû AL-ʾAWS and the Banû AL-KHAZRAJ, as well as other Arabs who had belonged to the Jewish tribes, were active in welcoming Muḥammad to the city and gave hospitality to those who made the *hijrah* with him or shortly afterwards. Even though there were those who were not active in supporting the Muslims or who acted in ways that hindered rather than helped the early community, after the death of the Prophet, all those who came from Madînah were grouped together under this designation. In the early history of the community, the *anṣâr* were never as influential as the QURAYSH of Mecca and became part of the pro-ʿAlid movement against the ʾUmayyads. When the ʿAbbasids came to power, the term generally lost significance as a political designation, although individuals would still bear the family designation Anṣârî. The term also designates a ṢÛFÎ activist political movement in the Sudan.

apostasy

See ILḤÂD; RIDDAH.

ʿaqîdah (Arabic: creed)

The QUR'ÂN indicates five basic articles of belief: belief in God, the prophets, angels, scripture, and the Day of Judgment, but does not formulate a formal creed. The later development of creeds in Islam are, for the most part, a result of sectarian disputes and are summaries of theological discussions. They are also sometimes short teaching texts to instruct children and converts. While there has never been a single, agreed-upon formulation of a creed, even among either the SUNNÎ or the SHÎʿÎ, most creeds have a number of concepts in common. The first is that ALLÂH is the only deity. He has no partners, was not born, and did not bear. This Qur'ânic formulation lies at the heart of Islam. The second is that He is the creator of all that exists and everything belongs to Him and will return to Him. It follows that any possessions humans have are transitory, a gift from God, and must be used in the right manner. Additionally, reward and punishment on the YAWM AD-DÎN are real and based on the contract set forth between Allâh and humans in the Qur'ân and in the model of His Prophet, MUḤAMMAD. Muḥammad is the last in a line of prophets sent by God to humankind, the first being Adam. Angels, devils, and JINN exist, and we interact with them according to God's plan. Some Shîʿî will add various concepts about ʿALÎ B. ABÎ ṬÂLIB, and the KHAWÂRIJ held that anyone committing a major sin had renounced Islam by that act. Unlike Christianity, Islam is not a religion dependent on creeds. There have been no great councils or synods called to decide a single formulation, and the SHAHÂDAH comes closest to a statement on which all Muslims can agree. Nor is Islam solely reliant on deeds. It is a middle way, requiring both belief (ÎMÂN) and acting correctly in the world.

'aqîlah (Arabic: to bind)

A term that designates the person(s) bound by Islamic law, SHARÎ'AH, to share the liability with someone who has committed a murder or inflicted bodily injury. The extension of liability varies among the several schools, (MADHHABS), of Islamic law, but generally it is confined to blood relatives, except in the case of ḤANAFÎ law, where the liability is extended to comrades in arms.

'aqîqah (Arabic: red)

The name of the customary sacrifice of an animal on the seventh day after the birth of a child, on which day the child's head is shaved and the child is named. The majority of the sacrifice is distributed as charity, but a ritual meal made from a portion of it, called a *walîmah*, should be consumed. If the ceremony does not take place on the seventh day, it can be performed later, even by the person him- or herself when they come of age. This practice, while widespread, is not based on Qur'ânic mandate and is customary.

'aql (Arabic: intelligence)

Among Islamic theologians, this term is used to designate a kind of natural intelligence or knowledge, as opposed to tradition. It is also used as a technical term in Islamic philosophy, referring to the Neoplatonic concept of a universal intellect.

'aqrab (Arabic: scorpion)

Because of the harmful or deadly character of the sting of the scorpion, verses of the QUR'ÂN are sometimes used as talismans against it in customary practice. The scorpion is also a sign in the zodiac and is used to interpret dreams.

'Arab

The designation 'Arab has, over time, been subject to a wide number of definitions. In the pre-Islamic period, ancient classical authors used the term "Arab" and "Arabia" to refer to a number of pastoral nomadic war-like people on the eastern edge of the Mediterranean world and into Arabia, which included the Sinai peninsula and the Syrian desert. Archaeological evidence indicates that some, but not all, of these peoples spoke or wrote languages that seem to be related to modern ARABIC. The first of these peoples appear in Assyrian records in the ninth century B.C.E. With the rise of Islam and Muslim interest in preserving the history of the forebears of MUḤAMMAD we get a complicated and somewhat legendary picture of the 'Arabs. According to some authors, the speakers of what would become the language of the QUR'ÂN were not the "true" or original 'Arabs, but had replaced those people in the area of the ḤIJÂZ. These new 'Arabs came, probably, from the coastal area of the Red Sea, as the name QURAYSH (probably "dugong") indicates. As the Qur'ân set the standard for the language of Arabic, it was also used by some to define who was an 'Arab by saying that anyone who spoke Arabic as his native tongue and participated in the culture of the 'Arabs was 'Arab. Under this definition, Jews and Christians have been considered 'Arab at various times. Sometimes, the term 'Arab meant being a pastoral nomad, a bedouin. One medieval chronicle asserts that the Kurds have 'Arab, meaning that there are those Kurds who have a bedouin lifestyle. For some, being 'Arab and being Muslim became more and more associated, so that we can, for example, speak of the

"Arab" countries of North Africa, even when most of the inhabitants are descended from Berber ancestors, because the countries were conquered by ʿArab Muslim forces and incorporated into the expanding Islamic world. The rise of modern nationalism has transformed the definition yet again to mean that an ʿArab is one who is a citizen of a self-designated ʿArab country.

Arabic

A Semitic language related to Hebrew and others, it is spoken in various dialects by the inhabitants of Arabia, the Middle East, and North Africa, including Muslims, Christians, and Jews. With the rise of Islam, it became the particular language of the QUR'ÂN, which became the dominant standard literary form, but did not eradicate the various spoken forms of the language, which differ from the written form to greater or lesser degrees. Some scholars of the language speak of a resultant "diglossia," or quasi-bilingualism, among speakers of Arabic because of the differences between the spoken and written forms. Muslim Arabic is written in a cursive script derived from Nabataean and Syriac scripts, but Jews and Christians have written Arabic in the scripts associated with their sacred liturgical texts. Thus, there is an extensive literature in Judeo-Arabic, written in Hebrew characters and incorporating many Hebrew words, often Arabized. Christians wrote Arabic in Greek, Syriac, or Roman scripts, depending on their confession. The language of Malta is a North African-derived Arabic written in Roman script. With the spread of Islam, Arabic has become the liturgical language of Muslims worldwide.

ʿArafah

A hill and plain east of MECCA featured prominently in the ḤAJJ at which the pilgrims assemble for the WUQÛF on the ninth of DHÛ-L-ḤIJJA, the month of pilgrimage. The name, which means knowledge, is associated with the sermon traditionally preached from that hill and from the recitation of the QUR'ÂN there.

architecture

Muslim religious sites, such as the mosques (MASJID), MADRASAH, MAQÂM, and RIBÂṬ, have been a mixture of local styles and aesthetics and the requirements of the religion. Some features usually associated with Islamic places of worship are the MINARET, a niche marking the direction of prayer (QIBLAH), and facilities for ritual ablutions. The universal character of Islam has allowed great creative variation in architectural styles and decorations, usually avoiding pictorial representations.

Islamic architecture is often highly decorative as demonstrated by this dome of the Shah Chiragh Shrine, Shiraz, Iran.

arkân al-Islâm

See PILLARS OF ISLAM.

Arkoun, Mohammed (born 1928)

Algerian-born Islamic philosopher and modernist whose works combine solid traditional Islamic scholarship with Western hermeneutics. His best known works are *Lectures du Coran* and *Ouvertures sur l'Islam*.

ʿaṣabah (Arabic: league, federation)

The Arabic word for the agnate heirs in Islamic INHERITANCE.

ʿaṣabiyyah (Arabic: group feeling)

The notion of group solidarity, usually based on tribal affiliation through birth or affiliation. Some Muslim authors, such as IBN KHALDÛN, have held this concept in high regard, but it was repudiated by MUḤAMMAD as contrary to the universal character of Islam in which all believers are interconnected as a group.

al-Asadâbâdî, Jamâl ad-Dîn

See AL-AFGHÂNÎ, JAMÂL AD-DÎN

Âṣâf b. Barâkhyâ

The name of the advisor to the prophet-king SULAYMÂN (Solomon), who reproved him for introducing idol worship into his kingdom. The name is not known from the QUR'ÂN, but derives from Jewish midrashic sources incorporated into the TAFSÎR traditions.

asḥâb al-kahf (Arabic: the companions of the cave)

The name used in Q. 18 to refer to the sleepers in the cave, called by Western scholars the Seven Sleepers of Ephesus, persecuted monotheists who sought refuge in a cave, and were put to sleep and caused to awaken by God. Post-Qur'ânic literature elaborates their story with material paralleling Christian hagiographic stories.

aṣḥâb ar-rass (Arabic: people of the well or ditch)

They are mentioned in the QUR'ÂN along with other unbelievers who were destroyed by ALLÂH for their unbelief. The Muslim exegetes know little of their history or identification.

aṣḥâb ar-ra'y (Arabic: adherents of personal opinion)

A term of opprobrium applied to certain schools (MADHHABS) and practitioners of Islamic law (SHARÎʿAH), who incorporated human judgment and analogic reasoning into their process of making legal judgments. No group has ever consented to be called by this term, since it was polemical on the part of the traditionists, who themselves incorporated RA'Y into their own reasoning.

aṣḥâb al-ukhdûd (Arabic: people of the trench)

A term from the QUR'ÂN. Muslim exegetes variously identify these people with the Christian martyrs of Najrân, supposedly burned in a trench by the Jewish king of South Arabia, Yûsuf Dhû Nuwâs, or with another group of people placed into a trench of fire to demonstrate their faith and the power of God. Other commentators understand the passage to refer to the future punishment of sinners in trenches filled with fire.

al-ʿasharah al-mubashsharah (Arabic: the ten who have been brought good news)

The ten persons promised Paradise according to the ḤADÎTH. The concept goes back to the earliest SUNNAH collections, but the term itself is fairly late. The list also varies but usually includes

MUḤAMMAD, ABÛ BAKR, 'UMAR, 'UTHMÂN, 'ALÎ, Ṭalḥah, az-Zubayr, 'Abd ar-Raḥmân b. 'Awf, Sa'd b. Abî Waqqâṣ, Sa'îd b. Zayd, and, sometimes, ABÛ 'UBAYDAH. When the last name is included, Muḥammad is dropped from the list.

al-Ash'arî, Abû-l-Ḥasan 'Alî (260/873–324/935)

Theologian and polemicist against the MU'TAZILAH, he was an early and leading practitioner of Islamic scholasticism (KALÂM) who united philosophical methods with traditional discourse. He was a descendant of the Companion Abû Mûsâ al-Ash'arî, and studied with the head of the Mu'tazilite school in BAṢRAH. He is said to have seen visions of the Prophet MUḤAMMAD urging him to return to "true tradition," without abandoning speculative theology (*kalâm*). Part of his reputation lies in his defense of traditionalism by using the Mu'tazilite arguments and the tools of Hellenized FALSAFAH. The subsequent school of theology, known as the Ash'ariyyah, took the opening that he provided and developed a full-fledged school of rationalist defense of traditional Islam that went well beyond the narrow intent of al-Ash'arî himself. At various periods, such as under the Buwayhids, the movement was persecuted, but by the fourteenth century, Ash'arism was the theology of the SUNNÎ mainstream.

Ash'ariyyah

See AL-ASH'ARÎ.

'Âshûrâ' (Arabic: ten)

A twenty-four-hour non-obligatory fast celebrated on the tenth of Muḥarram, it was first performed by MUḤAMMAD. Among the SUNNÎ, the day is marked as a commemoration of the day NÛḤ left the ark, and the door of the KA'BAH is opened for visitors. In North Africa the fast is broken by eating special dishes of fried cakes and flat bread. It is also a day to give charity for educational institutions. It is also a day of mourning for SHÎ'Î as the anniversary of the martyrdom of ḤUSAYN at KARBALÂ'. Both the name and the structure indicate a historic relation to the Jewish fast of the Day of Atonement.

Âsiyah

The name of the wife of FIR'AWN (Pharaoh) in the commentaries on the QUR'ÂN. She is a true believer, saves MÛSÂ, and generally functions in the same manner as Pharaoh's daughter in the biblical story of Moses. The traditions relate that because of her piety, her martyrdom at the hands of Pharaoh was without pain.

'askarî (Arabic: army)

The term designating the ruling, "military" class in the OTTOMAN EMPIRE. This included the families of the ruling elite, the members of the religious orders and even some Christians who owned land and had feudal association with the SULṬÂN. This caste was opposed to the majority *re'âyâ*, or "sheep" caste, which had its own religious establishment separate in many respects from the ruling 'ULAMÂ'. Many of the ṢÛFÎ TARÎQAHS and other popular movements were found in the *re'âyâ* but not the *'askarî* caste.

al-'asmâ' al-ḥusnâ (Arabic: the beautiful names)

The ninety-nine names or epithets of God, often used in personal devotion. In a ḤADÎTH from ABÛ HURAYRAH, we learn that ALLÂH has ninety-nine names by which He likes to be called, and whoever knows the ninety-nine names will enter Paradise. In the usual lists of the names, not all the names come from the QUR'ÂN and not all the names or epithets of Allâh in the Qur'ân are on the list. For this reason, there has always been some mystery as well as discussion about the names. In theological circles, the names have been equated with the attributes of God, with the attendant discussion of whether those attributes constitute part of God's essence or are accidental. (*See also* MU'TAZILAH; SUBḤAH.)

Assassins

A term of abuse applied to a group of ISMÂ'ÎLÎ SHÎ'Î who resisted the Crusaders. The name, through French, refers to the mistaken notion that they used HASHÎSH to induce a mystic state as a spur to assassination and terror. (*See also* NIZÂRIYYAH.)

astrology

The belief that the future fate of an individual can be predicted by an examination of heavenly bodies, this practice is firmly entrenched in Islamic popular cultures and has been generally condemned as antithetical to genuine Islamic teachings. Astrology was often inseparable from astronomy in the premodern Islamic world, and the Muslim scientific study of astronomy influenced the course of European scientific development in the fields of mathematics, navigation, and time-keeping, as well as in astronomy itself. Many star names are derived from the Arabo-Islamic astronomical tradition.

'atabât (Arabic: thresholds, steps)

The four SHÎ'Î shrine cities of Iraq: NAJAF, KARBALÂ', Kâẓimayn, and Samarrâ', which contain the tombs of six of the IMÂMS.

Atatürk, Mustafa Kemal (1881–1938)

Founder of the modern Republic of TURKEY, who sought to reform Islam on Western models and separate religion and politics. He abolished the caliphate in 1343/1924.

'Aṭṭâr, Farîd ad-Dîn (died *c.* 627/1230)

Persian mystical poet, whose *Manṭiq al-ṭayr* (Parliament of fowls) is an outstanding example of ṢÛFÎ writing.

Averroes

See IBN RUSHD.

Avicenna

See IBN SÎNÂ.

Avrupa Milli Görüş Teşkilati

Organization of Islamic Youth in Europe, an Islamist youth organization founded in 1985 from several previous groups.

Awami League

The People's League of Bangladesh, founded in Dacca in 1949, became one of two major political parties that achieved Bangladesh's independence.

'awrah (Arabic: lit. the genitals)

The areas of the body that must remain covered to maintain modesty. (*See also* DRESS.)

al-'Aws

One of the two chiefly Arab tribes in the city of MADÎNAH at the time of the Prophet. They were rivals of the other mainly Arab tribe, AL-KHAZRAJ, as well as the Jewish tribes. Like all the Arab tribes in the city, their tribe contained some Jews and the Jewish tribes contained some Arabs. Some of the clans of the 'Aws were slower to enter Islam, but after the battle of BADR they were active Muslims, and their rivalry with the Khazraj disappeared after the death of MUḤAMMAD.

ʾâyah (Arabic: sign, miracle, token; verse in the Qurʾân. Plural: *ʾâyat*)

In modern usage, the word almost always means a "verse" in the QURʾÂN, but Qurʾânic usage makes it clear that it often means a "miracle" or "wonder." Commentators have played with this range of meaning and speculated about a hierarchy of verses, if any, and the heavenly reward for reciting them. The convention in the Qurʾân is to place the number of the *ʾâyah* at the end, rather than at the beginning. For those who know the Qurʾân, it is sufficient to quote only the beginning of the verse to recall the whole verse. (*See also* ḤÂFIẒ.)

Aya Sofya

The largest mosque in ISTANBUL, it was originally the main church and seat of the Metropolitan of Greek Christianity, built by Constantius, the son of Constantine, in the middle of the fourth century. From an early time, it was called *Hagia Sôfia*, "Holy Wisdom." When the city was taken by Muslims in 1453, the interior of the church was stripped of its Christian symbols and converted to a mosque. As a church, it was oriented toward Jerusalem, so various changes were made to redirect the QIBLAH toward Mecca. During OTTOMAN times, it was the chief mosque. In 1934, ATATÜRK changed the mosque to a state museum.

âyatollâh

Honorific title in ITHNÂ ʿASHARIYYAH SHÎʿÎ Islam, from Arabic *âyât Allâh*, meaning "sign of God." The term is currently used to designate someone near the top of the Shîʿî ʿULAMÂʾ hierarchy.

ʿayn (Arabic: eye)

The evil eye. The superstition of the "evil eye" predates Islam. ABÛ HURAYRAH is attributed with the statement that the Prophet said that the "evil eye" is real, but other authorities quote traditions in which Muḥammad strongly condemned this belief. In popular practice, the "evil eye" is averted by pious utterances, holding out the hand, with its five fingers, or wearing an amulet made in the shape of a hand or an eye. Tourist travel to the Middle East has increased the prevalence of such amulets, and in the West they have become symbols of identification with the Middle East and Islam in some circles.

Ayyûb

The biblical Job. He is mentioned twice in the QURʾAN (Q. 21:83–84, 38:40–44) as a person noted for his suffering. Post-Qurʾânic legend greatly expands his story, based partly on the Bible and partly on Jewish legend. He is counted among the prophets in Islamic commentaries.

Ayyûbids

Kurdish dynasty in Syria and Egypt that flourished between 546/1169 and 648/1250, founded by Ṣalâḥ ad-Dîn (532/1138–589/1193).

Azâd, Abû al-Kalâm (1888–1956)

URDU journalist and Islamic reformer who, through his journal, *al-Hilâl*, sought to reform Indian Islamic society.

Azâr

The name of the father of Abraham in the QURʾÂN (Q. 6:75).

Azerbaijan (Persian *Âdharbâyjân*)

A region in extreme northwest Iran, it borders on Iraq and Turkey. The chief city is Tabrîz. In ancient times, it was ruled by the Medes, and was incorporated into the Persian empire. Zoroaster is said to have been born in this region.

Conquered by the Arabs in 18/639, it remained a Persian-speaking area, with a reported seventy languages or dialects spoken. In the sixth/eleventh and seventh/twelfth centuries, it was dominated by the SALJÛQ Turks. At the end of the ninth/fifteenth century, the ṢAFAVID dynasty arose in this area before ruling over the rest of Iran. The result of the Ṣafavid rise to power was the increasing domination of SHÎʿÎ Islam. When the Russians captured the northern portion in 1323/1905 with the aid of the British, it was estimated to be nearly eighty percent Shîʿî. Persian control was restored in 1340/1921, but lost again to the Soviet Union at the beginning of World War II. It became independent in 1412/1991 with the collapse of the Soviet Union. The state at present has no religious parties and professes religious freedom and tolerance.

al-Azhar

A mosque-university built by the FÂṬIMIDS in AL-QÂHIRAH (Cairo) in the fourth/tenth century as a center of ISMÂʿÎLÎ SHÎʿÎ learning and missionary training. Ṣalâḥ ad-Dîn changed its orientation to SUNNÎ in the sixth/twelfth century. It is one of the preeminent places in the Islamic world to study QURʾÂN, Islamic jurisprudence and related subjects, and statements by its faculty carry worldwide authority among Muslims.

B

Bâb (Arabic: gate, door)

Among the ṢÛFÎ, this refers to the SHAYKH through whom one enters into inner wisdom; among the SHÎ'Î, the *Bâb* is the senior disciple of the IMÂM. With the *Imâm* in GHAYBAH, he is the gate to the HIDDEN IMÂM. The title was assumed by the reformist Sayyid 'Alî Muḥammad Shîrâzî (1235/1819–1266/1850). His prediction of the imminent arrival of the HIDDEN IMÂM caused social unrest and his execution, and led to the creation of the BÂBÎ movement, which was a forerunner of the BAHÂ'Î faith. Among the NIZÂRÎ ISMÂ'ÎLÎ SHÎ'Î, it is a title indicating high rank in the DA'WAH organization. Among the 'ALAWIYYAH, the *Bâb* is identified with SALMÂN AL-FÂRISÎ and is thought to be reincarnated in each generation.

bâbâ (Persian/Turkish: father)

An honorific used for older men, it is used as the title/name of some ṢÛFÎ SHAYKHS.

Bâbî, Bâbism

The messianic movement of followers of the BÂB in nineteenth-century Iran. Ideas from this movement influenced the development of the BAHÂ'Î faith.

Badakhshân

A remote region of Pamîr in Central Asia, famous for its rubies, which is the home to many ISMÂ'ÎLÎ SHÎ'Î. Its capital is Khârôgh.

badal (Arabic: substitute)

According to some ṢÛFÎ doctrines, the world is preserved by a fixed number of "saints" and, when one dies, another is sent as a substitute to maintain the number.

Badr

The battle of Badr, southwest of MADÎNAH, was the first major conflict between MUḤAMMAD and his supporters in Madînah and the people of MECCA in 2/624 and the first military victory for the new community. In spite of overwhelming odds, the Muslims were able to win the day. The early sources attribute the Muslim victory to divine intervention, and some say that a band of angels rode with Muḥammad's troops. This battle dealt a severe blow to the Meccan military capability and prestige, but did not stop them completely. They felt the necessity of punishing Muḥammad, and began preparing for the next encounter, which was at Uḥud. For the Muslims, this was seen as a vindication of the truth of the faith, and many around Madînah saw it as such, also, because many bedouin tribes converted to Islam. In later Islamic literature, Badr has become a symbol of Muslim victory.

Baghdâd

The major city in Iraq, it was founded by the ʿABBÂSID caliph al-Manṣûr in 145/762 as the empire's capital. It was built on an ancient site, and the Arabs used the name after the ancient *Bagdadu*. Al-Manṣûr called the city *madinat as-salâm*, the "city of peace." It was a round city with gates opening to the cardinal points of the compass, in the center of which was a huge green dome, all of which meant to symbolize that this was the center of the world. It was a major cultural and intellectual center under the caliphate, boasting, among other institutions, one of the first universities of the Islamic world, the BAYT AL-ḤIKMAH. The city was sacked by the Mongols in 656/1258, ending the ʿAbbâsid caliphate. Under the Ottomans, it became a provincial capital and continued as an intellectual center of the region. As modern Iraq's capital, it was heavily bombed in the Gulf War of 1991.

Bahâ' U'llâh

The title of Mîrzâ Ḥusayn ʿAlî Nûrî (1233/1817–1309/1892), the prophet founder of the BAHÂ'Î faith. Originally a follower of the BÂB, he was persecuted, along with the other Bâbîs, imprisoned, and banished to BAGHDÂD, where he became the spiritual leader of the Iranian Bâbîs in exile. His growing popularity provoked another exile to ISTANBUL and later to Akka in Ottoman Palestine. In 1863, shortly before his departure from Baghdâd, he claimed to be the promised "divine manifestation" of the Bâbî tradition. His tomb is near Haifa, Israel, the headquarters of the Bahâ'î religion. To his followers, he is known as *Jamâlî-i-Mubârak*, "blessed beauty."

Bahâ'î

The faith of the followers of BAHÂ' U'LLÂH who believe that God is manifested in a chain of prophets by progressive revelation, including major figures of Judaism, Christianity, and Islam. All religions with prophets have intrinsic truth and are included under the faith's purview. Bahâ'îs have been regarded by some Muslims, particularly the ITHNÂ ʿASHARIYYAH SHÎʿÎ as heretics or non-Muslims and have been subject to persecution. The world-wide center of the Bahâ'î religion is in Haifa, Israel. For the Bahâ'î, God is transcendent but is mirrored through a constant series of prophets, starting with ADAM and proceeding through the Jewish and Christian prophets, Zoroaster, MUḤAMMAD, and then the BÂB. They believe in long cycles of history in which God is mirrored in the way best suited to the time. The moral precepts of the religion make it incumbent on the adherents to make the world a better place. They seek, among other things, to unify the human race, the unification of science and religion, gender equality, the elimination of prejudice, the elimination of extremes of wealth and poverty, and the rule of universal law.

Baḥîrâ (Aramaic: chosen)

The name of the Syrian Christian monk who, when MUḤAMMAD traveled as a boy with his uncle ABÛ ṬÂLIB to Syria, predicted his prophecy. In the various accounts of the event, the monk is supposed to have found a mark of prophecy on Muḥammad's body or seen a branch move to provide him shade regardless of where he moved. He said that he had found a prediction of Muḥammad's advent in his scriptures and warned Abû Ṭâlib to protect the boy from harm. This event took place, according to some traditions, when Muḥammad was twelve years of age, the same age as JESUS when he encountered the rabbis in the Temple. The figure of Baḥîrâ is found in Greek, Syriac, and Christian Arabic literature as a heretic monk who aided Muḥammad in the composition of the QUR'ÂN. These polemical works date from the early Islamic period and reflect the attitudes of some of the Christians of the time to the Islamic conquest.

Bairam, or Bayram (Turkish: festival)

The word refers to the Lesser Bairam, the 'ÎD AL-FIṬR, the three-day breaking of the fast of RAMAḌÂN, and the Greater Bairam, the 'ÎD AL-AḌḤÂ, the four-day feast of sacrifice beginning on the tenth of Dhû-l-Ḥijjah, in connection with the ḤAJJ.

Bairamiyya

An order of dervishes, a group of the NAQSHBANDIYYAH ṢÛFÎ ṬARÎQAH.

al-Bakka'î al-Kuntî, Aḥmad (1803–1865)

Sudanese religious and political leader and head of the QÂDIRIYYAH ṬARÎQAH, whose letters are an invaluable source of pre-colonial Sudanese Islamic history.

Ba'l, or Ba'al (Arabic from Hebrew: lord, master; owner)

When the word is used as a common noun, it means the possessor of something, but, in religious terminology, it is the name of the preeminent Northwest Semitic pagan deity, the head of the Phoenician pantheon.

Balkan states

The Muslim populations of the Balkan Peninsula are varied in ethnic origin and language, and are found in the countries of Hungary, Romania, Bulgaria, Albania, and the former Yugoslavia. They derive from three main sources: Turks from the conquest and occupation by the OTTOMAN EMPIRE, Muslims who settled in the area during the Ottoman period, and converts to Islam from the indigenous population. The Muslims of Hungary were at their peak in the tenth/sixteenth and eleventh/seventeenth centuries, but were slaughtered or forced to convert after the Christian reconquest. The Romanian Muslims, who had always been a small community, suffered under Communist rule and comprise less than fifty thousand individuals, mostly of Turkish ethnic origin. Bulgaria counted nearly fourteen percent of its population as Muslim in the middle of the last century, but recent campaigns to make every citizen a "Bulgarian" have made recent estimates more difficult. The indigenous Bulgarian Muslims are known as Pomaks. The Islamization of Albania under the Ottomans was so complete that over seventy percent of the modern state is Muslim. Of those, eighty percent are SUNNÎ and of Albanian ethnic origin. The other twenty percent followed the BEKTÂSHIYYAH ṢÛFÎ order, the practice of which is recognized as an official religion in Albania. In the former Yugoslavia, particularly in Bosnia–Herzegovina and Kosovo, conflict between Christian nationalists and the Muslim communities have seen the Muslims reduced in numbers by acts of slaughter, "ethnic cleansing," and genocide. When the Ottomans entered the area by defeating the Serbs in 792/1389 at the battle of Kosovo, many inhabitants converted to Islam, thus giving the region a large Muslim population. Under the Ottomans and into the middle of the last century, Muslims, Christians, and Jews lived together in an open society. Most identified themselves as Bosnians rather than by religious group, and most were secular. In the second half of the fourteenth/twentieth century, Muslims were favored under the reign of Marshal Tito. With the breakup of Yugoslavia and the rise of Serbian nationalism in the last decades of the last century, Muslims have been the victims of great atrocities, while the world communities have paid scant attention. The information being brought to light in the current war crimes trials in The Hague is only now beginning to indicate the extent of the disaster to the Balkan Muslim communities.

banks and banking

The prohibition in the QUR'ÂN of RIBÂ, speculation and interest, has meant that Islamic financial institutions have sometimes had to find alternative means for capital investment from Western models in which the time value of money determines profit and procedures. Islamic banks generally shun any transactions that are tainted by Qur'ânic and moral prohibitions. (*See also* GHARAR.)

al-Bannâ', Ḥasan (1324/1906–1368/1949)

Egyptian modernist reformer, founder of the Muslim Brotherhood (AL-IKHWÂN AL-MUSLIMÛN), who espoused ideals of Islamic statehood and social justice based on a return to the principles of the QUR'ÂN and SUNNAH. He demonstrated a spiritual bent at an early age, and, building on a solid religious education, was inducted into the Ḥaṣâfiyyah ṢÛFÎ order at the age of fourteen. He became a government schoolteacher in Ismâ'îliyyah in 1927, and was transferred to Cairo in 1933. Starting in 1928, he founded the movement and began public pamphleting and lobbying for reform. He was assassinated by Egyptian secret police in 1949.

Banû Isrâ'îl (Arabic: the children of Israel)

The usual Qur'ânic term for the Jews mentioned in the Hebrew Bible. This phrase is never used, to our present knowledge, in pre-Islamic poetry, although the term AL-YAHÛD is found frequently. In a few instances, the term Banû Isrâ'îl is used for Jews contemporary with MUḤAMMAD, although that depends on an interpretation of a verse from the QUR'ÂN. The term *al-yahûd* is also used for the biblical Jews as well as later Jews.

baqâ' (Arabic: subsistence, survival)

A ṢÛFÎ concept, the state of abiding or remaining with God after FANÂ'. It is generally understood to be the highest state in which the mystic, after "losing" the self in God, returns to the world, while still remaining with God, in order to do the work of helping perfect the world and lead others.

al-Bâqillânî, Abû Bakr Muḥammad b. aṭ-Ṭayyib b. Muḥammad b. Ja'far b. al-Qâsim (also Ibn al-Bâqillânî, died 403/1013)

He spent most of his life in BAGHDÂD, where he was a MÂLIKÎ jurist and judge, (QÂḌÎ). He is best known as an Ash'arite theologian, who was responsible for popularizing and systematizing that school of thought. He is credited with fifty-two works, of which six are extant. Of his best known works, the *Kitâb al-I'jâz al-Qur'ân*, a treatise on the inimitability of the QUR'ÂN, is a seminal work, and his *Kitâb tamhîd* is a good example of his religious polemic. He is frequently cited by later writers. (*See also* AL-ASH'ARÎ.)

Baqliyyah

A late third/early tenth-century sect of vegetarian QARMAṬÎ who did not eat garlic, leeks, and turnips. They abolished Muslim religious observance and displayed banners with the verses from the QUR'ÂN recalling the freeing of the BANÛ ISRÂ'ÎL from FIR'AWN.

barakah (Arabic: blessing)

Also commonly in the plural, *barakât*, blessings from God. In the ṢÛFÎ tradition, it is the blessings and supernatural powers brought from God through the mediation of a WALÎ or saint. In popular belief, *barakah* is associated with places as well as people.

Barelwî, Sayyid Aḥmad

(1786–1831)

Stringent north Indian reformer and proponent of JIHÂD, he opposed elements of ṢÛFÎ and SHÎʿÎ practice that he said were SHIRK.

Barelwis

Indian sect, followers of Maulânâ Aḥmad Riżâ Khân (1856–1921) with a strong veneration of MUḤAMMAD. The group has now spread beyond South Asia and has many adherents in Great Britain.

Barṣîṣâ

The name of the monk whom Muslim commentators on the QURʾÂN identify with the person who believes in the devil and then is abandoned by him (Q. 59:16). In several versions of the story, the monk is an ascetic who is overcome with temptation and ultimately loses his soul.

barzakh (Arabic from Persian: obstacle, barrier)

The boundary between the Heavens, Hell and the Earth, which prevents souls from traversing from one region to the other. For some, it is the intermediary place between Heaven and Hell, in which, however, there is no purgation of sins. In this last sense, it is better understood as "Limbo" rather than "Purgatory."

basmalah

The word meaning the utterance of *bismi-llâhi-r-raḥmâni-r-raḥîm*, "In the name of ALLÂH, the Merciful, the

Eastern Kufic calligraphy of the basmallah.

Compassionate," which precedes each chapter of the QURʾÂN except the ninth, *sûrat at-tawba*, and is said and written by Muslims as a preface to many activities, speech-acts and writings.

Baṣrah

A city in southern Iraq, it started as a military encampment during the early Islamic expansion. It quickly grew into a major religious center, in spite of the difficult climate. When ʿALÎ B. ABÎ ṬÂLIB employed the troops of the city in his fight against MUʿÂWIYAH, the city took on greater importance. In the second/eighth and third/ninth centuries, its dual role as a trading center and an intellectual center close to the ʿABBÂSID capital BAGHDÂD helped it become one of the major cities of Mesopotamia. After a period of decline, it revived as a center of SHÎʿÎ as well as SUNNÎ learning.

bast (Persian: refuge)

A term meaning a place of sanctuary in which a person could seek refuge free from fear of being harmed, even if guilty of a crime. In Islamic Iran, it was associated with a mosque or the tomb of a WÂLÎ, whose *barakât* was thought to protect the refugee. The term became associated with the Iranian 1905–11 constitutional revolution in which people sought refuge in mosques from political retaliation. (*See also* BARAKAH.)

basṭ (Arabic: delight)

The joyful state granted by God to ṢÛFÎs. It is the expansion of the heart to receive revelation and insight from God.

Ba'th Parties

Arab socialist parties of Syria and Iraq, which, while secular, regarded the coming of Islam to the Arabs as foundational to Arab identity.

bâṭin (Arabic: esoteric)

This is applied particularly with reference to understanding certain verses of the QUR'ÂN, as opposed to ẒÂHIR (exoteric, manifest).

Bâṭiniyyah

See ISMÂ'ÎLÎ.

bay'ah (Arabic: swear an oath of allegiance)

Usually thought to come from the Arabic word for sell, it has come to mean the making of an agreement, usually with a pledge or oath to abide by the terms of the agreed-upon contract. By extension, it has taken on the meaning of a pledge of loyalty to a person or a doctrine. It has been historically understood as the oath of allegiance to a caliph or ruler and the invocation of God's blessing on the ruler by the subjects. In modern Islamic political parlance, it has come to mean an "election" of an individual, implying, through the electoral process, the pledging of loyalty to the winner of the election. It should not, however, necessarily be understood to imply a "one person one vote" principle.

Bayram

See BAIRAM.

Bayt al-Ḥikmah

The institution of higher learning founded in BAGHDÂD by the 'ABBÂSID caliph al-Ma'mûn in 217/832. Its chief early activity was the collection, storage, and translation of the corpus of classical philosophical and scientific works and the promotion of the study of medicine and allied fields. It is credited with being the first, or one of the first, institution of higher learning in Islam, and provided a model for many later Muslim universities. It was also, indirectly, the model for the European and American state university system through its influence on the University of Naples.

bayt al-maqdis, also bayt al-muqqadas

The site of the Jewish Temple in Jerusalem. (*See also* AL-QUDS.)

Bâzargân, Mehdi (1325/1907–1416/1995)

Born into a devout family of Iranian merchants, Mehdi Bâzargân was a French-trained engineer, a lay Islamic scholar, and a long-time pro-democracy activist. He participated in a reform movement in the early 1960s aimed at democratizing the SHÎ'Î clerical establishment. Bâzargân was imprisoned several times during the 1960s and 1970s for his nonviolent opposition to the SHÂH through groups such as the Liberation Movement of Iran, which he cofounded in 1961, and the Iranian Human Rights Association, which he co-founded in 1977. After the revolution of 1399/1979, he served as interim prime minister, but resigned after a year over the move of the clerics to the right. He continued to serve in the Iranian parliament for several years, and then retired from politics but remained as a symbol of opposition to the radical Islamic regime.

Bektâshî, or Bektâshiyyah

Syncretic Turkish ṢÛFÎ order popular under Ottoman rule, but banned in modern Turkey. It is one of the official religions of Albania. (*See also* BALKAN STATES.)

bid'ah (Arabic: innovation)

In popular usage this has come to mean heresy. The accusation of fatalism associated with this term is obviated by the presence of the classifications of "good" innovations that were in accord with the QUR'ÂN and the SUNNAH of the Prophet.

Bilâl b. Rabâḥ (died 20/641)

Abyssinian slave appointed by MUḤAMMAD as the first MU'ADHDHIN on account of the carrying quality of his voice. He was an early convert to Islam and suffered greatly until purchased and manumitted by ABÛ BAKR. He became a close Companion to the Prophet and achieved considerable social status during his lifetime.

Bilqîs

The name given the Queen of Sheba in classical Islamic commentaries on the QUR'ÂN. Her story is popular in the TAFSÎR literature, describing her great power and wealth, which was overcome by SULAYMÂN. This led to her conversion to Islam. Whether she became a wife or concubine of Sulaymân was a subject of some speculation. (*See also* SABAEANS.)

Binyâmîn

The biblical Benjamin, who is mentioned in the QUR'ÂN but not named. In the TAFSÎR literature, his story is given with details close to the biblical version plus some haggadic additions. The complicated relationship between Binyâmîn and YÛSUF is used in Islamic mysticism (Ṣûfism) as a metaphor for the relationship between man and God or the disciple and the master.

birthday

See MAWLID.

birth rites

Islam has no official birth rites mandated by the QUR'ÂN, but many Muslim communities have customary practices including the use of prayers to MUḤAMMAD, the use of amulets, recitation of the Qur'ân, and the whispering of the BASMALAH in the ears of a newborn to keep the child from evil.

bismi-llâhi-r-raḥmâni-r-raḥîm

See BASMALAH.

black Muslims

See NATION OF ISLAM.

blasphemy

See SABB.

bohra, or bohorâ (Gujarati *vohôrvû*: to engage in trade)

A term used in western India to refer to SUNNÎ Muslims, ISMÂ'ÎLÎ Muslims, and even some Hindus and Jains. When used for Ismâ'îlî Muslims, it refers to those who do not follow the AGHÂ KHÂN. They are found primarily in western India and claim some descent from Yemenî Arabs. The greater portion of the Bohorâs are Ismâ'îlî and they tend to be a tight-knit community, governed by their own customs and officials. Historically, they have had connections with the MUSTA'LÎ branch of the Ismâ'îlî found in the Yemen and in East Africa.

Bosnia-Herzegovina

See BALKAN STATES.

Brazil

The earliest Muslims in Brazil were Africans brought as slaves in the sixteenth century. Brazil's modern Muslim population is mostly descended from SUNNÎ Lebanese migrants to Brazil, who came after World War II.

Brunei

The Sultanate of Brunei is officially a Muslim country, with the majority of its citizens Malay SUNNÎ Muslims belonging to the Shafi'î legal school (MADHHAB).

Bukhârâ

A famous caravan city in Uzbekistan and center of Islamic learning under the Sâmânid dynasty in the fourth/tenth century, it was part of the Bukhârâ Khânate from about 1500 to 1920, linked culturally and politically to Samarqand, Balkh, and Tashkent. In 1920, it came under Soviet domination as part of Soviet UZBEKISTAN.

al-Bukhârî, Muḥammad b. Ismâ'îl (194/810–256/870)

Famous collector of ḤADÎTHS, whose collection, known as the *Ṣaḥîḥ* (the "Sound"), became authoritative for SUNNÎ Muslims along with the collection of MUSLIM B. AL-ḤAJJÂJ. The *ḥadîth*s were selected from over a half million on the basis of their reliability and accuracy, and arranged by topic. He is credited with a tremendous memory. Both his teachers and, later, his colleagues were able to correct their collections from his memory. He also wrote a history of the persons whose names appear in the ISNÂDS of his great work.

Bukht Naṣṣar

The biblical Nebuchadnezzar is not mentioned in the QUR'ÂN, but is a prominent figure in the collections of TAFSÎR known as ISRÂ'ÎLIYYÂT. He is listed as one of the rulers of the world and as a Persian ruler. The mixture of legend and biblical text has given rise to much discussion among Muslim and Western scholars about the sources for the stories of his life, and even as early as the Muslim medieval commentators, scholars have questioned the legendary character of his representation.

Bûlâq

A small town near Cairo famous for its printing. A press was established in about 1821 by the state for military purposes, but it printed many editions of classical literary and religious works. The wide dissemination of its printed works contributed to the "Arab renaissance," and to the spread of much religious knowledge through its many printed editions of TAFSÎR and ḤADÎTHS.

al-Burâq (Arabic: lightning)

The traditional name of the winged horse-like creature that bore MUḤAMMAD on his ISRÂ' (night journey) from MECCA to AL-QUDS (Jerusalem), to a place near the Western Wall of the Second Temple, and from there to heaven on his MI'RÂJ. Traditions also say that al-Burâq was the mount of all the prophets. There is a disagreement among the early commentators about whether the journey was in the flesh or spiritual.

burdah (Arabic: cloak)

A long woolen cloak that can be used as a blanket or wrap at night. The *burdah* of the Prophet is reported to have been one of the treasures of the 'ABBÂSID caliphs that was destroyed by the MONGOLS in the sack of BAGHDÂD in 1258. An alternate tradition reports that the Prophet's cloak was not destroyed, but was preserved in ISTANBUL.

al-burhân (Arabic: proof)

The proof or demonstration of truth that comes from God. The QUR'ÂN itself is held to be the *burhân* of God's existence

Muslim woman wearing a burqu'.

and creative activity. In this sense, it is related to the concept of the Qur'ânic verse, the 'ÂYAH, as the sign of the miracle or the miracle itself.

Burhâniyya

A popular Egyptian ṢÛFÎ order named after its founder, Burhân ad-Dîn Ibrâhîm b. Abî al-Majd 'Abd al-'Azîz ad-Dasûqî (644/1246–687/1288). It is also known as the Dasûqî order.

Burhânuddîn, Sayyidnâ Muḥammad (born 1333/1915)

Current head of the Dâ'ûdî branch of the BOHRÂ ISMÂ'ÎLÎ community.

burqu', or burqa'

A long woman's veil that covers the body except for the eyes and the tips of the fingers. (*See also* CHÂDOR; DRESS; ḤIJÂB.)

bûstân (Persian: garden)

When the word comes into Arabic, it refers to gardens of a great variety. In religious usage, it refers to the garden of Paradise, AL-JANNAH.

Buzurg-Umîd, Kiyâ (died 532/1138)

The successor to ḤASAN-I ṢABBÂḤ of ALAMÛT as chief DÂ'Î of the NIZÂRÎ ISMÂ'ÎLÎ SHÎ'Î. Under his leadership, Ismâ'îlî influence expanded in the face of continuing hostility. His tomb has been the location of pious veneration.

C

Cairo

See AL-QÂHIRAH.

calendar

The Islamic religious calendar is a lunar calendar of twelve months and is, therefore, shorter than the solar calendar by about eleven days. Muslim festivals cycle through the solar year in a thirty-three-year period. The beginning of the calendar is the HIJRAH, which took place in 622 C.E. Some Western writings refer to the Islamic date with the designation A.H., an abbreviation for *Anno Hegirae*.

caliph

See KHALÎFAH.

Caliphate Movement

See KHILÂFAT MOVEMENT.

calligraphy

The decorative use of verses from the QUR'ÂN and pious phrases has been from early times a distinctive Islamic artform. Some attribute its development to statements by the Prophet and to Islam's aniconic tendencies.

call to prayer

See ADHÂN.

cassettes

In the last quarter of the twentieth century audio cassettes became both instruments of revolutionary mass communication, as in the period leading to the 1979 Iranian revolution, when the SHÂH controlled the mass media, and an easy means of spreading sermons and Qur'ânic study materials.

čelebî (Turkish: wise man)

Honorific title used in Turkish Muslim countries in pre-modern times.

châdor (Persian)

A large black cloak and head veil, which leaves the face open, worn in Iran and elsewhere. (*See also* BURQUʿ; DRESS.)

Calligraphy relief from the Myrtle Court, Alhambra, Spain.

charity

See ṢADAQAH; ZAKÂT.

China

Muslim merchants from the Middle East brought Islam to China as early as the eighth century. With the conversion of Central Asian peoples, such as the Khazakhs and Uighurs, Islam grew. Some Chinese Muslims, known as Hui, exist today, indistinguishable from the larger population except in religion.

Chiragh ʿAli (1844–95)

Indian modernist and reformer associated with Sir Sayyid AḤMAD KHÂN and the ALIGARH Movement.

Chishtiyyah

One of the major ṢÛFÎ orders of South Asia, named after Muʿinuddîn Chishtî (d. 1236), and characterized by the ecstatic listening (SAMÂʿ) to music and poetry. Its chain of authority (SILSILAH) is traced by its adherents to MUḤAMMAD through ʿALÎ B. ABÎ ṬÂLIB. Many of the members of this order are ascetic and practice their DHIKR silently, regulating the breath. Its syncretic harmonization of Islam with Indian culture has brought criticism from some Muslim jurists.

Children in a Muslim kindergarten, Xian, Shanxi province, China.

circumambulation

See ṬAWÂF.

circumcision (Arabic *khitân*)

Although widespread, male circumcision among Muslims is not mandated in the QUR'ÂN and there is debate whether it is FARḌ (legally obligatory) or SUNNAH of the Prophet. It is often associated with purification, and is then called ṬAHÂRAH. The age of circumcision varies from country to country, usually happening before or at puberty. Traditions relate the practice to the prophet Abraham.

clitoridectomy

"Female circumcision," the clitoridectomy, is pre-Islamic in origin and has no foundation in the QUR'ÂN, but is mentioned in some of the traditions of the Prophet, which aim to ameliorate this practice. In recent times, it has been outlawed in many countries (e.g. Egypt and Sudan) and is the subject of international women's and human rights campaigns advocating its eradication, but its elimination is widely resisted at the community level.

Companion

See ṢAḤÂBAH.

Companions of the Cave

See AṢḤÂB AL-KAHF.

Conseil National des Français Musulmans

A lobbying association aimed at the improvement of Muslim life in France.

consensus

See IJMÂʿ.

Constitution of Madînah

The agreement between MUḤAMMAD and the Jews and Muslims of MADÎNAH, establishing the Jews as one ʾUMMAH (religious community), and the Muslims as another, with mutual rights and obligations. This agreement and others made in the Prophet's lifetime formed the basis for establishing non-Muslims within the Islamic polity. (*See also* AHL AL-KITÂB; DHIMMÎ.)

conversion

Conversion may be understood as conversion to Islam, that is, submission to God (the meaning of the word Islam), or conversion away from Islam, regarded as apostasy. Following the Muslim belief that all humans are born Muslim, conversion to Islam can also be viewed as a return to that state. The formal ceremony usually involves the recitation of the SHAHÂDAH, the profession of faith, in the presence of witnesses, followed by the practice of the other PILLARS, most notably ṢALÂT (prayer). For males, CIRCUMCISION is often required, and in some communities the practice of adopting a "Muslim name" is common.

creed

See ʿAQÎDAH.

crescent

See HILÂL; RED CRESCENT.

customary law

See ADAT.

D

dâʿî (Arabic: caller)

One who summons someone to Islam, a missionary. The term was used in both SUNNÎ and SHÎʿÎ circles, but became associated with Shîʿî missionary activity at an early date. In ISMÂʿÎLÎ circles, the *dâʿî* is the representative of the IMÂM. The circles of *dâʿîs* are arranged hierarchically, culminating in the *dâʿî ad-duʿât*, the "Summoner of the Summoners" or, sometimes, the BÂB. At times when the *Imâm* was not in power, or at times of persecution, the circle of *dâʿîs* was secret or known only to a few. They served as political leaders but also carried on a strong intellectual and scholarly tradition, writing many of the major theological works of Ismâʿîlî Islam. The particulars of their functioning has varied among each of the groups of Ismâʿîlî in different historical periods. (*See also* DAʿWAH.)

ḍaʿîf (Arabic: weak)

This is applied as a technical term in classifying ḤADÎTH implying unreliability.

ad-Dajjâl (Arabic: the deceiver)

The term for the Muslim "anti-messiah," who will come at the end of time, rule over an unjust world for a period of forty days (or years), after which all who are left will convert to Islam before the Day of Judgment. This word and the associated traditions are elaborated through the use of Syriac Christian texts by the early commentators, some of whom see the figure of ʿÎsâ (JESUS) as one of those who helps destroy ad-Dajjâl. While this figure is not mentioned in the QUR'ÂN, the tradition has become associated with the story of DHÛ-L-QARNAYN (Alexander the Great) and his walling up of YA'JÛJ WA-MA'JÛJ (Gog and Magog). In many of the narrative geographies of the world, some attention is given to the location of the home of ad-Dajjâl, the conclusion generally being that it is just beyond the then current known world, to the east. (*See also* YAWM AD-DÎN.)

Damascus

See DIMASHQ.

dan Fodio, Usuman (ʿUthmân) (1754–1817)

Religious leader and reformer in Nigeria best known for his two-stage JIHÂD, the preaching *jihâd* or missionary activity, and the subsequent *jihâd* of the sword when preaching failed. Through his efforts, Islam became the dominant religion of Nigeria. (*See also* MAHDÎ; SOKOTO CALIPHATE.)

dâr al-ʿahd (Arabic: realm of treaty)

According to some commentators, there an exist lands, between the DÂR AL-ḤARB and the DÂR AL-ISLÂM, that are under covenant but not yet under Islamic control. The theorists say that such areas of land would be destined to become Islamic. Such an area is a place of non-belligerence and peace. (*See also* DÂR AṢ-ṢULḤ.)

dâr al-ḥarb (Arabic: realm of war)

In classical Islamic jurisprudence, these are the non-Muslim areas of the world opposed to Islam. Most of the theorists did not regard it as necessary to actually wage open warfare against this area of the world, but rather to conduct active missionary work DAʿWAH, to convert the area to Islam.

dâr al-islâm (Arabic: realm of submission)

These are the areas of the world under Islamic control. According to most theorists, these areas can include non-Muslims as part of the polity as long as they fall into the DHIMMÎ classification.

dâr aṣ-ṣulḥ (Arabic: realm of peace)

In Shâfiʿî jurisprudence a third area beside the DÂR AL-ḤARB and the DÂR AL-ISLÂM in which non-Muslims live in peaceful treaty agreement with Muslim states. (*See also* DÂR AL-ʿAHD.)

Dar Ul Arqam

A Malaysian non-governmental DAʿWAH movement that stresses Islamic revival.

Darul Islam

The Indonesian Islamic insurgent movement between 1948 and 1962.

darwîsh (Persian: poor)

Known in English as "dervish," a member of ṢÛFÎ orders such as the MEVLEVÎ "whirling" dervishes. In Islamic circles, the term also connotes a person who is a member of a mendicant order, sometimes called a FAQÎR, from the Arabic word meaning to be poor.

Dâʾûd, also Dâwûd, or Dahûd/Dahood

David, one of the pre-Islamic prophets mentioned in the QURʾÂN. He is associated with the ZABÛR (Psalms).

daʿwah (Arabic: summons)

Preaching; the missionary call to Islam; religious outreach. In the Qurʾânic usage, it means the call by Allâh to humans to adhere to the religion of Islam. While the term has been associated with the ISMÂʿÎLIYYAH, it is in common use in SUNNÎ circles, with many Muslim institutions of higher learning having departments of *daʿwah*.

dawlah (Arabic: state, government)

The word is often used to indicate an Islamic state. (*See also* ʾUMMAH.)

dawr (Arabic: age, revolution, turn, epoch)

A technical term among the ISMÂʿÎLÎ SHÎʿÎ referring to an era of religious history. *Dawr-i satr* is the age in which the Ismâʿîlî Shîʿî IMÂMS are in concealment, while *dawr-i kashf* is the epoch in which they are manifest.

dawsah (Arabic: step, tread)

A ceremony reported to have been performed by the SHAYKH of the ṢÛFÎ Saʿdî order in Cairo and elsewhere in which the shaykh would ride a horse over the backs of prostrate devotees without any injury. This ceremony was associated with the MAWLID celebration of the birth of the Prophet.

Deobandis

The reformist ʿULAMÂʾ associated with the school at Deoband, India, ninety miles northeast of Delhi, founded in

1282/1867 to reform Islam in India. They are of the ḤANAFÎ MADHHAB, practice IJTIHÂD, and rely on ḤADÎTHS to emulate MUḤAMMAD.

dervish

See DARWÎSH.

destiny

See QADAR.

devil

See IBLÎS.

dhabḥ (Arabic: slaughtering by cutting the throat)

All meat must be properly and ritually slaughtered in order to be ḤALÂL, or permissible. For large animals, this is done by orienting the animal toward the QIBLAH, pronouncing the name of God over the sacrificial animal, slitting its throat, and draining as much blood as possible. Different schools of Islamic law have more specific requirements for proper ritual slaughter. When *ḥalâl* meat is unavailable, it is permissible for Muslims to eat kosher meat.

dhabîḥah (Arabic: victim)

The name given to the properly chosen and prepared animal for the ritual slaughter during the time of the ḤAJJ. The rules governing the type of animal and its proper characteristics are spelled out in great detail in books of FIQH.

dhanb (Arabic: sin)

In Muslim legal practice serious sins are associated with ḤADD, punishment under the legal system (SHARÎʿAH). All sins may be mitigated or forgiven by sincere repentance (TAWBAH), a matter between the individual and God. The exception is the sin of SHIRK.

dhikr (Arabic: mention, remember)

Also pronounced *zikr* or *zekr* in some Islamic languages, it is the ritual utterance of the name of God or God's praise. In ṢÛFÎ usage it is the litany that is the core of worship, such as the repetition of a phrase like *Allâhu akbar* or the BASMALAH.

dhimmî (Arabic, from *ahl al-dhimmah*: people benefiting from protection)

Non-Muslim free communities living under Islamic law (SHARÎʿAH), who enjoy legal status and are subject to some restrictions and taxes. While it is usually limited to Jews, Christians, Sabaeans, and Zoroastrians, some Islamic courts in India also included those Hindus who supplied military assistance in exchange for land ownership. (*See also* AHL AL-KITÂB; IQṬÂʿ; JIZYAH; KHARÂJ.)

Dhû-l-Ḥijjah

The last month of the Muslim lunar CALENDAR in which the pilgrimage (ḤAJJ) occurs.

Dhû-l-Kifl

A prophet mentioned in Q. 21:85 and 38:48. Scholars have proposed several uncertain identifications with various biblical figures. The most usual identification is with Ezekiel, although certain features of his story have led some to identify the figure with AYYÛB (Job).

Dhû-l-Qarnayn (Arabic: the possessor of two horns)

A figure appearing in Q. 18:83–98, identified by some as Alexander the Great (al-Iskandar), who built a barrier against Gog and Magog (YA'JÛJ WA-MA'JÛJ). In the TAFSÎR literature, other figures are mentioned as Dhû-l-Qarnayn. It is generally agreed that he was a believer in Islam, and some even argue that he should be ranked among the prophets.

Dhû-n-Nûn (Arabic: the possessor of the fish)

An epithet of the prophet Jonah (Arabic Yûnus); Abû-l-Fayḍ Thawbân b. Ibrâhîm Dhû-l-Nûn al-Miṣrî (*c.* 180/796–*c.* 246/861), an Egyptian ṢÛFÎ famous for opposing the MU'TAZILAH on the issue of the createdness of the QUR'ÂN and of writing the first systematic treatise on Ṣûfî practice, only known, however, through later quotations.

dietary rules

The QUR'ÂN and the SUNNAH divide foods into permitted (ḤALÂL) and forbidden (ḤARÂM), or pure (*ṭâhir*) and impure (*najis*). Prohibited foods include pork, alcoholic beverages (KHAMR) and food improperly slaughtered or dedicated to an idol. Muslims are permitted to receive food from Jews and Christians, and at all times issues of health and survival take precedence over prohibitions and fasting.

Dihlawî, Shâh Walî Allâh

See WALÎ ALLÂH, SHÂH.

Dimashq

The city of Damascus is the largest city in Syria and one of the oldest cities in the world. It was conquered by Muslims in 14/635, and under the 'UMAYYAD caliph MU'ÂWIYAH became the capital of the 'Umayyad dynasty. It remained an important Islamic center even when the 'ABBÂSIDS moved the caliphate to BAGHDÂD in the 133/750. The city is rich in Islamic monuments, including the famous Great Mosque of the 'Umayyads built by the caliph Walîd I in the first/eighth century.

dîn (Arabic: religion, faith; judgment)

Faith or religion; in the phrase YAWM AD-DÎN, it means the "Day of Judgment."

divorce

While divorce is permissible in Islam, traditions from the Prophet declare it to be a hateful practice in the eyes of God. Legislation in the QUR'ÂN and the SUNNAH of MUḤAMMAD ameliorated the pre-Islamic practice of easy divorce without regard to the welfare of the wife or the children. Islamic law demands monetary settlement for a divorced woman and a waiting period of three menstrual cycles ('IDDAH) before she can remarry. Any offspring from a union belongs "to the bed of the father," making the father primarily responsible for the care of the children. The power to initiate divorce has been traditionally located with the man, although in some Islamic states, women have been granted that power. In SHÎ'Î Islam, the termination of a MUT'AH marriage does not require a divorce, since it is a time-limited union. In all cases, under Islamic law, divorce is a personal contract between two individuals rather than a state-sanctioned contract.

Djibouti

Small Muslim country on the coast of the Horn of Africa.

Dome of the Rock

See QUBBAT AL-ṢAKHRAH; AL-QUDS.

dowry

See MAHR.

dress

Muslim dress varies widely among different cultural regions, reflecting local custom and current ideology. There is no

Iranian Muslim women wearing the châdor.

one dress code among all Muslims. The QUR'ÂN enjoins both men and women to guard their modesty, and women are commanded to cover their bosoms. Women are permitted greater freedom of dress within the inner family circle than in public (Q. 24:30–1). Believing women are enjoined also to wrap their outer garments around them, as a mark of their belief and to forestall molestation (Q. 33:59). All Muslims are to dress appropriately for worship, with only indecency forbidden (Q. 7:31–3). Passages in the SUNNAH elaborate on Muslim dress, such as restricting men from wearing silk or gold. Among some Muslims, elaborate coverings for women, along with other restrictions, have become external signs of a religious commitment to fundamentalist principles. (*See also* 'ABÂ'AH; 'AWRAH; BURQU'; CHÂDOR; ḤIJÂB; MODESTY.)

Druze

A religion separate from Islam that developed from the teachings of Muḥammad b. Ismâ'îl al-Darazî (fl. 408/1017) that held that the sixth FÂṬIMID caliph, AL-ḤÂKIM BI-'AMR ALLÂH, was divine and did not die but went into GHAYBAH or occultation. The religion is esoteric, elitist, and its members are permitted to practice TAQIYYAH, or religious dissimulation, giving the impression that they are Muslims or of any other religion in circumstances in which it would be dangerous to reveal their religion. They call themselves *muwaḥḥidûn*, "unitarians." They are found chiefly in the areas around Lebanon, Syria, and Israel, and have played a major role in the shaping of modern Lebanon. In Israel they have enjoyed special status because of their separation from Islam and Christianity.

du'â' (Arabic: invocation)

Prayer or supplication, this term can refer to a formal, ritual prayer or an extra-rogatory prayer made at any time. In the second, personal, sense, the request to God can include anything and be uttered at any time. Jurists have tried to classify the circumstances when such a prayer would be more efficacious, but, in keeping with the tradition that nothing stands between the believer and God, such works have been hortative rather than legislative. (*See also* ṢALÂT.)

Duldul

The name of the mule given MUḤAMMAD by the Byzantine emperor Heraclius (Arabic Muqawqis), and which was the Prophet's mount in the battle of Ḥunayn. It is also reported that 'ALÎ B. ABÎ ṬÂLIB rode this mule in the battle of the Camel.

dunyâ (Arabic: nearest)

The term is used in the QUR'ÂN and in the religious tradition to mean the "world," that is, the physical, sensorial world, as opposed to the spiritual world. While some Muslims practice strong asceticism and rejection of this world, the overwhelming majority adhere to a balance between the quest for spiritual salvation and partaking in this life, following the maxim attributed to the Prophet, "There is no 'monkhood' in Islam."

Durrânîs

This dynasty, also known as the Abdalîs, was founded by ʾAḥmad Khân ʿAbdalî (1163/1747–1187/1772) in 1163/1747 in present-day AFGHANISTAN, and lasted until it was overthrown in 1393/1973 by a proto-Soviet military coup. At its height, the Durrânî empire stretched from Khurasan to Kashmir and the Punjab, and from the Oxus river to the Indian Ocean. It had the support of ethnic Uzbeks and Pashtuns, and was strongly influenced by ṢÛFÎ ideals. The dynasty declined through the thirteenth/nineteenth century, and in the fourteenth/twentieth century the rulers were primarily concerned with keeping the family in power rather than developing the country. The last king, Zâhir Shâh, who ruled from 1352/1933 to 1393/1973, is currently seeking to regain his throne and reestablish the dynasty.

Durûz

See DRUZE.

dustûr (Persian: one who exercises authority)

In pre-modern times, the word meant rule, regulation, or the person who exercised the office that enforced the rules and regulations. Hence it is included in the titles of viziers and other court officials. In modern Arabic, it has come to mean "constitution," as in the legislated constitutions of the various states.

E

Egypt

Over ninety percent Muslim and predominantly SUNNÎ, Egypt has been a major Islamic center since the time of the second caliph, ʿUMAR b. ʿAbd al-Khaṭṭâb (r. 12/634–23/644). Its capital is Cairo (AL-QÂHIRAH). Arabic speaking, home of AL-AZHAR, major publishing houses and a strong intellectual life, Egypt has been the center of much Islamic and Arabic thought. (*See also* BÛLÂQ.)

elephant

See FÎL.

Elijah

See ILYÂS.

Elijah Muhammad (1897–1975)

Born Paul Robert Poole, he was the leader of the Black Muslim movement the NATION OF ISLAM. Influenced by Fard Muḥammad, he taught that blacks in the United States were descended from the Arabian Shabazz tribe and that white people were descended from the devil. Under his leadership, the Nation of Islam movement was separate from worldwide Islam in its fundamental beliefs and lack of tolerance.

Enoch

See IDRÎS.

ensoulment

Many Muslims believe that the soul of a person is implanted in the body one hundred and twenty days after conception. This notion, found in the ḤADÎTH, has affected notions of ABORTION, INHERITANCE associated with the death of infant heirs, and other similar areas. Popular stories and practice, however, assume that the evil inclination of humans is implanted at birth, and some will recite the formula *bismi-llâh ar-raḥmân ar-raḥîm*, "In the name of God, the Merciful and Compassionate," to avert the devil's plan.

eschatology

Islamic views about the end of time, the Day of Judgment (YAWM AD-DÎN) and the AFTERLIFE (AL-ʾÂKHIRAH) vary greatly, but most Muslims agree that prior to the Day of Judgment, the forces of evil, led by AD-DAJJÂL, the Deceiver or false Messiah, and Gog and Magog (YAʾJÛJ WA-MAʾJÛJ) will clash with the forces of good, led by the MAHDÎ and/or JESUS. This will be followed by a general judgment of all souls, the righteous going to Heaven (see AL-JANNAH) and the evil going to torment in Hell (see JAHANNAM). (*See also* IBLÎS; MUNKAR WA-NÂKÎR.)

Eve

See ḤAWWÂʾ.

exegesis

See TAFSÎR.

Ezekiel

See DHÛ-L-KIFL.

Ezra

See 'UZAYR.

F

faḍâ'il (Arabic: excellence; sing. *faḍîlah*)

The genre of literature written in praise of, first, the QUR'ÂN, then the Companions (*ṣaḥâbah*) and other religious worthies, cities, provinces, and holy months. As a genre, it lists and extols the virtues of its subject. During the time of the Crusades, a considerable literature developed around Jerusalem, known as *faḍâ'il al-Quds*, which was intended to strengthen in the minds of Muslims their claim to that holy city. Material from this corpus is actively used today by Palestinians in the Palestinian–Israeli conflict.

Fadak

An ancient Arabian Jewish agricultural town, the inhabitants of which made a treaty agreement with MUḤAMMAD that they would be allowed to remain on their land, sharing the produce, which was used to aid the poor and travelers. After Muḥammad's death, his daughter FÂṬIMAH and the caliph ABÛ BAKR disagreed about whether she should inherit the proceeds from the town or whether they should remain state property. Abû Bakr's refusal to grant her claim is viewed by SHÎʿÎ as an injustice. Sometime during or after the reign of the caliph ʿUMAR, the Jews of Fadak were expelled, albeit with token compensation that recognized their ownership of the land.

Faḍlallâh, Muḥammad Ḥusayn (born 1935)

Lebanese SHÎʿÎ scholar and leader of the ḤIZBULLÂH (Party of God), named by Âyatollâh Rûḥollâh KHOMEINÎ as MARJIʿ AT-TAQLÎD, a source of imitation. He was instrumental in drafting the Lebanese Islamic constitution. His theology and views about revolutionary social action are intertwined, and he preaches that the Shiʿite Islamic revolution should be completed in Lebanon and throughout Palestine, with the resultant subjugation of Christians and expulsion of Jews. He espouses an activist UṢÛLÎ form of Shîʿism that stresses IJTIHÂD as a means to solve modern problems.

faith

See ÎMÂN.

Faith Movement

See ILYÂS, MAWLÂNÂ MUḤAMMAD.

Fakhr ad-Dîn ar-Râzî, Abû ʿAbd Allâh Muḥammad b. ʿUmar b. al-Ḥusayn (543/1149–606/1209)

One of the most prominent SUNNÎ theologians and religious philosophers, he studied in the town of Rayy. He engaged in religious polemic against the MUʿTAZILAH, who forced him to leave the city and undertake a series of trips, finally settling in Herât. He is said to have had an excellent memory, and to have been a great teacher and an excellent preacher. He was a prolific and encyclopedic writer whose works cover history, FIQH, TAFSÎR, KALÂM, and FALSAFAH, among others. Of his many works, his *Mafâtîḥ al-Ghayb*, his monumental commentary on the QUR'ÂN, demonstrates his anti-Mu'tazilite views, as it was written against the *tafsîr* of AZ-ZAMAKHSHARÎ. His *Munâẓarât al-'Allâmah Fakhr ad-Dîn* is an autobiographical exposition of his various intellectual encounters with other scholars and shows his positions on various subjects.

Fakhreddîn, Riẓâeddîn (1859–1936)

Russian Muslim reformist and educational advocate. He was an advocate of a modified pan-Turanism and of Islamic modernism.

falsafah (Arabic from Greek: philosophy)

This concept tends to be opposed to theology, KALÂM. The tradition of philosophical thought was derived from the Hellenistic Greek tradition and has been opposed by many Muslim thinkers, who have seen such speculative thought as antithetical to the religion of Islam. Nevertheless, many early groups actively promoted philosophical thinking and the use of the tools of philosophy, such as logic, to promote their causes. The SUNNÎ unease and rejection of philosphy has something to do with its association with SHÎ'Î speculative theology. In the course of arguments about religion, *kalâm* itself was strongly influenced by philosophy, and the Islamic philosophical tradition has been a strong one. Many famous Greek philosophers are known in whole or in part because of the preservation of their texts by Islamic philosophers.

family

The family and its extensions, the clan and the tribe, have been basic social units in Islamic societies up to and including modern times. The QUR'ÂN ameliorates the situations of women and children. Women are protected from divorce during pregnancy and nursing, and children are assured economic support in the Prophetic traditions by being assigned "to the bed of the father." In pre-modern agrarian societies, the extended family was the basic economic unit, and the family metaphor is often extended to all Muslims as "brothers" and "sisters" in the Islamic family. Pressures from the modern world are threatening the family structure in modern Muslim societies with the same range of reactions and transformations we see in the West.

family law

According to some, family law is the heart of the SHARÎ'AH, or Islamic religious law, but it has no distinct existence in the traditional treatises outside laws for marriage, divorce, women, inheritance, and other laws of personal status. In the last century, many Muslim states have adopted reforms in family laws, restricting polygamy, allowing for wife-initiated divorce, assuring equity in property rights between husband and wife, and, often following Western models, adopting codes for family law. These codes, which have been influenced in many instances by colonial forces, have fallen under stringent scrutiny and attack by Islamist activists, however, who see the codes as contravening their interpretation of the QUR'ÂN.

family planning

There is no unanimous opinion among Muslim jurists about family planning, meaning the limitation of the number of children. Some, arguing from

ḤADÎTHS that permit *coitus interruptus*, allow contraceptives. Some allow contraceptives only if the wife permits their use. Others, also relying on *ḥadîth*s and prohibitions in the QUR'ÂN, call contraception infanticide. The Grand MUFTÎ of Jordan, Shaykh 'Abdullâh al-Qalqilî, issued a FATWAH in 1964 allowing contraception as long as it was not injurious to the health. The use of ABORTION after 120 days of gestation is almost generally condemned and not allowed as a method of contraception.

fanâ' (Arabic: annihilation)

Among the ṢÛFÎ, this Arabic term indicates the passing away of the mystic's earthly ties and his absorption into God, without, however, the loss of individuality.

faqîh (Arabic: jurist; pl. *fuqahâ*)

An expert in FIQH, specialized legal knowledge.

faqîr (Arabic: pauper)

One who is poor or destitute. In religious terms, the word is used to refer to those renunciants who have given up all worldly possessions. They are, in some circles, regarded as having special spiritual powers. In popular use, the term refers to a beggar, and, since the time of the British in Islamic India, to a beggar who performs tricks and feats of magic for money.

al-Farâbî, Abû Naṣr Muḥammad b. Muḥammad (died *c.* 339/950)

One of the chief philospohers of medieval Islam; very little is known of his life. He was Turkish and was supported during his lifetime by Sayf ad-Dawlah, the SHÎ'Î ruler of Aleppo. Through a Christian Nestorian teacher he was introduced to the philosophical thinking of Aristotle. He saw Islam as the ultimate home for philosophical thought, and held that human reasoning was superior to all other forms of knowledge, including religious knowledge. He was a harmonizer between the views of Aristotle and Plato, holding that the differences resulted from a misunderstanding of the underlying truth. In the West, his works were translated into Latin and influenced the development of European medieval philosophy. He was known as Alfarabius, and was called the "Second Teacher," the first being Aristotle.

farḍ (Arabic: religious duty)

Religious obligations in Islam are divided between *farḍ 'ayn*, duties incumbent on each individual and *farḍ kifâyah*, those incumbent on the community. An example of the first would be daily prayer, incumbent on each individual. Of the latter, the responsibility of reciting a funeral prayer is fulfilled if at least one individual performs it, but the whole community sins if it is not performed. In most circles *farḍ* and *wâjib* are synonymous, except in the ḤANAFÎ tradition, where *farḍ* refers to those obligations derived directly from the QUR'ÂN and *wâjib* to those derived from reason.

al-Fârûqî, Ismâ'îl Râjî (1921–86)

Islamic activist scholar born in Palestine and educated in the Arab world and the United States. He sought the integration of Islamic knowledge and modern learning with the goal of revitalizing Islam and expanding its influence in the West. He served an active role in the Islam section of the American Academy of Religion and in the American Oriental Society. He and his wife, Lois Lamyâ' al-Fârûqî, were killed by an intruder in their home.

Courtyard of the al-Qarawiyyîn mosque in Fâs.

Fâs, also Fez

This important town in Morocco was founded in the second/eighth century by the Idrîsids but came into prominence under the Almoravids beginning in the fifth/eleventh century. It is known for its Hispano-Muslim monuments, the most famous of which is the al-Qarawiyyîn mosque.

fasting

See ṢAWM.

al-fâtiḥah (Arabic: the opening)

The first chapter of the QUR'ÂN. Early collections of the Qur'ân did not include this first chapter, and some regard it as an early liturgical prayer associated with the Qur'ân as early as MUḤAMMAD's lifetime. It is an important part of every prayer ṢALÂT, since it is recited at the beginning of each RAK'AH, or seventeen times a day. The chapter is used as an amulet in popular magic, and its recitation is thought to have curative powers for the sick; the seven letters of the Arabic alphabet missing from the chapter are also thought to have magical powers.

Fâṭimah (605–11/633)

The daughter of the Prophet MUḤAMMAD by his first wife, KHADÎJAH BT. KHUWAYLID. She married 'ALÎ B. ABÎ ṬÂLIB and bore AL-ḤASAN B. 'ALÎ and AL-ḤUSAYN B. 'ALÎ. She is one of the "people of the cloak" (*aṣḥâb al-kisâ'*), consisting of her, 'Alî, al-Ḥasan, and al-Ḥusayn, whom Muḥammad took under his cloak and pronounced as members of his family, an event of great importance to SHÎ'Î Muslims. She has received little attention in SUNNÎ historical sources, but Shî'î hagiographic traditions consider her one of the most important women in early Islam. Modern Western historical examinations of her life range between harshly critical and laudatory, reflecting the variances in Islamic sources.

Fâṭimids

The Ismâʿîlî Shîʿî dynasty that ruled in North Africa and Egypt from 297/909 to 567/1171. Its rich intellectual tradition and active missionary work failed to inculcate a permanent tradition of Shîʿî Islam among the Egyptians. Its rulers are regarded as Imâms in the Ismâʿîlî tradition. They are:

ʿUbayd Allâh	297/909–322/934
al-Qâʾim	322/934–334/946
al-Manṣûr	334/946–341/953
al-Muʿizz	341/953–365/975
al-ʿAzîz	365/975–386/996
al-Ḥâkim	386/996–411/1021
al-Ẓâhir	411/1021–427/1036
al-Mustanṣir	427/1036–487/1094
al-Mustaʿlî	487/1094–495/1101
al-Âmir	495/1101–525/1130
al-Ḥâfiẓ	525/1130–544/1149
al-Ẓâfir	544/1149–549/1154
al-Fâʾiz	549/1154–555/1160
al-ʿÂḍiḍ	555/1160–567/1171

fatwâ (Arabic: legal judgement)

A definitive legal pronouncement given in response to a question about an Islamic legal practice, it is given by a qualified muftî and based on authoritative precedents, not personal opinion alone. They are generally advisory and informative, with the inquirer agreeing to abide by the response to his question. Historically, *fatâwâ* have been separate from the judgments of the qâḍîs. In modern times the *fatwâ* has sometimes been associated in the popular practice with declarations of jihâd or with death decrees.

Fédération Nationale des Musulmans de France (FNMF)

This federation of approximately one hundred Muslim organizations in France was founded in 1406/1985 by a French convert to Islam, Daniel Youssef Leclerc, who is president of a group dedicated to increasing the quality of ḥalâl food in Paris. The goal of the organization is to assure French Muslims an Islamic standard of living according to a strict interpretation of sharîʿah.

feminism

The quest for rights for women and the creation of nonsexist postpatriarchal societies can be found throughout the Islamic world. While some argue that an original aim of Islam was to reform human conduct for the benefit of women and children, feminism in the modern sense has its roots in the late nineteenth century in letters, poems, and stories that questioned the exclusion of women from public society. By the mid-twentieth century, educated Muslim women were publishing scholarship about gender roles in Islam and proposing new religious interpretations aimed at redefining the understanding of Islam's foundation texts, the Qurʾân and the ḥadîth. Women's participation in the liberation movements of the twentieth century raised hopes for greater gender equality, but the rise of so-called fundamentalism has acted as a counter to the gains made in the mid-twentieth century. Groups like the Sisters in Islam in Malaysia and the Women's Action Forum in Pakistan have made steady progress, particularly through the use of Islamic liberation theology and the espousal of family rights.

Fez

See Fâs.

Fidâʾiyyân-i Islâm

A political and religious organization, founded in Iran in 1945. Its members advocated a Shîʿî Islamic revolution. Rigid in their social views, they espoused violence and terror to achieve their aims.

fîl (Arabic from Persian: elephant)

The title of sûrah 105 in the Qurʾân, it refers to the unsuccessful attack on

MECCA by the Ethiopian general ABRAHAH, who used a war-elephant. The TAFSÎR literature reports that the elephant, who was named Maḥmûd, refused to enter the sacred precincts and knelt before the KA'BAH. These events are supposed to have taken place in 570, the year of MUḤAMMAD's birth, but historians place the events somewhat earlier.

fiqh (Arabic: understanding, knowledge)

Usually understood as Islamic jurisprudence, it is the practice of discovering God's law (SHARÎ'AH), writing treatises about it, and relating the practice of law to revelation. Historically, *fiqh* arose from a systematic analysis of the QUR'ÂN and ḤADÎTH combined with rigorous analogic reasoning, QIYÂS. In both SHÎ'Î and SUNNÎ Islamic circles, this led to various "schools" MADHHABS, which were based regionally or on the ideas of an eponymous founder.

Fir'awn, or fir'awn

The Qur'ânic word for Pharaoh, and often used in a more general sense in the TAFSÎR for "tyrant."

firdaws

See AL-JANNAH.

fitnah (Arabic: smelt or assay, test, prove)

Trial, temptation, discord, civil war, strife; the term originally meant to test a metal by fire, and it retains a sense of this meaning in the QUR'ÂN, where the worth of the believers will be tested by the fire of the YAWM AD-DÎN. Subsequently, the term is often used to refer to the civil war that started with the killing of the caliph 'UTHMÂN and led to the formation of the KHAWÂRIJ and the SHÎ'Î. It can also refer to the trials that people will receive in the grave while awaiting the Day of Judgment. In common parlance, it refers to the temptation of wealth, children, and other things of this world that lead a Muslim toward sin.

fiṭrah (Arabic: nature)

The term is used in the QUR'ÂN to indicate the inherent characteristics of an individual created by God. This term has caused much discussion among theologians about how much of an individual's capacities are created by God and is therefore fixed, and how much is open to what we would term environmental influences, i.e. parents, learning, etc. In spite of some schools of thought that have exhibited a deterministic view, the Qur'ânic perspective promotes sufficient free will for almost everyone to be able to achieve salvation.

Followers

See TÂBI'ÛN

fundamentalism

Originally applied to nineteenth-century American Protestants, who were reacting strongly to the threats of modernism, the term has come to mean any religious group rigidly resisting change in the modern world. When applied to Islam, it is often understood as synonymous with terrorism, and, for this and all of its other pejorative meanings, many reject its applicability to Islam. Some scholars see fundamentalism as part of an ongoing reformist action in Islamic history, while others see it as a purely modernist movement. Despite its Western origins, the term has been translated into Arabic as 'UṢÛLIYYAH or SALAFIYYAH and used by Arab writers.

funerary rites

The proper conduct of a Muslim funeral is an obligation on the Muslim community, FARḌ *kifâyah*, and the details of the rites are a major subject of legal thought. Funeral concerns begin even before a person's death, with the SHAHÂDAH and a Qur'ânic SÛRAH, preferably *Yâ sîn* (*sûrah* 36), recited by relatives and friends. The dead should be prepared and buried as soon after death as possible. The body is washed three times by a relative of the same sex or by a spouse, taking care to preserve the modesty of the deceased, wrapped in a clean, white shroud made of three pieces of cloth for men and five for women, and scented with a non-alcoholic perfume. Funeral prayers (ṢALÂT AL-JANÂZAH) are recited standing with no prostration (*sujûd*). In the funeral procession, the mourners walk in front or beside the bier, and those who are riding or driving come behind. It is recommended that the mourners remain silent, without music or lamentation. The body is buried, facing MECCA, in a deep grave, without a casket, but with a covering to keep the dirt from the body. No bedding or other materials should be placed in the grave. The person who places the body in the grave should recite the *shahâdah* in the ears of the deceased. The grave can be marked with a small, simple headstone, but more elaborate monuments are discouraged by most scholars. Also, legal scholars have resisted the intrusion of local customs into the funeral practice, such as transferring the deceased to another country, reading the QUR'ÂN in the cemetery, putting offerings of food, water, flowers or money in or around the grave, slaughtering an animal for the funeral, maintaining mourning for a year, having the relatives of the deceased wear black, or planting flowers on the grave for the benefit of the deceased. (*See also* JANÂZAH.)

furqân (Arabic: proof)

This word is used in the QUR'ÂN to mean "criterion, salvation, discrimination, and separation." It is the title of *Sûrah* 25 in the Qur'ân, where it seems to mean the distinguisher between good and evil. It is also used in this sense when referring to the scripture received by MÛSÂ. In Q. 8:29 it is said, "O you who believe, if you fear God, He will assign you a *furqân* and forgive you your sins." Western scholars point to the Aramaic word *purqân*, meaning "salvation," as influencing the meaning of the Arabic word.

futuwwah

Related to the Arabic word for youth (*fatâ*), *futuwwah* organizations have been associated with ṢÛFÎ orders and craft guilds as well as popular movements in Islamic societies as fraternal orders. Often drawing from the impoverished and disenfranchised segments of society, the *futuwwah* groups have ranged from common gangs to instruments of religious and social reform.

Fyzee, Asaf 'Ali Asghar (1899–1981)

Noted ISMÂ'ÎLÎ SHÎ'Î Indian jurist and reformer, Fyzee's *Outlines of Muḥammadan Law* sought to explain Islamic law as a dynamic process in history and to influence the modernization of Islamic law to fit the needs of modern Muslim societies.

G

Gabriel

See JIBRÎL.

gambling

The QUR'ÂN and subsequent Islamic law forbids games of chance and gambling. This prohibition is extended to financial speculation. (*See also* BANKS AND BANKING; MAYSIR; RIBÂ.)

Garden (Paradise)

See AL-JANNAH.

Gasprinski (Gasprali), Ismâ'îl Bey (1851–1914)

Russian Tatar (Turkish) modernist, reformer and proponent of Jadîdism. He advocated the Westernization of the Russian Tatar community, which he sought to achieve through the creation of newspapers and an elementary school system. He also sought to create a national Turkish literary language, based on OTTOMAN Turkish.

geomancy (Arabic, *'ilm ar-raml*)

The popular practice of divination through the use of sand. Found in many parts of the Islamic world, it is condemned by 'ULAMÂ' as un-Islamic.

Ghadîr Khumm

The spot between MECCA and MADÎNAH where, according to the SHÎ'Î, MUḤAMMAD during the Farewell Pilgrimage declared 'ALÎ B. ABÎ ṬÂLIB as his successor. SUNNÎ tradition also recognizes the event but does not give it the same significance, or passes over it in silence. By report, the event took place on the eighteenth of the month of Dhû-l-Ḥijjah, which is marked by Shî'î as a day of solemn celebration.

al-Ghannûshî, Râshid (born 1941)

Tunisian modernist and reformer, who advocates democratic religious modernism with equality for men and women.

gharar (Arabic: risk, hazard)

The term is used in Islamic discussions of finance to indicate the risk of unknown elements in a transaction that would render the transaction invalid according to Islamic law. While some scholars allow a certain degree of risk, others seek a risk-free Islamic financial system.

gharîb (Arabic: strange, rare)

A term used in ḤADÎTH criticism to indicate a tradition that is not supported by multiple ISNÂDS.

Gharnâṭah or Granada

Granada was a major city in Islamic Spain and the last area of Spain to resist the Reconquista, falling in 897/1492. Its

The Alhambra Palace, Granada, Spain.

most famous monument is the Alhambra, the "Red Fortress," built by the Naṣrid dynasty. It is a series of buildings, and the best example of Islamic architecture and decoration in Spain.

Ghassânids

The pre-Islamic Arabian tribe, originally from the Yemen, that settled on the northwest border of the peninsula, allied with the Romans (Byzantines) as a client state, and formed a barrier between the settled areas of Rome and the interior of Arabia. They were Monophysite Christian and helped revive the Monophysite church. In the history of Arabia, they were a conduit of Roman ideas into the peninsula. They were eliminated as a tribe with the Islamic conquest, but some Syrian Christian families today can trace their ancestry to this tribe.

ghaybah (Arabic: occultation)

Originally an astronomical term for occultation, concealment, absence. In its religious use, it is found among both the SUNNÎ and the SHÎʿÎ, but it is most common among the Shîʿî. It most often refers to the absence in the physical sense of a person who is absent from the world but present with ALLÂH. In this sense, the term can apply to the figure of AL-KHAḌIR, whose presence is nevertheless felt through his activities in the world. This is the meaning usually applied to the occultation of the HIDDEN IMÂM of the ITHNÂ ʿASHARIYYAH SHÎʿÎ. In this doctrine, the *Imâm* is alive and hidden from the view of his followers, and will return at some eschatological time. By extension, the term can refer to the periods of time in which the *Imâm* is absent or hidden.

al-Ghazâlî (al-Ghazzâlî), Abû Ḥâmid Muḥammad b. Muḥammad aṭ-Ṭûsî (450/1058–505/1111)

Ashʿarî theologian, jurist, and ṢÛFÎ, he was trained as a jurist and practiced that profession for some time. He appears to have had a crisis in mid-career and left Baghdâd and a successful professorship. The reasons for his crisis have been much discussed, but he gives religious reasons as the cause. He returned to public life at the turn of the century, near the end of 499/1105, convinced of his role as the "Renewer of Religion," *al-Mujaddid*. In this period, he wrote his famous autobiographical work, *al-Munqidh min aḍ-ḍalâl* (The deliverance from error). In his philosophical/theological works, he criticized the thoughts and influence of philosophy. See, for example, his *Tahâfut al-falâsifah*. He also proposed an integration of theology, mysticism, law and ethics in his famous *Iḥyâʾ ʿulûm ad-dîn* (The revival of the religious sciences), in which he held that knowledge of the QURʾÂN and the SUNNAH of the Prophet was sufficient to be a Muslim. His autobiography, *al-Munqidh min aḍ-ḍalâl,* is a major testament to his spiritual and intellectual journey.

al-Ghazâlî, Muḥammad (1336/1917–1417/1996)

Egyptian reformer and former member of AL-IKHWÂN AL-MUSLIMÛN (the Muslim Brotherhood) and advocate of Islamic modernism. He is most noted for his limitation of the use of ḤADÎTHS that do not have a basis in the QUR'ÂN, allowing him to criticize both the extreme traditionalists and the radical left.

al-Ghazâlî, Zaynab (born 1336/1917)

Egyptian writer and teacher, founder of the Muslim Women's Association and member of AL-IKHWÂN AL-MUSLIMÛN (the Muslim Brotherhood). She believes in women's active participation in public life as long as it does not interfere with the sacred duty of being a wife and mother. She has been imprisoned for her views and the Muslim Women's Association was disbanded by the Egyptian government in 1964.

ghâzî (Arabic: raider, warrior)

Originally meaning a person who took part in a raid, or razzia, it came to be a term of honor, particularly among those nomadic and semi-nomadic Turks who used mounted cavalry attacks to spread their rule and Islam. At some times in history, the term refers to Turks in general, and more specifically those who were proponents of JIHÂD.

ghulât (Arabic: extremists, exaggerators)

A term of disrespect and opprobrium applied to various early SHÎ'Î groups that expressed radical revolutionary political doctrines and eclectic theological views from the perspective of the ITHNÂ 'ASHARIYYAH. In the early period of the development of Shî'î doctrines, a number of groups proposed speculative and widely varied ideas about a range of theological issues. Many doctrines that became standard among the Shî'î in later periods were deemed as exaggerations by some writers, including the GHAYBAH of the IMÂM.

ghusl (Arabic: washing)

The thorough washing of the whole body to achieve a state of ritual purity. It is usually performed before visiting a mosque, after sex, childbirth, contact with a dead body, and other major contaminations. In order for it to be a valid *ghusl*, as opposed to just a bath, it must be accompanied by the declaration of intent, NIYYAH, and be uninterrupted. The times when such an ablution is necessary and the particular practices for it vary among communities and schools of law (MADHHABS). (*See also* JANÂBAH.)

Ginân (Hindi)

Usually anonymous mystical poetry ascribed to various NIZÂRÎ ISMÂ'ÎLÎ PÎRS and used in devotionals.

God

See ALLÂH.

Gog and Magog

See YA'JÛJ WA-MA'JÛJ.

Goliath

See JÂLÛT.

Gospels (Christian)

See INJÎL.

Granada

See GHARNÂṬAH.

guardianship (Arabic, *walâyah*)

The guardian, or *walî*, is the protector of the minor, the orphan, and of the woman in marriage. It is also used to describe the relationship between the MAWLÂ, (client) and the *walî* in the early Islamic period when converts to Islam also became affiliates of Arab tribes. Among the ITHNÂ ʿASHARIYYAH SHÎʿÎ, the term signifies the foundation of the legitamacy of ʿALÎ B. ABÎ ṬÂLIB as the successor to MUḤAMMAD. After the 1979 Iranian revolution, *Imâm* KHOMEINÎ invoked this principle to justify the rule of the clerical elite. (*See also* WALÂYAH.)

H

Hâbîl wa-Qâbîl
See QÂBÎL WA-HÂBÎL.

habous (French, from Arabic *ḥubus*)
See WAQF.

ḥaḍânah (Arabic: embracing a child)
The right to custody of children in situations such as divorce. In most of the schools (MADHHABS) of Islamic law the presumptive right to custody of minor children rests with the mother, even though the father is obligated for child support. In respect to this principle, the right of *ḥadânah* lasts until about the age of seven for boys and until pre-puberty, or around nine years, for girls. For most schools, puberty will release a boy to dwell apart from both parents, while virgin girls are either bound or recommended to remain with the parents. This right of custody can apply to a non-Muslim parent unless that parent tries to turn the child from Islam, at which time the custody reverts to the Muslim parent.

ḥadath (Arabic: innovation)
A minor ritual impurity derived from contact with unclean substances, such as pus, urine, sperm, fermented beverages, etc. This impurity can be removed by a simple WUḌÛ' or, when water is not available, by TAYAMMUM. The SHÎ'Î include contact with unclean persons as well as substances, and the KHAWÂRIJ included such moral actions as unclean thoughts, perjury, obscene proposals, etc. While one is in this state of ritual impurity, it is not permitted to pray, touch the QUR'ÂN, or circumambulate the KA'BAH. Each school of Islamic law MADHHAB offers variants on the general principles mentioned here.

ḥadd (Arabic: limit, border; pl. *ḥudûd*)
The term generally refers to the punishment for certain crimes mentioned in the QUR'ÂN or in SHARÎ'AH, such as robbery, theft, drinking intoxicants, false accusation of unchastity, and adultery or fornication. While the punishments are severe, ranging from death to whippings, the actual practice of convictions is very difficult in Muslim courts. Evidence is hard to adduce and confessions can be withdrawn, making actual confessions virtually useless. In the field of speculative theology KALÂM the term refers to a definition.

ḥadîth (Arabic: speech, report; *aḥâdîth*)
In religious use this term is often translated as "tradition," meaning a report of the deeds and sayings of MUḤAMMAD and his COMPANIONS.

These reports form the basis of Islamic law, QUR'ÂN interpretation (TAFSÎR), and early Islamic history and lore. Each *ḥadîth* is composed of two parts, an ISNÂD or chain of authorities reporting the *ḥadîth*, and the main text, usually short, called a MATN. Criticism of each of these elements has resulted in the classification of each *ḥadîth* in SUNNÎ circles as ṢAḤÎḤ, ḤASAN, ḌA'ÎF, SAQÎM, or other classifications. The two most famous Sunnî collections of *ḥadîth*s are by AL-BUKHÂRÎ and MUSLIM B. AL-ḤAJJÂJ. In addition, four other Sunnî collections are added to the two to make a collection of six authoritative collections: ABÛ DÂ'ÛD, IBN MÂJAH, AN-NASÂ'Î, and AT-TIRMIDHÎ. The SHÎ'Î have their own collections based on lines of Shî'î transmitters. In modern times, Muslim reformers have often attacked over-reliance on *ḥadîth*s as leading to uncritical adherence to past authority (TAQLÎD), while others have seen it as a useful tool for reinterpretation of Qur'ânic prescriptions.

Collections of reports about the Prophet and the actions of the early Muslims started in the Prophet's lifetime and accelerated after his death, ultimately numbering in the tens of thousands. In the first Islamic century, there were no collections of *ḥadîth*s, only a collective memory of the reports and actions of the first generation. As a result, a great number of suspect traditions arose, reflecting both self-interested creations and pious redactions of family traditions, that is, those traditions transmitted within family and clan groups. Because of the importance of such reports in all aspects of the community, but particularly in the growth of Islamic law (SHARÎ'AH), a branch of learning known as the science of *ḥadîth* (Arabic *'ilm al-ḥadîth*) became one of the major branches of Islamic thought. The usual approach was to evaluate the *isnâd* or chain of authentication by examining the lives of the reporters. This has resulted in a rich and important biographical literature that aids both the scholar of *ḥadîth*s and the historian alike. Much attention has been paid to the authenticity of *ḥadîth*s by Western scholars, who have often criticized Islamic scholars for relying chiefly on *isnâd* criticism. While it is sometimes the case that "fabricated" traditions appear in the canonical collections, they usually represent the attitudes of the nascent schools of Islamic law. (*See also* SUNNAH.)

ḥadîth qudsî (holy *ḥadîth*)

These report sayings of God that are not found in the QUR'ÂN. They do not have the same holy character as the words of the QUR'ÂN, are not recited in prayers (ṢALÂT), and are not subject to the rules of ritual purity. Even though they have ISNÂDS that go back to God, they are assumed to be of a different nature than the words that came to humankind through JIBRÎL to the Prophet. Many of these traditions have clear parallels in the text of Jewish and Christian scripture.

ḥaḍrah (Arabic: presence)

This term can be used as the opposite of GHAYBAH. Its more usual use is among the ṢÛFÎ indicating the communal DHIKR, usually held on Friday, in which the devotees are imagined to be more fully present before God than in regular activities. The term is also used as a title of respect for saints and prophets, and sometimes it is pronounced *hazrat* in non-Arabic Islamic languages.

ḥâfiẓ (Arabic: preserve, memorize)

The term is applied to one who has memorized the entire QUR'ÂN. It is highly recommended that a Muslim commit large portions of the Qur'ân to memory, with the highest honors reserved for those who know it fully. In some circles it is considered extremely meritorious to write out copies of the sacred text from memory and donate them to places of worship. In medieval biographies, the number of copies of the Qur'ân so written out are indicated.

Ḥâfiẓiyyah

A branch of the ISMÂ'ÎLÎ SHÎ'Î formed in Egypt in the sixth/twelfth century. After the fall of the FÂṬIMID dynasty, the group was suppressed in Egypt and lost general support elsewhere.

Ḥâ'irî Yazdî, 'Abd al-Karîm

(1859–1936)

Prominent Iranian educator and cleric, who held the doctrine that one could follow more than one MARJI' AT-TAQLÎD on different aspects of Islamic law. His most famous student was *Âyatollâh* Rûḥollâh KHOMEINÎ.

Hâjar

The biblical Hagar, mother of ISMÂ'ÎL by IBRÂHÎM. She is said to have been an Egyptian, who bore Ismâ'îl and accompanied him when he was sent into the desert. Arabic legend tells of her compassion for her son, and her help in finding him a suitable wife.

al-ḥajar al-aswad

The Black Stone set in the corner of the KA'BAH. The stone is said to have been given to ISMÂ'ÎL and IBRÂHÎM when they built the Ka'bah. In Islamic narrative tradition, the stone was supplied from heaven by angelic intervention and then placed into the Ka'bah by the two patriarchs. When Western scholars read that the stone was from heaven, they rejected the possibility of divine intervention and asserted that it was a meteorite, as the most plausible secular explanation that still preserved the elements of the story. During the lifetime of MUḤAMMAD the Ka'bah was rebuilt, and the Prophet oversaw the replacement of the stone into its proper place by having a representative of each faction of MECCA hold the edge of a blanket. Muḥammad then rolled the stone onto the blanket with a stick, and all the Meccans lifted together on the blanket to raise the stone into its place. The Prophet then pushed the stone into place with his hands through the blanket. In this manner, no one could claim priority by saying that they, or their descendants, were better because they restored the stone. There is a legend that the stone was originally white, but that it turned black through the misdeeds of humankind. Pilgrims on the ḤAJJ and the *'umrah* try to kiss it if they can get close enough. In Western scholarship, it is still often asserted that the stone is a meteorite. This is based on speculation and a secular interpretation of TAFSÎR traditions.

ḥajj (Arabic: pilgrimage)

One of the five *arkân al-Islâm* (PILLARS OF ISLAM). It is required of each Muslim once during the lifetime provided that the person is of sufficient health, can afford it, and meets other conditions to make the pilgrimage to MECCA between the eighth and thirteenth of the month of Dhû-l-Ḥijjah, the last month of the Muslim lunar calendar. When the pilgrim arrives at the outskirts of the holy precinct around Mecca, the person, either male or female, puts on holy garments of unseamed white cloth, vows abstinence from sexual intercourse, the wearing of perfume and other acts of grooming, and is in a state of IḤRÂM. On the model of the Prophet's Farewell Pilgrimage, in which he set forth the pattern for the ceremony, Muslim pilgrims perform a number of rites including circumambulating the KA'BAH seven times, running between AṢ-ṢAFÂ and al-Marwah, and standing on the plain of 'ARAFAT on the ninth of the month. This standing, WUQÛF, around the

Muslims from around the world take part in the ḥajj *each year. Here Muslims traveling to Mecca arrive at the Ḥajj terminal at King Abdul Aziz airport, Jeddah, Saudi Arabia.*

Mount of Mercy, where MUḤAMMAD delivered his Farewell Sermon, is the central part of the *ḥajj*, without which it is invalid. Some scholars see this as a parallel to the standing around Sinai at the receipt of the Torah, and the plain of ʿArafat is thought by many to be the closest place to God. On the tenth, pilgrims sacrifice an animal and eat a ritual meal at MINÂ in commemoration of the intended sacrifice by IBRÂHÎM of his son, ISMÂʿÎL. Parts of the sacrifice are distributed as alms, and Muslims all over the world celebrate this day, called ʿÎD AL-AḌḤÂ, as one of the most important feast days in the Muslim calendar. The *ḥajj* has been an important social factor in unifying Muslims, and many teachings have spread throughout the world as a result of contacts made on the pilgrimage. Muslims who return from the pilgrimage are accorded special status in their communities and often incorporate a title in their names signifying that they have performed the rite. In numerous Muslim countries travel arrangements are organized by the government, and prospective pilgrims must register and receive instructions before they can go. At the end of the pilgrimage, many Muslims also add a visit to Muḥammad's tomb in MADÎNAH, although this is not a canonical part of the *ḥajj*. The lesser pilgrimage, the *ʿumrah*, which can be performed any time and has fewer requirements, does not satisfy the requirements of the *ḥajj*.

ḥakam (Arabic: judge)

This term is generally used for a person who is an arbitrator or who settles cases through the use of personal wisdom. Such "judges" are on the periphery of Islamic law (SHARÎʿAH), yet serve a useful function in adjudicating claims without resort to a full hearing under the strictures of *sharîʿah*. They often make use of Qur'ânic material and practices from the religious law courts.

al-Ḥakîm, Muḥsin (1889–1970)

Prominent Iraqî SHÎʿÎ MUJTAHID or interpreter of Islamic law, he was the architect of modern Shîʿî activism. He and his sons were persecuted by the Iraqî BAʿTH government, and he forbade Shîʿîs from being members of the Baʿth Party.

al-Ḥâkim bi-'Amr Allâh (375/985–411/1021)

He was the sixth caliph of the SHÎʿÎ FÂṬIMID dynasty in Egypt. He is famous for his persecution of Jews and Christians, his erratic behavior, and for the support accorded him by his followers, the DRUZE, who thought him to have divine qualities. He was declared caliph at the death of his father, when he was only eleven years of age. His reign was marked by a strong promotion of ISMÂʿÎLÎ beliefs and an active suppression of the SUNNÎ in his realm. He also issued edicts forcing Christians and Jews to wear five-pound religious symbols around their necks when in public and greatly reduced their economic and political roles. He issued various rulings, which were later retracted, so that he has earned a reputation for being arbitrary and erratic. On the other hand, he exhibited traits of piety, simplicity, and compassion, so that historians have difficulty fitting him into one category. He claimed for himself, and his followers claimed for him as well, that he was divine, or the manifestation of the divine on earth. One version of his ultimate end is that he was murdered by his sister, because he would not agree to let her marry the man she loved. The version given by his followers, those who would become the Druze, was that he went into GHAYBAH and still lives to guide the world. News of his persecution of Christians featured in the reports in the West that led to the Crusades.

ḥalâl (Arabic: clear, permitted)

The term is often used in opposition to the term ḤARÂM. In common use, it has come to mean food that is properly slaughtered and prepared for Muslims. The Qur'ânic food regulations are similar to the regulations found in the Torah, but are less strict than those found in rabbinic Jewish texts. The QUR'ÂN allows Muslims and Jews to eat together, avoiding those foods that have been offered to idols, are unclean (such as pigs), or have been improperly slaughtered. Historically, the term has a larger context in the discussion of acts that are permissible or impermissible.

Ḥalîmah bt. Abî Dhu'ayb

She was the foster mother of MUḤAMMAD and his wet nurse when he was with the bedouin tribe the Banû Saʿd b. Bakr. According to legend, she and her family prospered greatly while Muḥammad was with them, and she asked to keep him even after he was weaned. It was during the time he was with her that two angels appeared before the boy Muḥammad, cut him open, washed his heart in a pan of snow, weighed it against all of mankind, and restored it into him. This miraculous event, prominent in the SÎRAH, was an early literary indication of Muḥammad's immaculate nature.

al-Ḥallâj, al-Ḥusayn b. Manṣûr (244/857–309/922)

Famous and provocative mystic who proclaimed himself the "Divine Truth." His declaration of having achieved FANÂ', "*'Anâ al-ḥaqq*" ("I am the truth"), earned him a cruel execution. From an early age, al-Ḥallâj showed a keen interest in the esoteric side of religion. Before he was twelve years of age, he had memorized the entire QUR'ÂN and was seeking to discover the hidden meanings of the text. During his first pilgrimage (ḤAJJ), he vowed to remain in the holy site for a year, fasting and keeping silent. When this was finished, he gave up the ṢÛFÎ habit and began to preach more freely. Throughout his life, he maintained a monogamous marriage and a strict adherence to SUNNÎ Islam, in spite of his contact with a number of SHÎʿÎ and his use of Shîʿî terminology. By the time of his second pilgrimage he had a large following and a number of opponents, who accused him of sorcery and other impious acts. In response to these charges and to the charge that he had attained the beatific vision of God, he replied with the famous *shaṭḥ*, or ecstatic expression, "*ʾAnâ al-ḥaqq*," which resulted in his arrest and imprisonment for nine years. As a result of political intrigues, he was re-tried, found guilty, and sentenced to die by beheading. His legacy was to be a martyr for esoteric mysticism and to be the most famous of all Ṣûfî martyrs. (*See also* AL-ḤAQQ.)

ḥalqah (Arabic: circle)

This term is used particularly by the ṢÛFÎ to indicate a study group or a group of followers of a SHAYKH. It is also used more broadly to indicate a group of students gathered around a teacher (in a circle).

Ḥâm

One of the sons of NÛḤ (Noah), he is not mentioned in the QURʾÂN but is found in extra-Qurʾânic literature. There are numerous stories about this figure, including stories about him having sexual relations in the ark and assaulting his father, stories which are also known in Jewish legend. Some Muslim authors relate that ʿÎsâ, (JESUS) raised him from the dead for a while, in order to have him relate stories about the flood. Muslim authors also preserve the same genealogical relations with other nations that are found in the biblical account.

al-Hamadhânî, ʿAyn al-Quḍât (492/1098–525/1131)

Famous mystic, whose pronouncements resulted in his execution as a heretic. His most famous work was *Shakwâ al-gharîb* (The complaint of the stranger).

Ḥamâs

Ḥarakat al-Muqâwamah al-Islâmiyyah, the Movement of Islamic Resistance, was founded in December 1987 as an expression of Islamic religious resistance to Israel as opposed to the nationalistic ideology of the Palestine Liberation Organization. Claiming ties to AL-IKHWÂN AL-MUSLIMÛN (the Muslim Brotherhood), the group claims to perpetuate the JIHÂD against Israel, regarding Palestine as a perpetual WAQF for Islam. The group has rejected any peace initiatives that would compromise its aim of the elimination of Israel and the ultimate re-Islamization of Palestine.

ḥamdalah (Arabic)

The verbal form derived from the phrase *al-ḥamdu li-llâhi*, "Praise be to God," it means to utter that phrase. (*See also* BASMALAH.)

Ḥanafî, or Ḥanafiyyah

One of the four main schools of law in SUNNÎ Islam, named after ABÛ ḤANÎFAH. The school (MADHHAB) was chiefly the product of two of Abû Ḥanîfah's students, Abû Yûsuf and ash-Shaybânî, who built the system on the traditions of the Iraqî towns of BAṢRAH and KÛFAH. This school was favored by the early ʿABBÂSID caliphs and became well established in Syria and Iraq. It also spread eastward to Khurasân, Transoxania, and China. The school places emphasis on individual legal judgment (RAʾY), and today has its greatest following in the Middle East and South Asia.

Ḥanafî, Ḥasan (born 1354/1935)

Egyptian reformer and Islamic modernist, he is a prolific academic writer, whose main aim has been to revive Islam and place it intellectually and theologically in the center of world traditions. His *Muqaddimah fî ʿilm al-istighrâb* (Introduction to the science of occidentalism) stands as a critique of the West and an attempt to stem Western influence by showing that Islam is more universal and better suited to the human condition.

Ḥanbalî, or Hanbaliyyah

One of the four main schools of law in SUNNÎ Islam, named after AḤMAD B. ḤANBAL. The MADHHAB is generally regarded as the most stringent, a reputation enhanced by its adoption, in modified form, by the Wahhâbîs as the official school of law in Saudi Arabia.

ḥanîf (Arabic: monotheist)

A term found in the QUR'ÂN (e.g. Q. 10:105) and early literature meaning one who follows the true, monotheistic worship of God. In the Qur'ân, it is used particularly to refer to IBRÂHÎM as the paradigm of one who comes to follow true monotheism. In this usage, it is contrasted with those who worship idols. In some early texts, both Muslim and Christian, the term *ḥanîf* is synonymous with Islam. In this usage, there is the implied understanding that Islam represents true, pure monotheism, and there is some indication that the term was applied to the early Muslims before Islam became generally used. There is also an apologetic element in the use of the term, particularly among the extra-Qur'ânic authors, where the term is said to refer to those monotheists who are neither Jews nor Christians. The figure of Ibrâhîm is thus regarded as a person who was rightly guided to the right religion before Judaism's founder, MÛSÂ, Christianity's founder, ʿÎSÂ, and Islam's prophet, MUḤAMMAD. In the SÎRAH traditions, Ibrâhîm's legacy is thus open for claim by Muslims in their polemical discussions with Jews and Christians in the first two Islamic centuries. Similarly, the literary roles played by the early *ḥanîf*s contemporary with and slightly before the time of the Prophet serve a similar function.

ḥaqâ'iq (Arabic: truth; sg. *ḥaqîqah*)

Among the doctrines of some of the ISMÂʿÎLIYYAH is the notion that the truths of the universe are hidden in the QUR'ÂN and the law, (SHARÎʿAH). With the coming of the QÂ'IM, all hidden truths will become manifest, and the *ḥaqâ'iq* will be known to all and not just to the initiate elect. This eschatological end will come after a series of cycles have passed, and in this last time the Qâ'im will judge the world and rule triumphant. Until that time, the truths are held by the IMÂM in GHAYBAH and only released through a series of specially appointed teachers.

al-ḥaqq (Arabic: truth, correctness)

This term, meaning right, correctness, or certainty, has come to mean the Divine Truth. As such, it is one of the ninety-nine names (AL-'ASMÂ' AL-ḤUSNÂ) or attributes of God. The ṢÛFÎ mystic AL-ḤALLÂJ claimed this title for himself after he had had a beatific vision in which he felt himself to have been united with God, and his statement "*'Anâ al-ḥaqq*" ("I am the truth") earned him death at the hands of those who thought him to be a blasphemer.

ḥarâm (Arabic: forbidden, proscribed, sacred)

The Arabic root of this word yields a number of important Islamic terms. It has the base meaning of something sacred and, therefore, set aside from common use. From this use, it came to mean something forbidden or proscribed. *Ḥarâm* can mean the opposite of ḤALÂL, when referring to food, indicating the classes of forbidden food, such as pork and those animals not

Mecca, showing the sacred precinct, ḥarâm, *around the city.*

properly slaughtered. When referring to the holy cities of Islam, MECCA, MADÎNAH, and Jerusalem (AL-QUDS), it refers to the sacred precinct, *ḥarâm*, around each city in which a person must behave in accordance with the sanctity of the site. The pre-Islamic use of the term was applied to the sacred precincts around the KAʿBAH, which could not be entered without special rites and clothing. By extension, those animals and articles of clothing that were permitted in the sacred area were unavailable to those outside. The word *ḥarîm* (harem), derived from the same root, refers to the portion of the Muslim house in which women are protected from encountering males not entitled to enter the *ḥarîm*. IḤRÂM, a word also derived from the same root, designates the state of ritual purity on the pilgrimage, (ḤAJJ), and the ritual garments worn while in that state.

al-ḥaram ash-sharîf

Located in the Temple area of Jerusalem, this is the third of the three sacred precincts of Islam, the others being MECCA and MADÎNAH. It encompasses the QUBBAT AṢ-ṢAKHRAH, or the Dome of the Rock, and the al-Aqṣâ mosque. This area is located in the same area as the Jewish Second Temple, the wall of which, known as the "Wailing Wall" in popular parlance, bounds one side of the construct. The platform on which the modern structures stand was probably built by the emperor Herod as part of the Temple complex. The history of the importance of this site has developed over time. In the earliest period, most, but not all, Muslim scholars held that this was the location of the night journey, MIʿRÂJ, during which MUḤAMMAD traveled on the back of AL-BURÂQ from Mecca to Jerusalem and then ascended up to heaven. By the end of the second Islamic century, the majority of Muslim authors identified Jerusalem as the location, particularly because the *qubbat aṣ-ṣakhrah* had been constructed. Traditions about the sacrality of the site increased during the period of the Crusades, when a genre of literature known as *faḍâ'il al-quds,* "the virtues of Jerusalem," developed in part as propaganda to rally Muslim sentiment against the Crusaders. The sacredness of *al-ḥaram ash-sharîf* in modern times has become intermixed with the Palestinian conflict with the state of Israel over ownership of the territory. Some modern authors, relying solely on sources from the *faḍâ'il al-quds* literature, incorrectly deny any Jewish religious claim to this site. Christian claims to the rock that is under the Dome of the Rock are also ancient, with early pilgrims believing that the depression in the rock was the footprint of JESUS ('Îsâ), and not that of Muḥammad as Muslims claim. (*See also* ḤARÂM.)

al-Ḥaramayn, or al-Ḥaramân

The "Two Sanctuaries," i.e. MECCA and MADÎNAH. From an early date, both the KA'BAH in Mecca and the sites in Madînah associated with the Prophet's residence were places of pilgrimage, such that those on ḤAJJ would, if possible, visit Madînah as well. The sacrality of the two places extended in the minds of some to the whole of the ḤIJÂZ, as is seen in the prohibition of non-Muslims having permanent residence in the area in early times. In MAMLÛK and OTTOMAN times, the term *al-Ḥaramayn* also referred to AL-QUDS (Jerusalem) and AL-KHALÎL (Hebron), two sites that were WAQFS in the Ottoman Empire.

ḥarb (Arabic: war)

In Islamic law, all war is forbidden except that warfare that has a specific religious aim, JIHÂD, which is a FARḌ *kifâyah*, or communal duty imposed on a sufficient number of individuals but not necessarily all the members of the community. In the time of the Prophet, the wars involving the early community fell into this category because they either advanced the spread of Islam or were defensive, both categories permitted under the rubric of "holy war," or *jihâd*. The rules for warfare developed along with both the Islamic conquests and the growth of Islamic law (SHARÎ'AH). The prosecution of an authorized war was a communal rather than an individual duty and presumed the existence of an Islamic state, the head of which, either an IMÂM or caliph, would call the faithful to arms. It was presumed that a state of warfare would exist as long as there was an area not under Islamic control, which would only be modified in specific cases when there was a peace treaty in existence. No war against an enemy could be prosecuted unless the enemy was invited to Islam and refused. Muslim warriors were forbidden from shedding blood unnecessarily, from harming non-combatants, or wantonly destroying property. Since warfare is a religious duty, a considerable body of legal literature has developed governing every aspect of war, from training to concluding peace. During the period of the Crusades there was a marked increase of *jihâd* literature, which was paralleled by similar discussions in the Christian West about holy war. (*See also* DÂR AL-ḤARB; DÂR AL-ISLÂM.)

Harem

See ḤARÂM.

ḥarîr (Arabic: silk)

In the QUR'ÂN, it is said that silk will be the clothing of those in Paradise. On earth, however, many understand silk to be forbidden to men but permitted for women. This results from the ḤADÎTH that relates that the Prophet was given a silk robe to wear during prayer (ṢALÂT). He put it on, started to pray, and then stopped and removed the robe in disgust. Exceptions are for small decorations and those who suffer from irritations that silk helps alleviate.

Hârûn b. 'Imrân

Aaron, brother of Moses (MÛSÂ), in the QUR'ÂN. He is mentioned in the Medînan period of the Qur'ân as involved in the construction of the Golden Calf, but the primary responsibility rests with AS-SÂMIRÎ. Numerous legends occur in the TAFSÎR literature, including the account of Hârûn's death, in which he and his brother Mûsâ come upon a cave in which is a throne marked for the one who fits it. As it is too small for Mûsâ, Hârûn sits in it, at which point the angel of death appears and takes him. Mûsâ is later accused of having killed his brother, and Hârûn appears to testify on his behalf. In the ISMÂ'ÎLÎ SHÎ'Î tradition, Hârûn is designated as a ḤUJJAH, or living proof of the invisible God, along with his brother, Mûsâ.

ḥasan (Arabic: good)

A technical term in ḤADÎTH criticism, meaning "fair" or "good."

al-Ḥasan b. 'Alî (3/624–49/669)

The son of 'ALÎ B. ABÎ ṬÂLIB and FÂṬIMAH, daughter of MUḤAMMAD, he was the second SHÎ'Î IMÂM and is said by SUNNÎ scholars to have renounced the office of caliph in favor of the Sunnî MU'ÂWIYAH b. Abî Sufyân. Reports of Ḥasan's early life are filled with hagiographic details, which claim that he was the most like the Prophet and that he and his brother ḤUSAYN used to climb on the Prophet's back during prayer. After the death of his father, 'Alî b. Abî Ṭâlib, some people swore allegiance to him, but Mu'âwiyah immediately contested his claim to the office of caliph. After a period of negotiation and troop maneuvers, Ḥasan was attacked by one of the KHAWÂRIJ, who claimed that he had become an infidel like his father. As he was recovering from his wounds, negotiations continued with Mu'âwiyah and resulted in Ḥasan's abdication. The Shî'î and Sunnî accounts of the details of the abdication vary, and it is impossible to reconcile the two views. After a period of living with a great number of wives and concubines, he died after a long illness. Shî'î sources claim that his death was the result of poison at Mu'âwiyah's instigation, but the same sources say that there were seventy assassination attempts that were miraculously thwarted each time. Ḥasan is featured prominently in Shî'î religious drama.

Ḥasan al-'Askarî (230/844–260/874)

The eleventh IMÂM of the SHÎ'Î and father of the twelfth *Imâm*, MUḤAMMAD B. AL-QÂ'IM. Circumstances around his death caused questions about his succession. According to the traditions of the ITHNÂ 'ASHARIYYAH, he was elected *Imâm* after the death of his brother, Muḥammad Abû Ja'far. Since their father was still alive, some dissent arose among the faithful, who held that the imâmate entered GHAYBAH at that point. At his death, the majority of the Shî'î turned to Ḥasan's son, Muḥammad b. al-Qâ'im, who, at the age of five, made one appearance and entered *ghaybah*.

al-Ḥasan al-Baṣrî (21/642–110/728)

One of the TÂBI'ÛN noted for his piety and asceticism, he was a famous preacher and teacher. He admonished his listeners to live their lives with the YAWM AD-DÎN foremost before them. He was a strong critic of the political leaders of his time, calling them to account for what he perceived to be their lapses and straying from Islam. Because of his strong ascetic practices, he is regarded as the founder of Islamic mysticism, Ṣûfism. Few of his actual writings survive, but he is quoted extensively. The MU'TAZILAH claim that he was one of their own and had been present at the founding of the movement, when his student WÂṢIL B. 'AṬÂ' left his lecture to gather the early Mu'tazilite following.

Ḥasan-i Ṣabbâḥ (died 518/1124)

NIZÂRÎ ISMÂ'ÎLÎ SHÎ'Î leader and its first DÂ'Î. He captured ALAMÛT in 483/1090, fortified it, and made it the center of his opposition to the Crusaders and those SUNNÎ who opposed him. He was converted to the ISMÂ'ÎLÎ cause as a student and was trained in Egypt. On his return to Iran, he travelled extensively, fomenting rebellion against the Sunnî SALJÛKS. In 1092 his group broke with the Egyptian FÂṬIMIDS over issues of succession and were subsequently called Nizârî because of their support for Nizâr as IMÂM. He was an ascetic, intellectual leader, who demanded of his followers the same strict lifestyle he adopted for himself. He is said to have executed his two sons for grave sins. His surviving written works show him to have been a very logical apologist for the reformist Nizârî movement.

Hâshim

The great-grandfather of MUḤAMMAD, Hâshim b. ʿAbd Manâf, gave his name to Muḥammad's clan. He is credited with advancing the system of trade in MECCA and making the city the dominant trading center of Arabia.

Hâshimites

The dynasty that ruled MECCA from the fourth/tenth century to 1343/1924. They were SHARÎFÎ, that is, claiming relationship with and descent from MUḤAMMAD through the line that went back to his great-grandfather, HÂSHIM b. ʿAbd Manâf. This line provided the kings of Syria, Iraq and Jordan, and the dynasty took the title Hâshimite.

Hâshimiyyah

A SHÎʿÎ group that originated in KÛFAH and supported the ʿABBÂSID revolt against the ʾUMAYYADS. The original ʿAbbâsid claim to legitimacy seems to have been based on the tracing of a relationship to MUḤAMMAD through the HÂSHIMITE line. The third caliph, al-Mahdî, abandoned this claim in favor of the argument that they were legitimate because of their relationship to al-ʿAbbâs b. ʿAbd al-Muṭṭalib. From that point, SHÎʿÎ Islam concentrated its claims to legitimacy through the line of FÂṬIMAH and ʿALÎ B. ABÎ ṬÂLIB. The term Hâshimiyyah was also used by the ʿAbbâsids as the name of their administrative center before the building of the city of BAGHDÂD. This was not a single place, but the movable name of the location of the caliph.

ḥashîsh (Arabic: grass)

The name for Indian hemp, *Cannabis sativa*, which, when ingested or smoked, has psychotropic effects. It has a long history of cultivation and use as a narcotic in the Middle East and India, and stories of its use abound in popular literature. It was said, incorrectly, that the NIZÂRÎ ISMÂʿÎLÎ SHÎʿÎ used the drug to induce suicides to slay political opponents, giving the West the term "assassin" from it. The use of this drug to induce mystic visions is to be found chiefly in Western corruptions of Ṣûfism.

ḥawḍ (Arabic: basin, pool, cistern)

This term refers to the container of water used for ABLUTIONS in mosques. In ḤADÎTHS, it also refers to a pool in Paradise that will be used for purification on YAWM AD-DÎN. (*See also* GHUSL.)

al-hâwiyah

One of the seven ranks of Hell mentioned in Q. 101:9.

Ḥawwâʾ

The name of Eve in extra-Qurʾânic writings. She is unnamed in the QURʾÂN and only referred to as the "spouse." She was created from a left rib removed from ADAM by God, and Adam named her Ḥawwâʾ because she was formed from a living being. She is credited with leading Adam into the sin of eating the forbidden fruit, which is variously identified in the Muslim sources as grapes or wheat. After the expulsion from Paradise, Adam and Ḥawwâʾ went to Arabia.

The couple made a pilgrimage (ḤAJJ) to MECCA, where Adam fulfilled all the rites of that ceremony. Ḥawwâ' had her first menstruation there, and Adam dug the well of ZAMZAM with his foot to provide water for her purification. In many mystical circles, Ḥawwâ' is the symbol of the spiritual and mystical elements of Paradise.

ḥayḍ (Arabic: menstruation)

In Islamic law, menstruation is regarded as a natural event that nevertheless produces a state of impurity for the woman. She does not, however, contaminate men who have contact with her, except that sexual intercourse with a menstruating woman is condemned without penalty in the QUR'ÂN. A woman in such a state of impurity may not recite more than a few verses of the Qur'ân, walk through a mosque, fast during RAMAḌÂN, or perform the ṢALÂT. She may, however, attend the ḤAJJ, since ʿÂ'ishah began a period while setting out on the *ḥajj*, and the Prophet gave her permission to continue, wrapping herself with extra cloth. The *ḥayḍ* is used as a marker for the ʿIDDAH, or period of waiting after divorce (ṬALÂQ), before remarriage.

Heaven

See AL-JANNAH.

Hell

See AL-HÂWIYAH; JAHANNAM.

Hereafter

See AL-ÂKHIRAH.

heresy

See BIDʿAH.

heretic

See ILḤÂD; ZINDÎQ.

Hidden Imâm

Among some Shîʿî, it is believed that the last IMÂM did not die, but disappeared from view. (*See also* GHAYBAH, MUḤAMMAD AL-QÂ'IM.)

ḥijâb (Arabic: partition)

In modern and popular usage, the word *ḥijâb* means the veil or head covering worn by some Muslim women. In the QUR'ÂN, the word is non-gendered and means a separation, cover, screen or protection. It was the screen beyond which MARYAM (Mary) concealed herself from her family, and it referred to the separation of the wives of the Prophet from society. On the YAWM AD-DÎN, those who are saved will be separated from those condemned to Hell by a *ḥijâb*. In classical commentaries, the word *ḥijâb* refers to the institution of veiling, while other words are used for the actual veil itself. The wearing of such a veil marks the transition from childhood to adulthood, and is often taken at puberty, although some communities have girls of a younger age dress in a veil in imitation of their mothers. In some ṢÛFÎ writings, the *ḥijâb* is the curtain that separates us from the truth of ALLÂH, which can be penetrated by proper mystical devotion. In popular usage, this term has recently replaced the Qur'ânic word *khimâr*, the name of the garment that covers a woman's bosom. (*See also* BURQUʿ; CHÂDOR; (DRESS.)

al-Ḥijâz (Arabic: barrier)

The northwestern part of the Arabian peninsula containing the holy cities of MECCA and MADÎNAH. For Muslims this is the holy land, *al-bilâd al-muqaddasah*, the birthplace of Islam, and, as such, it has been restricted to Muslims in whole or part. After the death of the Prophet, the two cities of Mecca and Madînah became known as AL-ḤARAMAYN, the two cities that were ḤARÂM, or sacred.

Non-Muslims were excluded from these sites and, by extension, were allowed into the rest of the Ḥijâz only in limited ways. Until modern times, the area has been poor and dependent on pilgrim revenues to sustain its population.

hijrah (Arabic: dissociation, migration from one polity to another)

Meaning to migrate or change one's affiliation from one group to another, the term generally refers to the migration of the Prophet MUḤAMMAD from MECCA to MADÎNAH in 622 C.E., which became the first year of the Muslim CALENDAR on the establishment of the Muslim state. The Prophet lost the full support of his clan after the death of his uncle, ABÛ ṬÂLIB, who was replaced by ABÛ LAHAB, a supporter of Muḥammad's bitterest enemies and one of the people mentioned in the QUR'ÂN as condemned to Hell. After attempts to find a suitable affiliation with the inhabitants of aṭ-Ṭâ'if, the Prophet concluded the treaty of al-ʿAqabah with the Arab tribes of the city of YATHRIB, known as MADÎNAH. According to the traditions found in the SÎRAH, in the year 622 Muḥammad began to send his followers north to Madînah. His enemies among the QURAYSH plotted to kill the Prophet by having a representative of each of the clans simultaneously stab him, in order that the guilt would be spread evenly among them. When they arrived at Muḥammad's house, however, they found ʿALÎ B. ABÎ ṬÂLIB in his bed. The Meccans pursued the Prophet and ABÛ BAKR, but they hid in a cave, the entrance to which was miraculously covered by a spider's web, leading the Meccans to believe that the cave was uninhabited. According to tradition, they arrived by a circuitous route at the south side of the city on the twelfth of the month of ar-Râbiʿ al-'Awwal in the year 622. He loosed his camel, which went into the city, and where the camel stopped, he made his headquarters. The people who had been sent to Abyssinia in 615 and were brought to Madînah were counted as having made the *hijrah*. In subsequent Islamic history, the term has taken on a metaphoric sense to mean an Islamic religious journey.

hilâl (Arabic: crescent)

The crescent or new moon, it has become the symbol of Islam because of its association with the sighting of the new moon at the start and finish of the holy month of RAMAḌÂN. It is important in Islamic religious law (SHARÎʿAH), because the Muslim CALENDAR is lunar, and the beginnings of festivals are determined by the sighting of the new moon. The details of such sightings vary from one legal school (MADHHAB) to another. The crescent moon began to appear, usually accompanied by a five- or six-pointed star, in the first Islamic century as a symbol on coins and decorations. By the fifth/eleventh century, the crescent was used to replace the cross, when churches were converted to mosques. In Ottoman times, the crescent and the star became emblems on Muslim battle flags and royal standards. In the

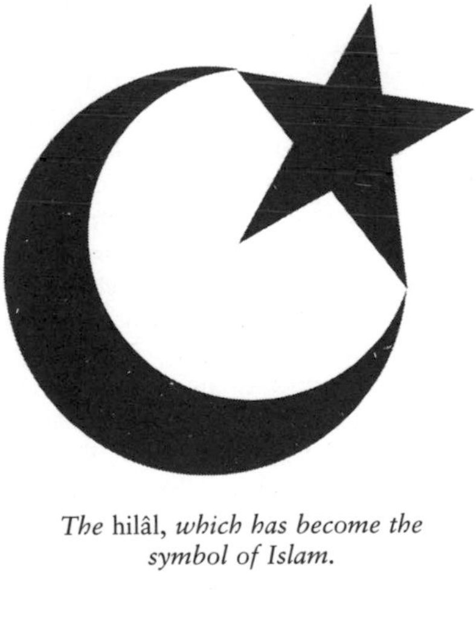

The hilâl, *which has become the symbol of Islam.*

twentieth century, these symbols became the flag of the Republic of TURKEY when it was declared in 1923. PAKISTAN also adopted it, as have a number of Muslim countries around the world. In the UNITED STATES, the crescent has become the official symbol for deceased Muslims in the United States military, parallel to the cross for Christians and the star of David for Jews.

al-Ḥillî, ʿAllâmah b. al-Muṭahhar (648/1250–726/1325)

Scholar and jurist of the ITHNÂ ʿASHARIYYAH SHÎʿÎ, prominent in the MUʿTAZILAH, and a theorist noted for his writings on IJTIHÂD. He is said to have written over five hundred works on all aspects of Islamic learning, only a few of which have been published. Two of his works, *al-Bâb al-ḥâdî ʿashar* and *Sharḥ tajrîd al-iʿtiqâd*, are regarded as foundational texts for Ithnâ ʿAsharî Shîʿism. His preaching converted the Ilkhânid ruler of Persia to Ithnâ ʿAsharî Shîʿism, making it the state religion of Persia for the first time.

ḥilm (Arabic: well-behaved, civilized)

This term is the opposite of the Arabic word *jahl*, from which we get the word JÂHILIYYAH, referring to the period before the coming of Islam. It is linked to the concept of ʿILM, which means knowledge or science, but it has broader civilizational aspects than those two terms usually imply in English. From the perspective of the coming of Islam, the eradication of the behaviors of the *jâhiliyyah* meant an end to the barbarities of that period and their social injustices. The term appears in the QURʾÂN to indicate kindness, forbearance, and patience, all aspects of the message that MUḤAMMAD strove to correct in his fellow QURAYSH. The link between *ḥilm* and *ʿilm* has profoundly affected Islamic views of education. Fundamental to a study of the sciences, particularly the religious sciences, is the notion that the student who studies the Qurʾân and related texts will become a moral person, a true Muslim.

ḥinnâʾ (Arabic: henna)

A plant used for dye, medicine, and, from its flower, perfumed oil. As a dye, it is widely used in the Islamic world to color the hair of both sexes, grey beards, and by women to decorate their hands and feet. In some communities, men use it to dye their beards on return from the ḤAJJ. There is no prohibition in the ḤADÎTHS against using it for decoration on the skin unless it resembles an all-over tattoo, so parts of the skin usually remain uncolored. In the popular imagination, the plant has properties to ward off evil as well as to cure certain illnesses.

Ḥirâʾ, Mount

The mountain northeast of MECCA in a cave of which MUḤAMMAD practiced *taḥannuth* (meditation). He also received his first revelation of the QURʾÂN from the angel JIBRÎL there. It is also called Jabal an-Nûr, the "Mountain of Light." (*See also* KHALWAH.)

al-ḥisâb (Arabic: reckoning)

The word is often used in the QURʾÂN in the sense of the final reckoning, the *yawm al-ḥisâb*. At the time of the final judgment of each soul, the person will receive a record of all their deeds, in the right hand if they are destined for Paradise, and in their left hand if destined for damnation. The imagery used in the Qurʾân is a commercial metaphor in which each deed is valued positively or negatively and made part of the final accounting. (*See also* YAWM AD-DÎN.)

ḥisbah (Arabic: reckon)

From a root meaning to reckon or sum up, the term refers to the institution in the Islamic state to regulate markets and maintain public order.

ḥiyal (Arabic: devices; sg. *ḥîlah*)

Legal stratagems designed to mitigate the severity or, sometimes, the unintended consequences of a law. Some of the earliest of these strategems were in the commercial field, where the prohibition of lending money at interest had the possible effect of eliminating business. In order to get around this, some people employed a simultaneous double sale, in which the object was sold at one price and re-purchased at a higher price to be paid in the future. The difference between the prices would be the equivalent of what would be termed interest in the West, and would satisfy the legal requirements of SHARÎʿAH. These legal fictions were favored by the ḤANAFÎ MADHHAB and condemned by the MÂLIKÎ and the ḤANBALÎ. AL-BUKHÂRÎ reserved a whole section of his *ṣaḥîḥ* for condemnation of the practice.

ḥizb (Arabic: one-sixtieth)

In the QUR'ÂN, the term refers to factions which weaken a religion and lead to its destruction. In modern usage, it means "party," as in ḤIZB ALLÂH, the "party of God," Q. 58:22. In Ṣûfism, the term refers to a particularly helpful prayer for a specific occasion, such as a prayer for traveling.

ḥizb Allâh (Arabic: party of God)

In the QUR'ÂN it is opposed to the *ḥizb ash-Shayṭân*, the party of the devil, Q. 58:19.

Ḥizb ad-Daʿwah al-Islâmiyyah

The Islamic Missionary Party, a major SHÎʿÎ party in Iraq in opposition to the Baʿthist regime.

Ḥizb an-Nahḍah

The principal Islamist party in Tunisia.

Ḥizb at-Taḥrîr al-Islâmî

The Islamic Liberation Party, founded in 1953 by a Palestinian, Taqî ad-Dîn an-Nabhânî. It seeks to establish a post-colonial Islamic state to replace the existing states, which are not founded on principles of SHARÎʿAH.

Ḥizbullâh

A militant revolutionary party formed in Iran after the revolution of 1979. It was used as a vigilante movement by the Islamic Republican Party, and as a paramilitary group to enforce their policies. Formed from Iranian roots, the party in Lebanon has developed a strong support base among the Lebanese SHÎʿÎ and has adopted a strong anti-American, anti-Israeli, anti-Phalangist stance. It has adopted the dual tactic of participating in parliamentary elections and committing acts of violence to further its aims of creating an Islamic state in Lebanon.

Ḥizkîl b. Bûdhî or Bûzî

The biblical prophet Ezekiel. His name is not found in the QUR'ÂN, but the TAFSÎR traditions equate him with the prophet sent to the people mentioned in Q. 2:243, who were killed by God and then brought back to life. In the ISRÂ'ÎLIYYÂT traditions, many features of Ezekiel's life are taken from Jewish and Christian commentaries.

holy war

See JIHÂD.

Houris

Properly *ḥuriyyah* or *ḥawrâ'*; in the QUR'ÂN, they are female companions in Paradise, e.g. Q. 52:20. In Islamic legend, they are perpetually virgins.

Hubal

The name of a major pre-Islamic deity. His statue was located in the KA'BAH, and divining arrows were cast before it. The practice of casting such arrows is condemned in Q. 5:90. The statue was guarded by a ḤIJÂB and seems to have been generally worshipped by the polytheistic QURAYSH.

Hûd

The prophet sent to the people of 'ÂD. Like MUḤAMMAD, he found his people strongly resistent to his message. As a punishment, God withheld rain from them for three years. Hûd suggested that they make a pilgrimage to MECCA to pray for rain, but they prayed to more deities than just ALLÂH, so God caused three clouds to appear. The leader of the people of 'Âd, Qayl, chose a black one, and God sent a terrible wind that destroyed all the unbelievers of 'Âd. Hûd and his small band of faithful then settled in Mecca.

al-Ḥudaybiyyah

A town near MECCA in which MUḤAMMAD and the Meccans signed a mutual non-aggression treaty in 6/628 granting the Muslims the right to make an *'umrah* (lesser pilgrimage) the following year in exchange for the return of those QURAYSH who had made the HIJRAH without their guardians' permission. The treaty was rendered moot by the Muslim conquest of Mecca in 8/630.

hudhud

The hoopoe bird, one of the few mentioned explicitly in the QUR'ÂN. In Islamic legend, it is regarded as a pious and faithful bird, monogamous and devoted to its parents. It has a major role in the story of SULAYMÂN and BILQÎS (Q. 27), where it reports finding the queen. In the TAFSÎR traditions, it also has the power to find water and carries important correspondence for Sulaymân.

ḥudûd

See ḤADD.

ḥujjah (Arabic: proof; the presentation of proof)

This term is used in various technical senses in philosophical and theological argument. Among the ISMÂ'ÎLÎ SHÎ'Î, it represents the person through whom the transcendent God becomes manifest. As such, it refers to a high level of rank in the DA'WAH organization.

Ḥujjatiyyah

From the Arabic word meaning proof, this ultra-conservative Iranian SHÎ'Î movement holds that the IMÂMS are the means by which those lower than they can achieve access to God. The group is violently anti-BAHÂ'Î. After 1979, the Ḥujjatiyyah were accused of opposition to the rule of clerics and driven underground, where its followers await the return of the HIDDEN IMÂM.

al-Hujwîrî (died 467/1075)

A well-known ṢÛFÎ who wrote the *Kashf al-maḥjûb* (Disclosure of the Concealed), in which he outlines the mystic path, while advocating that the mystic also follow the SHARÎ'AH.

al-Ḥusayn b. 'Alî (4/626–61/680)

The third IMÂM of the SHÎ'Î, the son of 'ALÎ B. ABÎ ṬÂLIB and Muḥammad's daughter, FÂṬIMAH. He, along with a small group of supporters, was massacred on YAWM 'ÂSHÛRÂ in 61/680 at the battle of KARBALÂ', an event commemorated by Shî'î to this day. For this reason, he is known as the Prince of Martyrs, and his death, remembered as heroic, has served as a paradigm of martyrdom.

ḥusayniyyah

Sites for the ritual ceremonies commemorating the martyrdom of AL-ḤUSAYN B. ʿALÎ, they were originally temporary tents in memory of the *Imâm*'s last encampment. The practice dates from the tenth century and has spread throughout the SHÎʿÎ communities in the Islamic world. Some *ḥusayniyyah* are permanent and endowed by WAQFS.

hypocrisy, hypocrites

See MUNÂFIQÛN.

I

ʿibâdah (Arabic: religious practice)

This word, mentioned in the QUR'ÂN, (Q. 18:110; 19:65), means the observances and devotional actions necessary to be a Muslim. In FIQH a distinction is made between *ʿibâdât* and *muʿâmalât*, the latter being the social requirements and obligations in Islam. In institutions like DIVORCE (*ṭalâq*) and MARRIAGE (*nikâḥ*), many scholars would divide between the two.

Ibâḍiyyah or Abâḍiyyah

The Ibâḍîs are a moderate branch of the KHAWÂRIJ named after ʿAbd Allâh b. Ibâḍ (fl. first/seventh century). They are tolerant of other sects of Islam, believing that Muslims who are not of their persuasion are not MUSHRIKÛN (polytheists), as the more extreme 'Azraqî Khârijites hold. This means that they reject the notion that those Muslims must be killed for apostasy. Marriage with non-Ibâḍîs is possible, but they are resistant to outside contact. They are found today chiefly in Oman, but also in East Africa and North Africa.

Iblîs

The name in the QUR'ÂN for the devil (e.g. Q. 2:34), derived from the Greek word *diabolos*. The Qur'ân lists Iblîs as the angel who refused to bow to ADAM, because he was made of clay. This caused ALLÂH to cast him out of heaven and be cursed until the end of time. Iblîs then requested that his punishment be deferred to the YAWM AD-DÎN and that he be given permission to lead astray all humans and JINN who are not steadfast and faithful. He started his temptations with ḤAWWÂ' (Eve) and Adam by persuading them to eat fruit from the forbidden tree, making both of them culpable. In the TAFSÎR literature he is said to have entered the mouth of the snake, which was at that time a beautiful creature. As part of the curse for tempting Adam and Ḥawwâ', the snake was stripped of its fine feathers and its legs and made to crawl forever in the dust as an enemy to humans. His usual approach to humans is to whisper in the ears. For this reason, the last two chapters of the Qur'ân are frequently recited at the perception of temptation or worn as amulets to ward off the evil. Parents will also say the BASMALAH in the ears of newborns to prevent Iblîs from having an influence on them. At the *yawm ad-dîn*, Iblîs and all his helping hosts will be cast into the fires of Hell. Some mystics hold out the hope that he will repent and be spared the final punishment. In extra-Qur'ânic literature, many popular stories about the Devil are elaborated. In one, NÛḤ (Noah) was supervising the loading of the ark when the pair of asses approached. Iblîs is said to have grabbed the tail of one of the asses so that it could not advance up the gangplank. Nûḥ, in exasperation, said, "Woe to you; enter, even if the devil is with you." This gave permission for Iblîs to enter the ark. There is extensive discussion about whether the devil is a fallen angel, a *jinn*, or both. The discussion hinges on the nature of angels and whether or not they are created sinless and obedient to God. Another point of discussion among commentators is the nature of Iblîs' sin. He was asked, so the argument goes, to bow to a human creature, which would be to disobey the command to worship only God and to bow to none else but God. Most see Iblîs' actions as derived from pride rather than humility, and that he was punished for his pride. Some ṢÛFÎs, however, see the connection between what they perceive to be true worship and what they are required to do in the world, and are sympathetic to Iblîs' plight. (*See also* SHAYṬÂN.)

Ibn ʿAbbâs (c. 619–68/688)

The common name for ʿAbd Allâh b. al-ʿAbbâs, a prominent early Companion, MUḤADDITH, and commentator on the QUR'ÂN. Because of his erudition, he is often called *al-Baḥr*, the "Ocean" of wisdom. He was born before the HIJRAH to a Muslim mother and was regarded as having been a Muslim all his life. Early in his life he began to collect sayings about the Prophet (ḤADÎTHS), and develop collections of material about the Qur'ân. These collections were both oral and written, and he used them as the basis for his daily public teachings on the entire range of Islamic topics. Because of his reputation as a scholar, he was frequently asked for legal opinions (FATWÂS) about matters, and was one of the first to engage in commentary on the Qur'ân, TAFSÎR. He had minimal involvement in the political turmoil of his time. He participated in several campaigns, but was not a central military figure. He was an advisor to ʿALÎ B. ABÎ ṬÂLIB and held some minor posts. He was involved in the appropriation of the town funds of BAṢRAH, but he seems to have been immune to scandal. He is best known to history as a great scholar whose extensive knowledge of the Qur'ân and *ḥadîth*s helped establish the basis for the development of the Islamic sciences.

Ibn ʿAbd Allâh (Arabic: son of the servant of Allâh)

This name is often taken by converts to Islam as their new patronymic.

Ibn ʿAbd al-Wahhâb, Muḥammad (1115/1703–1206/1792)

Founder of the Wahhâbî movement, which is based on the writings of IBN TAYMIYYAH and extreme Ḥanbalî thought. He was born in Arabia in a town in the Nejd called al-ʿUyaynah to a family of Ḥanbalî scholars. He began his education with his father by learning the QUR'ÂN by heart. After studying what was available to him in his home town, he left for a series of journeys "in search of knowledge." He went to MECCA on ḤAJJ, but was dissatisfied with what he learned there. While in MADÎNAH, however, he studied with ʿAbd Allâh b. Ibrâhîm an-Najdî, who was a supporter of Ibn Taymiyyah. He then went to Baṣrah, Baghdâd, where he married a wealthy woman and remained for five years, to Damascus and Cairo. He then returned to Arabia, wrote a treatise on the unity of God, and began preaching his reformist message against the veneration of saints and other innovations, (BIDʿAH). Some of the local Arabian SHÎʿÎ became alarmed at his preaching, and he moved to the town of Darʿiyyah, near present-day Riyâḍ, and secured the protection of the AMÎR, Muḥammad b. Saʿûd. His reformist ideology suited the ambitions of the *amîr*, and their association led to the beginning of a Wahhâbî state. He was active in writing and propaganda until his death at the age of eighty-nine. The movement he started took the doctrines of Ibn Taymiyyah to new lengths. He was opposed to all survivals among the bedouin of pre-Islamic practices, to any form of Ṣûfism and any kind of reliance on TAQLÎD, the adherence of a person to a doctrine because of the authority of others. This meant, also, that he was opposed to Shîʿî doctrines as well, which naturally relied on the authority of ʿALÎ B. ABÎ ṬÂLIB and the line of IMÂMS. The reports that Ibn ʿAbd al-Wahhâb was expelled from his home town by his own family seem to be exaggerated. On both religious and personal grounds, he was opposed to the OTTOMAN EMPIRE, which had killed his brother and condoned a wide variety of practices he saw as innovations and heresies.

Ibn al-ʿArabî, Muḥyî ad-Dîn

(560/1165–638/1240)

A famous ṢÛFÎ writer and master, dubbed *ash-shaykh al-akbar* (the great SHAYKH), he is best known for his doctrine of the oneness of being (*waḥdat al-wujûd*). Born in Spain, he spent the first thirty years of his life in and around Seville. As a result of a childhood illness, he changed his life and became more religious. The genuineness of this experience impressed his father and one of his father's friends, the famous philosopher IBN RUSHD. At the age of thirty, he left Seville and went first to Tunis and then to FÂS, where he began his writing. At the age of thirty-eight, he traveled to Cairo and then made the ḤAJJ to MECCA, where he stayed for two years. Additional journeys took him to BAGHDÂD and finally to DIMASHQ (Damascus), where he married several wives and lived a quiet life of teaching and writing. He was a prolific writer, credited with over four hundred different works. His best-known works are *The Bezels of Wisdom* (*Fuṣûṣ al-ḥikam*) and *The Meccan Revelations* (*al-Futûḥât al-makkiyyah*). Like many Ṣûfîs, Ibn al-ʿArabî believed that human knowledge is limited, and that knowledge acquired through sense perception and reason is inferior to religious knowledge acquired through inspiration from God to the soul. For this reason, he felt that humans should undertake spiritual journeys to God, insofar as they are able. The ultimate goal would be union with God while still living among humans on earth. At no point did he advocate abandoning the practice of the requirements of Islam – the daily prayers, the fasting, etc. He believed God to be completely transcendent, with emanations coming from Him that seem similar to Neoplatonic emanations, but he does not clearly explain how this process works. For him, knowledge from God comes to humans through these emanations, like the inspiration to the prophets, and must be received through faith, but humans must make the journey toward God in order to be receptive. Some are more receptive than others, like prophets chosen for their role, and Ibn al-ʿArabî regarded himself as particularly talented in this area. Without claiming prophethood, he regarded his writings as divinely inspired. The techniques he advocated for the spiritual journey involved silence, withdrawal from human contact, wakefulness, and hunger. At a final stage, the ḤIJÂB that separates humans from God is lifted, and the successful mystic perceives a manifestation of God. Ibn al-ʿArabî did not establish a ṬARÎQAH, so his influence is to be found among those who carried copies of his works to Iran and the Yemen. His greatest influence was in the OTTOMAN EMPIRE, where his works were used as school texts. In the West, he had some influence on the Catalan philosopher and missionary Raymondus Lullus (died *c.* 1315), and possibly on Dante's *Divina Comedia*.

Ibn ʿArûs, Abû al-ʿAbbâs Aḥmad (died 868/1463)

One of the most prominent and popular WALÎs (saints) of medieval Tunisia. He lived as an itinerant worker of miracles and violated the moral and religious codes, claiming that he was beyond those mundane restrictions. His popularity allowed him to withstand the criticism of the ʿULAMÂʾ, and he was buried in a ẒÂWIYAH, or tomb, that became the object of popular veneration. The ʿArûsiyyah ṬARÎQAH was named for him.

Ibn Bâdîs, ʿAbd al-Ḥamîd, also Ben Bâdîs (1307/1889–1359/1940)

Algerian Islamic reformer, head of the Algerian ʿULAMÂʾ, and architect of Algerian independent identity. Through his Islamic reform, he led the resistance to the French, restored Arabic as the national language, opposed the ṢÛFÎ orders, and interpreted the QURʾÂN in modernist terms, emphasizing human reason and free will. He studied at the Islamic University in Tunis, worked as a teacher and, in 1925, founded the newspaper *al-Muntaqid* (The critic). This short-lived publication was replaced by *ash-Shihâb*, which became a monthly platform for his reformist ideas, and continued until 1939. He was particularly devoted to ridding Algeria of the influence of the MARABOUTs, whom he saw as playing on ignorance and superstition, and the influence of French culture and ideals. Indeed, he saw the two elements as linked, to the detriment of Algerian independence and development. In 1931, he became the president of the Association of Algerian Muslim *ʿulamâʾ* and worked tirelessly promoting an Islamic cultural renewal. At his death in 1940, he was regarded as a "saint" for his efforts and his simplicity.

Ibn Bâjjah, Abû Bakr Muḥammad b. Yaḥyâ b. aṣ-Ṣâʾigh al-ʾAndalusî as-Saraqusṭî (c. 500/1106–533/1138)

Andalusian Islamic Neoplatonic philosopher, who influenced IBN RUSHD. He was also a well-known musician and poet, and the composer of popular songs. Little is known of his life. When his Iberian hometown of Saragosa fell to the Almoravids, he served as a WAZÎR until he was thrown into prison at a political change. He went to Seville and assumed another post as *wazîr* that lasted for twenty years. He died in FÂS, some say by poisoning. Ibn Bâjjah's main concern in his writings is the possibility of the union of man and God. He thought this could be achieved through the exercise of the intellect, by which a person is capable of comprehending increasingly abstract forms until the Active Intellect is reached. His work is decidedly Neoplatonic and based, apparently, on several Neoplatonic treatises that were available to him in Arabic translation. In the West, he was known as Avempace, and translations of his works helped bring knowledge of Neoplatonism and Aristotle to the West.

Ibn Baṭṭûṭah (703/1304–779/1369)

The most famous Muslim traveler, he tells in his *Riḥlah* (Travelogue) of his travels from the Middle East and Africa to China. He often earned his way by serving as a MÂLIKÎ judge (QÂḌÎ). His travel account combines both the genre of Muslim geography and the personal travel tale in such a way that he creates almost a new genre, of which he is the foremost example. His descriptions of India, the areas under Turkic domination and China contain a wealth of information not found elsewhere in Islamic literature of the time.

Ibn Ḥajar al-ʿAsqalânî, Shihâb ad-Dîn Abû al-Faḍl Aḥmad b. Nûr ad-Dîn ʿAlî b. Muḥammad (773/1372–852/1449)

A historian and scholar of ḤADÎTHs, he was a great writer of biographical encyclopedias that are rich sources of information about transmitters of tradition. His parents died when he was about three, but his mother left him a small fortune and he was able to live in the house of his birth and pursue his studies. After several RIḤLAHs, journeys for knowledge, and a good marriage, he started a career that saw him advance from lecturer to professor to judge in a relatively smooth path. His real fame lies in his works on ʿILM AL-ḤADÎTH, the science of tradition. He wrote immense biographical dictionaries, *al-Iṣâbah fî tamyîz aṣ-ṣaḥâbah* and *Tahdhîb at-tahdhîb* being the most famous. He also wrote biographies of Egyptian judges and a biography of famous men of his time. His commentary on the *Ṣaḥîḥ* of AL-BUKHÂRÎ, the *Fatḥ al-bârî*, is a model of juridical explication. He enjoyed a reputation of sound scholarship and criticism in his time, and his works are still standards to be consulted about *ḥadîth*s.

Ibn Ḥanbal

See AḤMAD B. ḤANBAL.

Ibn Ḥazm, Abû Muḥammad ʿAlî b. Aḥmad b. Saʿîd (384/994–456/1064)

Iberian jurist, theologian, poet, and specialist in comparative religion, he was a prolific writer and proponent of the ẒÂHIRÎ school of law (MADHHAB). He was born in Cordova, but little is known of his family background. His father was a WAZÎR in the court of the ruler, Manṣûr, and Ibn Ḥazm spent his early years in the court and in the harem. When his father fell from favor and the dynasty changed, Ibn Ḥazm became the *wazîr* to the ʾUMAYYAD claimant to the kingdom of Granada. At his sponsor's defeat, Ibn Ḥazm was put in prison for a time, a pattern that was repeated several times, until he went into semi-seclusion and withdrew from public life. His political writings reflect a strong bias against the MÂLIKÎ MADHHAB for its support of whoever might be in power, while his juristic writings reflect a strong bias against the ḤANAFÎ *madhhab*. In the West, he is best known for his treatise on love, *Ṭawq al-ḥamâmah* (The *dove's neckring*), as well as his writings on comparative religion, *Kitâb al-fiṣal fî al-milal wa al-aḥwâʾ wa al-niḥal*.

Ibn Hishâm, Abû Muḥammad ʿAbd al-Mâlik (died 218/833)

Editor of the first biography of MUḤAMMAD (SÎRAH), written by IBN ISḤÂQ. He spent his life in Egypt, but his family was of southern Arabian origin, and he wrote a work on the antiquities of South Arabia, called the *Kitâb at-tîjân*. His edition of the *sîrah* epitomized Ibn Isḥâq's original, confining it only to those materials that he felt were relevant to the life of the Prophet. He criticized Ibn Isḥâq for introducing elements that were problematic or shameful for a sacred biography, but his criticism reflected the changed and more insular attitudes of the Islamic community that had developed after the *sîrah* was composed.

Ibn Idrîs, Ahmad (1163/1749–1253/1837)

Eponym of the IDRÎSIYYAH ṢÛFÎ movement, he was born in Morocco, studied in FÂS, and spent his later years in the Arabian Peninsula. His son, ʿAbd al-ʿÂl, is credited with starting the movement formally, and his students carried his ideas to MALAYSIA and Africa.

Ibn Isḥâq, Muḥammad b. Isḥâq b. Yasâr b. Khiyâr al-Madanî (85/704–150/767)

Born in MADÎNAH to a MAWLÂ family of traditionists, he collected stories and poems about the Prophet and wrote the first complete biography of MUḤAMMAD, called the *Sîrat rasûl Allâh* or *as-Sîrah*. It started with the creation of the world and continued through the life of the Prophet up to the ʿABBÂSID CALIPHATE. It was later abridged by IBN HISHÂM to just the materials on the life of the Prophet, and is the most popular biography of Muḥammad in existence. Ibn Isḥâq was born into a scholarly family, for his father, Isḥâq, and his two uncles, Mûsâ and ʿAbd ar-Raḥmân, were transmitters of Prophetic tradition. We know little of his life, but he developed a solid reputation for his knowledge of *maghâzî* material, which included more than just the military aspects of the Prophet's career. At one point, Ibn Isḥâq seems to have earned the enmity of MÂLIK B. ʾANAS, probably for reasons of rivalry and their differing visions of what constituted proper sacred biography. Ibn Isḥâq went to Iraq and became associated with the newly forming ʿAbbâsid court, where he was the tutor to the young prince, al-Mahdî. It was partly as a textbook that he conceived the shape of *as-Sîrah*, which included a comprehensive history of the world from creation through the life of Muḥammad. He continued this history with a history of the Caliphs up to the ʿAbbâsids. While authorities differ about his reliability as a transmitter of legal ḤADÎTHs, all concur that he was a master at the Prophet's biography. *as-Sîrah* is the first to bring together a vision of the Prophet in a critical and comprehensive way, and set the pattern for our understanding of Muḥammad's life. All subsequent understandings of the Prophet are indebted to Ibn Isḥâq's vision and assiduous collecting of tradition. His vision of world history was so influential that it is said that the famous historian AṬ-ṬABARÎ used Ibn Isḥâq's material and plan as the basis for his universal history. (*See also* SÎRAH.)

Ibn Kathîr, Abû Maʿbad ʿAbd Allâh b. Kathîr al-Makkî (*fl. c.* 90/710)

Born in MECCA, he was a perfume dealer by trade, but became an authority on TAJWÎD, or recitation of the QURʾÂN. His reading is counted among the SUNNÎ as one of the seven canonical readings.

Ibn Khaldûn, ʿAbd ar-Raḥmân b. Muḥammad Walî ad-Dîn (732/1332–808/1406)

Historian, proto-sociologist, and social theoretician, he is best known in the West for his *Muqaddimah* (Introduction) to his historical writings, in which he sets forth a cyclical theory of the interactions between nomadic and urban civilizations. He describes a principle of group solidarity (Arabic: *ʿaṣabiyyah*) that makes a state cohere and, when lost, leads to decay and destruction. He was born in Tunis to a family that had left Seville before the advance of the Reconquista. He received an excellent traditional Islamic education, punctuated by the intrustion of political chaos and the Black Death. He moved to FÂS and became associated with the court there, continuing his studies. When he was twenty-eight years of age, he moved to GHARNÂṬAH. The political intrigues finally drove him back to North Africa and away from public office. He moved to Cairo (AL-QÂHIRAH), where he took a position as a teacher of MÂLIKÎ FIQH. His successes provoked jealousy, and he was dismissed from the post, a pattern that was repeated regularly. In addition to his *Muqaddimah*, Ibn Khaldûn wrote an autobiographical work that, unfortunately, does not give full insight into his motives and character. He also wrote a universal history, the *Kitâb al-ʿibar*, which has received less interest and scholarly attention. In part, this is because it does not meet the standards of historical thinking set forth in his *Muqaddimah*, and in part it is because of some serious historical lapses in the work. He is, for example, not always accurate on dates and on the beliefs of the groups he discusses. Western scholarship has discovered Ibn Khaldûn's *Muqaddimah* and has proclaimed him to be the "father" of sociology or social history. He has been judged unique, and it is hard to point to a predecessor who can be viewed as his model. It is also true that he left no successors, and his fame in modern times reflects his discovery or rediscovery within the context of contemporary social and historical theories.

Ibn Mâjah, Abû ʿAbd Allâh Muḥammad b. Yazîd (209/824–273/887)

A prominent MUḤADDITH, his collection of traditions, *Kitab as-Sunan,* is one of the six authoritative collections in SUNNÎ Islam. Born in Qazwîn, he traveled extensively in Iraq, Syria, Arabia, and Egypt to collect ḤADÎTHS. His collection, which contains over four thousand items, has been considered the weakest of the six canonical collections.

Ibn Masʿûd (died *c.* 33/653)

COMPANION to MUḤAMMAD and an early convert, was sent by the Prophet to Ethiopia, and later lived in MADÎNAH and KÛFAH. He was an assiduous collector of QUR'ÂN, although his recension differed from that of the caliph ʿUTHMÂN. The sources say that he was either the third or the sixth person to convert to Islam, and his zeal earned him a special affection from the Prophet. He was given the posts of carrying Muḥammad's sandals and making the toothpicks he used. This gave him daily contact with the Prophet, and he heard the Qur'ân directly from his mouth. He is said to have been the first besides Muḥammad to recite the Qur'ân in public, and was taunted by the non-Muslim QURAYSH for that. He was among those who made the little HIJRAH to Abyssinia, and returned in time to be among those who made the *hijrah* to Madînah. As a source of ḤADÎTHS, he has a mixed reputation due to the twin factors of his fall from public grace because of certain jealousies and his being credited with SHÎʿÎ tendencies. He is most famous for his recension of the Qur'ân, which differed slightly from the ʿUthmânic recension in the order of the SÛRAHS and in various readings.

Ibn Muljam, ʿAbd ar-Raḥmân al-Murâdî (died 40/661)

The chief conspirator and assassin of ʿALÎ B. ABÎ ṬÂLIB, he was a member of the KHAWÂRIJ. Much legend surrounds the motives for his assassination. It is said that he did it to win the love of a woman whose relatives had been slain at NAHRAWÂN, but general hatred of ʿAlî among the QURRÂ' seems to have been his main motive. He was slain in the attack, and it is only speculation that others in the conspiracy planned to slay Muʿâwiyah also.

Ibn Nubâtah, Abû Yaḥyâ ʿAbd ar-Raḥîm b. Muḥammad b. Ismâʿîl (died 374/985)

He was a prominent preacher in the Syrian court of Aleppo, and wrote religious and political sermons in rhymed prose, often using verses of the QUR'ÂN to end his lines. Some of his sermons had a topical theme of supporting the war against the Byzantines, but they have been preserved as models of literary sermons.

Ibn Qâḍî Shuhbah, Abû Bakr b. Aḥmad b. Muḥammad b. 'Umar Taqî ad-Dîn (779/1377–851/1448)

A judge, QÂḌÎ, and teacher of FIQH in DIMASHQ (Damascus), he is best known for his monumental biographical history of the Shâfi'î MADHHAB.

Ibn Qayyim al-Jawziyyah, Shams ad-Dîn Abû Bakr Muḥammad b. Abî Bakr (691/1292–751/1350)

Born and educated in DIMASHQ (Damascus), he was the most famous pupil of IBN TAYMIYYAH. His career was marked by conflicts with those opposed to neo-ḤANBALÎ views. He was the author of a considerable number of treatises on Ḥanbalism which are still today widely regarded in WAHHÂBÎ and Salafî circles.

Ibn Rushd, Abû al-Walîd Muḥammad b. Aḥmad (520/1126–595/1198)

Famous Iberian philosopher, judge, and doctor, he was known in the West as Averroes, and his commentary on Aristotle influenced both Islamic and Western philosophy. He came from a prominent Cordovan family and received an excellent Islamic education, although the science of law interested him more than ḤADÎTHS. He also studied KALÂM and medicine. His biographers do not give much information about his philosophical studies except to mention that he was attracted to the "Greek sciences." He apparently learned his philosophy from a physician, and, when he wrote his analyses of Aristotle, he criticized IBN SÎNÂ's philosophical understandings of Aristotle while still praising his medical writings. His approach to Aristotle involved viewing the Greek philosopher primarily as a logician. This allowed him to strip away much of the Neoplatonic overlay that characterized late Hellenistic and Islamic thought. One of the chief characteristics of Ibn Rushd's writings is his belief that religion and philosophy are ultimately able to be reconciled and that reason is a tool for faith. His most famous work, the *Tahâfut at-tahâfut* (The refutation of the refutation), a commentary on AL-GHAZÂLÎ's *Tahâfut al-Falâsifa,* sets out to restore philosophy and rid it of its Neoplatonic misinterpretations. Ibn Rushd probably enjoyed more of a reputation in the West than among his fellow Muslim philosophers.

Ibn Sa'd, Abû 'Abd Allâh Muḥammad b. Sa'd b. Manî' Kâtib al-Wâqidî (168/784–230/845)

He is known for his monumental biographical dictionary, *Kitâb aṭ-ṭabaqât al-kubrâ* (The book of classes), which was designed to assist in the assessment of the members of ISNÂDS in the study of ḤADÎTHS. He was born in BAṢRAH and made numerous journeys to find traditions for his work. He settled in BAGHDÂD and became the secretary to the famous historian AL-WÂQIDÎ. His dictionary includes biographical notices on 4,250 men and women who appear in *isnâds*. While his work is dependent on the work of his predecessors, he was a critical and careful scholar and produced a work of considerable reliability. Above all, it set a pattern for similar biographical dictionaries, which are a major part of Islamic historiography.

Ibn Sînâ, Abû 'Alî al-Ḥusayn (369/979–428/1037)

Philosopher, physician, and polymath, he was known in the West as Avicenna. His Neoplatonic interpretations of Aristotle influenced Thomas Aquinas, and his famous medical treatise, the *Qanûn fî aṭ-ṭibb* (The canon of medicine), enjoyed circulation in the West in translation. He was born near Bukhârâ and was a prodigy, who was teaching his teachers at the age of fourteen, directing physicians at sixteen and was regarded a master of the known sciences at eighteen, at least according to his biographers. He earned his living as a physician in various princely courts, but was sometimes the object of intrigues and jealousies, which caused him either to flee or, occasionally, be imprisoned. His *Kitâb ash-shifâ'* and his treatise on animals were translated into Latin and had a profound influence on Western thought at a time when Aristotle was little known in the West.

Ibn Sîrîn, Abû Bakr Muḥammad (34/654–110/728)

A renowned and reliable transmitter of ḤADÎTH, he is best known as the first Muslim interpreter of dreams. Dream interpretation, long known in the ancient world, was given a sanction by the story of YÛSUF in the QUR'ÂN. IBN SA'D mentions a long list of dreams interpreted by Ibn Sîrîn, but it is not until the third/ninth century that his fame as an interpreter reached its height. From that period, judging by the number of manuscripts on dream interpretation ascribed to him or by the number of quotations of his work, the field of dream interpretation was extremely popular. This has resulted in a number of spurious works ascribed to Ibn Sîrîn that are obvious forgeries. During his lifetime, he seems not to have made sufficient money, either from his dream interpretation or from his work as a cloth merchant.

Ibn Taymiyyah, Taqî ad-Dîn Aḥmad (661/1263–728/1328)

Influential ḤANBALÎ jurist, whose views have influenced modern SUNNÎ movements, particularly the WAHHÂBÎ. He was opposed to TAQLÎD (blind adherence to tradition) and regarded much of ṢÛFÎ practice to be BID'AH (innovation) along with many KALÂM and FALSAFAH doctrines. He held that the gate of IJTIHÂD was still open, that the QUR'ÂN, the SUNNAH, and the practice of the early Muslims were paramount, and that pietistic faith, ÎMÂN, was the source for an individual's choices. Born in Ḥarrân, he took refuge in Damascus (DIMASHQ) with the coming of the MONGOLS and was educated there in the Ḥanbalî MADHHAB. His hostile attitude toward *kalâm* and his strong anthropomorphism in the interpretation of the Qur'ân earned him enemies, who were to plague him throughout his life. He adopted a strong polemical attitude toward those with whom he disagreed, and used his association with the court to advance his views. He viewed himself as one who could reconcile the approaches of the exponents of *kalâm*, the Traditionists, and the Ṣûfîs, all the while preaching against them all. He was strongly opposed to all forms of *bid'ah*, which he saw in the veneration of WALÎs, in philosophy and theology, and in *taqlîd*. On matters of Qur'ân interpretation, he was a strict anthropomorphist and literalist, and he felt that God walked and talked just as humans do, citing evidence from the Qur'ân to back his point. He was strongly attracted to the doctrines held by the ṢAḤÂBAH (Companions), to those that came afterward, and was, in this sense, an advocate of SALAFIYYAH. He regarded himself as a *mujtahid*, that is, one able to interpret the primary sources of Islamic law, and did not regard the *bâb al-ijtihâd* to have ever been closed, at least not to those with his knowledge. He held that the state must exert power over humans to get them to act in the right manner, and was, therefore, a strong advocate of a powerful theocratic government. He was strongly critical of even the most revered Muslims, claiming at one point that even the caliph 'UMAR made mistakes. While he had great influence during his lifetime, the adoption of his views by the Wahhâbîs has done much to preserve his legacy.

Ibn Tûmart (*c.* 471/1078–524/1130)

He was known as the MAHDÎ of the Almohads. He was a religious reformer, who preached the doctrine of TAWḤÎD, the unity of God. He used ideas from both SUNNÎ and SHÎ'Î Islam. When his doctrine was combined with Berber ambitions, he founded a dynasty that ruled the MAGHRIB and AL-ANDALUS. (*See also* AL-MUWAḤḤIDÛN.)

Ibrâhîm b. Âzar

Abraham, a prophet and patriarch, father of ISMÂ'ÎL by HÂJAR (Hagar), and ISḤÂQ by SÂRÂ (Sarah). The QUR'ÂN regards him as a strong monotheist, a proto-Muslim, a ḤANÎF, who was neither a Jew nor a Christian. He turned from his father's tradition of idolatry to monotheism through a series of steps that show the powerlessness of idols and stars, was persecuted by a ruler identified in the commentaries as Nimrod, and was saved, according to those stories, by JIBRÎL (Gabriel). He was commanded by God to sacrifice his son, identified in later Muslim tradition as Ismâ'îl, who was saved by God's intercession. He and Ismâ'îl are said to have erected the KA'BAH and performed the ḤAJJ.

Ibrâhîm b. Muḥammad

The son of MUḤAMMAD and MÂRIYAH THE COPT. He died in infancy.

iconography

See IMAGES.

'Îd al-Aḍḥâ

The feast of sacrifice, celebrated throughout the Muslim world to mark the end of the annual pilgrimage (ḤAJJ). It is also known as the Greater BAIRAM, *qurbân bairam.* Not only do Muslims on *ḥajj* sacrifice, but, according to most authorities, it is incumbent on all free Muslims to sacrifice as well. Thus, on the day of sacrifice, Muslims around the world are united in the sacrifice and festive meal associated with it.

'iddah (Arabic: count, enumerate)

The legal waiting period before a divorced or widowed woman can remarry.

'Îd al-Fiṭr

The feast of the breaking of the fast of RAMAḌÂN, also known as the Lesser BAIRAM, *şeker bayram.* Even though it is known as the "lesser" festival, it is celebrated with great festivities, as it marks the end of the month-long period of fasting and the attendant hardships. It is customarily a time of paying the ZAKÂT if it has not been given beforehand.

'Îd al-Qurbân

See 'ÎD AL-AḌḤÂ.

Idrîs

A prophet named in the QUR'ÂN, (Q. 19:56), known for patience and righteousness. In extra-Qur'ânic writings, he is often identified with Enoch, and is said to have entered heaven alive and never to have died. In some stories he is credited with inventing writing and making clothing, and he is often regarded as a patron of craft guilds.

Idrîsiyyah

A ṢÛFÎ ṬARÎQAH founded on the teachings of IBN IDRÎS (1749–1837), with branches and influence from the Balkans to Indonesia.

ifranj (Arabic: Frank)

The Arabic term for Frenchman or European, also appearing as *faranj* or *firanj*. In the eschatological writings from the time of the Crusades, Europeans were regarded as a scourge from God and in the same category as disease, famine, and earthquake. This view led many Muslims to react to the incursion of the Europeans as a spur for religious revival and reform.

ʿifrît (Arabic: demon)

The term for a particularly malevolent class of JINN. In popular tales, it is a creature at least forty times larger and more powerful than a *jinn*, although it can be condensed and contained within a jar. They are divided into males and females and are capable of salvation as well as damnation, just as are all *jinn*.

ifṭâr

The first meal eaten to break the fast during RAMAḌÂN.

iḥrâm (Arabic: sacred state)

Both the state of ritual sacrality during the ḤAJJ and the two white seamless pieces of cloth that symbolizes the pilgrim state. (*See also* ḤARÂM.)

iʿjâz (Arabic: miracle)

The notion of the inimitability of the QUR'ÂN, whereby it would be impossible for humans to produce a book like it. The polemics between Muslims and Christians about the nature of scripture and the rise of speculative theology (KALÂM) gave rise to the doctrine that the Qur'ân was a miracle of speech from God that could not be imitated. While there seem to be few historical critics who advanced an argument that the Qur'ân could indeed be reproduced by humans, the notion of *iʿjâz* seems to parallel the Christian notion of the embodiment of God's word in Jesus by saying that the Qur'ân was God's embodied word. This notion seems to have given particular force to the argument between the MUʿTAZILAH and the Traditionists over the issue of whether or not the Qur'ân was created or eternal. From the doctrine of inimitability, many authors advanced elaborate theories of Arabic literature that took into account the Qur'ân's central role in forming the Arabic literary canon. (*See also* MIḤNAH.)

ijâzah (Arabic: authorization)

In the transmission of ḤADÎTHs, it means the authorization to transmit the tradition to another. In the early schools, this was usually indicated by having the transmitter, the professor, write out the permission at the end of the notes the students had written out. From this a tradition of diplomas arose, some of them written in rhymed prose (*sajʿ*), and quite elaborate.

ijmâʿ (Arabic: consensus)

In SUNNÎ Islamic jurisprudence, it is the doctrine that the consensus of those with sufficient knowledge to practice IJTIHÂD, or independent judicial reasoning, constitutes one of the sources of FIQH. According to classical Islamic jurisprudence, the consensus of all of the jurisprudents constitutes one of the main sources of Islamic law. This parallels the Western notion of the *consensus doctorum ecclesiarum*, and assumes that such a consensus must be divinely inspired. The KHAWÂRIJ denied this principle, this being one of the doctrinal views that set them apart from the rest of the Muslims. Over time, this principle has been applied to ratify the customary practices of certain communities, such as the inclusion of the practices of KÛFAH and MADÎNAH, and to include the veneration of WALÎs as the SUNNAH of the community.

ijtihâd (Arabic: strive)

A word derived from the same root as JIHÂD, to strive or make an effort, to exert oneself, in jurisprudence it means the exercise of independent judgment by one who has sufficient knowledge, as opposed to TAQLÎD, or the imitation of those precedents that went before. According to some SUNNÎ theorists, the so-called *bâb al-ijtihâd*, or gate of independent legal thought, was "closed" at the time of the canonization of the schools of Islamic law, but the HANBALÎ, particularly IBN TAYMIYYAH, held that the gate was never closed. Among the ITHNÂ ʿASHARIYYAH SHÎʿÎ, *ijtihâd* is the function of the MUJTAHID to determine the will of the HIDDEN IMÂM. As Islamic schools of law (MADHHABS) developed into hierarchical institutions, the notion developed that only certain individuals were entitled to challenge the fundamental tenets of the law, the so-called ʾUṢÛL AL-FIQH. In particular, this meant the ability to exercise independent reasoning in cases where there was insufficient precedent to decide a case. As a means of preserving the boundaries of each school, members were encouraged to remain within the bounds of the founding judgments that gave each school its identity. Reform movements in Islam have always been in a position of having to challenge such strictures, usually labeled as *taqlîd*, and encourage a renewed view of the interrelationship of QURʾÂN, ḤADÎTH, and human judgment (RAʾY) to achieve TAJDÎD.

ikhtilâf (Arabic: difference of opinion)

w>The opposite of IJMÂʿ, the acceptance of diverse opinions on legal matters assured the open and dynamic character of the schools (MADHHABS) of Islamic law by providing the interpretive space for new ideas and situations. The history of Islamic law is, in part, the history of the attempts to negotiate the inclusion of difference within each school while still retaining a distinct identity. The oldest schools of law recognized geographic differences, so that the schools of MADÎNAH, KÛFAH, and BAṢRAH were able to maintain differences in practice without condemning each other. When the schools became associated with particular individuals, this tolerance of difference was preserved, so that it was possible to have representatives of the several SUNNÎ *madhhabs* in the same city, but there was strong disapproval of an individual moving from one law school to another to engage in forum shopping. Within each school, difference was tolerated only when it was the result of the process of IJTIHÂD. Even then, there was an attempt to impose conformity on the members of the school. In the field of QURʾÂN interpretation and reading, Sunnî Islam recognizes seven canonical "readings" of the Qurʾân. These "readings" have primarily to do with manners of recitation, and do not represent differences in meaning from one practice to another. Movements that have attempted to abolish the differences among the schools have failed, and the maxim, *Ikhtalafa al-ʿulamâʾ* ("The *ʿulamâʾ* always disagree") represents the preservation of Islamic universalism.

al-Ikhwân al-Muslimûn

The Muslim Brotherhood, an organization founded in Egypt by ḤASAN AL-BANNÂʾ in 1928 as an Islamic reformist movement to return Islam to the fundamentals found in the QURʾÂN and the SUNNAH, and to oppose Western colonialism and imperialism. The organization was banned in Egypt in 1954, but has continued to operate underground. When the movement was founded in 1928 it spread throughout Egypt, setting up schools, hospitals, clinics, mosques, and commercial ventures, all designed to raise the standard of living of the poor. In 1936 the movement added the cause of the Palestinians, which gave it more international appeal. Al-Bannâ' was imprisoned during the period of World War II because of his strong opposition to the British, one of the founding principles of the movement. After 1949, when he was assassinated, the movement continued to act against the British, particularly in the Suez Canal area. During the time of Nasser, the Brotherhood was suppressed or tightly controlled, although their energy and ideology was useful to the regime. Their belief in the supremacy of the ideal of an Islamic state and the need to act against imperialism has been a popular idea, even when Islamic governments have been afraid of the revolutionary energies of the movement. It still is a vital force in the Islamic Middle East today.

Ikhwân aṣ-Ṣafâ'

The Brethren of Purity, a syncretic, mostly Neoplatonic philosophical movement in BAṢRAH in the fourth/tenth century. They were influenced by ISMÂʿÎLÎ SHÎʿÎ thought. Their work is contained in an encyclopedic body of fifty-two epistles (*rasâ'il*).

ʿIkrimah (died *c.* 105/723)

Starting as a slave to IBN ʿABBÂS, he became one of the distinguished members of the generation of TÂBIʿÛN (Followers), and was the main transmitter of information about the QUR'ÂN attributed to Ibn ʿAbbâs. He was regarded as a reliable transmitter, particularly by the older traditionists, but so many traditions were attributed to his master through him that later scholars came to suspect the authenticity of his transmission. He is said to have been one of the KHAWÂRIJ, but that did not seem to color his reputation as a transmitter.

ilḥâd (Arabic: apostasy, straying from the right path)

In the QUR'ÂN, it is said that those who willfully deviate from God's signs will earn a painful punishment. In the early history of the Islamic community, the term was applied to those who rebelled against the authority of the caliph. As such, the term was applied to the KHAWÂRIJ. In the ʿABBÂSID period, the term was applied to such people as materialists and atheists. The ISMÂʿÎLÎ were termed *mulḥid*s, as were all SHÎʿÎ and many ṢÛFÎs in the OTTOMAN period. (*See also* RIDDAH.)

ilhâm (Arabic: to swallow)

This term is normally paired with WAḤY, and both are understood to mean inspiration or revelation from God. *Ilhâm* is held to be the kind of individual inspiration given to WALÎs (saints), and is felt to be knowledge cast into the minds of those holy persons that does not have the status of scripture. *Waḥy*, on the other hand, is felt to be the kind of revelation given to prophets.

Îliyâ

Derived from the Latin *Aelia Capitolina*, this name is used as a synonym for AL-QUDS, Jerusalem, in early Islamic texts.

ʿilm (Arabic: knowledge; pl. *ʿulûm*)

A term used extensively in the QUR'ÂN for knowledge, learning, and science. It is contrasted with *jahl*, ignorance, and is related to ḤILM, civilized behavior. It is generally understood to be more than just common knowledge (*maʿrifah*), and implies the acquisition of such elements as wisdom (*ḥikmah*) and politeness (ADAB). Knowledge of the Islamic sciences are thought to be life-changing, and in Islamic tradition, knowledge is not merely passive but necessarily leads to action. Thus, the bifurcation that sometimes is expressed in Christian thought between belief (ÎMÂN) and deed (*'amal*) is not found in classical Islamic thought, since knowledge of God leads to belief, whch leads to action. (*See also* 'ULAMÂ'.)

'ilm ar-rijâl (Arabic: the study of persons)

This is the Islamic science devoted to the biographical study of individuals featured in the ISNÂDS of ḤADÎTH. The purpose is to determine the exact times and locations of their lives to discern whether the chain of authentication could have been possible and to determine the character and, insofar as possible, the veracity of the person. Also, since so many people have similar names, the science includes a determination of the exact name and genealogy of the individual. In the AL-JARḤ WA-T-TA'DÎL literature, of which this is a part, it is sometimes the case that *isnâd*s will, for example, include children under the age of two transmitting from aged transmitters and from people of bad character. This science has given rise to a major tradition of biographical literature that is one of the hallmarks of Islamic historiography.

Ilyâs

A prophet in the QUR'ÂN sometimes identified in the commentaries with the biblical Elijah/Elias. He is said to have been given power over rain by God, and he used it to turn his people away from sin. When they suffered from a drought, they came to him, claimed to repent, and he prayed for rain to deliver them from certain death. When they continued to worship idols and sin, he asked God to take him, so God sent him a horse of fire, and he rode on it to heaven, was clothed with feathers of fire, his need for food and drink removed, and he remained in heaven, half human and half angelic.

Decorative stonework from the tomb of Shah Rukn-i-'Alam, Multan, Pakistan.

Ilyâs, Mawlânâ Muḥammad (1302/1885–1363/1944)

Indian ṢÛFÎ and founder of the Faith Movement, whose mission was to bring Islam to the illiterate Indian poor.

images

Contrary to popular belief, the QUR'ÂN does not prohibit the making of images, but does prohibit idol worship. Some ḤADÎTHS assert that an artist who makes images will receive punishment on the Day of Judgment. Varying interpretations of the prohibition have produced an almost total ban on images associated with mosques and religious writings, while there has been a rich secular tradition of painting and sculpture at various times in some regions. It has also produced the elaborate art form of CALLIGRAPHY. The relationship between the ban in Islam and the Iconoclast Movement in the Greek Church remains an open scholarly question.

Imâm

The Arabic root of this word is cognate to the word *'umm*, mother, and 'UMMAH, religious community. Over time it has taken on several distinct meanings: (1) A leader, particularly a prayer leader, a function that might be assumed by any male Muslim over the age of majority. There are no special rites of ordination or sacerdotal powers necessary to assume this function. (2) Some of the early caliphs are also called *Imâms*. (3) The seven leaders of the NIZÂRÎ ISMÂʿÎLÎ SHÎʿÎ, descended from ʿALÎ and FÂṬIMAH, are called *Imâms*. (4) The twelve leaders of the ITHNÂ ʿASHARÎ SHÎʿÎ, descended from ʿAlî and Fâṭimah, are called *Imâms*. (5) In modern times it has been used as both a term of respect for the ÂYATOLLÂHS of Iran and, in a more ambiguous sense, as the title of Âyatollâh KHOMEINÎ, implying, according to some, that he was equal to or the embodiment of the HIDDEN IMÂM. (*See also* AGHÂ KHÂN.)

imâmah (Arabic: governance or rule)

The word is used in several senses in the Islamic world. Among the SHÎʿÎ, it refers to the rule of the IMÂM. Among the SUNNÎ, who use the word *imâm* in a more general sense, it refers to the leadership of the Islamic community after the death of the Prophet. For most Sunnî, this leadership is held by the person who is caliph.

Imâmî Shîʿî

See ITHNÂ ʿASHARIYYAH SHÎʿÎ.

imâmzâdah (Persian: *imâm*'s son)

Tombs of the IMÂMS visited and venerated by the SHÎʿÎ as shrines, some of the more popular being at KARBALÂʾ, MASHHAD, NAJAF, and QOM. Pilgrimage to these sites and the rites associated with them vary according to the site, but usually are determined by the season of the year. In the popular imagination these are locations of powerful blessings, *barakât*, that can effect healing, wealth, and other worldly rewards through the intercession of the tomb's inhabitant. (*See also* BARAKAH.)

Îmân (Arabic: belief, faith)

This word has the sense of not only belief, but also of safety and security. It is linked in this way with the very name Islam, since acceptance of Islam, submission, brings peace and security, SALÂM. For most commentators, *îmân* means both an inner state and an outward expression. Most schools of Islamic law are not satisfied merely with the expression of *îmân*. It must be accompanied by deeds that demonstrate that belief. At a minimum, after the declaration of faith (SHAHÂDAH), the believer must perform the daily prayers as proof of his belief.

India

Muslims comprise about twenty percent of the total population of India, are found in most areas of the subcontinent and have formed a significant part of Indian culture. Traders brought Islam to India in the eighth century, and by the twelfth century Muslim conquerers had established influential kingdoms. Until the establishment of the MUGHAL dynasty in the sixteenth century, Muslims from various ethnic origins came into India, both for trade and for conquest. The majority of Muslims are SUNNÎ, with a minority of all types of SHÎʿÎ including ISMÂʿÎLIYYAH. Islamic preachers and mystics have appealed to many in India, particularly among the lower castes. Converts to Islam in India have brought many ideas from Hinduism into popular Islamic practice, and in places like Bengal, worship at local shrines is similar for both Hindus and Muslims. In 1947, shortly before India's independence from Britain, many Indian Muslims left India for the newly formed Muslim state of PAKISTAN.

Indonesia

With a population of over two hundred million, ninety percent of whom are

Tomb of the Mughal emperor Humayun, New Delhi, India.

Muslim, Indonesia is the largest Muslim country in the world. Islam was brought by Muslim traders from India and from southern Arabia, chiefly the Hadhramaut, following pre-Islamic trade routes. By the thirteenth century Islam was well established, and by the eighteenth century the majority of Indonesians were SUNNÎ Muslims and followers of the Shâfiʿî MADHHAB. Hindu and animist beliefs were not obliterated but incorporated into the popular culture and Islamized. Throughout the last two centuries, Indonesian Islam has been informed by the great numbers of students who have studied in MECCA and other places in the Arab Middle East. In the second half of the twentieth century, Arab Muslims and Indonesians who have studied in the Arab world have engaged in DAʿWAH to rid Indonesian Islam of non-Islamic elements. Some of this has been played out against the background of anticolonialism against the Dutch and the Japanese, resulting in the intermingling of Arabism and Islamic reform. The revolution of 1419/1998 brought an end to the autocratic, non-Islamic rule of Suharto and led to the presidency of ABDURRAHMAN WAHID, a widely respected Muslim intellectual. In 1422/2001, however, he was charged with corruption himself, forced from office, and replaced by his vice-president, Megawati Sukarnoputra.

infidel

See KÂFIR.

inheritance

The Islamic system of inheritance, known in Arabic as *mîrâth*, relies heavily on verses in the QUR'ÂN, which has more to say on this subject than any other. Commentators agree that the Qur'ânic verses reform the pre-Islamic Arabian practices, particularly in allowing women to inherit. SUNNÎ and SHÎʿÎ theories and practice differ sharply. The Shîʿî view is that the Qur'ân totally supplanted all prior practice, while the Sunnî view holds that the inheritance of the agnates (Arabic: *ʿaṣabah*) is only ameliorated by the verses, thus giving male heirs a greater preference in the Sunnî practice. Inheritance rules restrict the amount of property that a person can dispose by testamentary bequest, and many Muslims use the instrument of the WAQF for estate control.

injîl (Arabic: Gospel)

This is the word in the QUR'ÂN for the Greek *Evangelion*, Gospel. The degree to which the Qur'ân represents the Gospels has been a subject of heated debate in the polemics between Muslims and Christians from the beginnings of the encounter between the two religions. Western polemicists assert that the Qur'ânic views of Jesus, MARYAM, and the Christian doctrines are confused or wrong. Muslims insist, on the other hand, that the Christian scripture has been corrupted (TAḤRÎF), and that the Qur'ânic view is the correct one. What is clear from both Qur'ânic and historical evidence is that many of the main ideas of Christianity were well known in Arabia during the lifetime of MUḤAMMAD, and that the references in the Qur'ân to Jesus reached listeners who understood the allusions with some subtlety. In post-Qur'ânic literature, the Gospels became quite well-known, both through their use among Christian Arabs and through translations into Arabic. There is, however, no evidence that there was a translation of the Gospels into Arabic prior to the rise of Islam. Arabic Christians lived under and among Muslims for a long time, and shared stories related to Gospel stories have found their way into popular literature. When Protestant missionaries came to the Islamic world, they brought with them the techniques of biblical scholarship, which they used to try to prove that the Qur'ân was false and that the Gospels were true. Muslim scholars soon used Western critical techniques against the variety of apochrypha and pseudepigrapha to counter those arguments and returned to the old argument that Christian scripture had been corrupted by *taḥrîf*.

innovation

See BIDʿAH.

inquisition

See MIḤNAH.

in shâ' Allâh

The Arabic phrase meaning "if God wills" is commonly used by Muslims to express God's control over the future.

Institute for Ismaili Studies (IIS)

The IIS was established in 1977 in London, with the object of promoting scholarship and learning of Muslim cultures and societies in general, the intellectual and literary expressions of Shîʿîsm in general, and ISMÂʿÎLÎ SHÎʿÎ in particular. Through the sponsorship of the AGHÂ KHÂN and the Ismâʿîlî Shîʿî community, the IIS continues a tradition of DAʿWAH on an intellectual and ecumenical level.

intention

See NIYYAH.

intercession

See SHAFÂʿAH.

interest

See BANKS AND BANKING; RIBÂ.

Internet

The growth of the use of the Internet has increased the dissemination of Islamic knowledge greatly. It is possible to find many major Islamic texts available online, either in translation or in the original Islamic languages. It is possible, for example, to access multiple translations of the QUR'ÂN as well as copies of the Qur'ân in Arabic, recited in Arabic, and explained. It is also possible to learn how to perform the HAJJ or the *ʿumrah*, schedule transportation and link up with other Muslims from an on-line computer. For Muslims in small communities, where resources are limited, it is possible to find on-line ordering sites for Islamic needs, such as clothing and books. Several problems arise with the use of the Internet that are parallel to problems in research in general. The sites are often anonymous, so their biases are not easily detected, and they are ephemeral as they migrate from one service provider to another. (*See the bibliography at the back of this book for a short list of Islamic URLs.*)

interpretation of the Qur'ân

see TAFSÎR; TA'WÎL.

intiẓâr (Arabic: waiting)

A term introduced by the Iranian SHÎ'ÎTE theologian 'Alî Sharî'atî (died 1977), meaning both the active waiting for the return of the HIDDEN IMÂM and the rejection of the status quo.

Iqbal, Muhammad (1877–1938)

Poet, philosopher, theologian, and advocate for an independent Muslim state, he was born in Sialkot in the Punjab, educated in Lahore, Munich, and Cambridge, and served as a politician, lawyer, professor, and mentor to Muslim intellectuals. He composed speculative TAFSÎR and was an advocate of IJTIHÂD. His *The Reconstruction of Religious Thought in Islam* was an attempt to harmonize Islamic and Western thought, and his advocacy of an independent Muslim state led him to be regarded as the intellectual father of the state of Pakistan, formed after his death. While he was a student in Lahore, he met the British Islamicist Thomas Arnold, who encouraged him to go to England to study. While there, he studied Hegelian philosophy, which led him to Munich for his Ph.D. After his return to Lahore he taught philosophy and developed his legal practice, but experienced a crisis when comparing the state of development between Europe and India. He came to feel that an Islamic renewal was needed to vitalize the Muslim world, and he began to express these ideas in both URDU and PERSIAN. His notions of the strengthening of the ego rather than its annihilation (FANÂ') were not well received at first, but by 1928 he delivered a series of lectures titled "Six Lectures on the reconstruction of religious thought in Islam," which sought to harmonize European and Islamic thinking. At the same time, he expressed the need to form a separate Islamic state in the area of present-day Pakistan. He was also instrumental in the foundation of the University of Kabul in AFGHANISTAN. Iqbal's thought is a true synthesis of Western and Islamic thinking. Influenced by Nietzsche, he believed that ALLÂH is the supreme ego, but that each human is given an ego that must be developed. This does not lead to a separation between God and humans, but, because the development comes through prayer and the QUR'ÂN, to a closer union. Through the resulting cooperation between God and the human ego, the divine will can be carried out, with the result that the Islamic mission is strengthened. Since his death, his philosophy has been criticized, but in Pakistan any criticism is regarded as near sacrilege.

iqṭâ' (Arabic: fief)

Land granted under feudal tenure, which, in South Asia under the MUGHALS, allowed some Hindus to be included as part of the DHIMMÎ class. These grants of land were also called JÂGÎRS in India.

Iram

Identified with the biblical Aram, the son of Shem, he is said to be an ancestor of the tribe of 'ÂD and the tribe of THAMÛD. It is also identified on the basis of Q. 89:7 as a place in pre-Islamic Arabia that God destroyed because of the wickedness of the people.

Iran

Known in pre-modern times as Persia, it came under Muslim political domination in 16/637 by the Arabo-Muslim invasion, becoming predominantly Muslim in religion only after the ninth century. The populace retained the Persian language, which became Arabized through the script and the extensive use of Arabic vocabulary. Until the sixteenth century, Iran was mostly SUNNÎ, with small pockets of SHÎ'Î, but after the ṢAFAVID DYNASTY, it was chiefly Shî'î. In modern times, the secularizing and Westernizing Pahlavi dynasty was overthrown by the revolution of 1399/1979 that established an Islamic republic, strongly Shî'î and intolerant of political and religious dissent, particularly that of the Marxists, the *mujâhidîn*, and the BAHÂ'Î.

Courtyard of the Masjid-i Shah (Royal Mosque), Isfahan, Iran.

Iraq

The area of the confluence of the Tigris and Euphrates rivers had been home to Arabs from before Islam, and Muslims found allies in the Muslim conquest of 13/635. With the founding of the 'ABBÂSID CALIPHATE and the construction of the capital city of BAGHDÂD, Islam was established in the middle of ancient Jewish and Christian centers. With the decline of the caliphate in the thirteenth century, Iraq became a province of the Persian, OTTOMAN or British empires until the twentieth century. Modern Iraq has a mixed population of Arabs and Kurds, SHÎ'Î and SUNNÎ Muslims, and is currently ruled by a secularist dictatorship.

'Îsâ

This Arabic name for Jesus is used as a personal name among Muslims, as are the names of other figures common to the Bible and the QUR'ÂN. The long association between Muslims and Christians in the Iberian peninsula has given rise among Spanish-speaking Christians to the use of the name Jesus, a practice not generally found elsewhere in the Christian world. (*See also* JESUS.)

Isaac

See ISḤÂQ.

Isḥâq

The biblical Isaac, the son of IBRÂHÎM (Abraham), by SÂRÂ. He was the younger brother of ISMÂ'ÎL (Ishmael). The foretelling of Isḥâq's birth is mentioned in the QUR'ÂN, and commentators see his birth as a reward for Ibrâhîm's willingness to sacrifice Ismâ'îl. The earliest Muslim interpreters of the story of Isḥâq disagree as to which of the two sons of Ibrâhîm was the intended sacrificial victim. By the end of the second/eighth century, most scholars agreed that it was Ismâ'îl and argued polemically with Jews and Christians on this point.

ishârât as-sâ'ah (Arabic: the signs of the hour)

This means the signs of the *eschaton.* Numerous signs are mentioned in the QUR'ÂN, such as the oven giving forth water, mountains collapsing, and seas boiling. Many more signs are mentioned in ḤADÎTH and TAFSÎR literature, including worldwide corruption, wars with AD-DAJJÂL and YA'JÛJ WA-MA'JÛJ, the appearance of the MAHDÎ and JESUS, and, according to some, the appearance of MUḤAMMAD.

Ishmael

See ISMÂ'ÎL.

'ishq (Arabic: love, desire)

This word, which does not appear in the QUR'ÂN, has come to mean passionate love of the sort that indicates a strong need in the individual. SÛFÎs have adopted this term to express the lack in humans that drives them to love God and seek union with the divine.

ishrâqî (Arabic: radiant)

The term for "illuminationism" in ṢÛFÎ and gnostic circles, and particularly associated with the writings of as-Suhrawardî.

al-'Iskandar

See DHÛ-L-QARNAYN.

iṣlâḥ (Arabic: reform)

In modern times this term has come to be associated with MUḤAMMAD 'ABDUH and RASHÎD RIḌÂ, although others, including conservatives, have tried to claim the reformist title. The term has its roots in the QUR'ÂN and in early Islamic literature, where humans are enjoined to act as holy, righteous persons, *ṣâliḥ* (also used as a common given name). The term for pious acts, *'amal ṣâliḥ*, also comes from this same root. It is this sense of piety that underlies the mission of modern reformers as they try to connect the modern community with the pious deeds of the first generation of Islam.

Islam

The name of the religion of MUSLIMS is derived from an Arabic root meaning "peace." In this form, it means "submission," to the will of God. In the message of the QUR'ÂN, humans are told that following correct action brings the surety of reward. In this sense, the "peace" was understood by the early Muslims as a lack of the anxiety associated with polytheism, in which the individual is unsure of which deity to assuage and whether any action would produce positive results. Muslim commentators believe that Islam is the original, authentic monotheistic worship of God and that MUḤAMMAD was the last of the line of Muslim prophets sent to humankind to preach Islam. Islam is also understood as the name of the religion of God. In Q. 5:3 we read, "This day have I perfected for you your religion, DÎN, and completed My favor on you and chosen for you Islam as a religion." The word for religion, *dîn*, means also the debt or obligation that the believer owes to ALLÂH, so Islam implies a series of actions as well as belief. This is seen in Q. 49:14–15: "The dwellers of the desert say: We believe. Say: You do not believe but say, We submit; and faith has not yet entered into your hearts; and if you obey Allâh and His Apostle, He will not diminish aught of your deeds; surely Allâh is Forgiving, Merciful. The believers are only those who believe in Allâh and His Apostle then they doubt not and struggle hard with their wealth and their lives in the way of Allâh; they are the truthful ones." In other words, faith, ÎMÂN, for a Muslim results in the interior change of the person, submission, ISLÂM, which results in the outward deed that demonstrates the person's Islam. The relationship between deed and faith has resulted in Islam having fewer creeds than Christianity and striking a balance between belief and action. This is seen in the centrality of Islamic law, (SHARÎ'AH) as the main expression of the individual's religion, and Islam becomes all-pervasive in its sacralization of daily life. Thus, even the most mundane and seemingly secular acts fit within *sharî'ah* and are part of what it means to be a Muslim. The location of the Muslim within the law also indicates an additional feature of the religion, the connection with community. Muslims understood both from the Qur'ân and from the Prophet's example that the obligation, *dîn*, was to fellow humans as well as to God. The ideal of the solitary mystic is less frequent in Islam than in, for example Christianity or Hinduism, because of the community connection. Modern reformers invoke this sense when they call for IṢLÂḤ and TAJDÎD. Many additional words and terms are derived from the same Arabic root, s-l-m, the most frequent of which is the greeting *Salâm*, "Peace."

Islâm-bol

See ISTANBUL.

Islamic calendar

See CALENDAR.

'iṣmah (Arabic: sinless, without error)

The doctrine of impeccability, or sinlessness, was first articulated by the SHÎ'ÎS, who hold that MUḤAMMAD, FÂṬIMAH, and each of the IMÂMS are without sin. Among the SUNNÎ, this notion is applied to Muḥammad and to the prophets, but it is regarded as a gift from God and not part of their natural state. This allows for certain occasions of inadvertance, such as, for example, the time that the Prophet neglected to say "*in shâ' Allâh*." The doctrine is also invoked by some scholars in association with IJMÂ' (consensus), holding that the totality of the Muslim community cannot agree on error.

Ismâ'îl

The prophet Ishmael, the son of IBRÂHÎM by HÂJAR. He is mentioned in the QUR'ÂN as a prophet and a messenger, who helps his father build the KA'BAH and establishes monotheistic worship in MECCA. Popular legends develop the themes of the Qur'ân and tell that, when he was young, Ibrâhîm, responding to divine command, escorted him from the family and took him with his mother, Hâjar, into the desert, where they wandered until they came to Mecca. There, by a miracle, he found the water of the well of ZAMZAM and was saved. We are told that he married, but not well, and was visited by Ibrâhîm, who advised him to get another, more pious wife. He is said by most commentators to be the ancestor of the Arabs in the Abrahamic line and the intended sacrifice commanded by God, although this doctrine did not take hold until the polemics of the second Islamic century. We are also told that he was patient and instructive to his father as his father bound him for sacrifice. He is said to have comforted his father and helped keep him steadfast, so that Ismâ'îl becomes the model for proper piety and steadfastness in the face of adversity.

Ismâ'îlî, or Ismâ'îliyyah

Those SHÎ'Î who hold that the seventh IMÂM, ISMÂ'ÎL B. JA'FAR was the last of the line of *Imâms* before going into GHAYBAH, or occultation. From this, they are also called Seveners. They hold to esoteric (*bâṭinî*) interpretations of the QUR'ÂN, as well as exoteric (*ẓâhirî*) interpretations and are referred to also as the Bâṭiniyyah. The FÂṬIMID DYNASTY was ruled by members of this group and was responsible for patronizing many Ismâʿîlî Neoplatonic theologians and sending missionaries to many parts of the Islamic world. They are found all over the world with major communities in South Asia, East Africa, and the United States of America. (*See also* ÂGHÂ KHÂN, ASSASSINS.)

Ismâʿîl b. Jaʿfar (died 145/762)

The eldest son of JAʿFAR AṢ-ṢÂDIQ, the IMÂM and eponym of the ISMÂʿÎLÎ SHÎʿÎ.

isnâd (Arabic: support)

The genealogic chain of authorities attached at the head of a ḤADÎTH to indicate the line of transmission from its source. Scholars use this chain to authenticate *ḥadîth*s. The development of the science (ʿILM) of *ḥadîth*, and the association of *isnâd*s with the traditions has had a profound effect on Islamic historical consciousness and a sense of connection with each generation of Muslims back to the time of the Prophet. The use of the *isnâd* started in the pre-Islamic period, when traditions of the "battle days" of the Arabs were accompanied by a recitation of the noble genealogies from that event to the time of the listener. Early Muslims adopted this custom when reciting the major events in the life of the Prophet and the community (ʾUMMAH), and it soon became conventional to apply this to all traditions reported about the Prophet and the early Companions (ṢAḤÂBAH). In order to determine the veracity of the individuals involved and whether or not they could have been connected with the other members of the chain, Muslim scholars developed an elaborate science of biographical dictionaries that are the major characteristic of Islamic historiography. (*See also* ʿILM AR-RIJÂL.)

al-isrâʾ (Arabic: night journey)

The night journey of MUḤAMMAD from MECCA to the MASJID AL-AQṢÂ, usually identified with AL-QUDS (Jerusalem), on the back of AL-BURÂQ, depicted in Islamic paintings as a winged horse with a human head. From the location of the Masjid al-Aqṣâ, it is believed that Muḥammad made an ascent (MIʿRÂJ) and a tour of heaven. Reports of his journey caused some consternation among the faithful, and provoked ridicule from Muḥammad's enemies. Countering this, Muḥammad was able to describe the location of some lost animals and predict the arrival of a caravan that he saw while on the journey. Early traditions reflect an ambivalence about whether this was a physical or spiritual journey, but in the popular stories about Muḥammad it was a miraculous story of great appeal. ṢÛFIS see in this story the possibility of both a heavenly ascent and the beatific vision of God. (*See also* AL-ḤARAM ASH-SHARÎF; JIBRÎL.)

Isrâfîl

The archangel who is assigned the task of blowing the trumpet to signal the YAWM AD-DÎN. He is not mentioned in the QUR'ÂN, but Islamic extra-Qur'ânic legend contains many stories about him. He is a huge angel, with his feet under the lowest level of the earth. His head reaches up to the throne of God. He has four wings and is covered with hair and tongues, which indicate his main function of reading out divine decrees to the rest of the archangels. He is said to have been MUḤAMMAD's guide into prophecy before JIBRÎL brought the Qur'ân. He is also said to have met DHÛ-L-QARNAYN when he traveled to the land of darkness. His trumpet will not only signal the beginning of the *yawm ad-dîn*, but will also have the power of raising the dead and refreshing those in Paradise.

isrâ'îliyyât

The term designating the Jewish, and sometimes Christian, stories about biblical figures and motifs that were incorporated into early Islamic commentaries on the QUR'ÂN and in the SÎRAH. After the second Islamic century, collecting and elaborating this material fell out of favor, but by that time, it had become an important component of TAFSÎR. In the first Islamic century, many stories, legends, and literary traditions were used by commentators on the Qur'ân, polemicists, and popular preachers (*qâṣṣ*) to explain and advocate for Islam. Much of this material came from Jewish and Christian sources through the medium of converted Jews and Christians in the Arabian Peninsula. A number of famous transmitters are associated with the transmission of this material, including KA'B AL-AḤBÂR and Wahb b. Munabbih. IBN ISḤÂQ incorporated some of their traditions in his famous biography of the Prophet, *Sîrat rasûl Allâh*, but even more was uncritically used by popular preachers. Booksellers in the major metropolitan centers enjoyed a brisk business translating and selling material they claimed to be the seventy scriptures revealed in the seventy languages of humankind. By the middle of the second Islamic century, interest in *isrâ'îliyyât* had diminished, and Muslims made greater use of Islamic and Arabic materials to explain the Qur'ân. This corresponded to the time that Jewish and Christian communities were settling into their respective roles in the developing Islamic empire. *Isrâ'îliyyât* literature has had a major impact on Islamic literature in two ways. Much of the content for *tafsîr* on the prophets and biblical figures comes from this source. Additionally, the literary patterns of *tafsîr* have been influenced by the patterns of commentary on scripture found among Jews and Christians.

Istanbul

The capital of the OTTOMAN EMPIRE from its capture in 857/1453 to the end of the empire in 1342/1923. The name of the city, which had been Constantinople, was a Turkish derivitive from the Greek, *'es tên polis*, "This is the city," which reflects the popular name used by the Greek inhabitants. Muslims also called the city Islâm-bol, meaning "the place where Islam is abundant." When the Turks captured the city, they transformed a number of churches into mosques, the most famous of which was the AYA SOFYA, the Church of Holy Wisdom, which became the central mosque of the city. Under the Ottomans, the city grew in size and changed into a more characteristically Middle Eastern city. Craft guilds and workers were clustered by trades around market areas, and central markets were distributed throughout the city for ease of control and tax collection. Many of the resulting neighborhoods and their mosques were established by WAQFs that assured their continued upkeep. In addition to shops and lodging for resident merchants, provisions were made for foreign merchants in shops called *khân*s. These, too, were clustered in groups, often according to either the type of goods or the nationality of the merchants. The Ottomans improved the harbor for both commercial and military use, and the city became one of the major world cities. The city became even more internationalized after the influx of refugees from Spain after 1492, and after the expansion of the empire into the Mediterranean in the next century. Istanbul lost its role as the seat of government with the development of the Republic of TURKEY under Mustafa Kemal ATATÜRK in 1923, and also lost its central position as one of the world's centers for Islamic learning. It has retained its role as the chief city of Turkey, and, in recent years, has seen a resurgence of Islamic institutions, which were diminished during the initial periods of secularization under the republic.

istinjâ' (Arabic: escape)

The purification that a believing Muslim must do after fulfilling natural needs. This must be done immediately. Failure to do so places the person in a state of ritual impurity that would render invalid any prayer (ṢALÂT), recitation of the QUR'ÂN, or other action that requires ritual purity. (*See also* GHUSL; JANÂBAH; WUḌÛ'.)

istinshâq (Arabic: sniff)

The recommended practice of inhaling water into the nostrils during the performance of the ritual cleansing, WUḌÛ' and GHUSL.

istisqâ' (Arabic: seek water)

The communal prayer for rain. Although the practice is attested in the pre-Islamic period, it is because of the actions of the Prophet that the modern-day custom continues. It is reported that MUḤAMMAD led the community in asking for rain by standing atop a MINBAR (pulpit) erected for him, raising his arms, and turning his cloak inside out. In popular practice, the petitioners turn their clothes inside out, make babies cry, and, if it is at the site of a WALÎ, invoke the name of the saint as well as ALLÂH. Sometimes objects are cast into a body of water. Among the theologians, none of the folkloric practices are condoned, and only prayers to Allâh, sometimes coupled with repentance and the reading of passages from the QUR'ÂN that have to do with God's withholding rain, are allowed.

Ithnâ 'Ashariyyah Shî'î

The Twelver Shî'î, so-called because of their belief in a line of twelve IMÂMS in the line from MUḤAMMAD. The twelfth *Imâm*, MUḤAMMAD AL-QÂ'IM, disappeared, or went into GHAYBAH, in 329/940, and Twelver Shî'îs wait his return. The Twelvers are the majority group among the SHÎ'Î, living in Iran, Iraq, and Lebanon. Ithnâ 'Ashariyyah Shî'î share with all Shî'î the view that rightful rule of the Islamic community ('UMMAH), was passed by Muḥammad to 'ALÎ B. ABÎ ṬÂLIB and a line of IMÂMS who were his heirs. They are:

1. 'Alî b. Abî Ṭâlib (died 41/661)
2. al-Ḥasan b. 'Alî (died 49/669)
3. al-Ḥusayn b. 'Alî (died 61/680)
4. 'Alî b. al-Ḥusayn Zayn al-'Âbidîn (died 95/714)
5. Muḥammad al-Bâqir (died 126/743)
6. Ja'far aṣ-Ṣâdiq (died 148/765)
7. Mûsâ al-Kâẓim (died 183/799)
8. 'Alî ar-Riḍâ (died 203/818)
9. Muḥammad Jawâd at-Taqî (died 220/835)
10. 'Alî an-Naqî (died 254/868)
11. al-Ḥasan al-'Askarî (died 260/874)
12. Muḥammad al-Qâ'im (entered *ghaybah* 260/874).

During the period in which the *Imâm*s were living in the world, they functioned as both temporal and religious leaders with a divine mandate. Their position as *Imâm*s authorized them to interpret scripture and to make pronouncements about the conduct of the community. For this reason, their sayings and actions were collected in a manner similar to the way the SUNNÎ collected the sayings of the Prophet and the companions (ṢAḤÂBAH). In addition to these collections of ḤADÎTHS, two works, the NAHJ AL-BALÂGHAH (The way of eloquence), a collection of sayings, letters, and sermons attributed to 'Alî b. Abî Ṭâlib, and the *Ṣaḥîfah sajjâdiyyah* (Page of prostration), attributed to 'Alî b. al-Ḥusayn Zayn al-'Âbidîn, complement the traditions and the QUR'ÂN. While the Shî'î reject for the most part the *ḥadîth*s of the Sunnî, their use of Shî'î *ḥadîth*s looks in both form and content like their Sunnî counterpart, and there have been periods in Islamic history in which legal scholars have studied in each group's schools of law. With the major *ghaybah* of Muḥammad al-Qâ'im, the community began to collect and compile their literary collections and construct their institutions of ʿULAMÂ' to deal with the absence of their leader as a present, accessible source for law and interpretation. It has been the post-*ghaybah* period that has seen the development of the great theological works. The Ithnâ ʿAshariyyah Shîʿî practices are similar to those of the Sunnî, and do not differ from them any more than the several Sunnî groups differ among themselves. They do place emphasis on visiting and venerating of the tombs of the *Imâms* and WALÎs. For many Shîʿî, the expectation of the coming of the *Imâm* in *ghaybah* is linked with the *eschaton*, YAWM AD-DÎN, in the same way that the Sunnî expect the MAHDÎ.

iʿtikâf (Arabic: devote oneself fully)

The practice of secluding oneself in a mosque, fasting, reciting the QUR'ÂN, and engaging in prayer (ṢALÂT). This is usually done for a fixed number of days in response to a vow. The person who undertakes *iʿtikâf* must not leave the mosque, except to perform necessary acts of nature and to perform necessary ABLUTIONS to maintain ritual purity. As in all such vows, the individual is restricted in the fasting to those periods of time in which the body will not be harmed, for all the schools of law, (MADHHABS) regard such over-fasting as a grave sin.

ʿIzrâ'îl

The angel identified with the angel of death, *malak al-mawt*. He is said to be so large that if all the water on earth were poured on his head, none would reach earth. He has four thousand wings, and his body is covered with eyes and tongues, the number of which corresponds to the number of those alive on the earth, both humans and JINN. He is a pitiless angel, which is the reason God appointed him the angel of death. He is said to carry a scroll containing the names of those who are about to die, but he is ignorant of who will die when, that matter being reserved to God.

J

jabr (Arabic: fate, predestination, compulsion)

This word was a technical theological term used in debates over free will and determinism.

Jacob

See YA'QÛB.

Ja'far aṣ-Ṣâdiq (80/699–148/765)

The sixth SHÎ'Î IMÂM, he was recognized by both the ISMÂ'ÎLÎ (Seveners) and the ITHNÂ 'ASHARIYYAH (Twelvers). He was a noted transmitter of ḤADÎTHS, pious and learned. It is said that the 'ABBÂSIDS offered him the position of caliph (KHALÎFAH), which he refused. After his death, the Shî'î split over the succession of the imâmate. He held a unique position as the first of the *Imâm*s recognized for his leadership by the SUNNÎ as well as the two branches of the Shî'î, the Ismâ'îlî and the Ithnâ 'Asharî. When he died in 148/765, there were rumors that he had been poisoned by the caliph al-Manṣûr, and was buried in MADÎNAH. His tomb was the object of pious veneration and pilgrimage until it was destroyed by the Wahhâbîs. His death provoked a crisis of succession. He had designated his son, Ismâ'îl as his heir, but he predeceased his father. There were those who said that Ismâ'îl was not dead but in GHAYBAH, and these formed the nucleus of those who would become the Ismâ'îliyyah Shî'î. Others accepted 'Abd Allâh, Ismâ'îl's brother, but he too died within a few weeks. For the majority of Shî'î, the imâmate passed to Mûsâ, whose mother, Ḥamîdah, was a slave. Those who regarded MÛSÂ AL-KÂẒIM as the *Imâm* became the Ithnâ 'Asharî. Some Muslims held that Ja'far himself did not die, but went into *ghaybah*. These are called the Nâwûsiyyah. Ja'far is credited with being one of the greatest *Imâm*s. He is said to have written on magic, alchemy, divination, and to have been a master ṢÛFÎ.

jafr (Arabic: divination through letters)

The SHÎ'Î believe that the IMÂMS inherited through FÂṬIMAH the power to foretell the future of individuals and nations. One esoteric tradition narrates that when MUḤAMMAD was dying, he told 'ALÎ to wash his body and then clothe him and sit him up. When 'Alî did so, the Prophet told him all that would happen from that time to the YAWM AD-DÎN. 'Alî passed this information on to his sons, who, in turn passed it on to the line of *Imâm*s. Many esoteric traditions became associated with this concept, such as the interpretation of texts (including the QUR'ÂN) by means of number letter substitution in the manner of the late ancient Neopythagoreans.

Both the body of literature and particular books attributed to JA'FAR AṢ-ṢÂDIQ and to 'Alî were titled *jafr.*

jâgîr (Hindi: grant of land)

A grant of land given in India to those who had rendered government service. The holders were exempt from taxation on the land and were regarded as DHIMMÎ. Many of the land holders were Hindu and continued polytheistic worship even while holding dhimmî status. (*See also* IQṬÂ'.)

jahannam (Arabic from Hebrew: Gehenna)

This word, mentioned frequently in the QUR'ÂN, is used either for Hell generally or for one of the seven ranks of Hell. It is a synonym of AN-NÂR, the fire, and is often used interchangeably with the range of the words for Hell. At other times, commentators regard *jahannam* as a particular location in Hell with particular punishments. In those traditions, it is one of the upper areas of Hell designated for Muslims who have committed grave sins for which they have not repented, but, according to some commentators, the possibility exists for some inhabitants to repent and move to Heaven.

jâhiliyyah (Arabic: ignorance)

This word refers to the period before the rise of Islam in Arabia. It can also mean the period before the coming of Islam to various specific localities. It is derived from an Arabic root that means "ignorance," but it means more than just a lack of knowledge. It is generally contrasted with the word "Islam," so it means all the values that are the opposite of Islam. It is the antonym of both 'ILM, "knowledge," and ḤILM, "good behavior, kindness." These notions speak to one of the central characteristics of Islam, namely that knowledge of God and the QUR'ÂN will have a transformative effect on the believer so that he will behave well. Morality comes from God and is known best by humans through the revelation of scripture and through the model of MUḤAMMAD's behavior. Many Muslims have felt that the study of literature, art, music, rhetoric, etc. will make one *'adîb*, "polite and well-mannered," which has been the basis for Islamic support for education and the arts. In some modernist circles, the term *jâhiliyyah* refers to Western secularism.

al-jaḥîm

One of the seven ranks of Hell.

al-Jâḥiẓ, Abû 'Uthmân 'Amr b. Baḥr (160/776–255/868)

A distinguished Mu'tazilî writer and advocate of the belletristic style of *adab*, his writings greatly influenced Arabic prose style. (*See also* MU'TAZILAH.)

Jahm b. Ṣafwân (executed 128/746)

Early Mu'tazilî theologian who held that Hell and Paradise are not eternal, that the attributes of God are allegorical, that the QUR'ÂN is created, and that human actions are predetermined. A sect called the Jahmiyyah was named after him. (*See also* MU'TAZILAH.)

Jâlût

The biblical Goliath, who attacked ṬÂLÛT (Saul). From the one Qur'ânic story (in Q. 2:249–51), commentators attach a number of stories of the ISRÂ'ÎLIYYÂT variety. As an example, DÂ'ÛD, when he comes to kill Jâlût, gathers three stones, which represent the biblical patriarchs. These stones combine into one, and Jâlût is killed with the force of the patriarchs. Commentators also make Jâlût into a paradigm oppressor of the faithful, and the conflict between the outnumbered Muslims and the Meccans at the battle of BADR is seen as a repetition of the conflict between Jâlût and the BANÛ ISRÂ'ÎL.

jamâ'ah (Arabic: group, community)

This term meaning "community" comes from post-Qur'ânic usage as a synonym of 'UMMAH. It is connected to another word from this root, *Jum'ah*, "Friday," meaning the day on which the community gathers together for prayer (ṢALÂT).

Jamâ'at-i Islâmî

A fundamentalist revivalist party founded by Sayyid Abû al-A'lâ MAWDÛDÎ in the early 1940s with the aim of transforming Pakistan into a theocratic Islamic state.

al-Jamâ'at al-Islâmiyyah (Arabic: Islamic organizations)

A loose federation of Islamic groups in Egypt that operate through independent mosques and student groups with the general aim of promoting Islamic resurgence and revival.

jamâ'at khânah, also jamatkhana

A prayer-hall for ISMÂ'ÎLÎ SHÎ'Î.

jâmi' (Arabic: general)

A *masjid jâmi'* is the term for a central mosque where Friday prayers are said and a sermon delivered. (*See also* MASJID.)

al-Jâmi' as-Sayfiyyah

The principal educational institution of the Dâ'ûdî BOHRA ISMÂ'ÎLÎ, founded in 1814 in Surat, India.

al-Jamrah (Arabic: pebble)

Three locations in the valley of MÎNÂ, which are visited by pilgrims on the ḤAJJ for the lapidation or stoning of IBLÎS (the devil). This action is in emulation of IBRÂHÎM, ISMÂ'ÎL, and ḤÂJAR, each of whom was tempted by the devil, as well as the actions of MUḤAMMAD in the "Farewell Pilgrimage." It is a mandatory part of the pilgrimage.

janâbah (Arabic: major ritual impurity)

A major ritual impurity, such as contact with blood and other bodily fluids, that renders one unfit for prayer. Such an impurity can be removed by a major ritual ABLUTION. While in this state, the Muslim cannot engage in prayer (ṢALÂT), circumambulate the KA'BAH, or recite the QUR'ÂN, beyond uttering phrases of the scripture to ward off evil. (*See also* GHUSL.)

janâzah (Arabic: bier)

The corpse, the bier on which the corpse is placed, or the funeral procession. (*See also* FUNERARY RITES.)

Janissaries (Turkish *yeniçeri*: new troops)

Muslim slave troops in the Ottoman army. They were recruited from among Balkan Christians, converted to Islam, given a thorough education, and placed in high rank in Ottoman military society.

al-jannah (Arabic: garden)

This is a common Qur'ânic name for Paradise (*firdaws*), the place of reward for the deceased Muslim faithful. The QUR'ÂN describes many of the wonders of AL-JANNAH, including the food, drink, and companionship that the faithful will enjoy. The ḤADÎTHS elaborate on the rich Qur'ânic details. It is located under the throne of God in heaven, and is different from the garden out of which God expelled ADAM. There are different levels of the garden, each with different rewards for specific actions. In this, *al-jannah* parallels the levels and specificity of Hell, where the punishments are different for different transgressions. Different Muslim groups have debated whether or not the Qur'ânic verses should be interpreted literally or allegorically, and there is no single, authoritative teaching on this that is common to all Muslims. That said, belief in reward and punishment for actions is fundamental to being a Muslim.

al-jarḥ wa-t-ta'dîl (Arabic: the disparaged and the trustworthy)

A genre of ḤADÎTH criticism that analyzes the ISNÂDs and the biographies of the transmitters to determine the degree of acceptability of the *ḥadîth*. With the proliferation of traditions and reports about the Prophet and the early Companions (ṢAḤÂBAH), questions arose about the authenticity of the transmission of *ḥadîth*s. This was particularly so in the face of contradictory and obviously anachronistic traditions. In addition to the content of the traditions, commentators began to evaluate the *isnâd*s, or chains of authentication, to determine whether the transmitters were trustworthy and would have been in a position to transmit the *ḥadîth*. A large body of biographical dictionaries and encyclopedias arose that became the hallmark of Islamic historiography. These dictionaries tried to determine the exact name, dates of birth and death, and location of each individual who figured in the chains of transmission. Additionally, they tried to determine whether the individual was a good Muslim, was truthful and reliable, had a history of sound transmission of traditions, and was of generally good character. Contradictory reports arose about some individuals, resulting in complexities that the genre of *al-jarḥ wa-t-ta'dîl* attempted to solve.

jarîmah, also jurm (Arabic: crime, offense, sin)

In many modern Muslim countries, this word has come to be used as the ordinary word for crime. This includes both secular crimes and those traditionally punishable under Islamic law (SHARÎ'AH). (*See also* ḤADD.)

jâsûs (Arabic: spy)

The QUR'ÂN (Q 49:12) says that believers should not spy on one another and should avoid suspicion. Islamic law does not, however, forbid espionage on an enemy.

jâwî

This is the name for Muslims from Southeast Asia, originally derived from the name for the Javanese peoples. It is also the name in Indonesia and Malaysia for the Arabic script when used to write one of the languages of the area.

Jerusalem

See AL-QUDS.

Jesus (Arabic 'Îsâ)

A prophet mentioned prominently in the QUR'ÂN. Muslims regard Jesus as human, the son of MARYAM, and as having performed miracles. The Qur'ân and Muslim literature strongly deny that Jesus is the son of God. Some extra-Qur'ânic stories also hold that he was without sin. His prophetic book is called the INJÎL (Gospel) in Arabic, and he will be one of the party of judgment at the *eschaton*. He is called AL-MASÎḤ, which is Arabic for "Messiah" but without the Judeo-Christian religious sense, NABÎ (prophet), RASÛL (messenger), and Ibn Maryam, the son of Mary. This last term for Jesus indicates one of the central views of him in Islam, indicating both his humanity and the importance of his mother. Before his birth, JIBRÎL appeared to Maryam in the form of a perfect man and announced his birth to make her a sign, or ÂYAH, for humans and a mercy from God. When Jesus was born, he spoke from the cradle to those who were scandalized by Maryam bearing a child, telling them that he was a servant of ALLÂH and a prophet (*nabî*). As a youth, he made clay birds and breathed life into them. During his mission, he cured a blind man, a leper, and raised a man from the dead, all with the permission of and direct intervention from God. He caused a table already prepared to descend from heaven for his disciples. On the basis of Q. 61:6, Muslim commentators see Jesus as predicting the coming of MUḤAMMAD after him. According to the Qur'ân, the real Jesus was neither killed nor crucified, only a likeness of him. The TAFSÎR traditions expand on the Qur'ânic statements and make Jesus a prominent member of the entourage of the YAWM AD-DÎN. He will, according to some of these traditions, appear in AL-QUDS dressed in white with his head anointed with oil. He will kill AD-DAJJÂL, the "Antichrist," and then pray the dawn prayer with the *Imâm*. He will break all the crosses, kill all the pigs, and slay all those who do not believe in him and Islam. There will then be one religion, Islam, and peace will prevail. In the wake of Muslim–Christian polemic and dialogue, Muslim tradition has strengthened the view that makes Jesus more like Muḥammad. Also, the role of Maryam is emphasized, particularly in the face of Protestant missionaries, whose lack of veneration of Maryam made them, in the eyes of some Muslims, deficient Christians. In spite of the miraculous nature of the life of Jesus, for Muslims he was a man, a prophet, and called humans to Islam.

Jews

See AL-YAHÛD.

Jibrîl, also Jibrâ'îl

The archangel Gabriel. He is the greatest of all the angels in Islamic cosmology. He brought the QUR'ÂN to MUḤAMMAD, showed IBRÂHÎM and ISMÂ'ÎL how to build the KA'BAH and NUḤ how to build the ark. He protected Ibrâhîm from the fire of Namrûd and the Children of Israel from the armies of FIR'AWN. Throughout Muḥammad's prophetic career, Jibrîl was at his side, bringing him revelations from ALLÂH, warning him of plots against him, and heading a band of thousands of angels at the battle of BADR. According to tradition, he appeared only twice to Muḥammad in the form in which he was created rather than as a more ordinary person. Jewish and Christian tales about Jibrîl found their way into the ISRÂ'ÎLIYYÂT literature, adding details to the Qur'ânic accounts. He is depicted as huge, with his feet astride the horizon, covered with six hundred pairs of wings. He appeared on horseback at the time that MÛSÂ split the Red Sea, and it was his footprints that AS-SÂMIRÎ picked up and threw into the gold that helped create the Calf of Gold that the Children of Israel worshiped. He and MÎKÂ'ÎL are the two angels that opened the young Muḥammad's breast and washed his heart, and he was the one who escorted Muḥammad to heaven. All believers will encounter him on the YAWM AD-DÎN, as part of Allâh's judging entourage.

jihâd (Arabic: striving)

This word is often mistranslated as "holy war." For classical commentators, *jihâd* is divided into greater *jihâd* and lesser *jihâd*. The greater striving is the struggle against sin within the individual and the quest for a perfect spiritual life. It is regarded as the harder of the two and the one with the greater rewards. The lesser striving includes missionary activity and active armed conflict with evil. In the latter sense, some groups, such as certain of the KHAWÂRIJ and some modern activists, regard the armed struggle as an essential feature of faith, with the aim of creating Islamic states wherever possible. During the period of the Crusades, Muslim jurists developed detailed codes of Islamic warfare based on earlier thinking, which limited the barbarity and harmful effects on non-combatants. In the modern period, some Muslim thinkers have argued that it is the duty of every Muslim to wage armed struggle against those states that are not Islamic, and even against those traditionally Muslim states that have not fully implemented the SHARÎ'AH. This has given rise to a number of *jihâd* organizations that utilize the Islamic concept to promote support for primarily political, post-colonial liberationist and nationalist movements.

al-Jîlânî, 'Abd al-Qâdir (470/1077–561/1166)

Eponym of the QÂDIRIYYAH ṬARÎQAH, he was a ḤANBALÎ ascetic with a reputation for great piety. What is known of his life is mostly legendary and hagiographic, with wondrous tales of his calling an assembly of all the saints (WALÎs), as well as MUḤAMMAD. His tomb in BAGHDÂD is a pilgrimage site.

jinn (Arabic)

Intelligent creatures made of fire, often invisible, they are like humans in their capacity to receive God's word and be saved, since the QUR'ÂN mentions that it was sent to both humans and JINN (Q. 72:1ff.). In the Qur'ân, IBLÎS is said to be a *jinn*, but he is also said to be an angel. This has caused considerable trouble to the commentators, and many theories have developed about the relationship between *jinn* and angels. It is generally held, however, that one of the main differences is that *jinn*, like humans, are capable of both sin and salvation and that the Qur'ân and MUḤAMMAD's mission was to both groups. There is an immense folkloric literature about the *jinn*. They helped SULAYMÂN with his activities, as they were able to take various shapes and carry out heavy work almost instantly. The "genie" of the lamp in Western versions of the *Thousand and One Nights* is a folkloric version of the *jinn*. They are believed to sit on the walls around heaven, trying to listen in on God's councils with the angels, and shooting stars are caused by the angels throwing things at them to drive them away. *Jinn* can appear as animals – a black cat, a dog, a fox – or as humans, either ordinary or grotesque. They can be helpful or harmful to humans, depending on whether or not they are of an evil nature or have been annoyed by humans. Pious behavior on the part of humans is the best defense against them.

Jinnah (Jinâḥ), Muḥammad 'Alî (1293/1876–1367/1948)

British-trained Indian lawyer who became president of the MUSLIM LEAGUE that promoted the foundation of the independent Muslim state of PAKISTAN. He became the first president of the country's constituent assembly. He was born in Karachi and educated there and in Bombay before he was sent to England for his legal training. He adopted English customs in dress and speech, speaking English rather than URDU. He returned to India in 1896 and worked as a lawyer in Bombay. He became a member of the Indian National Congress as the representative of the Muslims of Bombay. While a member of the Congress, he joined the Muslim League, but resigned from the Congress in 1919 over issues of Muslim repression by the police. He was also disaffected from many of his fellow Muslims, who were supporters of the

KHILÂFAT MOVEMENT. In 1935, he became active again in the League, and began to press for a separate Muslim state. By 1946, it was clear that he had a majority of Muslims on his side, and he participated in the negotiations for partition. At midnight on 14–15 August, 1947 Pakistan came into existence, and he became the first president of the constituent assembly. He died on 11 September 1948, having created a new Muslim state.

Jirjis

Saint George the Martyr. The story of Saint George the Martyr was included in Islamic stories about holy persons by the end of the first Islamic century as a person whose piety and forbearance caused ALLÂH to bring him back to life each time he was killed by Dâdân (Diocletian). He lived in Palestine during a time of persecution of Christians, and was tortured to death three times. His steadfastness and his resurrection impressed Diocletian's wife, who converted and was herself killed. After being brought back to life three times, Jirjîs asked God to let him remain dead, and his wish was granted. The veneration of this saint and martyr is shared in some communities by both Christians and Muslims, and its springtime festivities are symbolic of vernal renewal.

jism (Arabic: body)

Many Traditionists, in opposition to the MU'TAZILAH, held that God has a body, *jism*, that is physical and corporeal. These are grouped under the term *mujassimûn*, usually translated as "anthropomorphists." While the majority of Muslims came to accept a view that God does not have a body in the same manner as humans, ALLÂH's possession of hands, eyes, etc. is still part of most Muslims' conceptualization of God.

jizyah (Arabic: tribute)

A capitulation tax or poll tax paid by non-Muslim members of the Islamic state, the AHL AL-KITÂB, who also paid a land tax, the KHARÂJ.

Job

See AYYÛB.

John

See YAḤYÂ.

Jonah

See DHÛ-N-NÛN.

Joseph

See YÛSUF.

judge

See ḤAKAM; QÂḌÎ.

Juḥâ

A fabulous figure in stories and legends, he is a jester, a fool, a wise bumpkin, and a prankster. While the majority of these stories are told for amusement, some of them have a religious didactic character and are used by ṢÛFÎs to instruct initiates in the complexities of the world.

Jum'ah

See JAMÂ'AH; *Ṣalât*; YAWM AL-JUM'AH.

al-Junayd, Abû al-Qâsim b. Muḥammad b. al-Junayd al-Khazzâz al-Qawârîrî (died 298/910)

He was a ṢÛFÎ whose work is accepted within SUNNÎ "orthodoxy." His written works mostly survive as fragments of letters he wrote explaining his mystical experiences and his views about God and mysticism. His careful use of language and clear explanation of the mystic experiences in terms that non-mystics could understand and accept earned him high praise and enabled him to lay the foundations for later Ṣûfism.

jurisprudence

See FIQH.

jurm (Urdu: crime)

See ḤADD; JARÎMAH.

al-Juwaynî, Abû al-Ma'âlî 'Abd al-Malik b. al-Juwaynî

(419/1028–478/1085)

Known as *Imâm al-Ḥaramayn* because of the reputation he earned teaching in MECCA and MADÎNAH, he was a famous writer on Shâfi'î jurisprudence. He was an expert on 'UṢÛL AL-FIQH as well as KALÂM. While his works never became widely popular, his exposition of those two subjects was based on principles of rational logic, partly derived from Aristotle, which influenced later writers. He was the teacher of AL-GHAZÂLÎ.

K

Ka'b al-Aḥbâr, Abû Isḥâq b. Mâti' b. Haysu' (died *c.* 32/653)

He was a Jew from the Yemen who converted to Islam. He is the attributed source for many ISRÂ'ÎLIYYÂT traditions found in Islamic literature. His title, *al-Aḥbâr,* indicates that he had scholarly status among the Jews. He came to MADÎNAH during the caliphate of 'UMAR B. AL KHAṬṬÂB and went with him to AL-QUDS (Jerusalem), where he advised 'Umar about the initiation of worship at the *ṣakhrah*, the rock at the Temple Mount. It is likely that he converted at the time of that journey, and, after his conversion, he was on close terms with the caliph. After 'Umar's death, which he is said to have predicted, he became an advisor and supporter of 'UTHMÂN. He is credited with the reliable transmission of information about 'Umar, but it was his profound knowledge of the Bible, of Jewish tradition, and of Yemenite traditions that earned him his reputation. Almost all traditions regarding the pre-Islamic prophets bear some mark of his erudition.

Ka'bah (Arabic: cube)

The cube-shaped shrine in the center of the great mosque in MECCA toward which all Muslims face in prayer. According to Islamic traditions, the foundations of the shrine were laid by ADAM, but the building was constructed by IBRÂHÎM and ISMÂ'ÎL, and they are the ones who placed the Black Stone, AL-ḤAJAR AL-ASWAD, in the eastern corner as the cornerstone. According to popular belief, this stone was brought from heaven by the angel JIBRÎL. The shrine is also the object of the ḤAJJ and the *'umrah*, during which pilgrims try to touch the Black Stone. The shrine was rebuilt during MUḤAMMAD's lifetime, and was destroyed and rebuilt between 64/683 and 74/693. Each year, the shrine is covered by the KISWAH, and pieces of the old covering are prized possessions of the *ḥajj*. Contrary to Western belief, the shrine is not worshiped, but is used as the focal point of the worship of God. The name, Ka'bah, was due to its cube-like appearance, and appears to have been applied to a number of pre-Islamic shrines, most notably in Ṣan'ah in the Yemen and aṭ-Ṭâ'if. The corners of the shrine are roughly at the compass points, with the Black Stone set in the eastern corner. The shrine is hollow, with a door in the northeast facade. Inside are three columns that support the roof rising from a marble floor and a ladder leading to the roof. There are numerous hanging lamps and building inscriptions, but nothing remains of the paintings that existed during the time of the Prophet. Little is known of the history of the Ka'bah outside Islamic tradition, but there is reason to believe that the shrine was an active pilgrimage site as early as the second century C.E. The geographer Ptolemy calls the city "Macoraba," with the significance of *miqrab*, "temple." During Muḥammad's lifetime but before he received the prophethood, the Meccans rebuilt the Kaʿbah, enlarging it from its height of no taller than a person. Muḥammad is said to have effected the compromise by having a representative of each clan help replace the Stone. When Mecca was conquered by the Muslims, there were over three hundred and sixty idols in and around the Kaʿbah, and the Prophet had them all removed, the shrine cleansed, and Muslim worship instituted. In 64/683, during the attempt of ʿAbd Allâh b. az-Zubayr to gain the caliphate, the Kaʿbah was nearly destroyed by the siege and a subsequent fire cracked the Black Stone into three pieces. When the siege was lifted the stone was repaired with a band of silver, and the Kaʿbah was rebuilt and enlarged. In 74/693, the ʾUMAYYADS conquered Mecca, killed az-Zubayr, and re-did many of his alterations, returning the Kaʿbah to a simpler form, much as it is today. In 317/929, the QARÂMIṬAH carried off the Black Stone, which was returned after a twenty-year absence. In Islamic sacred geography, the Kaʿbah is the center of the world, and it has fulfilled that function for Muslims since the time of the Prophet. It is the daily reminder in prayers (ṢALÂT) of the unity of Muslims, and the *ḥajj* has brought Muslims from all over the world to Mecca for study and the dissemination of ideas as well as for worship. All groups within Islam have accepted the centrality of the Kaʿbah.

kaffârah (Arabic: expiation)

An act performed for the expiation of sins.

kâfir (Arabic: to conceal, be ungrateful)

One who is "ungrateful" to God, an unbeliever, an atheist. Almost all groups hold that a *kâfir* will be condemned to Hell. The KHAWÂRIJ held that anyone who had committed a grave sin was a *kâfir*, while the MURJIʾAH held that the determination of who goes to Hell is left to God's judgment. The various schools of Islamic law (MADHHABS) spell out how a Muslim is to deal with a *kâfir*, but generally the AHL AL-KITÂB are not included in the category of unbelievers, since they believe in God and are recipients of God's revelation.

kâhin (Arabic: prognosticator, priest)

A seer or soothsayer among the Arabs in the JÂHILIYYAH, who usually spoke *sajʿ*, or rhymed prose. In the pre-Islamic period, there was a class of religious figures who claimed the power to tell the future, find lost animals, and determine paternity. They would often go into mantic trances and utter cryptic sayings that would subsequently be interpreted for their clients. They used techniques of dowsing to find water and phrenology to determine paternity. Their magic is reported to have been generally of the "white" sort, but they were also reported to have been able to cause impotence, various illnesses, and other maladies. One of their techniques, mentioned in Q. 113:4, was to partially tie a knot, utter a curse and spit into the knot and pull it tight. The knot had to be found and untied before the curse could be lifted. The last two SÛRAHS of the QURʾÂN are often thought to be prophylactic against that sort of magic. MUḤAMMAD was accused by his pagan detractors of being a *kâhin* because of the *sajʿ* of the Qurʾân and his prophetic powers.

kalâm (Arabic: speech)

The word *kalâm* is used in the QURʾÂN at least three times to refer to the speech of ALLÂH, which the commentators understand to be both the Qurʾân itself and the previous revelations to prophets, such as

MÛSÂ. Historically, this leads to discussions about the nature of God's speech, whether speech is inherent in God, and whether or not the Qur'ân was the created or uncreated speech of God. These discussions led to the second definition of the term *kalâm*, speculative scholastic theology. The *'ilm al-kalâm*, the science of theology, became one of the Islamic sciences. While it is hard to date the beginnings of this science, it most probably started with the MU'TAZILAH. *Kalâm* is distinguished from FALSAFAH (philosophy), even when the subjects of discussion and the content appear to be similar, as *kalâm* always remained God-centered and part of the training of religious scholars. In later periods it became as much a method of argument as a method in inquiry, and usually assumed a real or hypothetical opponent against which arguments were made.

karâmah (Arabic: generosity; pl. *karâmât*)

Understood as the favors shown by God to humans; in popular parlance, the miracles performed by a WALÎ (saint). It is generally felt that ALLÂH bestows special gifts to humans through holy persons, prophets, and *walîs*. These gifts come outside the natural order of things and fall into the category of "miracles." Different schools of Islamic thought have had strongly different reactions to the possibility of such miracles. The MU'TAZILAH and the WAHHÂBÎ have been strongly opposed to the notion of miracles. ṢÛFÎs and many SHÎ'Î, on the other hand, regard such divine intervention as a usual part of the order of the universe. Many thinkers distinguish between the *karâmât* and *mu'jizât*, or the miracles performed by prophets and the IMÂMS. (*See also* MIRACLE.)

Karbalâ'

City in Iraq holy to the ITHNÂ 'ASHARIYYAH SHÎ'Î because of the shrine-tomb of AL-ḤUSAYN B. 'ALÎ and the proximity to the battleground where he was martyred in 61/680 by 'UMAYYAD troops. By as early as 65/685 there was active veneration of the tomb, which the 'ABBÂSID caliph al-Mutawakkil tried to stop in 236/850. This having failed, the city continued to prosper, boasting a large MADRASAH and a good hostel to accommodate the pilgrims. The city has the reputation of assuring Paradise to those who are buried there, so many aging and ill pilgrims go there to die, and bodies are sent there for burial.

kasb, also iktisâb (Arabic: acquire)

A term used to refer to the doctrine of "acquisition" in the thought of some speculative theologians, by which humans "acquire" actions that are really created by God. This notion is meant to provide a separation between God's creation and human free will, so that there will not be any action in the universe that cannot be said to have been created by God. (*See also* KALÂM.)

Kemal, Mustafa

See ATATÜRK.

khabar (Arabic: report; pl. *akhbâr*)

This word refers to reports or traditions that have a form similar to ḤADÎTHs but carry historical rather than legal importance. In the first Islamic century, this distinction was not always clearly defined, and some commentators and traditionists used the terms *khabar* and *ḥadîth* interchangeably. A *khabar* will have an ISNÂD as well as the text (MATN), and can be subject to the same types of scrutiny as a *ḥadîth*.

Khadîjah bt. Khuwaylid (died 619 C.E.)

First wife of MUḤAMMAD. It is said that she was the first to accept ISLÂM. She was a wealthy widow, somewhat older than Muḥammad, who owned property and engaged in trade. Muḥammad's first association with her was as a trading agent, which duties he is said to have performed admirably. At the time they were married, Muḥammad was reported to be twenty-one, twenty-three, or twenty-five, and Khadîjah anywhere from twenty-eight to forty. She bore him two sons, who died in infancy, ʿAbd Allâh and AL-QÂSIM, and four daughters, FÂṬIMAH, RUQAYYAH, ʾUMM KULTHÛM, and Zaynab. Muḥammad was monogamous until her death two years before the HIJRAH. Through marriage, she provided Muḥammad with material and emotional support that helped him turn toward the religious life.

al-Khaḍir, also al-Khiḍr

A mysterious, mystical figure in popular and ṢÛFÎ legend, who is said to be the unnamed sage in the eighteenth chapter of the QURʾÂN who instructs MÛSÂ in esoteric wisdom. When Mûsâ goes on a journey in search of the confluence of the "two rivers," he and his companion find that they have forgotten a fish they had for provisions; the fish finds its way into the water, comes back to life, and swims away. While searching for the fish, they encounter the unnamed figure who agrees to instruct Mûsâ in wisdom if he can refrain from challenging his actions. Mûsâ promises, but is ultimately unable to keep from asking about the esoteric actions that seem wrong or contradictory in the exoteric world. As a result, Al-Khiḍr is understood as the master of esoteric wisdom and is credited as the founder of many Ṣûfî orders. Many scholars, particularly in the West, have remarked on the parallels between the story of al-Khiḍr and the Alexander Romance, which is itself derived from the story of Gilgamesh. In popular stories, al-Khiḍr often appears in the guise of a beggar or some other unlikely person and rewards the person who gives charity and punishes the person who acts selfishly.

Khâlid b. al-Walîd b. al-Mughîrah (died 21/641)

A contemporary of MUḤAMMAD who opposed the Muslims at the battle of Uḥud but later (*c.* 6/627) converted to Islam, and earned the title "Sword of Islam." After the death of the Prophet, the caliph ABÛ BAKR sent him against the rebels in the RIDDAH wars, where he inadvertently killed some Muslims and married the widow of one of his victims. Abû Bakr forgave him, however, and sent him into Iraq. He is said to have been a great general, and his loyalty to Muḥammd and to Islam after his conversion is unquestioned.

khalîfah (Arabic: successor, caliph)

The head of the Islamic community in SUNNÎ Islâm, the office was regarded as elected, but without a specified process. The office was terminated, in the minds of some, with the capture of BAGHDÂD in 656/1258 by the MONGOLS, but there have been subsequent claims to the title, and the KHILÂFAT MOVEMENT sought to revive the office. According to SHÎʿÎ tradition, before MUḤAMMAD died he designated his closest male relative, ʿALÎ B. ABÎ ṬÂLIB, as his successor. According to Sunnî tradition, the Prophet did not designate a successor, but he had appointed ABÛ BAKR to lead the community in prayer (ṢALÂT) during the period of his last illness. Using that role as precedent, the community chose Abû Bakr as its leader and the political successor to Muḥammad. Through the reigns of the first four caliphs, the shape and duties of the office expanded. Abû Bakr developed the duties as community leader and commander of the armies of defense and conquest. ʿUMAR further developed the military role, calling himself the 'Amîr al-Mu'minîn, the Commander of the Faithful. He also developed the bureaucratic aspects of the position by appointing deputies to manage the fiscal and military aspects of rule. ʿUthmân added a religious aspect by making and promulgating an official recension of the Qur'ân. Throughout this earliest period, several different conceptions of power and authority existed side by side, and some of these came to a head with the murder of ʿUthmân and the conflict between the supporters of ʿAlî, the Shîʿî, and the supporters of Muʿâwiyah, the 'Umayyads. At base were issues of hereditary Arab privilege, rule by the principles of the Qur'ân, and rule by the household of the Prophet's family. In addition, there were those who felt that the leadership of the community should be open to any Muslim. These views and variations of them were distributed across both Arabs and newly converted non-Arabs, so that the civil war that resulted in the rise of the 'Umayyads further fractured the community. 'Umayyad rule was characterized by hereditary Arab leaders ruling in the name of Islam. With the advent of the ʿAbbâsid Caliphate (from 132/750), the rulers regarded themselves as members of the family of the Prophet, rivaling the claim of the Shîʿî, and felt themselves to be ruling as Muslim rulers commanding a theocratic state. At the same time, they began ruling an empire that contained Christians, Jews, Zoroastrians and others, and the caliphate took on the trappings of an ancient Near Eastern kingship. The caliph became a distant, semi-divine potentate, removed from his subjects and heading a giant bureaucracy. At the periphery, in places such as Spain, local rulers, who had been calling themselves kings, began to call themselves caliphs, and the idea of a unified caliphate, while remaining an ideal, became impossible to achieve. Toward the end of the caliphate, the caliphs were controlled by military rulers, who were given the title sulṭân, and who kept the caliphs as virtual puppets to ratify their rule. (*See also* Imâm.)

al-Khalîl (Arabic: the friend)

The title borne by Ibrâhîm as "friend" of God and a name of the town of Hebron, regarded as Ibrâhîm's town.

khalwah (Arabic: seclusion, solitude)

Among the Ṣûfî, the practice of seclusion and solitude is one means to develop the soul on the mystic journey. The model of Muḥammad was often invoked for the practice, and this meant that it resulted in periodic retreats from the community rather than a life of complete isolation, as was the ideal expressed in the stories of the Christian Desert Fathers. Indeed, complete retreat from community was regarded as un-Islamic. The retreat is usually limited to forty days, but even during this period, deeds of charity are performed, again following the sunnah of the Prophet.

Khalwatiyyah

A Ṣûfî order (tarîqah), found from Central Asia to North Africa. Its central tenets include adherence to the sharîʿah, the bond between disciple and master, and the practice of a periodic retreat (khalwah), after which the order was named.

khamr (Arabic: fermented beverage, wine)

The fermented beverage prohibited by Muslim jurists; wine. While wine was produced in Arabia in the pre-Islamic period, most wine consumed in Arabia was imported by Jews and Christians from Syria and Iraq. The sale of wine was associated with debauched entertainments, and public drunkenness seems to have become a mark of status in MECCA. Passages in the QUR'ÂN concerning wine can be interpreted to reflect an ambivalence toward wine, but are generally regarded as holding wine drinking to be more of a sin than a benefit (Q. 2:219). In post-Qur'ânic interpretation, wine is forbidden by most jurists, although it is said that it will be the drink of the faithful in Paradise. Some schools of law, taking a strict interpretation of the Qur'ânic passages, prohibit those fermented beverages made from substances known to MUḤAMMAD, such as grapes and dates, but allow the consumption of fermented beverages made from such things as grain, fruits, and other substances unknown in early Arabia. Consumption, however, is limited to an amount that will not produce drunkenness. For most schools of law (MADHHABS), contact with *khamr* renders one ritually impure and a complete GHUSL (ablution) is necessary. Among the ṢÛFÎ, the image of wine consumption is allegorically linked to the mystic journey, with intoxication by the love of ALLÂH as the substitute for alcoholic drunkenness.

khamsah (Arabic: five)

The number five has a magical value for many people of the Middle East, and the notion has spread with Islam. The five fingers of the right hand are thought to be able to ward off evil, particularly the evil eye. Amulets in the shape of hands, sometimes known as the "Hand of Fâṭimah," are worn to ward off evil, and houses in North Africa and Egypt are sometimes decorated with hands painted in henna. Thursday, the fifth day of the week, is regarded as a fortuitous day for travel, ceremonies, etc.

khân, or Khân

Title of the leader of Central Asian tribal leaders, an administrative and honorific title in Persian, a Muslim surname in Pakistan, and a part of the title for spiritual leaders of the ISMÂ'ÎLÎ SHÎ'Î.

Khandaq (Arabic from Persian: ditch, trench)

In 627, MUḤAMMAD and the Muslims of MADÎNAH were besieged by the forces of MECCA. Outnumbered, Muḥammad on the advice of SALMÂN AL-FÂRISÎ, dug a moat or trench across the open area leading into the town. This prevented the Meccans from using their superior camel cavalry and, when they tried to maintain a siege of the city, they were unsuccessful. This victory for the Muslims was one of the last defeats for the Meccans before their capitulation. Several Prophetic miracles are reported to have happened during the digging of the trench, for example, Muḥammad was able to restore the sight of an injured person and to feed the entire town on a mere handful of dates.

khânqâh (Persian: residence)

A residential teaching center for ṢÛFÎ disciples. Often compared with Christian monasteries, these building complexes were designed to house Ṣûfîs, provide places for communal worship, feed the residents and guests, and are sites of the burial and subsequent veneration of the masters. As the institution spread, it never adopted a distinctive architectural form, but developed according to local need and custom. (*See also* RIBÂṬ; ZÂWIYAH.)

kharâj (Arabic: tax)

The land tax. When the Muslims entered into the newly conquered territories, they imposed a tribute tax on the yield from the land along the same models as previous rulers. This tribute tax was parallel to the JIZYAH tax, or poll tax, paid by non-Muslims. When the landowners converted, the tax remained on the land and continued as a general levy. The confusion between the *kharâj* and the *jizyah* taxes in later sources reflects a conflation of the two sources of revenue. Eventually the tax as a distinct source of revenue fell into disuse.

Khârijites

See KHAWÂRIJ.

Khâtam an-Nabiyyîn, also Khâtam al-Anbiyâ'

The Seal of the Prophets, a title from the QUR'ÂN borne by MUḤAMMAD.

khatm (Arabic: seal)

The recitation of the whole of the QUR'ÂN from beginning to end.

Khatmiyyah

A ṢÛFÎ order introduced to the Sudan in the early nineteenth century devoted to the veneration of MUḤAMMAD through the practice of the recitation of a poetic biography written by the founder, Muḥammad 'Uthmân al-Mîrghânî (*fl.* early thirteenth/nineteenth century).

Khawârij, also Khârijites

The name given to a number of groups who defected from the support of 'ALÎ B. ABÎ ṬÂLIB in his struggle with MU'Â-WIYAH. They are alternately described as democratic, allowing a "black slave" to be caliph (KHALÎFAH), and fanatical, defining very narrowly who can be a Muslim and who is without sin. Many of them became "terrorists," and were eradicated in conflicts that resulted from their activities. When 'Alî b. Abî Ṭâlib accepted the offer made by Mu'âwiyah at the battle of ṢIFFÎN in 657, a group from 'Alî's army defected, saying that judgment belonged only to ALLÂH and not to a human conference. By successive defections, the group grew in size and in the conviction that both 'Alî's claim to the caliphate and that of 'UTHMÂN, who was being defended by Mu'âwiyah, were wrong. The defectors split into a number of groups, the most radical of which held that anyone who did not believe as they did was an infidel (KÂFIR), and deserved to be killed. Several important ideas about the community's governance became associated with this movement. One was an egalitarian notion that any Muslim could be caliph. They were opposed to the legitimist ideas of the SHÎ'Î, and the later 'ABBÂSIDS, as well as the ideas of quietism and the deferral of judgment espoused by the MURJI'AH. They held that only those members of the community who acted their faith could be regarded as among the faithful, so that mere profession of faith was insufficient to make one a Muslim, and one could lose one's Muslim status by committing a sin. So strict were some of the groups that one even removed SÛRAH 12, the *Yûsuf sûrah*, from the canon of scripture, because it was too worldly. In conflicts with the 'UMAYYADS and then the 'Abbâsids, the Khârijites lost politically and were virtually wiped out, but their ideas were an important catalyst in the formation of Islamic theology, and the views of both the SUNNÎ and the Shî'î were profoundly affected by reaction to them.

al-Khazraj

One of the two main Arab tribes of MADÎNAH. They were rivals of AL-'AWS, but the two tribes joined in welcoming MUḤAMMAD and the Muslims into the city at the time of the HIJRAH. After the *hijrah*, their identity, along with al-'Aws, was merged into the larger group known as the ANṢÂR, the "Helpers."

al-Khiḍr

See AL-KHAḌIR

Khilâfat Movement

The movement in India between 1919 and 1924 to advance the claim of the OTTOMAN SULTAN as the caliph of all Muslims. Notions of the revival of the caliphate had existed in the Islamic world for some time before World War I, but the defeat of the Ottoman *sulṭân* was a major psychological blow to many Muslims in the world. The Ottomans had been successful in claiming that they were the rightful heirs to the caliphate and the good protectors of the Islamic holy places in Arabia. For Indian Muslims, this was threatened not only by the success of the British and Allied powers, but also by the rise of Arab nationalism, which threatened to make Arabia into an Arab rather than a Muslim location. The movement became most active in 1919 and held that the preservation of the caliphate and full Muslim control over the holy places was a central part of their religion. They presented this to the viceroy and to the British government directly, without, however, any success. The movement then became associated with Indian nationalism, and they enlisted the support of the Indian National Congress and Ghandi, who became a member of the Central Khilâfa Committee. In 1920, some thirty thousand Muslims made a HIJRAH to Afghanistan, but returned disillusioned by their reception. This marked a break with the Hindus. Another blow came from Turkey itself, when Kemal ATATÜRK abolished the caliphate in 1924. Some followers of the movement tried to redirect the cause to addressing Hindu–Muslim problems, but by 1928 even they had ceased activity.

khirqah (Arabic: patch)

A mystic's patched, woolen robe, which is often a sign of the investiture of a particular disciple by a ṢÛFÎ SHAYKH. Assuming the rough *khirqah* has been a mark of the beginning of the mystic journey since the third/eighth century. It seems to continue a pre-Islamic Christian ascetic practice of wearing coarse cloth as a sign of penance. In addition to referring to the robe itself, the word *khirqah* also means the initiation ceremony itself, which can involve handclasps, the passing of a SUBḤAH (rosary), and other ceremonials, depending on the ṬARÎQAH.

khitân

See CIRCUMCISION.

khiṭbah (Arabic: demand in marriage)

This term refers to the betrothal, which involves a promise and an acceptance, but is not, according to most schools of Islamic law (MADHHAB), a contract. The man has the right to see the woman, and has right over all other men to have right of first refusal for marriage. Either party can dissolve the betrothal unilaterally, but any presents that have been exchanged have to be disposed of properly, depending on the condition under which they were given, and damages can be sought by either party for the breaking of the betrothal.

Kho'i, Abol-Qâsem (1317/1899–1413/1992)

Popular MUJTAHID of the ITHNÂ ʿASHARIYYAH SHÎʿÎ in Iraq, he opposed KHOMEINÎ's declaration of *wilâyat al-faqîh* (government by jurist) declared that goods brought from Kuwait after the Iraqî invasion of the country in 1990 were stolen, and advocated the rights of and education for women. Through his establishment of mosques and publishing houses and through his students, he has had influence throughout the SHÎʿÎ world. He was regarded as MARJIʿ AT-TAQLÎD.

khojas (Hindi from Persian *Khwâjah*: "Sir")

The name for the Nizârî Ismâ'îlî Shî'î Muslims of India and Pakistan. Their practices, some of which derive from Hinduism, have caused some to accuse them, falsely, of being non-Muslims.

khojkî

A script especially developed by the khojas for private records and secret writings.

Khomeinî, Rûḥollâh al-Mûsâvî (1320/1902–1409/1989)

The spiritual and political head of Iran during and after the revolution of 1399/1979. Having been exiled to Turkey, Iraq, and France by the shâh, Rezâ Pahlavi, he organized the revolution, returned at the Shâh's overthrow and ruled Iran until his death as the supreme cleric. His declaration of *wilâyat al-faqîh* (government by jurist) placed him at the pinnacle of the hierarchy of clerics, and he stood, in the minds of some, as this generation's embodiment of the twelfth Imâm.

A portrait of Rûḥollâh al-Mûsâvî Khomeinî hangs at the entrance to the Masjid-i Naw (New Mosque), Shiraz, Iran.

khums (Arabic: fifth)

This was at first the one-fifth of booty taken as tax for the community. In later Shî'î Islam, it was held that the descendants of the Prophet, the Imâms, were entitled to the *khums*.

khuṭbah (Arabic: sermon)

This is preached at the Friday noon congregational prayer. The person who delivers the sermon, the *khâṭib*, must be in a state of ritual purity, and it is usual for him to recite praise of Allâh, invoke prayers on the Prophet, and recite a portion of the Qur'ân. The sermon is usually delivered from an elevated place in the mosque. The sermon can be on any topic, from commentary on the Qur'ân to discussions of the condition of the community and its problems. In the history of Islam, sermons have served as important public declarations of political and social directions. In modern times, they have served as rallying points against oppression and colonialism.

kihânah (Arabic: divination)

There is a ḥadîth that states that there is no divination after the coming of prophecy (*lâ kihânah ba'd an-nubuwwah*), but this hortatory injunction failed to end the practice of divination among Muslims. Diviners, or people who claimed to have such powers, used dream interpretation, phrenology, palmistry, sand-pouring, flights of birds, and astrology to predict the future. Never sanctioned at an official level, each area of the Islamic world has its own variety of divinatory practices. (*See also* jafr.)

al-Kindî, Abû Yûsuf Ya'qûb b. Isḥâq (died *c.* 252/866)

One of the earliest Islamic philosophers, whose major contribution was the development of Arabic philosophical terminology. He lived in a time of considerable intellectual turmoil in the areas of philosphy and KALÂM, and was probably influenced by the thought of the MU'TAZILAH. He was of noble birth and high standing, and was received in the courts of the 'ABBÂSID caliphs al-Ma'mûn and al-Mu'taṣim, and his defense of philosophy was developed with the caliph in mind. He borrowed from Aristotle, often without acknowledgment, in his arguments that humans must pursue knowledge no matter the source and that philosophy and religion are not antithetical. In one of his treatises, he invokes ALLÂH to guide him in his philosophical pursuits. He departed from the Greek philosophers when they contradicted the QUR'ÂN. He tried in his works to use terms that can be used for both philosphy and religion and to define them carefully. He left few pupils and established no "school," but helped integrate philosophy into Islamic thought, and so he earned the title of "Philosopher of the Arabs."

Kirâm al-Kâtibîn

The "Two Noble Scribes," a pair of angels assigned to each individual to record their good and bad deeds.

al-Kirmânî, Ḥamîd ad-Dîn Aḥmad b. 'Abd Allâh (died *c.* 412/1021)

Major FÂṬIMID ISMÂ'ÎLÎ SHÎ'Î missionary to Iraq and Iran.

al-Kisâ'î, Abû al-Ḥasan 'Alî b. Ḥamzah b. 'Abd Allâh (119/737–189/805)

Famous grammarian, philologist, and QUR'ÂN reader. His reading of the Qur'ân is one of the seven canonical readings. He was born into a Persian family and moved to southern Iraq for his education. He had trouble with Arabic, so lived among the bedouin to improve his knowledge of the language. The wealth of information he collected there is reflected in his philological works, but he did not either care much for or know much about poetry.

al-Kisâ'î, Muḥammad b. 'Abd Allâh

This otherwise unknown author is known as *Ṣâḥib Qiṣaṣ al-'Anbiyâ'*, or the author of the *Qiṣaṣ al-'Anbiyâ'*, the famous collection of stories of the prophets. It is a collection of ISRÂ'ÎLIYYÂT and other legendary accounts of the prophets from ADAM to MUḤAMMAD.

kiswah (Arabic: clothing)

The black cover of the KA'BAH that is made of silk and cotton is changed each year. Pieces of the *kiswah* are prized relics from the ḤAJJ.

Koran

See QUR'ÂN.

Kosovo

See BALKAN STATES.

Kûfah

One of the two "camp cities," in Iraq, the other being BAṢRAH. These two cities started as military camps, since the Islamic armies of expansion were not quartered in existing towns. As they attracted the families of soldiers and other camp followers, they grew in size and importance into major cities. With the conflict between 'ALÎ B. ABÎ ṬÂLIB and Mu'âwiyah, the cities became political centers as well. Immigrants and converts soon joined the population, and both cities developed into major centers of Islamic learning. When BAGHDÂD became the capital, Kûfah retained a provincial conservative character, while still attracting SHÎʿÎ elements, which influenced Shîʿî Islam in Iran. In addition to its fame as a center of Shîʿîsm, the city is famous in Islamic intellectual circles for its contributions to Arabic grammar.

kufr (Arabic: unbelief)

See KÂFIR.

al-Kulaynî, Abû Jaʿfar Muḥammad b. Yaʿqûb b. Isḥâq ar-Râzî (died *c.* 328/940)

He was a prominent Imâmî SHÎʿÎ traditionist, whose *Kitâb al-kâfî* was a guide to Imâmî doctrine and legal thinking. He is also said to have written on the interpretation of dreams. He had only a slight reputation during his lifetime, but eventually his *Kitâb al-kâfî* became regarded as one of the four canonical collections of traditions among the ITHNÂ ʿASHARIYYAH SHÎʿÎ. His tomb in BAGHDÂD is a much-visited shrine.

kuttâb (Arabic: writing school)

Elementary school for the study of the QUR'ÂN. A typical *kuttâb* education would include the memorizing of the Qur'ân, learning to write, and other practical subjects. One of the earliest plans for such elementary education also included swimming and other physical activities. The system of education that started with the *kuttâb* probably dates from the earliest 'UMAYYAD period, although there are claims of its coming from the time of the Prophet and the Companions (ṢAḤÂBAH). The schools were an important instrument in spreading knowledge of Islam and of assimilating non-Arab elements into the society. The schools have been closely connected with the mosques, and have often been supported by WAQF funds as well as by the fees from parents of the pupils. Education was segregated by gender but not by age, and boys from about four to nine or so would all study together in the same room, each student progressing at his own rate. Like Jewish schools of the same type, the rooms were noisy, filled with the recitation aloud of Qur'ân and other lessons. The teacher was a *mudarris*, so-called because the word for study also meant to beat, and the teacher would use a large stick to keep order. Prior to modern times, the *kuttâb* was the closest institution to general education in the Islamic world. While there were differences between rich and poor neighborhoods and between the city and the country, the curriculum was standardized around the Qur'ân and those subjects needed to make a good Muslim. In recent times, with the secularization of many Islamic states, the institution has suffered, but almost all Islamic countries have tried to incorporate some of the traditions of the *kuttâb* into their systems of primary education.

L

labbayka (Arabic: at your service)

The *talbiyah*, the saying of a phrase meaning "I am here at Your service," as part of the ritual of the HAJJ.

Lamasar, or Lanbasar

One of the complex of fortresses of the ISMÂʿÎLÎ SHÎʿÎ around ALAMUT.

laqab (Arabic: nickname)

In the Arabic naming pattern, which was adopted in various forms by Muslims around the world, the addition of an honorific or descriptive "nickname" was common. Sometimes the names were given ironically or in jest, but more often it was a name meant to bring about good fortune or, when given later in life, to indicate status or power. Caliphs assumed such regnal nicknames as *Sayf ad-Dawlah*, the "Sword of the State," or *Ṣalâḥ ad-Dîn*, the "Savior of Religion." In the period of the great empires, the honorific nicknames became more elaborate and lengthy, so that they were not usually used in everyday discourse. Titles like *Bey* and *Efendi*, however, became part of everyday names, and were sometimes passed on to children as heritable titles.

al-Lât (Arabic: the goddess)

One of the three most venerated deities in the pre-Islamic pantheon, she was, according to some sources, imagined as the consort of ALLÂH. Her cult was of great antiquity, with her name being found in Akkadian inscriptions. Her cultic center was aṭ-Ṭâʾif, where there was a KAʿBAH, evidently with a white stone. The story of Abraha's confusion of aṭ-Ṭâʾif for MECCA can be explained by the similarity of the names and typology of the two cities' chief deities. Shortly before the rise of Islam, the QURAYSH had transferred her worship and the worship of her sister deities MANÂT and AL-ʿUZZÂ to Mecca and had installed images of them in the Kaʿbah as part of their federation of the Arab tribes.

law

See SHARÎʿAH.

lawḥ (Arabic: board, plank)

The ark built by NÛḤ (Noah) is called a *dhât alwâḥ*, a "thing of planks." The word also has the sense of a tablet on which something is written, and thus preserved. In the ḤADÎTH, the expression *bayn al-lawḥayn*, "between the two boards," is found, meaning the QURʾÂN.

al-lawḥ al-maḥfûẓ (Arabic: the preserved tablet)

This tablet, mentioned in Q. 85:22, is to be found in Heaven and contains the original words of the QUR'ÂN, from which JIBRÎL took verses to MUHAMMAD. Also called the 'UMM AL-KITÂB, the tablet has been important for ṢÛFÎS, with a glimpse of the tablet as part of the mystical quest.

laylat al-miʿrâj (Arabic: night of the ascension)

The night of the celebration of MUHAMMAD's ascension to Heaven (the twenty-seventh of Rajab). (*See also* MIʿRÂJ.)

laylat al-qadr (Arabic: the night of power)

This is celebrated between the twenty-sixth and twenty-seventh of RAMAḌÂN as the night of the first revelation of the QUR'ÂN.

Lezgh, also Lezghin

The name of a Muslim people in the Caucasus and their language. Lezghin is a northeast Caucasian language that has been influenced by Azerî Turkish, and exists in several dialects, of which Kürin is the literary language. Legend says that Islam was brought to the region as early as the second/eighth century, but complete Islamization did not occur until some seven centuries later. In the late nineteenth century, Lezghin became a literary language, written in Arabic script, but it did not replace Arabic. With the Russian revolution, the script changed first to the Latin script and then to the Cyrillic alphabet. Since before the fall of the Soviet empire, some Lezghins have advocated the formation of an independent Lezghistan that would embrace all the Lezghins in Dagestan and Azerbaijan. The majority of the population is SUNNÎ, although there is a significant SHÎʿÎ minority. Current estimates indicate that there are between a half million and a million Muslim Lezghins.

lithâm (Arabic: half-veil)

A half-veil that covers the nose and lower part of the face. This was worn by both sexes among the bedouin to protect the face from dust, heat, and cold. It also had the function of masking the identity of a person and could be used to avoid blood-vengeance in raids. In some of the descriptions of the angel ISRÂFÎL, one of his four wings covers the lower part of his face like a *lithâm*. Versions of this form of the veil are used by women in some Islamic societies.

Liu Chih (fl. twelfth/eighteenth century)

Little is known of the personal life of this prolific Chinese-speaking Muslim. He dedicated his life to translating Islamic works from Persian and Arabic into Chinese and attempting to harmonize Islam and Confucian thought. He is credited with several hundred manuscripts. His monumental work was a biography of MUHAMMAD, *An Accurate Biography of the Arabian Prophet*, published in 1193/1779 and translated into a variety of languages, including French and English. His tomb outside Nanking was a pilgrimage site for Muslims.

Luqmân b. ʿÂd

A fabulous wise man from the pre-Islamic period, and a giver of good advice. Some stories represent him as a monotheist. He features in much early Arabic poetry and has been compared to Aesop. The thirty-first chapter of the QUR'ÂN is named after him. In addition to his wisdom, he is supposed to have had a very long life. As a reward for his piety in the face of the wickedness of his people, he was given a variety of choices about how long to live. He chose the lives of seven vultures, which were supposed to have long lives, according to the Arabs. Accordingly, he lived as long as thirty-five hundred years. Post-Qur'ânic commentators took the brief mention of Luqmân in the Qur'ân and collected proverbs and wisdom literature ascribed to him: Wahb b. Munabbih is supposed to have read over ten thousand chapters of his wisdom, and homiletic wisdom books were in popular circulation. He was not a prophet, and, when given the choice between being a prophet or a wise man, he chose being wise. Stories about him make him a slave who bests his master with his wisdom. In one example, Luqmân is ordered to slaughter a sheep and set the best parts before his master. He gives him the heart and the tongue. When asked to slaughter another sheep and give him the worst parts, he gives him the heart and the tongue, with the explanation that there is nothing better than a good heart and tongue, and nothing worse than a bad heart and tongue. Among the ṢÛFÎ, Luqmân is considered a wise, pious ascetic who moves in and out of adversity and slavery with ease and equanimity, and such tales are used as models for proper ascetic behavior.

Lûṭ

Identified with the biblical Lot, he is one of the messengers mentioned in the QUR'ÂN who is sent to warn his city of destruction. Because of their sins of sodomy, all are destroyed except Lûṭ and his family, including his wife, who lingered in the city. In post-Qur'ânic literature, the sins of Lûṭ's people are identified with a lack of hospitality and with homosexuality. The term *liwâṭ*, sodomy, derives as a denominative from this name, because of the many passages in the Qur'ân that associate this sin with Lûṭ's people. The city associated with him, which was destroyed by God, is understood to be Sodom. The city was destroyed by *sijjîl*, stones of baked clay, similar to those that destroyed the armies of Abraha. Lûṭ's wife also perished both because she looked back against God's command and because she betrayed her husband to the evil townfolk. The Dead Sea is often called *Bahr Lûṭ*, Lûṭ's Sea, in Arabic.

luṭf (Arabic: kindness, benevolence)

Among theologians, *luṭf*, used in the QUR'ÂN to mean God's kindness and benevolence to humans, is used to indicate God's grace or help. The MU'TAZILAH used this concept to explain how humans could have freedom of choice and action in the face of God's omnipotence and prescience. Derivative forms of this root are used commonly among Arabic-speaking Muslims as given names, such as Luṭuf and Laṭîfah.

M

Madanî, ʿAbbâsî (born 1931)

Algerian Islamist, and founder in 1989 of the Islamic Salvation Front (FIS), after serving with the National Liberation Front (FLN) to free Algeria from the French. He espouses an Islamic-based program meant to counter Western humanistic and political influences in the Islamic world.

madhhab (Arabic: movement; pl. *madhâhib*)

In SUNNÎ Islam, the word is primarily used to refer to one of the four major "schools" of Islamic law, the ḤANAFÎ, the ḤANBALÎ, the MÂLIKÎ, and the Shâfiʿî. It also implies one's doctrine, creed, or philosophy of life.

Madînah (Arabic: city)

The city of the prophet in the western part of the Arabian Peninsula. In pre-Islamic times, it was known as YATHRIB, and was an agricultural town inhabited by Jews and polytheistic Arabs. The two main Arab tribes were AL-'AWS and AL-KHAZRAJ. The Jews who were settled in the town probably came after the destruction of the Temple in 70 C.E. as part of a general migration of Jews from Palestine into Arabia. There is evidence, however, that a number of Arabs had converted to Judaism and settled in the town. The population was so intermingled that there were Jews in "Arab" tribes and vice versa, and all tribes had relations with bedouin tribes surrounding the town. This complexity and the lack of resources had produced serious tensions among all the inhabitants and seems to have been one of the reasons that MUḤAMMAD was invited to come to mediate. When Muḥammad made his HIJRAH from MECCA in 622, the city submitted to his rule, but the process of converting all the population was a slow one. The mixed population was ruled by the CONSTITUTION OF MADÎNAH, which established each religious group with rights and obligations, with Muḥammad as the arbiter of disputes. This agreement and its implementation formed the basis for later Islamic rules for non-Muslims. The stresses of the battles of BADR and Uḥud identified the ambivalent converts and those who were in collusion with the Meccan forces, and they were removed from the city. Some of the major Jewish tribes were expelled, but a large Jewish population remained in the city until well after Muḥammad's death. From the period of the *hijrah* to the death of the Prophet, the inhabitants of the city participated in many of the raids, and when the armies of expansion went north into Syria and Mesopotamia, they were well represented. One of the results was that captured non-Arabs were brought back to the city, and many of them converted to Islam and were

Pilgrims at the Prophet's Mosque, Madînah.

manumitted. This helped make Madînah a center for the non-Arab Muslim political sentiment that focused around ʿALÎ B. ABÎ ṬÂLIB. When the conflict over the caliphate moved to Syria, Madînah became a provincial town out of the mainstream of Islamic politics. As it dropped from the political scene, it grew as an intellectual center and one of the leading locations for the development of the Islamic sciences and Islamic law (SHARÎʿAH). In modern times, the city has prospered somewhat from pilgrim traffic and from an immigration of retired Muslims who wish to spend their last days in the Prophet's city. It is now part of the WAHHÂBÎ kingdom of SAUDI ARABIA, and it is reported that the Wahhâbis, when they first entered the city in the mid-1920s, destroyed the elaborate tombs of the Companions, (ṢAḤÂBAH) and the Prophet's family out of puritanical zeal. Most of the population is SUNNÎ, but there are some SHÎʿÎ living there, including a servile pariah class, the *nakhâwilah*, who are not allowed to live in the city, stay overnight, or bury their dead in the cemetery. They perform menial tasks and rent their houses to Shîʿî pilgrims during the ḤAJJ. Madînah has the epithets *al-munawwarah*, "the radiant" and *al-fâḍilah*, "the virtuous." By custom, it is one of the sites visited by pilgrims when on the *ḥajj*.

madrasah (Arabic: school)

A place of study, a school or college, usually for religious education and early associated with mosques. A *madrasah* was both a place of study and a residence for students and teachers. It was often subsidized by the charitable endowment of a WAQF and was the foundation of Islamic learning, teaching literacy through the study of QUR'ÂN and ḤADÎTH. As a part of Islamic education, the mosque started as a center for Islamic learning, particularly those mosques that were not the central, congregational mosques. These mosque-schools soon attracted students who lived near or in the mosque, and apartments and refectories were added to the complex. As these became subsidized by *waqf*s, they took on a permanent character of centers of learning with places of worship attached. The architectural development took place at the same time as the transformation of the Islamic curriculum. What had been a simple curriculum of Qur'ân and *ḥadîth* evolved into a set of Islamic sciences centered on the rise and study of Islamic jurisprudence (FIQH). As the different schools of law (MADHHABS) evolved, each developed its own schools and curricula. In addition to instruction in law, these schools trained the bureaucrats for the state, which meant that additional subjects were added. In the face of FÂṬIMID SHÎ'Î missionary activity, the SUNNÎ SULṬÂN Ṣalâḥ ad-Dîn b. 'Ayyûb is credited with founding a great number of *madrasah*s as a means of educating his subjects to be loyal to Sunnî Islam and to train them for government service. While medicine was normally taught in separate institutions, over time it, together with other sciences, was added to the curricula of some *madrasah*s. This was the exception, and most *madrasah*s remained schools of Islamic learning. The institution of the *madrasah* had a profound effect on Western education through its influence on the University of Naples. The emperor Frederick II Hohenstaufen was influenced by the *madrasah* system he knew in Egypt, and recreated it in his foundation of the University of Naples in the early thirteenth century as the first state university in Europe for the training of loyal state functionaries. The idea soon took hold, and the majority of universities in Europe two centuries later were on this model. The building of *madrasah*s has been an important part of the spread of Islam throughout the world. India, Pakistan, Malaysia, and Indonesia, to name a few Islamic countries, have developed *madrasah*s as part of their education systems. (*See also* KUTTÂB; PESANTREN.)

Maghrib (Arabic: the place of the sunset)

The west; North Africa. There is no agreement on the eastern limit of this geographic term, but it generally excludes Egypt. To the west, it reaches to the Atlantic Ocean. When Muslims dominated Sicily and Iberia, those regions were included as well. To the south, the designation goes as far as the limits of the Sahara desert and excludes the rest of Africa. The *ṣalât al-maghrib* is the sunset prayer.

Mahdî (Arabic: the one who is rightly guided)

The Mahdî is a figure who is prominently featured in the eschatology of all branches of Islam. He will come at the end of time to restore right religion and justice and will rule before the world comes to an end. The term does not appear as such in the QUR'ÂN, but the root h-d-y, meaning "divine guidance," does occur frequently. Some of the earliest uses of the term occur with the SHÎ'Î in reference to the IMÂM AL-ḤUSAYN after he was martyred. The Shî'î identify this figure with all the *Imâm*s and the role is said to have been passed from one to another until the present *Imâm*, who is in occultation, (GHAYBAH), to return at the *eschaton*. Among the Sunnî, there is no consistent belief that a rightly guided figure will appear at the last days to restore Islam. The 'ABBÂSIDS claimed the role, and the second caliph was called al-Mahdî, but they had little success in persuading the majority of Muslims. In the various speculations about the YAWM AD-DÎN, the Mahdî is given differing roles and importance. In ṢÛFÎ thought, the Mahdî is expected to come with JESUS as his WAZÎR to impose true Islamic rule. A number of political figures throughout history have made the claim to be the Mahdî, including MUḤAMMAD 'UBAYD ALLÂH, the first FÂṬIMID Caliph, IBN

TÛMART, the founder of the Almohad movement, Shaykh Usuman DAN FODIO of Sokoto, who established a JIHÂD-based Islamic rule in Nigeria, and MUḤAMMAD AḤMAD B. ʿABDÛLLAH of the Sudan.

Mahdiyyah

The movement named after MUḤAMMAD AḤMAD B. ʿABDULLAH al-Mahdî, which, in the last two decades of the nineteenth century succeeded in forming the Republic of Sudan on Islamic principles.

maḥmal (Arabic: bearer)

The ornate palanquin sent by Islamic rulers in medieval times on the ḤAJJ as a sign of their wealth, authority, and political power.

Maḥmûd, Muṣṭafâ (born 1921)

Egyptian Islamist writer, philosopher, and scientist, he was trained as a physician and practiced from 1952 to 1966, when he turned his full attention to Islamist writings. One of his main causes has been social welfare and health care on Islamic terms. He is an outspoken critic of recent proposed reforms at AL-AZHAR and also presents a popular television program on Qur'ân and science.

mahr (Arabic: dowry)

The bride-price given by a bridegroom to a bride. The *mahr* belongs to the bride and is hers to keep in the case of divorce. She is entitled to half if the marriage ends before consummation. The amount varies widely, since an amount is not stipulated in SHARÎʿAH. It forms a necessary part of the marriage contract, and the marriage is not valid without it. There is concern in Islamic law that the *mahr* should not be either too high or too low. In legal discussions, it is clear that it should not be regarded as purchase money, because the bride in Islam is not to be regarded as property. By custom, the amount of the *mahr* is negotiated by the agents of the two who are to be married, and the station of each is taken into consideration in calculating the amount.

majlis (Arabic: a place to sit)

From a pre-Islamic use meaning a meeting place or tribal council, under Islam it came to mean the public audience granted by the caliph or the SULṬÂN. Sometimes the *majlis* would be for public entertainment, in which the ruler would invite guests and musicians, and serve food and drink. More regularly, the term was understood to be a public forum for the conduct of political matters and judgment. In legal and academic circles, when a professor held a *majlis* the session would be for teaching and would normally take place in a MASJID (mosque) or a MADRASAH. Among the ISMÂʿÎLÎ SHÎʿÎ, the term means a formal session of religious instruction. Among SHÎʿÎ in India, the *majlis* is an assembly for mourning the martyrdom of AL-ḤUSAYN at KARBALÂ'. In modern Islamic circles, it has been applied more widely to mean a parliamentary body with legislative or deliberative powers, or in revolutionary circles as the revolutionary council.

al-Majlisî, Muḥammad Bâqir (1037/1628–1110/1698)

A late ṢAFAVID SHÎʿÎ writer whose prolific output in both Persian and Arabic did much to promote Shîʿî thought in Iran and to discourage Ṣûfism. After receiving a broad education, he decided to specialize in traditions about the Prophet, even though that was a less lucrative career path. He then devoted himself to lecturing and studying Shîʿî thought and translating what he learned into Persian for easy dissemination among his students. He was appointed SHAYKH AL-ISLÂM or MULLÂBÂSHÎ in 1098/1686, and began to repress and eliminate everything he regarded as heresy (BIDʿAH), such as the prevalent ṢÛFÎ practices. Some of his more famous pronouncements on Shîʿî doctrine include his declaration that the SUNNÎ caliphs ABÛ BAKR, ʿUMAR, and ʿUTHMÂN were hypocrites, (MUNÂFIQÛN), and were cursed by God. His works continue to be studied in Iran today.

majûs (Arabic: Zoroastrian)

The *majûs*, a term originally applied to an Iranian caste of ruling priests, was applied by the Arabs more generally to anyone who was a Zoroastrian. Relying on interpretations of the QUR'ÂN, the Zoroastrians were counted among the AHL AL-KITÂB.

Makhzûm

An important tribe of the QURAYSH. They were a source of strong opposition to MUḤAMMAD, but became reconciled. One of their most famous members, KHÂLID B. AL-WALÎD, became a prominent Muslim general.

Makkah

See MECCA.

makrûh (Arabic: hateful)

In Islamic Law, an act that is hateful.

maktab (Arabic: a place for writing)

This term is sometimes used for a primary school. (*See also* KUTTÂB.)

maktabah (Arabic: library)

The development of the institution of the library is closely linked to the development of the MADRASAH. Often, libraries were associated with those institutions of higher learning, and rulers prided themselves on their library collections. The ʿABBÂSID BAYT AL-ḤIKMAH was just such an institution, and the caliph and his WAZÎRS endowed both the collection of books, and the places to house them. Libraries were catalogued according to subject, and many were open to the public, providing paper, pens, and ink for the patrons. Usually a fee was charged if a book were taken from the building. Some private libraries had funds in their endowments to lodge scholars from distant lands. (*See also* WAQF.)

malak

See ANGEL.

Malaysia

The predominantly Muslim country of Malaysia, strategically located between the Indian Ocean and the South China Sea, has a mixed population of Chinese, Indian, and Malay peoples. Before the advent of Islam in the fifteenth century, the country was influenced by Hindu, Buddhist, and animist religions, some elements of which remain in the popular culture. The Muslim population is predominantly SUNNÎ, following the Shâfiʿî MADHHAB but influenced by ṢÛFÎ thought. Since independence from the British in the 1960s, Malaysians have sought to build an Islamic-based, pluralistic society independent of outside influences. The official languages are English and Bahasa Malaya, but Arabic is widely taught in Muslim schools.

Malcolm X (1925–65)

Born Malcolm Little in Omaha, Nebraska, he converted to Islam after enduring a life of racism and imprisonment for larceny. In 1948, he joined ELIJAH MUḤAMMAD's NATION OF ISLAM and was appointed head of the Harlem Temple in New York. By 1964, he had risen to such political and

The New Federal Mosque, Kuala Lumpur, Malaysia.

religious prominence that he was forced to withdraw from his position of leadership. His advocacy of changes in the direction of the Nation of Islam, to bring it more in line with SUNNÎ Islam, promote the teaching of Arabic, and increase the association of members of the Nation of Islam with other Muslims in the world caused his expulsion from the organization. That event and his experience of the ḤAJJ transformed him, and he took the name El-Hajj Malik El-Shabazz. He was assassinated on 21 February 1965 by members of the Nation of Islam, with the reputed complicity of some American government authorities. His *Autobiography* is a staple in anti-racist curricula in American schools.

Mali

The Republic of Mali has been an Islamic region for over nine hundred years, during which time it has been a center of trade, with Timbuktu as its most famous city. During French colonial occupation, WAHHÂBÎ influence increased and has come in conflict with the older ṢÛFÎ-influenced practices, with the result that a number of Islamist movements have successfully resisted the socialist and secular governments that have ruled the country since its independence in 1960.

Mâlik

The angel who is the guardian of Hell.

Mâlik b. ʾAnas, Abû ʿAbd Allâh (94/716–179/795)

The eponym of the MÂLIKÎ MADHHAB of Islamic law. He was the author of the first major treatise on FIQH, *al-Muwaṭṭaʾ*. He spent most of his career in MADÎNAH, teaching disciples, who developed his ideas into a *madhhab* in his name. A legend, arising from a misinterpretation of a saying attributed to him, says that he spent three years in his mother's womb. Another tradition says that he wanted to become a singer, but was advised by his mother to become a traditionist, because he was too ugly. He studied with a great number of traditionists. He achieved a good reputation and, while he tried to remain aloof from politics, was ill-treated during some of the changes of governance of Madînah. In his monumental work, which is the earliest surviving work on Islamic law, he set out to write a survey of all law, justice, ritual practice, and religious conduct in Madînah according to the SUNNAH of the city. His work was not, however, finished in a definitive edition, but comes to us in some fifteen different versions. Nevertheless, the mere fact of codifying the law had a profound effect on Islamic legal development, since it provided a basis for the further elaboration of the principles of law (ʾUṢÛL AL-FIQH.)

Mâlikî

The MADHHAB named after MÂLIK B. ʾANAS. It is based on the legal practices developed in the city of MADÎNAH. This SUNNÎ school of law is regarded as somewhat conservative and dependent on tradition. The Mâlikî *madhhab* is similar to the other schools of law in Islam, but differs on some specific points. It remains neutral about the legitimacy of the succession of ʿALÎ B. ABÎ ṬÂLIB. It also adds the IJMÂʿ (consensus) of Madînah to that of Muslims in general. The school is particularly harsh on schismatics, ṢÛFÎs and SHÎʿÎ. This made it a popular and useful school for the ʿABBÂSIDS. The school was quite active in sending out missionaries, and it is found among Muslims around the world, particularly in North Africa.

Mamlûk, or mamlûk (Arabic: owned, possessed as a slave)

This became the name of the dynasty that ruled in Egypt, Syria into southeast Asia Minor, and the northeast quadrant of Arabia from 648/1250 to 922/1516–17. It was founded by Turkic and Circassian slave-soldiers, and Mamlûk armies defeated the MONGOLS in 658/1260 at the battle of ʿAyn Jalût in Palestine, and ushered in a golden age of Egyptian high culture. Baybars, an uncle of the ʿABBÂSID caliph in BAGHDÂD who had been killed by the Mongols, was installed in Cairo as SULṬÂN in 1260, with the aim of restoring the caliphate in Egypt. The dynasty was defeated by the OTTOMANS in 922/1516–17, but the dynasts continued as local rulers and princes under the Ottomans until Napoleon Bonaparte's invasion of Egypt in 1798. The institution of slave dynasties has been a hallmark of pre-modern Islamic societies. From an early date, many free Muslims regarded association with the government as corrupting and distasteful. The rulers found themselves in need of standing armies that would be loyal to them and protect their power. A ready source of such military might was to be found among the Turks who were being conquered along the expanding frontiers. These Turks, already trained as soldiers, found the duty and privileges attractive and became the palace guards for many rulers. Since they had no natural support base in the larger society in which they were slaves, their loyalties were toward their masters, the rulers. They were brought by Muslim merchants and placed in special barracks for their training. This training consisted of military education and education in the basics of Islam. Once they graduated from this training, they were manumitted and made simple soldiers, with, however, the possibility of rising to the rank of officer because of their superior training. Even when freed, the *mamlûk* retained ties to his owner/patron and was dependent on the influence of that individual for his advancement. The children of the *mamlûk*s could not themselves be in the same military order, and many of the more powerful

Mamlûks established WAQFS for their children to provide a livelihood for them. They were separated from the rest of society by their customs and their language, which was, for the most part, Turkish. They provided a formidable army for the states in which they ruled, and the Mamlûk army of Egypt was the force that stopped the Mongol invasion of the Middle East. Religiously, they were quite staunchly SUNNÎ, and sought to maintain their religious views where they reigned. The Mamlûk sultanate ruled over Egypt from 648/1250 to 922/1517, and over Syria from 658/1260 to 922/1516.

Manâf

Pre-Islamic god worshipped among the QURAYSH and other tribes of northwest Arabia. We know little about this deity except the lists that are preserved by Muslim scholars. From the name, it would appear that he was an astral deity. His idols were located in the KA'BAH and menstruating women kept away from them.

al-Manâr (Arabic: the light)

An Islamic journal published by RASHÎD RIḌÂ, it was a source for ideas about resistance to colonialism and the restoration of Islam. It appeared in Cairo from 1898 to 1940.

Manât

Important female deity of the pre-Islamic period, she is usually associated with AL-LÂT and AL-'UZZÂ as the so-called "daughters" of ALLÂH. Evidence from the ancient Near East shows that this goddess was very ancient. Her name appears in early Akkadian, and is one of the names associated with Ishtar. In Palmyra she is shown as a seated deity, holding a scepter, and is represented as the goddess of fate. In Arabia, her worship location was close to YATHRIB/MADÎNAH, and she was worshiped by the two Arab tribes of that city, AL-'AWS and AL-KHAZRAJ. She was linked with al-Lât and al-'Uzzâ, probably as part of the process of the federation of the cult by the Meccans, but Ugaritic evidence has three linked female deities as the daughters of Ba'al, so this linkage may represent a similar phenomenon.

mansûkh

See NÂSIKH WA-MANSÛKH.

maqâm (Arabic: site, place pl. *maqâmât*)

A sacred place or the tomb of a saint. Among the ṢÛFÎ, it refers to a stage of spiritual development.

marabout (from Arabic *murâbiṭ*)

A term used primarily in North Africa for an ascetic sequestered and trained in a garrison called a RIBÂṬ and who attained spiritual and military prowess. The term can refer to a "saint," either male or female, who can perform miracles, and it can be passed as an epithet to the descendants. The term is also applied to garrisoned soldiers, particularly along a frontier.

al-Marâghî, Muṣṭafâ (1881–1945)

A protégé of MUḤAMMAD 'ABDUH, he served as rector of AL-AZHAR in 1928 and from 1935 to 1945. He promoted the introduction of modern science in the curriculum and advocated modernist reforms of Islam in Egypt, while still keeping Islam and the role of the 'ULAMÂ' central.

Mâriyah the Copt

The Christian slave given to MUḤAMMAD by an Egyptian notable. She became his concubine, and he was very devoted to her. She became the mother of his son, IBRÂHÎM B. MUḤAMMAD, who died in infancy. According to tradition a solar eclipse occurred that day, which, if true, meant that he died on 27 January 632, shortly before Muḥammad's death. She was honored by ABÛ BAKR and given a pension that lasted until her death in 637.

Marji' at-Taqlîd (Arabic: the source of imitation)

An epithet of the ÂYATOLÂHS in SHÎ'Î Islam of the highest rank, who have the privilege of IJTIHÂD. *Âyatollâh* Rûḥollâh KHOMEINÎ was regarded by his followers in this category, as was the Iraqî Abol-Qâsem KHO'I. The title implies that lay people can and should follow their views.

marriage

The QUR'ÂN provides the basis for Islamic law on marriage, but, as with other laws of personal status, either attenuates existing practice or is complemented by provisions in SHARÎ'AH. These provisions vary by region, legal school, or division of Islam. Fundamentally, marriage is a contract between a man and a woman over the age of majority and/or her WALÎ, or guardian, subject to the terms of the negotiated contract. While it is supervised under Islamic law, it is not regarded as a religious sacrament, as in Christianity. Polygamy is permitted by the Qur'ân, but restricted by rules of fairness and equity. This has led some to declare that only monogamy may be practiced by ordinary Muslims, a position that has been incorporated into Tunisian law. Just as past regional practice was both tolerated and sometimes incorporated into *sharî'ah*, modern law codes in Muslim countries have incorporated both regional customs and Western practices. In a number of Muslim countries, scholars are harking back to the time of the Qur'ân and early community practice, when women had more status, political freedom, and autonomy, as a means of reforming modern Islamic marriage laws and other laws of personal status. In ITHNÂ 'ASHARIYYAH SHÎ'Î Islam, a temporary marriage, called MUT'AH, is permitted, the term of which ends at a preset time, rather than by DIVORCE.

A Pakistani Muslim couple on their wedding day.

martyr

See SHAHÎD.

Maryam (Arabic)

The name of the mother of 'Îsâ (JESUS) in the QUR'ÂN. She is the only woman called by her proper name in the Qur'ân, and her life and position are expanded and exalted in the TAFSÎR literature. The Qur'ân honors Maryam greatly, saying in Q. 23:50: "We made the son of Maryam and his mother a sign." The angel JIBRÎL comes to her in the form of a perfect man and announces the birth of ʿÎsâ. The "virgin" birth is mentioned in Q. 66:12, where God says that He breathed His Spirit into her. When ʿÎsâ was born, he spoke from the cradle to those who were scandalized by Maryam's bearing a child, telling them that he was a servant of ALLÂH and a prophet (NABÎ). Maryam is highly venerated in Muslim popular religion. In places where Muslims and Christians live together, such as Egypt, Muslim women have taken Maryam and FÂṬIMAH as models for behavior and sources of solace in times of trouble. In AL-QUDS (Jerusalem), for example, Jews, Christians, and Muslims visit the *ḥammâm sittî Maryam*, the bath of Maryam, where it is believed that Maryam bathed. It is thought to be a cure for childlessness. In the nineteenth century, when Protestant missionaries came to the Near East, some Muslims chided them for not being good Christians, because they did not hold Maryam in sufficient reverence. Maryam is also the name of the nineteenth chapter of the Qur'ân.

masâ'il wa-ajwibah (Arabic: question and answer)

One of the techniques that developed in Muslim higher education was the instruction of students by means of a set of questions and answers. The student was to memorize both the questions and answers, and, when examined, be ready to take either part. This technique started with Qur'ânic instruction and then moved into the legal curriculum. From there, it became part of the medical and scientific curriculum. At its most advanced form, it was part of the training for missionary activity (DAʿWAH). There is some evidence that this technique influenced the medieval European *quaestiones et responsiones* pedagogic techniques through the translations of Islamic scientific works into Latin.

mâ shâ' Allâh (Arabic: what God willed)

This phrase occurs in several places in the QUR'ÂN, and has passed into general use in the Islamic world. Its primary use indicates acceptance of what has happened as having come from the will of ALLÂH. It is also used to express wonder or surprise. In some Islamic countries, the phrase is thought to have a prophylactic effect when worn written on amulets or on the sides of taxicabs and trucks. It can also be used as a personal name.

maṣḥaf (Arabic: book, volume)

A complete copy of the text of the QUR'ÂN. The word was applied to the earliest collections of the text, but there is some debate about whether that meant a collection of the complete text between boards or pages of the text, *suḥûf*. By the second Islamic century, the word was applied to a physical copy of the full text of the Qur'ân, bound and in proper order.

Mashhad (Arabic)

An important city in the northeastern area of Iran. The town, close to the pre-Islamic town of Ṭûs, is the site of the tomb of the ʿABBÂSID caliph Hârûn ar-Rashîd and the tomb of the eighth SHÎʿÎ IMÂM, ʿAlî ar-Riḍâ. The name Mashhad means "a place where a hero or saint has died," as well as "a funeral cortege." For the ITHNÂ ʿASHARIYYAH SHÎʿÎ the term refers to the tombs of the *Imâm*s, all of whom died as martyrs, and it is from the Shîʿî use and the veneration of the tomb of the *Imâm* that the city gets its name. It seems to have grown from a little village to a major city on the strength of pilgrim traffic, which was operative as early as the eighth/fourteenth century, according to the famous traveler IBN BAṬṬÛṬAH. It is currently an industrial and agricultural center as well as a place of pilgrimage.

al-Masîḥ (Arabic: the anointed)

An epithet usually associated with JESUS, it is related to the Hebrew word for Messiah. The Qur'ânic usage, however, differs from the Jewish and Christian meaning, since Jesus in Islam does not have the same function as a messiah. It seems, rather, to be used as a title or epithet indicating Jesus' exalted role as a prophet. In the HADÎTHS, we are informed that those who say, "We have worshiped *al-Masîḥ* b. Maryam" will have earned a place in Hell. In personal names in Arabic, al-Masîḥî indicates a Christian.

masjid (Arabic: a place of prostration)

A mosque. In Qur'ânic and early Islamic usage it merely meant a place of prayer, and so could be any ritually acceptable place. One of the fundamental notions in Islam is that one can pray anywhere, since God is everywhere. This meant that the institution of the SAJJÂDAH or prayer carpet as a portable holy spot for worship could be taken around the world, or, even, into space. The communal need for fixed places of worship with facilities to become ritually pure for prayer developed quickly as the community grew in MADÎNAH after the HIJRAH. As Muslim religious ARCHITECTURE developed *masjid* came to refer to a place of congregational worship that had facilities for ABLUTIONS, a MINARET for the call to prayer, a *minbar* or pulpit for a sermon, and a MIḤRÂB or niche to indicate the QIBLAH, the direction of prayer. It was used as a center for worship, but also the center of community life. So important was the model that MUḤAMMAD had established by building the *masjid* in Madînah, that Muslims established mosques wherever they went spreading Islam. Architectural styles of mosques vary, often reflecting the style of the region and the time period. Sometimes mosques have been converted churches, and sometimes they have been built to look like churches, depending on the local architectural idiom and aesthetic. Mosques in America have usually been built with strong Near Eastern architectural characteristics to set them apart from other houses of worship and mark the distinctiveness of the community. In some communities, however, there are store-front mosques, and mosques in apartments. In this, they follow the patterns of both churches and synagogues. Many American mosques have added functions as Islamic community centers, with kitchens and banquet facilities for life-cycle events. Some mosques house the bodies of deceased saints and serve as shrines for veneration as well as places for prayer. An active mosque will have a place for ablutions, GHUSL and WUḌÛ', and will have carpets on the floor. It will contain lamps, both for reading and as a symbol of God as Light, (NÛR). There will be some indication of the direction of MECCA, the *qiblah*, particularly if the original orientation of the building is not toward the KA'BAH. There will also be a *minbar*, for the delivery of the sermon. Most mosques are financed by the community, but some are endowed with WAQFS. There is no official priesthood in Islam, but from early times caretakers have been appointed to look after the property. The earliest of these mosque employees were the popular preachers (*qâṣṣ*) who also served as educators. In larger mosques, the prayer leader or (IMÂM), is assisted by a financial manager and a staff. In many Muslim countries the organization and maintenance of the mosques is seen as a state duty and handled through the state bureaucracy, including the appointment of the *imâm*. Another important member of the mosque staff is the MU'ADHDHIN, the person who calls to prayer. While this function is being taken over by automated recordings in some modern communities, the heirs of BILÂL have served an important function in calling the faithful to the five daily prayers.

al-Masjid al-Aqṣâ (Arabic: the most remote place of worship)

By community consensus since the second Islamic century, this has meant AL-QUDS (Jerusalem). In some of the earliest commentaries on the QUR'ÂN, however, it was understood to be a location on the edge of the sacred precinct around MECCA. The site, wherever it is, is connected with MUḤAMMAD's night journey and his ascent to heaven (MI'RÂJ), which is also connected to Jerusalem. It now refers to the mosque that is located on the south side of the platform that is AL-ḤARAM ASH-SHARÎF, that is, south of the Dome of the Rock (QUBBAT AṢ-ṢAKHRAH). The present structure has been built over an earlier structure, access to which is still possible, and the lower level is used for worship. (*See also* ISRÂ'.)

al-masjid al-ḥarâm

The Great Mosque in MECCA. (*See also* KA'BAH.)

maskh (Arabic: metamorphosis)

In several places in the QUR'ÂN, we are told that God transformed sinners into animals. Q. 2:65 says that Sabbath-breakers were turned into apes, and Q. 5:60 that sinners were turned into monkeys and pigs. Commentators confronted with the reality of the Qur'ânic statements and with the pre-Islamic legend of Isâf and Na'ilah, who were turned to stone in the KA'BAH, discussed both the theology and the physics of such transformations. Some, noting that no transformations had occurred after the rise of Islam, concluded that this was not a punishment used by God in this era.

maṣlaḥah (Arabic: public welfare)

The principle in the SHARÎ'AH of public interest or public welfare by which new circumstances and the requirements of the law can be accommodated to meet the needs of Muslims in any age.

matn (Arabic: prose text)

The prose body of the text of a ḤADÎTH, usually short, containing the message of

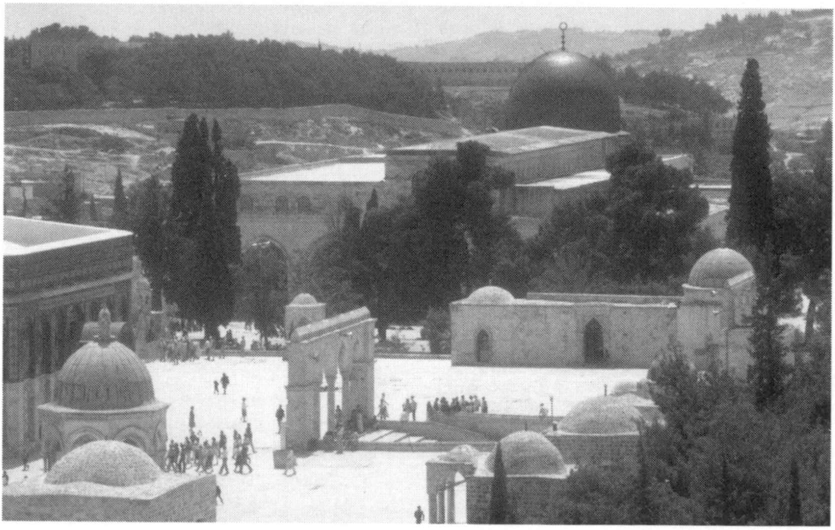

Al-Masjid al-Aqṣâ Mosque, al-Quds (Jerusalem).

the tradition, as opposed to the authenticating chain of transmitters, the ISNÂD. The word was used in the pre-Islamic period meaning prose text, and was associated with the *ayyâm al-Arab* (battle days of the Arabs) traditions.

al-Mâturidî, Abû Manṣûr Muḥammad b. Muḥammad b. Maḥmûd as-Samarqandî (died 333/934)

The titular founder of Mâturîdism, one of the two orthodox SUNNÎ schools of theology, the other being the school founded by AL-ASH'ARÎ. Almost nothing is known about his personal life except that he led an ascetic life and that there were miracles (*karâmât*) ascribed to him after his death. He was a member of the ḤANAFÎ MADHHAB, unlike the other schools of KALÂM in Sunnî Islam. He was a rationalist in his views and a strong polemicist against other religions. He held, among other things, that humans have the capacity and the obligation to learn about, thank, and worship God through the powers of reason given us by God. Prophetic revelation is a gift from God. The anthropomorphic expressions about God in the QUR'ÂN are, for him, metaphors, but he ultimately held that Prophetic revelation should be accepted without question. He believed, against the views of the MU'TAZILAH, that the beatific vision was possible, but not in the usual, corporeal sense. He also held that God's speech, *kalâm*, was an eternal attribute of God, but that it could not be heard by human ears. He took an intermediary position on the question of free will, holding that humanity has real and not just illusionary free choice, so that God's rewards and punishments are just. The school of *kalâm* to which he gave his name remained in the Ḥanafî *madhhab* and was less influenced by philosophy and science than were the Ash'arîtes.

Mawdûdî, Sayyid Abû al-A'lâ (1321/1903–1398/1979)

Muslim writer, thinker, and political activist. His prolific output has influenced the course of many Muslim movements in the twentieth century. Born in South Asia under British colonial rule, he came from a family that produced a number of spiritual leaders. He received a sheltered Muslim education at home, and, when his father died, went to work as a journalist. He became involved in the KHILÂFAT MOVEMENT, and, through this, got to know many 'ULAMÂ', who helped him learn Arabic. He also learned English at this point. After a period of study of the history and nature of Islam, he began preaching to his fellow Muslims that they were a separate people within India and that Islam has a universal message for all peoples. Mawdûdî developed a strong anti-colonial and, later, a strong anti-nationalist attitude that helped shape his pan-Islamic program of Islamic revival. In his view, the dialectic struggle between Islam and non-Islam should energize religious piety toward social activism to bring about an Islamic state that would effect sweeping social reforms. He was not, however, an advocate for violent, mass-movement revolution and held that education was essential for social change. The formation of PAKISTAN gave him a forum for his ideas, and he was instrumental in shaping the new country's constitution. Mawdûdî was a prolific writer on almost all Islamic and social topics. His *Tafhîm al-Qur'ân* is the most widely read translation and commentary in URDU. His ultimate aim was to create a system of Islamic thought that would counter the modern world on Islamic and not reactionary terms. He drew heavily on the past for his ideal, but did not neglect the problems of the present. His thought continues to have wide influence throughout the Islamic world. (*See also* JAMÂ'AT-I ISLÂMÎ.)

mawlâ (Arabic)

Derived from the Arabic verb *waliya*, "to be close or near," the term can mean "master," "slave," "client," or, with the definite article, *al-mawlâ*, "the Master," i.e. God. In early Islamic circles, it often referred to a non-Arab Muslim who had become a client of an Arab tribe or had been a slave and was manumitted. In this case, although the word implies a degree of equality, the *mawlâ* is the social inferior of the Arab master. It is sometimes used in this sense as synonymous with *ʿajam*, non-Arab or Persian. Because many non-Arabs became prominent in governmental and clerical positions, the term came to be commonly used as a title of respect for government and religious authorities, as in its Persian form, *mullâ* or *mullah*, a person who has attained the lowest rank of the SHÎʿÎ ʿULAMÂʾ and is authorized to teach, preach, and officiate at religious rituals. In the form *mawlây*, meaning "my lord," it is applied to ṢÛFÎ saints and high government officials.

Mawlawiyyah

See MEVLEVÎ.

mawlid, or mîlâd (Arabic: birthday, anniversary)

The *mawlid an-nabî* is the birthday celebration of the Prophet, celebrated on the twelfth of Rabiʿ al-ʾAwwal in the Islamic lunar calendar. Except in SAUDI ARABIA, where WAHHÂBÎ prohibitions forbid, it is marked throughout the Muslim world with happy festivities. The celebration of the Prophet's birthday became a regular part of Islamic festivities only fairly late. The first recorded public celebration is from the sixth/twelfth century, although pious pilgrims had been visiting his birthplace, which had been enlarged into a shrine by the mother of the ʿABBASID caliph Hârûn ar-Rashîd (145/756–169/785). The main feature of the celebration of the *mawlid* is the recitation of a poetic panegyric that begins with praise of God, lists MUḤAMMAD's ancestry, tells of the annunciation to ÂMINAH of the Prophet's birth, and then tells of his birth. These panegyrics, also called *mawlid*s, are usually recited in Arabic, but are also found in the variety of Islamic languages throughout the world. Popular poems are printed and distributed widely. When the *mawlid*s are sponsored by states and rulers, the processions and poetry recitations are very elaborate. Celebratory meals also accompany the *mawlid*s, often including the eating of sweets with honey, the Prophet's favorite treat. In some parts of the Islamic world, the *mawlid* does not need to follow the Islamic calendar and can be celebrated on the occasion of other births or at the rite of passage of boys into adulthood. The term *mawlid* also refers to the birth or death anniversary celebrations of holy persons, or WALÎs, who are thought to be bringers of *barakât* (blessings). Such celebrations usually focus around the tomb of the holy person and feature a ZIYÂRAH, or circumambulation of the shrine and the offering of food and/or incense. In some communities, this is the occasion for the circumcision of young boys. Many *mawlid* celebrations include non-Muslims as well as Muslims in the veneration of the holy person and the ceremony of the *ziyârah*. Often the celebration has a fair-like atmosphere with entertainments and markets. Wahhâbî prohibition of the *mawlid* celebration is an extension of their general opposition to the veneration of saints, and the fact that women are active participants in these celebrations in many parts of the Islamic world.

mawlidiyyah (Arabic)

A panegyric poem composed and recited in honor of the Prophet for the MAWLID.

Many of these poems are in Arabic and follow classical Arabic ode patterns, but poems exist in almost all Islamic languages, each reflecting the poetic idiom of the language. Thus, for example, we find poems in Tamil written in the style of poems in praise of the baby Krishna, while the URDU poems follow the verse-idiom of South Asian songs.

Maymûnah bt. al-Ḥârith (died 61/681)

The last of MUḤAMMAD's wives, she was the sister of his uncle al-ʿAbbâs and survived the Prophet.

maysir (Arabic: easy; left-handed)

The QUR'ÂN forbids a game of chance that was popular in pre-Islamic Arabia, in which animals were slaughtered and divided into ten parts. Specially marked arrows were then drawn for the parts, with the winner taking an assigned portion of the slaughtered animal. Evidently large numbers of animals were slaughtered to play the game, resulting in great losses for some. The game seems also to have had some connection with pre-Islamic religious practice, and the casting of arrows was used to predict the future. This game became the symbol for all forms of gambling and gaming in Islam. By extension, all forms of games of chance were forbidden, including financial speculations, like the stock market, lending and borrowing money at interest, etc. In modern Islamic financial circles, ways around such prohibitions have been found. *See also* BANKS AND BANKING; RIBÂ.)

maytah (Arabic: something dead)

Anything killed without ritual slaughtering. Most schools of Islamic law (MADHHABS) prohibit the eating of animals that have not been properly slaughtered according to Islamic requirements even when they are otherwise permissible. Exceptions are locusts and fish, which do not have to be ritually slaughtered to be eaten. Some jurists permit the skin of a *maytah* to be tanned and used for leather, but others forbid its use. (*See also* HALÂL; ḤARÂM.)

maẓlûm (Arabic: ill-treated)

This is a term applied to the IMÂMS and others who show forbearance in the face of oppression. In SHÎʿÎ thought, the IMÂMS are thought to be, as a class, the victims of oppression and tyranny, and to have personified the virtues of modesty and forbearance under that oppression. They characterize the willingness of the *imâms* to accept martyrdom, to become a SHAHÎD. The model of this behavior is *Imâm* AL-ḤUSAYN, whose example shows the way to live and die in this world in order to achieve salvation in the next.

Mecca

Known to the ancient geographers as Macoraba and to the Arabs as Makkah, or sometimes Bakkah, it is the holiest city in Islam. Located in Northwest Arabia, it is the site of the KAʿBAH and the holy well of ZAMZAM, both objects of veneration in the ḤAJJ. The Prophet MUḤAMMAD was born there around 570 C.E. and received his first revelation in 610. He left the city for MADÎNAH in 622, but returned at the end of his life to cleanse the city of polytheistic worship and demonstrate the *ḥajj*. The city has a long history well back into pre-Islamic times. The ancient name Macoraba means "temple" in various Semitic languages. This probably referred to the Kaʿbah, which was an ancient place of sacrifice for the Arabs. According to Islamic legend, the city was founded by ADAM. It was the location to which HÂJAR and ISMÂʿÎL came after they were sent into the desert by IBRÂHÎM, and it was where Ibrâhîm and Ismâʿîl built the Kaʿbah. Arab tradition holds that the original Arabs were supplanted by the QURAYSH, probably some time in the fourth or fifth century, when they moved their trade from the Red Sea inland and onto camel caravans. By the time of Muḥammad, the city had become a major commercial center and had formed federations with the major tribes in the region. The Quraysh also federated Arabian worship and, after the manner of the Romans, had transferred the worship of all the local deities to the central shrine in Mecca, the Kaʿbah. Worship, then, was conducted by visiting the city for religious and trade fairs. The attack by the Ethiopian general ABRAHA was partly caused by Meccan commercial success, and is said to have happened in 570 C.E., the year of Muḥammad's birth. The city lost its political importance after the death of Muḥammad but retained its holy importance. It was the site of pilgrimage (*ḥajj*), but there are reports that it also became a center for singing girls and debauchery. It was unable to rival its sister city, Madînah, for intellectual activity, but its schools became places of study for students from all over the world. With the advent of the WAHHÂBIS, many of the shrines and coffee houses were razed out of puritanical zeal. In modern times and as a result of oil revenues, the city has been rebuilt, its shrines refurbished, and is better able to receive the annual throngs that visit it.

Mecelle (Turkish from Arabic *majallah*: law code)

The OTTOMAN ḤANAFÎ law code dating from 1285/1869.

Medina

See AL-MADÎNAH.

menstruation

Blood during the period of menstruation renders a woman ritually impure, during which time she is enjoined from touching the QUR'ÂN or engaging in ṢALÂT, but, according to a ḤADÎTH, she may perform the rites of the ḤAJJ. When the cycle is complete, GHUSL (ritual washing) removes the impurity. Three menstrual cycles or three periods of purity constitute the ʿIDDAH, or waiting period before a divorce becomes final.

Mernissi, Fatima (born 1940)

Moroccan sociologist, writer, and Islamic feminist, she received her Ph.D. in sociology from Brandeis University. Her writings have been both descriptive and activist. In her first book, *Beyond the Veil: Male–Female Dynamics in Modern Muslim Society* (1975), she sought to release Islamic discourse from patriarchal control. In her most recent book, *Islam and Democracy: Fear of the Modern World* (1992), she advocates a reformist approach free of fearful reactions to the West.

messenger

See RASÛL.

messianism

Muslims do not believe in a Messiah in the same sense as Jews or Christians, but the belief in an end-time figure, such as the MAHDÎ, who will come to deliver believers from tyranny and repression, has been a part of Muslim belief from the beginning. SUNNÎ and SHÎʿÎ views differ in their identification of the end-time figure, the ITHNÂ ʿASHARIYYAH SHÎʿÎ holding that the twelfth IMÂM is the awaited Mahdî.

Mevlevî, or Mevleviyya (Turkish)

Known in the West as the whirling dervishes because of their use of dance for their DHIKR or SAMÂʿ, this important ṢÛFÎ order was inspired and named after the Persian mystical poet Jalâl ad-Dîn

RÛMÎ, who held the epithet *mawlânâ*. The order had great influence on OTTOMAN art and music. It was banned by ATATÜRK in 1925 but their *samâ*ʿ continues to be performed at various places around the world.

Michael

See MÎKÂ'ÎL.

mîḍâ'ah, or mîḍa'ah (Arabic: washing place)

The fountain associated with a mosque for the WUḌÛ', or ABLUTIONS before prayer.

mi'dhânah, or ma'dhanah (Arabic)

See MINARET.

migration

See HIJRAH.

miḥnah (Arabic: test, trial)

The inquisition imposed by the ʿABBÂSID caliph al-Ma'mûn (170/786–218/833) to test his subjects' adherence to the notions of the MUʿTAZILAH, including the belief that the QUR'ÂN was created and not eternal. The inquisition continued until the reign of al-Mutawakkil (206/822–247/851). Several theological and political issues converged in this inquisition, which is remembered vividly in SUNNÎ hagiography. Many traditionalists (*ahl al-ḥadîth*) were tested and forced to renounce their belief that the Qur'ân was God's speech and was, therefore, eternal with God, for they could not imagine that God could have ever been silent. Those who did not were imprisoned and beaten. The most notable among those who refused was AḤMAD B. ḤANBAL, who became the symbol of resistance. From the perspective of the caliphs, their imposition of Muʿtazilite doctrine was an effort to assure that a correct, non-corrupted form of Islam was being taught, since they feared that Islam might deviate from the correct path in the way that they believed Judaism and Christianity had done. They were also interested in preserving centralized power over religious ideology against the developing power of the popular traditionists. The failure of the caliphs to impose the *miḥnah* ended their ability to assert freely that they were *khalîfat Allâh*, caliphs of God. They no longer had the ability to dictate the course of Islam. This triumph of traditionalism over caliphal authority made room for the development of Sunnî Islam. (*See also* MUḤADDITH.)

miḥrab (Arabic: niche)

The niche in a mosque indicating the QIBLAH or direction of prayer, it is usually highly decorated with tiles and mosaics. (*See also* MASJID.)

Mîkâ'îl

An archangel mentioned in the QUR'ÂN along with JIBRÎL, he is the guardian of places of worship. He and Jibrîl, were the two angels who opened Muḥammad's breast, washed his heart, and weighed him against all humankind.

mîlâd

See MAWLID.

millah

See MILLET.

millet (Turkish, from Arabic *millah*)

In Qur'ânic and early Islamic use, *millah* means "religion" and "religious community," as in the "religion of Ibrâhîm," (Q. 3:95). When the word is used with the definite article, *al-Millah*, it means the religious community, the 'UMMAH of Islam. Otherwise, it came to mean religious communities other than Islam, and usually People of the Book, AHL AL-KITÂB. In heresiographic literature, it was paired with *niḥal* (sects), and meant religious groups other than Muslims. In this latter sense, it was adopted as an OTTOMAN legal and administrative term to designate the religious groups in its empire. These groups were administered separately, each with its own code of law for governing internal affairs, and its own set of rulers. Eventually, Muslims came to be regarded as one of a group of religious claimants for recognition and court patronage. With the collapse of the empire and the identification of religious groups as national entities, the word has taken on the sense of "nation" in modern Turkish.

Minâ

A small town about three miles from MECCA that is central to the rites of the ḤAJJ. In the valley near Minâ, there are small stone pillars where pilgrims perform the lapidation, or stoning, of the devil. On the tenth of the month of DHÛ-L-ḤIJJAH, an animal is sacrificed as part of the *ḥajj*. The *ḥajj* ceremonies were practiced in pre-Islamic times, including the stone-throwing. (*See also* RAJM.)

minaret

Derived from the Arabic word *manârah*, "a light tower," the minaret is one of the most distinctive architectural symbols of Islam. Usually called a *mi'dhânah* or *ma'dhanah*, it is the place from which the ADHÂN or call to prayer is given, either in person by the MU'ADHDHIN or, in some modern settings, by recording. The minaret has assumed many different forms around the world and is considered a major component of a mosque, although not all mosques have them. (*See also* MASJID.)

minorities

See AHL AL-KITÂB; DHIMMI.

mîqât (Arabic: times)

This term is used in FIQH literature to refer to the fixed times for properly performing religious duties, such as the times for prayer (ṢALÂT), the times for beginning and ending fasting, and the times for putting on or taking off the IḤRÂM. Exact time-keeping became one of the major religious and intellectual activities of Muslims, which led to advancements in many scientific fields. Astronomy, mathematics, engineering, and navigation are all areas that benefited from the quest for more accurate ways to measure the passage of time. Modern time-pieces, which are the heirs to these earlier efforts, are capable of determining the exact time for each of the five prayers, the direction for prayer (QIBLAH), and announcing the call to prayer (*Adhân*).

miracle

Miracles associated with God's prophets are generally termed in Arabic *mu'jizah*. These are generally understood as God's direct intervention in the natural order of things to demonstrate His power in order to promote belief and confound and make weak those who disbelieve. For MUḤAMMAD, the miracle was the QUR'ÂN itself, although popular legend has him multiplying food and healing the wounded. Among Muslim literary critics, the miraculous nature of the Qur'ân was translated into the notion of the inimitability of the sacred text, I'JÂZ. For saints, the term is *karâmât*, understood as special favors granted by God through the saint to believers. This terminology is particularly associated with the practice of visiting the tombs of saints (WALÎs), or, for the SHÎ'Î, the tombs of the IMÂMs, called *mashhad*s. Throughout the history of Islam, there have been groups that have argued against any miracles. One such group is the WAHHÂBÎ, who are strongly opposed to the notion of miracles of any sort. (*See also* KARÂMAH.)

mi'râj (Arabic: ladder)

The term has come to mean the ascension of MUḤAMMAD to heaven after his ISRÂ', or night journey, from MECCA to the MASJID AL-AQṢÂ, usually interpreted as AL-QUDS (Jerusalem). The brief references in the QUR'ÂN, in *Sûrat an-najm* and *Sûrat al-isrâ'*, are greatly elaborated in TAFSÎR literature and legend. In brief, the archangel JIBRÎL took Muḥammad through the seven heavens, where he met with MÛSÂ and others and received the commandment for the five daily prayers (ṢALÂT), reduced by negotiation from as many as five hundred. While there, he is supposed to have met with all the past prophets, including Mûsâ, IBRÂHÎM, and JESUS ('Îsâ). The ladder motif is used in the SÎRAH to equate Muḥammad with the ladder vision of the biblical Jacob. ṢÛFÎ interpreters have used the journey as a model for the mystical experience, and some commentators regard *ṣalât* as the *mi'râj* of the ordinary believers, taking them to heaven. In this view, the souls of those who pray are transported up to heaven and are near to God. There has been considerable debate about whether the journey was physical or spiritual. Translations of some of the Islamic stories about the Ascension may have influenced Dante's *Divine Comedy.*

miswâk (Arabic: toothstick or toothbrush)

Another word for this device is a *siwâk*. Following the model of MUḤAMMAD, the use of a toothstick as part of regular ablutions is recommended. There are preferred woods for making the toothstick, but it should be a wood of medium hardness that can be formed into a brush-like appearance at the end, either by incising it or by chewing it, as 'Â'ishah did for the Prophet during his final illness. While it is not obligatory, its use falls into the class of highly recommended, except, according to some, during the daylight hours of the fast of RAMAḌÂN. There, the foul breath of the fasting believers is said to be sweet-smelling to God.

modesty (Arabic *tawâḍu'*)

Freedom from arrogance and vanity is enjoined in the QUR'ÂN for all Muslims in both mental attitude and demeanor. The sin of IBLÎS is regarded as related to vanity and arrogance, and stories are told that his form as a serpent was the punishment that reduced him from the most beautiful animal to the most repulsive. Some interpreters have used the Qur'ânic injunctions to dictate dress for women, while others have argued that the commandments for modesty apply equally to men and women (Q. 24:30–31, 60; 33:59; 7:31–33). (*See also* DRESS.)

Moghuls

See MUGHALS.

Mongols

One of the Turkic-speaking peoples from Central Asia who entered the Islamic world. They created a massive empire in the seventh/thirteenth century, sacking BAGHDÂD in 656/1258, ending the 'ABBÂSID CALIPHATE. They were stopped by the MAMLÛKS at 'Ayn Jâlût in 658/1260. Many converted to Islam, and the South Asian empire of the MUGHALS derives from them.

monotheism

The belief that there is only one deity is central to Islamic belief. (*See also* ALLÂH; TAWḤÎD.)

Moors

The term applied in most European languages until the twentieth century to the Muslims of Spain and North Africa. Of uncertain origin, it was first used by the Greek writer Polybius. Through the influence of Spanish and the polemical literature of the Reconquista, the term has taken on a negative connotation in most Western languages, reflecting the political, religious, and ethnic conflict between the Islamic world and Europe. The term is seldom used today except in archaizing polemic.

Moriscos

The term refers to those Muslims who remained in Spain after 1492 and were converted, at least on the surface, to Christianity. They retained many elements of the Muslim identity, however, including a strong literary tradition in a mix of Spanish and Arabic, known as Aljamiado. They were known as *Nuevos Christianos* or *Convertudos de moros*, "new Christians," or "Moorish converts." By a FATWÂ of 910/1510, they were allowed to practice TAQIYYAH, religious dissimulation, to be crypto-Muslims in an increasingly hostile environment. The expulsion of this population in 1609 recognized their genuine Islamic identity, and many refugees went to Tunisia, where they resumed the open practice of Islam, but continued their literary tradition in Aljamiado. (*See also* ALJAMIA.)

Morocco

Islam came to Morocco with an Arab invasion in 682, marking the end of Byzantine rule of the coastal areas. The indigeneous Berber, who had ruled the interior, converted to Islam and joined in the Islamic conquest of Iberia. A series of Arab-Berber dynasties ruled through the beginning of the seventeenth century, when Muslims and Jews, expelled from Spain, came to Morocco and helped usher in a golden age. This was also the beginning of European domination of Morocco under Portuguese, Spanish, and French colonial rule. Islam in Morocco has been marked by tensions between scripture-based 'ULAMÂ' and popular Ṣûfism. Since independence from France in 1956, public discussion about the directions of Islam have been influenced by the growth of SALAFIYYAH movements.

Moses

See MÛSÂ.

mosque

See MASJID.

Mozarab (Spanish *mozarábe*)

A word derived from the Arabic *musta'rib*, to become like an Arab, the term is applied to Christians of the Iberian peninsula who adopted Muslim customs and modes of life without converting to Islam. Another explanation of the origin of the term comes from Latin texts that called the Christians living among the Muslims as *mixti arabes*, those whose blood was mixed with that of Arabs. Both possible etymologies reflect the interconnected culture of Islamic Iberia, where Muslims, Christians, and Jews lived in close cultural and economic cooperation. As the Reconquista became more successful, many of the autonomous Mozarab Christians moved to Christian territory, bringing with them Islamic artistic tastes, customs of dress, and features of Arabic that were incorporated into the developing Spanish language. Mozarab artistic and architectural production was a vehicle for Islamic influence on the development of Spanish culture.

mu'adhdhin (Arabic: one who makes the *adhân*, or call to prayer.)

The first *mu'adhdhin* was BILÂL B. RABÂḤ, a person with a stentorian voice, whom MUḤAMMAD appointed to call the faithful to worship. With the development of Islamic architecture, the *mu'adhdhin* issued the call from a MINARET, a practice that has become custom. In some modern areas, the *mu'adhdhin* is being replaced by sound recordings of the ADHÂN.

Muʿâwiyah b. Abî Sufyân

(died 60/680)

Founder of the Syrian-based 'UMAYYAD dynasty. While he had opposed Islam at first, he converted before the conquest of MECCA. After the death of MUḤAMMAD, he was a leader in the battles against the Byzantines. When the third caliph, ʿUTHMÂN, to whom he had been related, was assassinated, Muʿâwiyah assumed the role of family head of the 'Ummayad clan and sought to bring the killers to justice. This put him in direct opposition to forces supporting the caliphate of ʿALÎ B. ABÎ ṬÂLIB. Muʿâwiyah was formally recognized as caliph by his Syrian supporters in 40/660. When ʿAlî died the next year, he was generally recognized as caliph. His reign was marked more by his use of tribal and clan alliances to enforce his authority than by any appeals to a divine right to rule.

muezzin

See MU'ADHDHIN.

muftî (Arabic: one who gives a *fatwâ*)

Someone empowered to give a FATWÂ or religiously based judgment on issues of daily Islamic life. The *muftî* has not historically necessarily been a QÂḌÎ. The role of the *muftî* in the development of Islamic law has been significant. The judgments of the *muftî*s were collected into manuals that would guide the community in its legal practices and help determine the IJMÂʿ of the community. A *muftî* can be a woman, a slave, or blind or dumb, but must be a person of good standing, have legal knowledge, and the capacity to use reasoning to solve problems. In popular tales, one hears of the lowest members of society besting their superiors in this capacity. *Fatwâ*s may be given to anyone, and magistrates are recommended to seek opinions from those who might be of assistance. As the institutions of religion and government developed, some rulers appointed *muftî*s, who were paid out of the state treasury. Often, these people were also the close advisors to the ruler, ruler and *muftî* deriving mutual benefit from the arrangement. Modern Islamic states do not have the need for *muftî*s, but the use of *muftî*s by private individuals continues, particularly where there is disaffection from the state.

Mughals

The name Mughal means MONGOL and shows the relationship of the empire created by Bâbur (888/1483–937/1530) in the Indian subcontinent to the great Mongol empire of Chingis Khan. Under the Mughals, all but the extreme south of India was brought under Islamic rule. The empire ended with the beginnings of British colonialism in 1858. Some of the greatest monuments in the subcontinent were built by the Mughals, including the famous Tâj Maḥal.

muḥaddith (Arabic: one who transmits a *ḥadîth*; pl. *muḥaddithûn*)

Often translated "traditionist," this term refers to a person who transmits a ḤADÎTH, or an individual who is involved in the dissemination of traditions.

muhâjirûn (Arabic: emigrants)

Those who made the HIJRAH with MUḤAMMAD. In the initial period of the community in MADÎNAH, the Emigrants who came with the Prophet were charity wards of the city's Arab inhabitants. As raids were successful, however, the Emigrants began to prosper and acquire land from Jews and hypocrites, (MUNÂFIQÛN), who were expelled or forced to give up their holdings. These Emigrants formed a strong part of the city during the lifetime of the Prophet and shortly after, but became assimilated into the larger Muslim community by the end of the first Islamic century. The term is also applied to those who made the little migration to Abyssinia. In the early period of the OTTOMAN EMPIRE, the term applied to those Muslims who fled Christian reconquest of Ottoman territories and fled to the interior. Among some ṢÛFÎ groups, the term is used in a spiritual sense for those who make a spiritual journey from sin to Islam.

Muḥammad ʿAbduh

See ʿABDUH, MUḤAMMAD.

Muḥammad b. ʿAbdullâh

(570–10/632)

The Prophet Muḥammad and founder of Islam was born in MECCA in the year 570 C.E. into the HÂSHIMITE clan of the tribe of QURAYSH, the dominant group in the city. Little is known of his earliest life aside from what little is known from the QUR'ÂN and found in the SÎRAH. His father died before he was born, and his mother, ÂMINAH, shortly afterwards. Under the care of his uncle, ABÛ ṬÂLIB, he learned the town's business of trade but also experienced what it was like to be an orphan and poor in a materialistic society. When he was twenty-five years old, he married a rich widow, KHADÎJAH, and attained a new measure of social status and wealth. His response was to contemplate the source of his good fortune, which he did in a series of annual retreats outside Mecca in a cave in Mount Ḥirâ'. In 610 C.E., when he was forty years old, he received his first revelation of the Qur'ân on one of these retreats, during the month of RAMAḌÂN. Starting with the first five verses of the ninety-sixth SÛRAH of the Qur'ân, he received revelations from God through

The cave of the Prophet, Mount Ḥirâ' outside Mecca.

an intermediary, the archangel JIBRÎL for the rest of his life. As Muḥammad began to preach his message of Islam, the Meccan oligarchy resisted his reforms, since it would have diminished their social and economic stranglehold on the ḤIJÂZ. He, with a small band of his followers, was forced to make the famous HIJRAH to the city of MADÎNAH, where he was able to establish Islam politically as well as socially, but not without warfare with the Meccans and their bedouin allies. In three significant battles, BADR, Uḥud, and KHANDAQ, he led the Muslim forces to victory over the Meccan coalition, established religious dominance in the area, and, in 10/632, led the paradigm Farewell Pilgrimage that set the model for the ḤAJJ. He died after a short illness in 10/632 in MADÎNAH in the arms of his favorite wife, ʿÂ'ishah. He died without male heirs and FÂṬIMAH was the only daughter to survive him. Little of Muḥammad's life can be learned directly from the Qur'ân, but some material can be found in the *sîrah* and ḤADÎTHS, sources which only hint at the depth and greatness of his character. Later Islamic biographies are, naturally, hagiographic, and are generally based on the Arabic primary sources. In some communities in South Asia, poetic biographies, which show some Hindu influence, are recited at the MAWLID celebrations. Until recently, Western biographies of Muḥammad have generally been negative and polemical, with exceptions, such as Thomas Carlyle's *On Heroes, Hero Worship, and the Heroic in History*. Recent scholarship on the biography of Muḥammad in the West has been influenced by a search for the "historical" Muḥammad patterned on the search for the "historical" Jesus. The trend among Western academic Islamicists has been to attempt to expunge the earlier negative views of the Prophet and present him in a more positive and comparative light.

Muḥammad Aḥmad b. 'Abdullâh (*c.* 1258/1834–1302/1885)

The self-proclaimed MAHDÎ of the Sudan, he was an initiate in the Sammâniyyah ṢÛFÎ ṬARÎQAH. Claiming to have been visited by the Prophet, JIBRÎL, and AL-KHAḌIR, who appointed him as Mahdî to cleanse the world of corruption and rule over lands held by the Ottomans and the British, he led military expeditions against the British in Khartoum, where he killed the British garrison, including General Gordon. He died shortly after, probably of typhus. Among his religious innovations was the addition of his name to the SHAHÂDAH, replacing ḤAJJ with JIHÂD, and making the recitation of extra prayers obligatory. The Mahdist rule of the Sudan ended in 1898 when the British retook Khartoum.

Muḥammad al-Bâqir (57/676–*c.* 126/743)

The fifth IMÂM in the SHÎ'Î tradition, he was the grandson of the second Imâm, AL-ḤASAN B. 'ALÎ. Shî'î tradition holds that he was martyred and was buried in MADÎNAH.

Muḥammad b. Ismâ'îl (*c.* second/eighth century)

The eighth IMÂM for the ISMÂ'ÎLÎ SHÎ'Î. Before the death of JA'FAR AṢ-ṢÂDIQ, some of his followers recognized his son ISMÂ'ÎL B. JA'FAR as the rightful successor. He died before Ja'far, so they passed their allegiance to Ismâ'îl's son, Muḥammad b. Ismâ'îl. Those who follow this line of succession are called "Seveners," or Ismâ'îlî, and those who follow Ismâ'îl's brother, Mûsâ al-Kâẓim, are the ones who became the "Twelvers," the ITHNÂ 'ASHARIYYAH.

Muhammadiyyah

A reform movement in Indonesia founded in 1912 by a SANTRI, Mohammad Darwisj, who changed his name to Kiyai Hadji Ahmad Dahlan after a sojourn in MECCA. His message combines Islamic traditionalism and social concerns that seek to provide stability in the period of rapid change after Dutch colonialism.

Muḥammad al-Qâ'im (*c.* 255/868 to his *ghaybah* in 260/874)

The twelfth SHÎ'Î IMÂM, he was the son of the eleventh *Imâm*, ḤASAN AL-'ASKARÎ. He is said to have made a single appearance at this father's funeral and then entered GHAYBAH. He is the "awaited one," hence his epithet *al-Muntaẓar*, and the "rightly guided," al-MAHDÎ, who will return to signal the advent of the YAWM AD-DÎN. (*See also* ITHNÂ 'ASHARIYYAH SHÎ'Î.)

Muḥammad Jawâd at-Taqî
(195/810–220/835)

The ninth IMÂM of the ITHNÂ 'ASHARIYYAH SHÎ'Î, he attained the imâmate when he was seven years of age, lived in BAGHDÂD, married a daughter of the SUNNÎ caliph al-Ma'mûn, and was martyred at her hands.

Muḥammad 'Ubayd Allâh
(died 323/934)

First FÂṬIMID caliph, who came to power through the use of both SHÎ'Î and Mahdist ideologies. (*See also* MAHDÎ.)

Muḥarram (Arabic)

The first month of the Islamic lunar calendar, it is known as the Month of Mourning, particularly among the SHÎ'Î, because it was in this month that AL-ḤUSAYN B. 'ALÎ was martyred at KARBALÂ'. In many places in the Islamic world, the tenth of this month, called 'ÂSHÛRÂ', is not only a time for fasting but also for the performance of plays of lamentation and the recitation of poetry commemorating the tragic event.

muḥâsabah (Arabic: accounting)

In religious terms, this is the accounting that one does of the soul and the accounting that will be done at the YAWM AD-DÎN by God and the band of those judging humans. According to tradition, those who will be saved will receive their account books in their right hands, and those who will be damned will receive them in their left hands. The use of this term fits the extensive commercial metaphors found in the QUR'ÂN.

al-Muḥâsibî, Abû 'Abdullâh Ḥârith b. Asad al-'Anazî (165/781–243/857)

Shâfi'î theologian and one-time member of the MU'TAZILAH, he used the techniques of KALÂM to argue against them, and was one of the first to renounce them. He is also one of the first SUNNÎ mystics to have had a thoroughgoing theological education. His main work, *Ri'âyah li-ḥuqûq Allâh*, influenced the theologian AL-GHAZÂLÎ.

muḥkamât (Arabic: clear verses)

The precise, clear verses of the QUR'ÂN, as opposed to the MUTASHÂBIHÂT. The Qur'ân divides itself into two categories of verses, those that are clear and unambiguous and those that are obscure. The *muḥkamât* are often regarded as the "essence" of the Qur'ân. (*See also* TAFSÎR.)

mujâhid (Arabic)

One who engages in JIHÂD.

Mujâhidîn

In Afghanistân the general name for the JIHÂD fighters against Soviet occupation.They were a Sunnî movement, influenced by the writings of the IKHWÂN AL-MUSLIMÛN. There were at least seven different groups, which united to expel the Soviets and replace the Communist government. Their rule has been replaced by that of the ṬÂLIBÂN.

Mujâhidîn-i Khalq (Persian)

The Sâzimân-i Mujâhidîn-i Khalq-i Îrân (The Holy Warrior Organization of the Iranian People) was formed in IRAN in the 1960s as a revolutionary, religious, socialist armed movement against the Pahlavi government and contributed to the fall of the SHÂH in 1979. Their subsequent conflict with the leadership of the Islamic republic forced their leadership into exile and diminished their popular base within Iran.

mu'jizah

See MIRACLE.

mujtahid (Arabic)

One who practices IJTIHÂD.

mukhâṭarah (Arabic: risk)

A legal device or stratagem to evade a rule of Islamic law (SHARÎʿAH). The term was usually applied to the system of the double sale to avoid usury (RIBÂ), where the difference in the prices between the first sale and the second constitutes the unearned profit. The Arabic word was borrowed into Latin as *mohatra*, with the same meaning. (*See also* BANKS AND BANKING; MAYSIR.)

mullâ, or mulâ

See MAWLÂ.

mullâbâshî (Persian)

A term used in the eighteenth and nineteenth century as a title for the head of the Iranian *mullahs*.

mullah

See MAWLÂ.

Mullâ Ṣadrâ, Ṣadr ad-Dîn Muḥammad b. Ibrâhîm Qawâmî Shîrâzî (979/1571–1050/1640)

Persian mystic, philosopher, and theologian of the ṢAFAVID period, who propounded the notion of different levels of being or existence. He studied in his native town of Shîrâz and in Iṣfahân, and was forced to retire from public life because some of his early writings on mysticism were condemned. Called from retirement to a teaching post in Shîrâz, he began to write the foundation of a new school of Shîʿîsm that combined elements of a number of existing schools. He is credited with moving SHÎʿÎ theology away from its reliance on Aristotelian philosophical concepts and creating a new terminology that expresses reality in terms of God's light. In his system, mysticism, theology, philosophy, QURʾÂN studies and ḤADÎTH studies are all compatible.

mu'min (Arabic: believer, one who preserves safety)

Muʾmin has come to mean "believer," but it is related to other formations from this root which mean safety and surety. ALLÂH is called *al-Muʾmin* in Q. 59:23, apparently with this meaning. These senses of the word relate closely to the sense of safety and surety in the word Islam itself, and the concept of belief and acceptance seems to imply the surety of being in God's protection.

munâfiqûn (Arabic: dissemblers)

These are the hypocrites, mentioned in the QURʾÂN as those who feign belief in Islam. They are condemned to the lowest part of Hell. While Arab lexicographers know of the meaning of the root, "to pay money," they prefer to see the term as related to a word indicating the back door of a gerbil's den, where the animal enters one hole and escapes through another. Historically, they have identified the hypocrites with those Muslims in MADÎNAH who seemingly supported the Muslims but proved faithless when the city was attacked by the Meccan forces. In ṢÛFÎ discussions, the concern is more spiritual, and they contrast the word *nifâq* (hypocrisy) with *wifâq* (harmony), and see the *munâfiqûn* as bringers of disharmony to the community.

Munkar wa-Nakîr

The two angels, not mentioned in the QURʾÂN, who guard the grave and are involved in an individual's punishment. According to popular belief, the dead will be asked about MUḤAMMAD. The righteous will answer that he is the apostle of ALLÂH, and they will be left alone until the *yawm ad-dîn*. The rest will be tortured in the grave every day except Friday until the Day of Judgment. The MU'TAZILAH rejected the notion of an actual punishment in the grave, and in the controversies between them and the traditionists, SUNNÎ doctrine crystalized around the actuality of punishment. By the third/ninth century, various creeds developed that expressed the "reality" of punishment in the grave.

al-murâbiṭûn (Arabic: dwellers in forts)

Known in Western literature as the Almoravids, this dynasty in North Africa and Spain started in the fifth/eleventh century through the reform efforts of a Ṣanḥâjah Berber chieftain, who had become inspired on a ḤAJJ. He built a fort (RIBÂṬ), from which his political and religious movement spread. The *ribâṭ* gave the name to the movement that ruled until their defeat by AL-MUWAḤḤIDÛN in 540/1146.

murîd (Arabic: seeker)

An initiate of a ṢÛFÎ ṬARÎQAH. Entrance into this state is usually marked by a public ceremony in which the MURSHID, the guide, gives the initiate an object, such as a SUBḤAH (rosary), a KHIRQAH (woolen cloak) or other mark of the new status. The length of time a person remains in this role and the obligations vary from one *ṭarîqah* to another.

Murîdiyyah

A prominent ṢÛFÎ ṬARÎQAH in Senegal, founded by Amadu Bamba M'Backe (*c.* 1850–1927).

Murji'ah (Arabic)

The Murji'ites, an early group within Islam that held the punishment of sinners would be "postponed," and, in contrast to the KHAWÂRIJ, that Muslims who sinned did not cease to be Muslims because of their sin. They held a political position between that of the SHÎ'Î and the Khawârij and formed the foundation for the development of SUNNÎ Islam. In the early controversies between the Shî'î and the Khawârij, a central issue was the status of those who had committed a grave sin. Both sides regarded the other as having committed apostasy by their actions, the Shî'î for supporting 'ALÎ B. ABÎ ṬÂLIB's decision to enter into negotiations with MU'ÂWIYAH, and the Khawârij for leaving the community and declaring all who did not believe as they did to be apostates and sinners. The middle way between those two was labeled *irjâ'*, deferral or postponement of judgment. They held that judgment was up to God, who would decide when He willed. They held that both ABÛ BAKR and 'UMAR were above reproach, and they deferred judgment on both 'UTHMÂN and 'ALÎ. They held that the nature of faith (IMÂN) was defined by belief independent of acts. Politically, they represented the center majority against what were perceived as radical groups. They translated this into political theory by supporting a more open view of the caliphate than the Shî'î, but more restrictive than the Khawârij. Their middle doctrine became marginalized as traditionalist Sunnî Islam developed, and AḤMAD B. ḤANBAL was vehemently opposed to the Murji'ites, declaring them to be excluded from the community, ('UMMAH). Not all schools held such a strong view, and many Murji'ite views became mainstream Sunnî doctrine.

murshid (Arabic: guide)

One who gives right guidance along the mystic way. Often used as the term for someone who guides an initiate, or MURÎD, into a ṢÛFÎ ṬARÎQAH. (*See also* SHAYKH.)

murtadd (Arabic: one who turns back)

An apostate is one who either returns to a former religion, in the case of a convert, or one who denies Islam in either speech or action. A person, born a Muslim, who treats the QUR'ÂN with disrespect would be accused of being a *murtadd* even when there was not a "return" *per se*. Such individuals are described in the Qur'ân as having earned punishment in the next life. In the ḤADÎTH, there are numerous statements attributed to the Prophet that call for the killing of the one who changes religion away from Islam. The different schools (MADHHAB) of Islamic law vary about the possibility of repentance, but almost all make a distinction between male and female apostates and whether or not the apostasy was under compulsion, in which case it is forgiven. (*See also* RIDDAH.)

Mûsâ (Arabic)

The prophet Moses, mentioned in the QUR'ÂN. The Qur'ânic picture of Mûsâ is similar to the biblical and Jewish Haggadic story of Moses, and is one of the longer and more developed narratives in the Qur'ân. Mûsâ is presented as a precursor to MUḤAMMAD and similar to him both in mission and in the reception of his people. What is not found explicitly in the Qur'ân was supplied by early commentators, so we know that FIRʿAWN (Pharaoh) decreed that all Israelite first-born boys were to be slain. His mother placed him in a chest and cast him in the Nile, where he was found by Pharaoh's wife, who took him into the palace to raise him. When he would not nurse, burning the breasts of all who tried, his own mother was hired as a wet-nurse. When he reached his majority, God gave him understanding and he recognized the social injustices against his people. His speaking out caused the elders to plot against him, so he fled to Midian, married, and received his prophetic mission from God through a burning bush. He then returned to Egypt, and, with his brother, HÂRÛN (Aaron), encountered Pharaoh in a series of tests and led the Israelites from Egypt, during which God killed Pharaoh and his army in the Red Sea. When they reached Sinai, God gave him the TAWRÂT (Torah). He then guided the Israelites toward the Holy Land, but God sent angels to take him before he reached that destination. In the post-Qur'anic stories, Mûsâ burns his mouth on coals when Pharaoh offers him gold, and he becomes a stammerer. His meeting with AL-KHAḌIR is a story particularly popular in ṢÛFÎ commentaries, and is meant to demonstrate that there are other truths beside just the exoteric ones. An interesting development in the TAFSÎR literature is the creation of a Mûsâ AS-SÂMIRÎ, Moses the Samaritan, who was responsible for the creation of the golden calf idol that the Israelites worshiped. The purpose of this narrative creation seems to be to explain away Hârûn's role in the affair.

Mûsâ b. Ja'far aṣ-Ṣâdiq al-Kâẓim (*c.* 128/745–183/799)

The seventh IMÂM for the ITHNÂ ʿASHARIYYAH SHÎʿÎ, he was a son of JAʿFAR AṢ-ṢÂDIQ. After his father's death, his claim to the Imâmate was supported by those who became known as the "Twelvers," the Ithnâ ʿAsharî.

Musaylimah

A younger contemporary of MUḤAMMAD and a pretender to prophecy, who led his tribe, the Banû Ḥanîfah, in revolt in the RIDDAH wars. According to Islamic stories, he wrote to Muḥammad offering to share the role of prophet, which earned him the nickname *al-Kadhdhâb* and the declaration that he was a liar. He died in a bloody battle in the year after Muḥammad died. Little is known about the content of his supposed prophetic message, except for some statements ascribed to him.

mushrikûn (Arabic: associators)

Those who engage in SHIRK (polytheism) or the association of other deities with God.

Muslim (Arabic: one who submits)

The name, derived from the Arabic root s-l-m, meaning "peace," indicates that the person who submits to God is granted the peace and surety of certain reward for good actions and certain punishment for evil, unlike the uncertainty of trying to appease multiple deities in polytheism. (*See also* ÎMÂN; MU'MIN.)

Muslim Brotherhood

See AL-IKHWÂN AL-MUSLIMÛN.

Muslim–Christian dialogue

The movement to promote understanding between Muslims and Christians started by the World Council of Churches in the middle of the twentieth century, but expanded to include a number of religious groups interested in interfaith communications. The goals are to promote mutual understanding without attempts at conversion in a nonjudgmental environment, and are modeled on Jewish–Christian dialogue. Many Muslims are reluctant to participate because of the long history of hostile interfaith communication, the memory of colonialism and the identification of Christianity with the oppression of Muslims. In spite of the difficulties, however, there has been considerable success at local levels in promoting mutual understanding and respect where Muslim and Christian groups participate.

Muslim b. al-Ḥajjâj, Abû al-Ḥusayn (*c.* 202/817–261/875)

A famous collector of ḤADÎTHS. His collection, along with that of AL-BUKHÂRÎ, is called SAḤÎḤ, "sound." His collection is ranked just below that of al-Bukhârî among the top six collections. He was born in Nîshâpûr and traveled extensively from an early age in pursuit of traditions. The strength of Muslim's collection is in the organization of each chapter, which deals with only one subject, unlike others, which may contain numerous subjects in one chapter, and allows for a careful scrutiny of both the content of the MATN and the extent of the proliferation of the ISNÂD.

Muslim–Jewish dialogue

The model for Muslim–Jewish dialogue is Jewish–Christian dialogue, but it has been less successful because of mutual suspicions on both sides and the interjection of the politics of the Palestinian–Israeli conflict into the discussion, in which nationalism and religious identity are strongly intertwined in both groups. In spite of the problems, there have been successful dialogue groups operating since the mid-1970s in both the United States and in Israel.

Muslim League

A political group founded in 1906 in India, the aim of which was to establish an independent Muslim state. It was a major factor in the formation of PAKISTAN.

Musta'lî

The branch of the ISMÂ'ÎLÎ SHÎ'Î who recognized the FÂṬIMID caliph al-Musta'lî (487/1094–495/1101) as IMÂM.

mut'ah (Arabic: enjoyment)

Temporary marriage, contracted for a negotiated bride-price, or MAHR, and terminated at a fixed time rather than by divorce. This legal arrangement is sanctioned only by the laws of the ITHNÂ 'ASHARIYYAH SHÎ'Î. Those who sanction this marriage arrangement see Q. 4:24

as a source, but the SUNNÎ commentators argued from an early date that the passage only discussed lawful marriages and the equity rights of women. In the ḤADÎTHS, there is some evidence that it was a pre-Islamic practice. There are also contradictory traditions, with some saying that the Prophet permitted the custom and those who said that he forbade it.

mutashâbihât (Arabic: unclear)

The term applied to the ambiguous or unclear verses of the QUR'ÂN. (*See also* MUḤKAMÂT; MYSTERIOUS LETTERS OF THE QUR'AN; TAFSÎR.)

muṭawwif (Arabic: guide to circumambulation)

The guide for the ḤAJJ who assists pilgrims through the rituals of the pilgrimage to assure that all is done correctly. These guides also make arrangements for food and water, lodging, tent arrangements, and other necessaries. Current arrangements have many of these guides formed into guilds, each in charge of a specific group of pilgrims from a particular geographic area.

Mu'tazilah

A theological movement that created speculative dogmatic theology in Islam. It began in the same religious and political climate as the SHÎ'Î, the KHAWÂRIJ, the MURJI'AH and other sectarian groups. They adopted an "intermediate" stance between those who felt that the commission of sin caused immediate apostasy and those who felt that sin had no impact on belief. They called themselves the "people of justice and unity" (Arabic *ahl al-'adl wa-t-tawḥîd*), holding that God was absolutely just and unitary. Their most famous doctrine held that the QUR'ÂN was created, argued to prevent a plurality of eternals. This doctrine was used in the MIḤNAH of the early 'ABBÂSIDS and earned the Mu'tazilah a bad reputation. Their speculative theology influenced all later theological movements in Islam and is being revived in some circles today as a counter to anti-intellectual fundamentalism. (*See also* KALÂM.)

al-muwaḥḥidûn (Arabic: unitarians)

This is the name given to the members of a reformist movement also known as the Almohads, that ruled in North Africa and Spain in the sixth/twelfth and seventh/thirteenth centuries. The founder of the movement, IBN TÛMART, brought reformist ideas from his study in the east and had instilled ideas of reform and conquest among the Maṣmûdah Berber tribes, who were protesting against the rigid rule of the AL-MURÂBIṬÛN. Their capital was Marrâkesh, and at the height of their rule governed Spain and North Africa.

Muzdalifah

A place near MECCA where pilgrims on the ḤAJJ spend the night after running between there and MINÂ.

Mysterious Letters of the Qur'ân

The name in Western literature for the letters found at the beginning of twenty-nine of the SÛRAHS of the QUR'ÂN. Over the years, both Muslim and Western commentators have tried to decipher the meaning of the letters. To date, each theory has failed to adequately satisfy every critic, and one is left to conclude that they are among the most obscure of the MUTASHÂBIHÂT, whose meaning is with God alone. Some of the letters have found their way into popular use in amulets and as given names of individuals.

N

nabî (Arabic: prophet)

This is the usual word for prophet in the QUR'ÂN and in Arabic literature. It implies that the recipient has been chosen for prophethood by God and has received WAHY (revelation) and scripture from God. MUḤAMMAD is the last in the line of prophets in Islam, which starts with ADAM. In popular tradition, God is said to have revealed His scripture to seventy prophets in the seventy languages of humankind.

nabîdh

A slightly alcoholic beverage fermented from barley, dates, raisins, and/or honey. This drink was permitted in moderation by some ḤANAFÎ jurists and by others as a medicinal compound, but in recent times the word has come to mean any alcoholic beverage and, therefore, forbidden.

Nafîsah, as-Sayyidah (died 209/824)

The great-granddaughter of AL-ḤASAN B. ʿALÎ, she gained a reputation as a worker of *karâmât*. Her tomb in Cairo is an object of pilgrimage and veneration. (*See also* KARÂMAH.)

nafs (Arabic: self, spirit, soul)

This word for soul seems to have a sense of personal identity, as opposed to RÛḤ, which means "breath" or "wind." Different theologians have speculated about whether the body will be resurrected after death or only the soul, but Muslims generally hold that the soul is immortal.

nahḍah (Arabic: to rise)

This term has come to mean an awakening or a renaissance. It has been used to refer both to the Arab renaissance from the middle of the nineteenth century to the end of World War I and to the rise of Arab and Islamic movements in the modern period in general.

Nahdatul Ulama

An important Islamic social organization founded in 1926 in INDONESIA, the purpose of which is to foster relationships among the four SUNNÎ schools of law, promote proper Islamic education, attend to the needs of the poor, and promote a lawful Islamic economy. Under the leadership of ABDURRAHMAN WAHID, the movement has tried to become a proponent of a democratic and harmoniously Islamic Indonesia.

Nahj al-balâghah (Arabic: the way of eloquence)

A collection of sayings, letters, and sermons attributed to ʿALÎ B. ABÎ ṬÂLIB. In spite of some doubt as to whether all of it may be accurately attributable to

ʿAlî, the work has enjoyed considerable popularity and generated numerous commentaries and translations into other languages.

an-Nahrawân

The location east of the Tigris river where ʿAlî b. Abî Ṭâlib fought with the Khawârij in 38/658. The battle saw the death of many of the Khawârij, and ʿAlî was roundly condemned by his contemporaries for the slaughter. A member of the Khawârij assassinated him, and the movement continued to exist under the reign of the ʾUmayyads.

Najaf

A city near Kûfah that contains the tomb of ʿAlî b. Abî Ṭâlib. The site and the surrounding locations are regarded as holy among the Shîʿî and receive much pilgrim traffic. It is also referred to as a *mashhad*, which means a tomb of an Imâm.

Nakîr

See Munkar wa-Nakîr.

namâz (Persian: obligatory prayer)

See ṣalât.

namâzgâh (Persian: place of prayer)

In India, this is the name for a place of prayer, built on the side of town closest to Mecca (the west), with only a wall, the miḥrab (the indicator of the direction of prayer), and the *minbar* (the pulpit). The resulting partial enclosure is often large enough to accommodate the entire male population of the town. It is used for the celebration of the ʿÎd al-Fiṭr and the ʿÎd al-Aḍḥâ, and usually has no special place for ablutions. These enclosures are not regarded with the same sanctity as a mosque and can be destroyed and rebuilt without special concerns. (*See also* masjid.)

names and naming

Names under Islam have a special significance. A tradition reportedly from Muḥammad enjoins Muslims to give pleasant and beautiful names to their children. There is also the Qurʾânic principle to call children after their true fathers. This has led to a patronymic system among Muslims, even outside the sphere where Arabic is used. Additionally, in many places the *laqab* or "nickname" is used as well as the *nasab* or location/tribal name. Titles, such as *Ḥajjî* for someone who has completed the ḥajj, or Sharîf, claiming descent from the Prophet, are also added. In the modern period and in response to Western influence and the necessities of having surnames as index names, the strict patronymic system is changing. Children may be named after prophets in the Qurʾân, including Muḥammad and ʿÎsâ; the latter custom may have influenced the Spanish to be the only Christians to name their children after Jesus. Converts to Islam regularly adopt Islamic names.

Namrûd

He is only alluded to in the Qurʾân, but is identified with the biblical Nimrod as the one who cast Ibrâhîm into the blazing furnace. Extra-Qurʾânic stories add many details to the short version in the Qurʾân. He is thought to be one of the three or four kings who ruled the world. He, like Firʿawn (Pharaoh), is told that a child will destroy his kingdom, so sets out to kill all the male children. Ibrâhîm, the prophet of his age, is born in secret and matures so rapidly in both mind and body that he cannot be taken for one of those slated for death. When Ibrâhîm begins preaching to him, Namrûd claims to have power over life and death, but the prophet is able to restore birds to life. Namrûd is credited with building the tower of Babel to assault heaven, as well as to fly to Heaven to attack God by using an eagle-powered flying chest. In frustration, he throws Ibrâhîm into a fire, but angels cool him with their wings. After ruling for four hundred years, he is tortured for four hundred by a gnat that enters his brain through his nose and torments him to death.

Nâmûs (Arabic)

This word, thought to be a name, which occurs in the SÎRAH, is identified as the archangel JIBRÎL who brought the QUR'ÂN to MUḤAMMAD. WARAQAH B. NAWFAL, the cousin of KHADÎJAH, said that this is the same Nâmûs who came to MÛSÂ. Other traditions and comparisons with Syriac and Greek texts show that this word means "law," in the sense of scripture, and the tradition understands that Mûsâ and Muḥammad both received scripture from ALLÂH.

Naqshbandiyyah

A major ṢÛFÎ order found in Turkey, Central Asia, and the Indo-Pakistani subcontinent, it is rarely found among the Arabs and has had only a slight influence in Iran, in spite of the fact that many of its major works were first composed in PERSIAN. The order adheres to a spiritual and interior DHIKR and has only occasionally been a major political force in modern times, particularly in late OTTOMAN Damascus (DIMASHQ).

nâr (Arabic: fire)

This is the word used in the QUR'AN for hell-fire, occurring 111 times with this meaning. It also means "fire" in the more normal sense, and is used to name the fire into which IBRÂHÎM was cast by NAMRÛD, and the fire that burned in the bush when God spoke to MÛSÂ.

an-nâr (Arabic: Hell or the fire)

This is one of the most common terms for the place of punishment for the wicked in the AFTERLIFE.

an-Nasâ'î, Abû 'Abd ar-Raḥmân Aḥmad b. Shu'ayb (died *c.* 303/915)

The author of one of the six major compilations of ḤADÎTH. Little is known of his life or death.

naṣârâ (Arabic)

Christians, particularly those living under Islam. It is used fifteen times in the QUR'ÂN to refer to Christians, and is thought by most commentators to come from the place-name an-Nâṣirah, Nazareth, the hometown of 'Îsâ (JESUS). It may also reflect a use of the word Nazarene, an early term for Christians.

Nâṣif, Malak Ḥifnî (1886–1918)

Egyptian feminist and Islamic reformer, who wrote under the name *Bâḥithat al-Bâdiyah*, "Searcher in the Desert." Among other reforms, she advocated equality for women under Egypt's Muslim Personal Status Code and for women to be able to participate fully in congregational worship.

nâsikh wa-mansûkh (Arabic: abrogating and abrogated)

The doctrine in QUR'ÂN interpretation that holds that verses revealed later may abrogate some of those revealed earlier. This doctrine allows the removal of apparent contradictions within the Qur'ân. The abrogated verse (*mansûkh*) remains, however, in the Qur'ân. (*See also* ABROGATION.)

Nasr, Seyyed Hossein (born 1933)

Iranian-born, Harvard-educated historian of science, philosopher, and advocate of traditional Islamic mysticism. His writings advocate a balance between the sacred and profane world, casting Western individualism as the opposite of the true freedom of the ṢÛFÎ knowledge of the relationship of the individual to God.

Nation of Islam

The movement among black Americans started by Wallace D. Fard in Detroit, Michigan, in the 1930s. He used both the Bible and the QUR'ÂN in his preaching, promoted black separatism from the United States, self-help for the members of his Temple of Islam, and established his own style of worship. When he disappeared mysteriously in 1934, ELIJAH MUHAMMAD assumed leadership and put his own stamp on the movement. He taught that ALLÂH was a black man, and that he knew him personally and was his anointed messenger. He promoted black self-help, self-improvement, and a conservative lifestyle. His movement recruited actively in the poorest neighborhoods and in the prisons, enjoying great success. It established a network of small businesses nationwide, selling healthful and useful products to the black community. Central to his doctrine was the notion that white persons were products of an evil scientist named Yacub, who made the white race temporarily dominant in a rebellion against Allâh. At the end-time, through the battle of Armageddon, the black race would again dominate the earth under Allâh. In the period from 1952 to 1964 the movement was also led by MALCOLM X, but a difference in ideology caused Malcolm X to leave the movement; he converted to SUNNÎ Islam just a year before he was assassinated by members of the movement. The leadership was then assumed by Louis Abdul Farrakhan. When Elijah Muhammad died in 1975, one of his six sons, Imâm Warith Deen Mohammed, was named supreme minister of the Nation of Islam. He set about dismantling the organization of the movement, repudiating the racist doctrines and moving his followers into the mainstream of Sunnî Islam, ultimately abandoning a distinctive name for the movement. This led to a splintering off of some members under the leadership of Louis Farrakhan, who claimed the leadership and the name of the movement, retaining many of its racist and separatist notions that puts it outside the mainstream of Islam.

Nawrûz (Persian: new day)

Originally an Iranian vernal festival and Zoroastrian new year, it has become Iran's foremost national festival, marked with celebrations and exchanges of gifts. In SHÎ'Î tradition, it was on this day that MUḤAMMAD designated 'ALÎ B. ABÎ ṬÂLIB as his heir, that the ark of NÛḤ came to rest, the idols were cleansed from the KA'BAH and the day that MUḤAMMAD AL-QÂ'IM will appear to defeat AD-DAJJÂL and signal the end of time.

Niger, Republic of

This republic is predominantly Muslim, having first been missionized by traders crossing the Saharan trade routes. The ṢÛFÎs have historically had strong influence in the region, and there are several ṬARÎQAHS represented. The republic maintains close ties to the rest of the Islamic world, and shows influence from the various movements current in other Islamic countries.

Nigeria

Approximately half of the population is Muslim, with the next largest group Christians, generally located in the southeast of the country. In the twentieth century, ṢÛFÎ brotherhoods were a major way for Muslims to organize and relate to each other, but in the 1970s a reformer named Abubakar Gumi started a reform movement in which he challenged the brotherhoods, translated the QUR'ÂN into Hausa, and advocated interpreting the Qur'ân to accommodate modern needs. Because Nigeria is multiethnic and traditional ties to the brotherhoods have been hard to dissolve, the Islamic communities, while reformist, have not developed a unified religious or national approach.

nikâḥ (Arabic: marriage, marriage contract)

See MARRIAGE.

Ni'matullâhiyyah

An Iranian SHÎ'Î ṢÛFÎ ṬARÎQAH, started in the eighth/fourteenth century as SUNNÎ and changing in the ninth/fifteenth. It is currently found both inside and outside Iran. Its current leader is Dr. Javâd Nûrbakhsh, a retired psychiatrist who lives in London. He advocated the practice of constant, silent DHIKR and the importance of love over intellect. The movement has attracted a number of converts to Islam as well as expatriate Iranians.

Nimrod

See NAMRÛD.

ninety-nine names of God

See AL-'ASMÂ' AL-ḤUSNÂ.

niyyah (Arabic: intent)

Most actions in Islam are judged by both the action itself and the intention. ṢALÂT is not regarded as valid unless the person who prays declares the intent to pray that prayer. *Niyyah* is required before washing, prayer, giving charity, making the ḤAJJ, observing a fast (ṢAWM), or any other religious act. It must immediately precede the act, and the intention must be maintained in the mind until the act is completed. In this regard, Islam strikes a balance between extremes of orthodoxy or orthopraxy. The word does not occur in the QUR'ÂN, but it is found in the ḤADÎTH.

Nizâriyyah, also Nizârî Ismâ'îlî Shî'î

These are members of the group of ISMÂ'ÎLÎ SHÎ'Î who supported the accession of Nizâr, the eldest son of the FÂṬIMID caliph al-Mustanṣir. One of the leading figures in the development of this branch of Islam was ḤASAN-I ṢABBÂḤ, who not only led the movement politically but also helped develop the role of the IMÂM as the central interpretive figure in this branch of Shî'îsm. This branch of Islam is found throughout the world, with their current headquarters in London, and Aiglemont, France. (*See also* AGÂ KHÂN.)

Noah

See NÛḤ.

nubuwwah (Arabic: prophethood)

See NABÎ; RASÛL.

Nûḥ

This is the prophet Noah, who was instructed by God to build a ship to rescue the righteous members of his family from a devastating flood that covered the earth. While the Bible does not regard Nûḥ as a prophet, he is the first of the so-called prophets of destruction in Islamic tradition. When God sends him to his people, who are known only as the People of Nûḥ, he warns them that they will be destroyed if they do not repent. When they scorn him, God commands him to build an ark and be ready to sail with two of every creature when the "oven" boils, an indication that the primordial waters are coming up from under the ground. Nûḥ's family comes aboard except for a son, named Yâm, who refuses to take his father's or God's instruction and is drowned. This feature, which is not found in the Bible, makes the account given in the QUR'ÂN very personal. TAFSÎR literature has many stories, including that of a giant named 'Uj, who clings to the ark and is saved. There are also etiological stories, such as the story of the origin of the pig, created by having the elephant sneeze in order to have an animal that would eat the offal on board the ark. Also in the *tafsîr*, we learn the names of Nûḥ's sons who survive with him on the Ark, Sâm, ḤÂM, and Yâfith. In similar vein to traditions found in Jewish commentary on this story, Nûḥ's wife is described as a sinner, who described her husband as crazy and undermined his mission.

nûr (Arabic: light)

This is identified with coming from God, as God's wisdom and teaching, and with the Prophet MUḤAMMAD. The most famous expression of the concept of God being light is found in the "light verse," Q. 24:35. Islamic philosophers discussed this nature of God extensively, relating it to concepts found in Aristotle and in the Neoplatonists. For the ṢÛFÎ, the concept of light represented the divine spark and featured prominently in mystic speculations.

Nûrbakhshiyyah

A ṢÛFÎ ṬARÎQAH named after Muḥammad b. Muḥammad b. 'Abdullâh Nûrbakhsh (795/1393–869/1465), a peripatetic teacher who claimed to have mastered all knowledge and was called both MAHDÎ and caliph (KHALÎFAH) by some of his followers. The group claims spiritual connection with the philosopher-mystic Shihâb ad-Dîn as-Suhrawardî, and has been mainly found in South and Central Asia.

Nurculuk

A Turkish religious movement named after Bediüzzaman Said Nursî (1876–1960), who proposed uniting all Turkish Muslims under the twin ideals of Islam and modernism. Although accused of establishing a new ṢÛFÎ order (Nursî had been educated by the NAQSHBANDIYYAH), he and his followers claimed a wider purpose. The movement has found appeal among educated intellectuals as well as in the rural, poorer areas.

nûr Muḥammadî (Arabic: the light of Muḥammad)

This means the pre-existence of the soul of the Prophet, created by God as one of the first acts of creation. Among the SHÎ'Î, this light is transmitted from MUḤAMMAD to the IMÂMS.

Nuṣayriyyah

See 'ALAWIYYAH.

O

Organization of the Islamic Jihâd

The Munaẓẓamat al-Jihâd al-Islâmî was formed out of the ḤIZBULLÂH party in Lebanon in 1982 as the covert and militant wing of Ḥizbullâh. It was the instrument for the bombing of the United States embassy in Lebanon in 1983 and for a series of kidnappings from 1982 through 1991. The group has adopted an extreme rejectionist stand in respect to a negotiated settlement of the Arab–Israeli conflict.

Ottoman Empire

The dynasty was named after its founder, Osman I (656/1258–727/1326), a member of a branch of the Oğuz Turks, although the name itself was derived from Arabic (ʿUthmân). The dynasty expanded from a remote outpost in Anatolia to encompass the Middle East to the borders of Iran, Anatolia, Europe to the northern borders of Hungary, and the coast of North Africa almost to the Atlantic Ocean. Building on their GHÂZÎ heritage, which embraced cavalry warfare, a JIHÂD ideology, and a SUNNÎ notion of a religious state, they offered non-Muslims DHIMMÎ status, which meant that they could incorporate them into the state without forcing the population to convert. The influx of Jewish refugees from Iberia after 1492, who brought international trade and new techniques of manufacturing, helped finance a rapid expansion of the empire in the early sixteenth century. Ottoman society was divided into two main classes: the *osmanlılar* or ruling class, and the *reʿâyâ*, or "protected flock" class. The religion of the ruling class was Sunnî Islam of the ḤANAFÎ MADHHAB mixed with elements from ṢÛFÎ practice, pre-Islamic Turkish beliefs, and elements brought in by Christian converts to Islam. The religions of the subject class were governed by their own religious rules, since each religious group was divided into MILLETS, or separate religious communities. The Muslims of the subject class were strongly influenced by Ṣûfî orders and popular charismatic leaders, which ultimately meant that there was a disconnection between the two classes religiously. During the period of decline in the nineteenth century and leading up to the dissolution of the empire after World War I, numerous reforms were attempted to correct the social and religious problems of the empire, but these generally resulted in bringing in greater Western influence in the areas of technology and education. Unable to sustain itself economically or militarily, the empire was dissolved after World War I by the victors, the British, the French, the Italians, and the Russians. Many of the borders of modern Middle Eastern states were drawn to reflect colonial interests rather than the needs and history of the indigenous populations, resulting in political and religious conflicts throughout the twentieth century. With the fall of the empire, many saw the last hope for the restoration of the caliphate disappear. (*See also* ATATÜRK; KHILÂFAT MOVEMENT.)

P

pâdishâh (Persian)

The term, combining the two Persian words, *pâd*, "lord," and *shâh*, "king," became a regular term for Muslim emperors.

Pahlavi, Muḥammad Rezâ Shâh (1919–1980)

The second and last ruling monarch of the Pahlavi dynasty in IRAN, he was installed by combined British and Russian influence after they ousted his father, Reza Shâh. His reign was marked by a feeling that his rule was illegitimate and under the influence of the West. That feeling increased when he was restored to his throne in 1953 by a combined American and British coup after having lost it when the popular vote challenged the role of the monarchy and Mohammad Mossadegh was elected as prime minister. As part of the *shâh*'s effort to maintain control, in 1963 he exiled a number of activist clerics, among whom was *Âyatollâh* Rûḥollâh KHOMEINÎ. After systematically reducing the power of the groups that opposed him, he was left to face the *mullah* class, who participated in a secular, Marxist revolution in 1979 that ousted him. The clerics subsequently installed an Islamic republic led by Âyatollâh Khomeinî.

painting

Painting in an Islamic religious context is iconoclastic, and avoids the use of figures and images, so mosques are traditionally decorated with abstract designs, CALLIGRAPHY, and mosaic patterns. In religious manuscripts, the tradition is different. Under the influence of miniature painting from South and East Asia, Islamic religious manuscripts can be filled with paintings of birds, animals, flowers, people, and, in the case of depictions of

Miniature depicting musicians.

the MIR'ÂJ, images of the Prophet, though usually veiled so as not to show his face. In the court traditions of the OTTOMANS and the ṢAFAVIDS, there was a fine tradition of portraiture, increasingly influenced by Western models. In many places in the contemporary Islamic world, Muslim painters are producing works of art, some of which are pictorial and some of which are abstract, reflecting the trends in modern painting in the West while incorporating traditional themes and motifs.

Pakistan (Urdu: pure land)

Pakistan came into being as an Islamic republic in 1947 with the partition of British India. It is the only country that was created in the name of Islam, and is primarily SUNNÎ, of the ḤANAFÎ MADHHAB, but there are SHÎ'Î as well from both the ITHNÂ 'ASHARIYYAH and ISMÂ'ÎLÎ groups. Its national language is URDU, but there is no single language that is common to all Pakistanis. Less than four percent of the population is non-Muslim. The religious history of the country has been marked by tensions among secular modernists, those who desired a religiously based Islamic republic based on the QUR'ÂN and SHARÎ'AH, liberal reformist Muslims, and those influenced by ṢÛFÎ traditions. These debates have been carried out against the background of external threats from India, internal threats of civil war, and military dictatorship. Islamic modernism is the least strong element in the current debate, particularly after the departure of the movement's leader, FAZLUR RAHMAN.

Pandiyât-i jawânmardî

A collection of religious and devotional writings attributed to the NIZÂRÎ ISMÂ'ÎLÎ SHÎ'Î Imâm al-Mustanṣir, and accepted by them as a sacred text. These are mostly poetic works that contain religious and moral messages.

pan-Islam

The notion of the unity of all Muslims is as old as the religion itself, although like

Tomb of Shah Rukn-i-'Alam, Multan, Pakistan.

the ideal of the unity of all Christians or all Jews, it has remained only an ideal. In the modern sense, the pan-Islamic ideology is a product of nationalism, like pan-Arabism or pan-Turanism. As an active idea, it was most vital during the declining years of the OTTOMAN EMPIRE and the period of the KHILÂFAT MOVEMENT. In the last half of the twentieth century it was used for its emotional appeal rather than as a serious program for the unification of all Muslims.

Paradise

See AL-JANNAH.

Partai Islam Se-Malaysia

Known by its initials, PAS, this nationalist and fundamentalist Islamist political party in MALAYSIA, founded in 1371/1951, seeks to establish an Islamic state. At present, they rule the state of Kelantan, where they have established the rule of *syariat* (Bahasa from Arabic, SHARÎʿAH).

Partai Persatuan Pembangunan

The Development Unity Party in Indonesia, known by the initials PPP, is a moderate Islamist party that succeeded in the 1970s and the 1980s in effecting a greater inclusion of Islamic ideals in Indonesian politics.

pashah

An abbreviated form of PÂDISHÂH.

Patani United Liberation Organization

A liberation movement in the four southern provinces of THAILAND that seeks to form a mostly ethnic Malay state based on Islamic principles.

pbuh

Used by English-speaking Muslims after writing the name of the Prophet, indicating "Peace be upon him," meant as the equivalent of the Arabic "*ʿalayhi-s-salâm.*"

People of the Book

See AHL AL-KITÂB; DHIMMÎ.

PERKIM

An acronym for Pertubuhan Kebajikan Islam SeMalaysia, the All Malaysia Muslim Welfare Association, the aim of which is to promote a multi-ethnic Muslim community in Malaysia in which non-Malays can feel welcome.

Persian

One of the major Islamic languages, Persian is a member of the Indo-European family of languages. In its modern Islamic form, it is known as Farsî and is written in the ARABIC script and has a great number of Arabic lexical items. It is the official language of IRAN. It was the court language of the MUGHAL and OTTOMAN empires as well as empires in Persia. Old Persian was written in cuneiform and has been attested as late as the third century B.C.E. Middle Persian, often called Pahlavi, was written in the Aramaic script and was the official language of the pre-Islamic Sassanian kings. Zoroastrian and Manichaean religious documents were written in Pahlavi. Dialects of Persian are spoken by peoples in Afghanistan, Central Asia, and Eastern Anatolia.

pesantren (Javanese: place of study)

Second-level schools in Indonesia that teach Islamic subjects, including ARABIC grammar, QUR'ÂN recitation, TAFSÎR, KALÂM, FIQH, ethics, logic, history, and mysticism. Under modern pressures, these schools have added more subjects, but appear to be losing ground to other more modern forms of education.

Pharaoh

See FIRʿAWN.

Philippines

Muslims comprise only about nine percent of the population of the Phillipines, and live in the island of Mindanao. Conversion took place as a result of Islamic traders arriving as early as the thirteenth century, being well established when the Spanish conquered the area in the sixteenth century. The Spanish called the Muslims the Moros, after the Moors of Spain, and failed to convert them to Catholicism as they did the rest of the inhabitants. The last half of the twentieth century saw a Moro liberation movement to establish an independent Islamic state in Mindanao, with the resultant conflict unresolved.

philosophy

See FALSAFAH.

pilgrimage

See ḤAJJ.

Pillars of Islam (Arabic *arkân al-islâm*)

There are five actions that Muslims agree are foundational for being a Muslim: SHAHÂDAH, the declaration of faith, ṢALÂT, the five daily prayers, ZAKÂT, the giving of charity, ṢAWM, fasting during the month of RAMAḌÂN, and ḤAJJ, making the pilgrimage. While these are not in the QUR'ÂN, they are found in traditions from the Prophet, and the elements were agreed on early by most Muslims. Each of these five actions require an internal spiritual commitment and an external sign of intent (NIYYAH) as well as the faithful completion of the action, showing Islam's medial position between the extremes of orthodoxy and orthopraxy. Over time, some groups have added to or modified this list, with JIHÂD as the most common addition.

pious foundations

See WAQF.

pîr (Persian: elder)

A term used to designate a ṢÛFÎ teacher who initiates a MURÎD into the ṬARÎQAH. Critics of Ṣûfism contend that the *pîr* is an uneducated person whose only claim to authority is his ability to confer *barakât* (blessings), and who often acts contrary to the QUR'ÂN and the SHARÎʿAH. This tension is a theme that is part of the story tradition within Ṣûfism. (*See also* BARAKAH.)

Pîr Ṣadr ad-Dîn Muḥammad (died *c.* beginning of the ninth/fifteenth century)

Credited with the founding of the KHOJAS (NIZÂRÎ ISMÂʿÎLÎ SHÎʿÎ) in India, by converting Hindus and giving them the title *khoja*, meaning "sir." Biographical information about him is derived from GINÂNS, making them more hagiographic than historical.

Pîr Shams (*fl.* eighth/fourteenth century)

A NIZÂRÎ ISMÂʿÎLÎ SHÎʿÎ leader who is credited with beginning the *satpanth*, or "True Path," in the area of Sind. Little certain is known of his biography except through the GINÂNS attributed to him. (*See also* SATPANTHÎ.)

polygyny

See MARRIAGE.

Potiphar

See QIṬFÎR.

prayer

See ṢALÂT.

prophethood

See NABÎ.

puberty rites

There are no obligatory puberty rites of passage dictated in the QUR'ÂN or in the SHARÎ'AH. Nevertheless, regional custom includes male CIRCUMCISION (*khitân*), between the ages of three and fifteen, and is said to be a practice of the pre-Islamic prophets, particularly IBRÂHÎM. Ceremonies surrounding male circumcision are elaborate and often mark the entry of the male into full participation of the rites of Islam. The CLITORIDECTOMY, so-called "female circumcision," is a pre-Islamic practice that has little authority or foundation in Islam.

purdah (Persian/Urdu *pardah*: veil, curtain)

The custom of separating and secluding women from the public sphere. This notion has come under scrutiny as scholars in many Islamic countries have tried to align modern Islamic practice with the practices of greater freedom for women at the time of MUḤAMMAD.

purification

Purity is one of the central notions in Islam and necessary for a Muslim to conduct a daily religious life. Food must be ḤALÂL, which includes notions of purity as to both type and preparation, and the individual must be free from contaminants, such as blood, feces, etc. before performing prayer (ṢALÂT). Removal of contaminants through ABLUTION, changing clothes, and other external acts is prescribed in detail in SHARÎ'AH. Spiritual purity is equally important and requires repenting of sins as well as acts of atonement. Muslims in some communities will go to great lengths to lead lives that avoid major contaminants, such as pork, dogs, and touching non-Muslims or wearing clothes worn by them. Modern science and traditional notions of purity have sometimes combined both to find a scientific basis for religious purity and to provide a religious foundation for public health issues. (*See also* GHUSL; ṬAHÂRAH; WUḌÛ'.)

Q

Qâbîl wa-Hâbîl (Arabic)

Cain and Abel, sons of ADAM, not mentioned in the QUR'ÂN, but prominently featured in TAFSÎR. Qâbîl is the first murderer in human history, killing his brother and burying him after watching the crow scratch in the earth. According to ISRÂ'ÎLIYYÂT traditions, one of the causes of the enmity between the two brothers was that each of them had a twin sister. Each brother was supposed to mate with his brother's twin, but Qâbîl preferred to marry his own sister, since they had been born in Paradise (AL-JANNAH.) (*See also* 'ANÂQ.)

qadar (Arabic: divine decree, fate, predestination)

The term has the sense of fixed limit and was probably originally related to concepts in Greek and Northwest Semitic cultures that humans had a fixed portion of fate allotted to them. Because of the extensive use of this term in the QUR'ÂN, coupled with the related notions that God decides salvation or damnation for whom He wills, many have felt that human free agency was limited. Even among the most "fatalistic," however, humans are seen as having the freedom to choose between good and evil. Of all of God's sentient creatures, only the lower angels are deprived of that faculty. (*See also* KALÂM.)

Qadariyyah (Arabic)

The name for a number of theological movements in early Islam that held that humans have free will and are not limited in their actions by QADAR, or predestination.

qadhf (Arabic: defamation)

A false accusation of unchastity (ZINÂ'), which is severely punished under Islamic law. The revelation of the requirements for four eye-witnesses for fornication comes from the experience of 'Â'ISHAH bt. Abî Bakr, wife of MUḤAMMAD, who became separated from a raiding party when she was accompanying the Prophet. She was found and returned the next day by a young Muslim, but rumors were spread that she had had improper relations with him. After a period in which she was sent back to her father's house, the revelation came that made the requirement for four eye witnesses. The punishment of eighty lashes is also thought to relate to this incident by most commentators. In Islamic law (SHARÎ'AH), this extends to calling someone a bastard, because this is tantamount to accusing the mother.

qâḍî (Arabic: judge)

A person empowered by the ruler of an Islamic country to judge cases under SHARÎ'AH law. The powers of a *qâḍî* have historically been broad, but in some Muslim countries in the premodern period, criminal and political cases came under the jurisdiction of a *shurṭah* or police court, thus avoiding the protections of *sharî'ah*. The earliest *qâḍîs* were appointed from the ranks of popular preachers. In many modern Islamic states, the religious connection of the *qâḍî* has been modified by the creation of secular judicial systems and laws. The *qâḍî* may or may not also function as a MUFTÎ.

Qâdiriyyah

A prominent early ṢÛFÎ ṬARÎQAH founded by 'Abd al-Qâdir AL-JÎLÂNÎ in BAGHDÂD. While he left no complete guide, his sons organized the rites of the order. It is found today throughout the Islamic world.

Qâf

The mountain range in Irano-Islamic cosmology that is said to surround the earth. The mountain is either made of or rests on a giant emerald, and is said to be the foundation that supports the earth to keep it stable. All the world's mountains are linked to this mountain, and through it God can cause earthquakes. No one can get to it or go beyond it, and the realm of the eternal life is said to be beyond this range.

al-Qâhirah (Arabic: the victor; the planet Mars)

Cairo, the capital of EGYPT, is one of the Islamic world's most important cities. It was founded in 359/970 by the FÂṬIMID caliph al-Mu'izz near the old camp city of al-Fusṭâṭ, the site of the military camp built by the Muslim conquerors of Egypt. The city is rich with mosques and monuments. Of Islamic importance today is the University of AL-AZHAR. Surveys of Islamic monuments list over seven hundred major Islamic monuments. In addition, the city is filled with small neighborhood mosques and other places of local Islamic interest.

qahwah (Arabic: coffee)

Originally, this term meant wine, but by the eighth/fourteenth century, it had come into common use to mean coffee. Because this beverage was not part of the store of things known to the Prophet in his lifetime, a number of groups have sought to have it banned on religious grounds as an innovation (BID'AH). So far, these moves have proved unsuccessful.

al-Qâ'im

See MUḤAMMAD AL-QÂ'IM.

Qâjârs

The Iranian dynasty that succeeded the ṢAFAVID dynasty, ruling from the twelfth/eighteenth century to 1342/1924, when they were succeeded by Rezâ Shâh PAHLAVI. They were ITHNÂ 'ASHARIYYAH SHÎ'Î. During their reign, Western influence in Iran increased.

qânûn (Arabic from Greek: law)

This means especially codified legislated law, as opposed to the religious law, of the SHARÎ'AH.

Qarâmiṭah, or Qarmâṭî (Arabic)

The Carmathians (also spelled Karmathians). An offshoot of the early ISMÂ'ÎLÎ SHÎ'Î, they were a revolutionary group founded by Ḥamdân Qarmaṭ (disappeared *c.* 286/899). Their doctrines show a mixture of extreme Shî'î thought, Gnosticism, and other philosophical systems. They are infamous for their capture of the Black Stone from the KA'BAH in 317/929, which they kept for over twenty years. With the rise of the FÂṬIMIDS, the main thrust of the movement was absorbed into the mainstream of Ismâ'îlî Shî'îs.

al-Qâsim

The son of the Prophet MUḤAMMAD and KHADÎJAH. Because of him, Muḥammad was known as Abû al-Qâsim. He died at the age of two.

Qaynuqâ'

One of the major Jewish tribes of MADÎNAH. They were expelled from the city, and migrated to Syria.

Qayrawân

Kairouan, an Islamic city in TUNISIA, it was one of the major cities of Islam, founded in the seventh century by 'Uqbah b. Nâfi', the conqueror of North Africa. Like other early Muslim cities, it started as a military camp, since the early Muslim armies of conquest were not quartered among the conquered populations.

qiblah (Arabic)

The direction of prayer toward the KA'BAH in MECCA. The determination of the *qiblah* is a prerequisite for observing the rite of ṢALÂT (prayer). In a mosque, this is marked by the MIḤRÂB. As Muslims traveled throughout the world, they developed sophisticated techniques to determine the direction of prayer, and those techniques enhanced their ability to navigate accurately. Modern advances in these techniques have yielded watches that tell the times for prayer, recite the ADHÂN, and indicate the *qiblah*.

qiṣâṣ (Arabic: retaliation)

Islamic law allows retaliation within the bounds of justice for individuals who are wronged. This system replaces the pre-Islamic notion of revenge that saw no bounds and led to blood feuds.

Qiṭfîr

The name of Potiphar, the Egyptian who purchased YÛSUF, is not mentioned in the QUR'ÂN, but is identified in the TAFSÎR literature as a tyrant and a sexual deviant, whose actions forced his wife to falsely accuse Yûsuf of misconduct.

qiyâs (Arabic: analogical reasoning)

This term is used in FIQH to refer to the strict deductive reasoning that allows one legal case to be linked to another by analogy.

Qom

A small Iranian town south of Tehran, it is the site of a major SHÎ'Î shrine, the tomb of Ḥazrat-i Ma'ṣûmah, the sister of the eighth IMÂM and the location of the leading theological seminaries for the ITHNÂ 'ASHARIYYAH SHÎ'Î.

qubbah (Arabic: dome)

The tombs of saints and other holy places are locations of spiritual power and significance in Islam. As such, they are the destinations of pilgrimages and the locations of supplication and worship. While worship practice varies by location, the rites often involve performing prayers (ṢALÂT), circumambulation (ṬAWÂF), and sacrifices or offerings of food. In many locations where there are mixed religious groups, the shrines are shared by all the worshipers. (*See also* WALÎ.)

qubbat aṣ-ṣakhrah (Arabic: the dome of the rock)

See AL-QUDS.

al-Quds (Arabic: the holy)

This is the Arabic name for Jerusalem. Jerusalem is considered Islam's third holiest city after MECCA and MADÎNAH. It first figured in Islamic religious consciousness as the location of the MASJID

The Dome of the Rock, al-Quds (Jerusalem).

AL-AQṢÂ from which MUḤAMMAD ascended to Heaven on the night of his ISRÂ' and MI'RÂJ. Muslim commentators after Muḥammad's death also made much of the correlation between Mecca and Jerusalem as centers of the earth. When the city was captured in the early years of the conquest, those holy sites, which were in the same location as the ruins of the Jewish Second Temple, were marked with the building of mosques and the *qubbat aṣ-ṣakhrah*, the Dome of the Rock. Over time, the location was further enhanced to become a major shrine center. During the period of the Crusades, a body of literature developed that was designed to enhance the prestige and importance of the city in the minds of Muslims to encourage them to recapture it from the Crusaders. This *faḍâ'il al-Quds* literature collected ḤADÎTHS about the city and combined them with stories adapted from Jewish and Christian lore, with the result that al-Quds became an object of veneration and pilgrimage. The city was part of the OTTOMAN EMPIRE until it became the capital of British Mandate Palestine. It is now included in the state of Israel, and ownership of the city, particularly the sites holy to Jews, Christians, and Muslims, is one of the most sensitive and contentious issues in the Middle East.

Qur'ân (Arabic: recitation, proclamation)

This is the scripture for Muslims brought to the Prophet MUḤAMMAD from God through the mediation of the archangel JIBRÎL.

There are 114 SÛRAHS, or chapters, each divided into 'ÂYAT, or "verses," but, more properly, "signs." Each *sûrah* except for the ninth is preceeded by the BASMALAH formula, "In the name of God, the Merciful, the Compassionate." Each *sûrah* has a name derived either from a prominent term or from the major theme of the chapter. Muslims refer to the *sûrah*s by name, while Western scholarship refers to them by number. During Muḥammad's prophetic career, we are told that Jibrîl reviewed the revelations annually for accuracy and twice before the Prophet's death. Muḥammad's secretary, ZAYD B. THÂBIT, headed a commission some two decades after his death to make an official recension under the sponsorship of the caliph 'UTHMÂN, and by the fourth/tenth century, a system of orthography was fixed that reduced the number of variant readings to approximately seven.

The Qur'ân is the culmination of God's revelations, which started with the prophet ADAM. It is a revelation both to humans and to JINNS, who are regarded as created, with souls, and as capable of salvation and damnation. It is viewed as the completion of all previous scripture and a correction of errors that have entered the preserved versions of those scriptures. For Muslims, previous scripture is valid only as it agrees with the Qur'ân. Each part of God's word can

Decorative frontispiece from the Qur'ân, opening page of Sûrah *1.*

be found in heaven in a "well-guarded tablet," the *'umm al-kitâb*, and is held to be God's immutable speech. As such, it is comparable to the notion of *Logos* in Christianity, but, unlike Judaism and Christianity, Muslims regard the words of the Qur'ân divine in and of themselves and as signs and proofs of God. For this reason, Muslims approach the text in a state of ritual purity. The ideal is to internalize God's word by memorizing the Qur'ân. Regardless of the native language of the individual Muslim, the Qur'ân remains in Arabic, any translation being a commentary, TAFSÎR.

By its own account, the Qur'ân was sent by God as a guide and a warning. Both of these functions are presented in various forms: as direct command, as direct prohibition, as story, and as parable. Sometimes the Qur'ân has clear passages, MUḤKAMÂT, and sometimes ambiguous or obscure passages, MUTASHÂBIHÂT. In all cases, the style of the passages facilitates timeless interpretation, not bound by specific historical circumstances or cultural locations. When the Qur'ân refers to stories and events mentioned in Jewish and Christian scripture, it does so as a reminder, and leaves off mentioning all of the details. It rather sets out the meaning of the stories for their moral purpose and as a guide to right behavior. It sets forth a clear notion of a "contract" between God and His creatures that good actions will be rewarded and evil actions punished at the end of time. In this sense, it is regarded as the foundation for Islamic law (SHARÎʿAH).

Muslims are said to live under the Qur'ân, meaning that it is a protection in every part of their daily lives. It provides the basis of ethical behavior and a guide for conducting all life's activities. Muslims recite the opening chapter as well as other portions during each of the five ṢALÂT and one-thirtieth each night during the month of RAMAḌÂN. Portions are recited at public events and in connection with important life-cycle events. The aesthetic dimension of recitation, TAJWÎD, is important in Muslim life, and Qur'ân reciters often enjoy celebrity status in Islamic countries. Calligraphic designs made from Qur'ânic passages are used for decoration throughout the Islamic world, and, in their most abstracted forms, have given way to arabesques in Western art.

Modern trends in Qur'ân interpretation are generally characterized by two competing strands. Under the general rubric of "fundamentalism," some are proposing a narrow, "literalist" reading of the scripture as a means of anchoring their political and social views in the Qur'ân. Others are turning to the same text to counter those interpretations and to overturn blind adherence to authority (TAQLÎD). These modern trends also characterize the polar tensions in Qur'ân interpretation throughout the history of Islam, during which the Qur'ân has served as a firm anchor and guide to individual Muslims and to the 'UMMAH in general.

Qur'ânic recitation

See TAJWÎD.

Quraysh (Arabic)

The tribe of MUḤAMMAD and the dominant tribe in MECCA during his lifetime. The name is associated with an aquatic mammal, possibly a dugong, indigenous to the Red Sea and Indian Ocean, suggesting the origin of the tribe as a sea-trading group that moved inland for trade advantage. Descendants of the tribe, because of their relationship to Muḥammad, were eligible to assume the office of caliph (KHALÎFAH) in SUNNÎ Islam.

Qurayẓah

One of the major Jewish tribes of MADÎNAH. They were accused of treachery during the battle of KHANDAQ and punished by having their men killed and their women and children enslaved.

qurbân (Arabic: sacrifice)

See 'ÎD AL-AḌḤÂ.

qurrâ' (Arabic: villagers; sg. *qâri'*)

The political group(s) in early Islam grouped together under the name *qurrâ'*, often but incorrectly translated as "Qur'ân reciters." They were Iraqis, who were represented in the armies of both 'ALÎ and MU'ÂWIYAH in their conflict, but ended by blaming 'Alî more for the failure of their cause. Their political ambitions were not based solely on religious grounds. They were, for the most part, from southern Iraq, and under the expansion of Islam, were losing their positions of privilege, particularly under the policies of the caliph 'UTHMÂN. Their support for 'Alî seems to have been based, in part, on their hope that an 'UMAYYAD defeat would result in their regaining their privileges. They formed some of the constituent elements of the KHAWÂRIJ and proved to be some of the most fanatical in those groups.

Qurṭubah

Cordova was one of the major cities of Islamic Spain, AL-ANDALUS. The town was conquered by Muslims in 92/711 and became the capital of al-Andalus in 99/717. Its major period of prosperity was during the 'UMAYYAD period, starting in 138/756. From 422/1031, it was ruled by various dynasties, including the Almoravids (AL-MURÂBIṬÛN) and the Almohads (AL-MUWAḤḤIDÛN). It was taken in the Reconquista by Ferdinand III of Castile in 1633/1236. Of the major Islamic monuments, the most striking is the Great Mosque, known in Spanish as *La Mezquita*. Numerous Islamic scholars were born in the city, including IBN ḤAZM and IBN RUSHD.

al-Qurṭubî, Abû 'Abd Allâh Muḥammad b. Aḥmad b. Abî Bakr b. Faraj al-Anṣârî al-Khazrajî al-Andalusî (died 671/1272)

A writer of MÂLIKÎ FIQH and TAFSÎR. His monumental *tafsîr*, *Jâmi' li-aḥkâm al-Qur'ân*, is a complete treatise on the subject of scriptural exegesis. It makes extensive use of ḤADÎTHS and assists the reader in understanding the relationship between the Qur'ânic verses and law.

Quṣayy

Ancestor of MUḤAMMAD and father of 'Abd Manâf and 'Abd al-'Uzzâ.

al-Qushayrî, Abû al-Qâsim 'Abd al-Karîm b. Hawâzin (376/986–465/1074)

Writer on KALÂM and defender of AL-'ASH'ARÎ's thought as well as a ṢÛFÎ. In his treatises on metaphysics, he both defended al-ʿAshʿarî from accusations of heresy and attempted to harmonize mysticism with metaphysics. He also wrote a mystical TAFSÎR on the QUR'ÂN.

quṭb (Arabic)

As a technical term in Ṣûfism, it means the "axis" or "pole," i.e. the center of the hierarchy of saints. (*See also* WALÎ.)

Quṭb, Sayyid (1324/1906–1386/1966)

Influential Islamist thinker associated with AL-IKHWÂN AL-MUSLIMÛN (the Muslim Brotherhood). His writings include opposition both to the West and toward leaders in Islamic countries he saw as violating the precepts of Islam. His participation in Brotherhood activities led to his execution in Egypt in 1966. His writings have inspired numerous Islamist revolutionaries.

R

ar-Rabb (Arabic: the Lord)

This is applied exclusively to God. The word occurs as a common noun in Arabic meaning "master," or "owner," but a ḤADÎTH forbids slaves to refer to their masters as *rabb*.

Râbiʿah al-ʿAdawiyyah (*c.* 95/713–185/801)

A famous female ṢÛFÎ, she was born in BAṢRAH, stolen into slavery, and freed because of her piety. She spent the rest of her life in mystic seclusion, preaching the doctrine that the mystic love of God and the seeking of His companionship is the object of every true believer. She also likened the beatific vision to the lifting of the veil of the bride, the Ṣûfî, by the bridegroom, ALLÂH. She is depicted as carrying fire in one hand and water in the other. When asked where she was going, she replied that she was going to throw fire into Heaven and water onto Hell, so that both would disappear and leave humans to contemplate Allâh alone, without either the temptation of reward or the fear of punishment.

ar-râfiḍah (Arabic: rejectors)

A term of abuse used by SUNNÎ against the SHÎʿÎ, who rejected the legitimacy of the first three caliphs in favor of the caliphate of ʿALÎ B. ABÎ ṬÂLIB. The ITHNÂ ʿASHARIYYAH SHÎʿÎ turned the term into a label of praise, claiming that they were the ones who turned from or rejected evil. They claim that this was a term applied to HÂRÛN, reinforcing the notion that ʿAlî's position with respect to MUḤAMMAD was like Hârûn's to MÛSÂ. The city of QOM became the intellectual center for the Ithnâ ʿAsharî Shîʿî movement. They were strongly anti-Sunnî, but were, at first, politically quietist. They held that ʿAlî had been designated by Muḥammad as his IMÂM and KHALÎFAH. They allow the practice of TAQIYYAH, or religious dissimulation, to protect themselves and their community. Ideas of the early Râfiḍiyyah influenced the development of Shîʿîsm in general and the Ithnâ ʿAsharîs in particular.

rahbâniyyah (Arabic: monasticism)

This term occurs once in the QUR'ÂN (Q. 57:27) in a passage that has given rise to numerous interpretations. Several ḤADÎTHS attribute to MUḤAMMAD the statement that there is no monasticism in Islam. According to a tradition quoted by AḤMAD B. ḤANBAL, Islam has replaced monasticism with JIHÂD: "Every prophet has some kind of *rahbâniyyah*; the *rahbâniyyah* of this community is *jihâd*."

Râḥîl

The biblical Rachel, wife of YAʿQÛB (Jacob). She is not named in the QUR'ÂN, but in Q. 4:23, marrying two sisters is prohibited except when that has happened in the past. Some commentators see this as a reference to Ya'qûb's marriage to both Liyâ and Râḥîl.

ar-Raḥîm (Arabic: the Compassionate)

One of the ninety-nine AL-'ASMÂ' AL-ḤUSNÂ, or beautiful names of God and part of the BASMALAH.

ar-Raḥmân (Arabic: the Merciful)

One of the ninety-nine AL-'ASMÂ' AL-ḤUSNÂ or beautiful names of God and part of the BASMALAH.

Rahman, Fazlur (1919–88)

Born in what would become PAKISTAN, he became the twentieth century's foremost voice of liberal Islamic reform. Educated at Punjab University and Oxford, he taught for a time in Pakistan until he was forced to leave after criticism of his reformist views. He moved to North America, where he became a professor of Islamic studies at the University of Chicago. He believed that fundamentalist approaches to Islam were misguided attempts to maintain a secular status quo, and that the problems of the Islamic world were a result of poor religious education. He regarded himself as a MUJTAHID, and earned a reputation as the "destroyer of ḤADÎTH" from his view that every tradition should be reviewed in light of the overall Qur'ânic message. His writings have greatly influenced Islam in North America and Islamic reformers around the world.

Rajab (Arabic)

The seventh month of the Islamic lunar calendar, it was a "holy" month in pre-Islamic times. It is the month in which the ISRÂ' and MI'RÂJ of the Prophet are said to have taken place.

rajm (Arabic: stoning)

The lapidation or stoning of the devil during the rites of the ḤAJJ. The word can also mean "cursed," and is used in the form *rajîm* as an epithet of the Devil. (*See also* MINÂ.)

rak'ah (Arabic: bowing)

This term has come to mean a unit of worship in the ṢALÂT. The number of units varies with each prayer, with the first having three, the second, fourth, and fifth having four, and the third having two, making a total of seventeen units that are obligatory each day. (*See also* FARḌ.)

Ramaḍân

The ninth month of the Muslim lunar calendar and the month of fasting in Islam. It is the month in which the QUR'ÂN is said to have been first revealed. (*See also* 'BAIRAM; ÎD AL-FIṬR; ṢAWM.

Rashîd Riḍâ, Muḥammad (1865–1935)

Modernist Islamic revivalist and advocate of reform, he was born and educated in Syria and moved to Egypt to join MUḤAMMAD 'ABDUH, where he became one of his close associates. Through his influential publication AL-MANÂR, he advocated a return to the foundational sources of Islam, the QUR'ÂN, the SUNNAH, and IJMÂ' as a source for reform, believing that Islam was fundamentally compatible with the modern world. His writings have had great influence in the modern Islamic world.

Râshidûn (Arabic: the rightly guided)

A term generally applied by the SUNNÎ to the first four caliphs after the death of MUḤAMMAD: ABÛ BAKR, 'UMAR,

ʿUTHMÂN, and ʿALÎ. This was a polemical title designed to counter SHÎʿÎ rejectionist claims that only ʿAlî should have been caliph. (*See also* AR-RÂFIḌAH.)

rasûl (Arabic: messenger)

MUḤAMMAD is termed a *rasûl* because of his message of warning and hope. (*See also* NABÎ.)

râwî (Arabic: transmitter)

A transmitter of ḤADÎTH, stories, and poetry. In pre-Islamic times, the *râwî* was an important figure in the chain of preservation of the poetry of the *ayyâm al-ʿArab* (the battle days of the Arabs). They were often apprentice poets or poets in their own right, who would memorize lines of poetry and preserve them. When a poet needed to recover a section of poetry, he would go to his *râwî* and have the lines recited. He might then amend them and have them committed again to memory. When this custom was brought into the Islamic period, it became one of the patterns for the preservation and transmission of the QUR'ÂN and ḤADÎTHS, even after the introduction of writing.

Rawzah khvânî (Persian)

The narrative lamentations of the martyrdom of IMÂM ḤUSAYN B. ʿALÎ. Among the ITHNÂ ʿASHARIYYAH SHÎʿÎ of Iran, these are performed by both men and women, sometimes at great length, with professional performers paid on the basis of their rhetorical skill and ability to evoke sad emotions from their hearers.

ra'y (Arabic: opinion, idea)

In Islamic law, the term has the sense of individual legal opinion or judgment. (*See also* FIQH; QIYÂS; SHARÎʿAH.)

Rayḥânah bt. Zayd (died 10/632)

Concubine of the Prophet MUḤAMMAD.

reʿâyâ

See ʿASKARÎ.

Red Crescent

The Islamic equivalent of the Red Cross. (*See also* HILÂL.)

Regional Islamic Daʿwah Council of Southeast Asia and the Pacific

Known as RISEAP, the organization was founded in 1980 to coordinate the region's missionary efforts.

relics

The veneration of relics of holy persons and souvenirs of holy places is often condemned in Islam but has been part of Islamic practice from an early period. Pieces of the KISWAH, the covering of the KAʿBAH, are treasured by persons returning from the ḤAJJ as possessing the power to bestow *barakât* (blessings). The same is true of the possessions and remains of saints (WALÎs). Some of the ʿULAMÂ' have declared that the practice is un-Islamic, but other groups have defended the practice on the basis of QUR'ÂN and ḤADÎTH.

repentance

See TAWBAH.

revelation

See WAḤY.

revival, renewal

See TAJDÎD.

ribâ (Arabic: usury)

Unearned profit, usury, this financial practice is condemned in the QUR'ÂN

(Q. 2:275ff.). *See also* BANKS AND BANKING; MAYSIR.)

ribâṭ (Arabic)

Fortified Islamic monastery in North Africa. It also refers to the military and mystical institution that developed around it. The development of the *ribâṭ* system is linked to the development of JIHÂD practices in North Africa. The fortifications themselves offered refuge and protection to the troops and to the surrounding countryside in case of attack. As with such fortifications elsewhere, they became the centers of urbanization when other conditions were favorable. Within the *jihâd* organization, the troops regarded themselves as dedicated to God and members of a brotherhood, often in the manner of Islamic mystics (ṢÛFÎ). Some of these fortifications became the tombs of saints (WALÎs), and were the objects of pilgrim veneration. (*See also* KHÂNQÂH; MARABOUT; ZÂWIYAH.)

riddah (Arabic: apostasy)

Under SHARÎʿAH, apostasy is judged to be a most severe transgression. At various times, some Muslim groups have held that grave sin will constitute apostasy. This was the view held by the KHAWÂRIJ and recently by those who condemned Salman Rushdie, in spite of his protests that he had not left Islam. (*See also* ILḤÂD; SABB.)

Riḍwân (Arabic)

The angel in charge of Paradise, who will be in charge of taking care of the blessed at the YAWM AD-DÎN.

Rifâʿiyyah

A major ṢÛFÎ ṬARÎQAH named after Aḥmad b. ʿAlî ar-Rifâʿî (499/1106–578/1182) in southern Iraq. His group was known for using fire and snakes in their devotions. In modified forms, it has spread widely in the Islamic world.

Rightly Guided Caliphs

See RÂSHIDÛN.

riḥlah (Arabic: journey)

A journey taken to obtain religious knowledge. The early collectors of ḤADÎTHs traveled widely to obtain their collections, and the institution of the ḤAJJ has promoted travel for religious purposes. In Persian, the word also means to travel to the next life, to die.

rûḥ (Arabic: spirit, soul, breath)

See NAFS.

Rûmî, Jalâl ad-Dîn (604/1207–672/1273)

Influential Persian mystic and poet, whose poem the *Mathnawî*, has achieved almost cultic status among Persian speakers and many New Age mystics in North America. He was called by many *Mawlânâ*, "Our Master," which has given rise to the MEVLEVÎ ṢÛFÎ ṬARÎQAH.

Ruqayyah bt. Muḥammad (died 2/624)

A daughter of MUḤAMMAD and KHADÎJAH, she was married to ʿUTHMÂN B. ʿAFFÂN. She died during the battle of BADR of an illness, so that her husband, who was nursing her, was not present at the battle.

ru'yâ (Arabic: vision)

As a technical term in Islamic mysticism, it refers to the Beatific Vision of God. This concept has caused considerable controversy in Islamic theological circles, with many claiming that it is impossible for humans to see God. The MUʿTAZILAH, in particular, denied the possibility of the Vision, and this became one of the test questions in the MIḤNAH.

S

as-sâ'ah (Arabic: the hour)

This is one of the terms in the QUR'AN for the *eschaton* and the time of the end of all things. While it is often synonymous with such terms as YAWM AD-DÎN, the Day of Judgment, and YAWM AL-QIYÂMAH, the Day of Resurrection, some commentators use it to refer to a specific point in time among all the events of the end-time.

Sabaeans, or Sabeans

A group of people mentioned in the QUR'ÂN regarded as AHL AL-KITÂB (people of scripture), entitled to special privileges under Islamic rule. Scholars have identified the group with either the residents of the kingdom of Sabâ', or Sheba, in South Arabia, or a group of star worshipers in northern Syria in the area of Ḥarrân. This latter group is said to have asserted its claim to religious protection after Syria had been conquered by the Muslim armies. The South Arabian group is identified with the people of BILQÎS, the Queen of Sheba, who visited SULAYMÂN. Post-Qur'ânic tradition has made much of that visit, the involvement of JINN, and the strategems used by Sulaymân to determine whether or not Bilqîs was of half-demonic parentage.

sabb (Arabic: insult)

Blasphemy, in the sense of insulting God, the Prophet, or any important aspect of Islam.

sacrifice

Sacrifice in Islam is interpreted as blood sacrifice, that is, the ritual slaughter of animals, and personal sacrifice, such as charitable donation. Martyrdom is viewed as the supreme personal sacrifice, and combines the two categories. The details of the exact manner for performing a sacrifice are the subject of much discussion in ḤADÎTH collections and books on FIQH. Blood sacrifice is part of the obligatory rites of the ḤAJJ, during the 'ÎD AL-'AḌḤÂ, and is optional on that day for Muslims not on *ḥajj*. Tradition holds that this sacrifice is in commemoration of IBRÂHÎM's intended sacrifice of his son. Some Muslims also sacrifice animals at the birth of a child, two for a boy and one for a girl, in a customary rite called 'AQÎQAH. In all the cases of blood sacrifice, a portion of the meat is distributed as alms, and the believer is enjoined to regard the sacrifice as thanks to God. In the cases of charity, either ZAKÂT or ṢADAQAH, the sacrifice is to be given freely, with thanks to God, and not in an amount that would impoverish the giver.

ṣadaqah (Arabic: alms)

Voluntary charitable giving, it is usually distinguished from the more organized almsgiving of ZAKÂT. As with all charity in Islam, the amount is supposed to come from the surplus of what one has after one has set aside enough to keep oneself and family, and in any case must not be an amount that would impoverish the giver.

ṣadr (Arabic: breast)

A title used chiefly in Iran and Central Asia to refer to someone of high rank among the ʿULAMÂʾ of both the SUNNÎ and the SHÎʿÎ. When the office of *ṣadr* became institutionalized and hereditary, the term also became used as a "last" name.

aṣ-Ṣadr, Muḥammad Bâqir (1935–80)

Influential SHÎʿÎ thinker and political figure from IRAQ, he wrote on TAFSÎR, FALSAFAH, ʾUṢÛL AL-FIQH, and other Islamic topics, but his work on interest-free banking was his most widely known work. In it, he advocated a simple means of avoiding RIBÂ through a single contract system in which the bank served as a mediator between the borrower and the capital holder. As a political figure, he opposed the Baʿathist regime in Iraq, and he was taken from his home town of NAJAF and executed along with his sister.

aṣ-Ṣadr, Mûsâ (1928–1978?)

Founder of AMAL, the popular SHÎʿÎ movement in Lebanon, Mûsâ aṣ-Ṣadr was born into a prominent clerical family and educated in IRAN and in NAJAF, IRAQ, under some of the leading teachers of Shîʿî FIQH. When he visited Lebanon in 1957, he impressed the Shîʿî population so that they invited him to become the senior religious authority in Tyre. His practical work in establishing educational and social institutions as well as his spiritual and political leadership earned him the title *Imâm* Mûsâ. In the Lebanese civil war, the politics of the Lebanese Shîʿî community became religiously charged, resulting in the defeat of the PLO at the hands of the Israelis in 1982. Some sources claim that this event was supported and applauded by Lebanese Shîʿî in the name of aṣ-Ṣadr, although others deny that. He disappeared in 1978 while on a visit to Libya and is regarded by his followers to be in GHAYBAH.

Ṣafâ

A small hill in MECCA that, along with a companion hill, Marwah, are the terminus points of the running in the ritual of SAʿY in the ḤAJJ and the *ʿumrah*. The two hills are now enclosed within the Great Mosque.

Ṣafavids

The dynasty that ruled IRAN from 907/1501 to about 1134/1722, it took its name from Ṣafî ad-Dîn Isḥâq (died 735/1334), the founder of the mystical order of the Ṣafawiyyah. Situated between MUGHAL India and the OTTOMAN EMPIRE, the dynasty formed an alliance with the Qizilbash tribe, whose beliefs were partially SHÎʿÎ. This led eventually to the Ṣafavids adopting the Shîʿism of the ITHNÂ ʿASHARIYYAH (Twelvers) as their state religion and promoting a Persian-based literary and intellectual renaissance under state sponsorship. The religious culture they developed survived their political collapse and helped form the basis for modern Iran.

Ṣafiyyah bt. Ḥuyayy

One of the wives of the Prophet, she was a Jewish captive, taken at the battle of Khaybar, and manumitted after her conversion to Islam.

Ṣafavid mural, Chihil Sutun Palace, Isfahan, Iran.

ṣaḥâbah (Arabic: companion; sg. *ṣâḥib*)

Companions of the Prophet MUḤAMMAD. The term refers to the close associates of the Prophet who converted before the fall of MECCA. Other scholars count all those Muslims alive in his generation who had contact with him, however fleeting. They were the first generation of transmitters of ḤADÎTH materials, and their eye- and ear-witness accounts of the sayings and deeds of the Prophet are a source of Islamic law and lore. (*See also* SUNNAH.)

ṣaḥîfah (Arabic: leaf, page)

In Islamic religious usage, the term refers to a page from the QUR'ÂN or to a page from one of the revelations to prior prophets.

ṣaḥîḥ (Arabic: true, sound)

A technical term in ḤADÎTH indicating the greatest degree of reliability of its transmission and authenticity of its origin. The term is also used as a title for two *ḥadîth* collections, one by AL-BUKHÂRÎ and the other by MUSLIM B. AL-ḤAJJÂJ. The two are often referred together as the "two *ṣaḥîḥ*s," or *aṣ-ṣaḥîḥayn* and are regarded as the two most reliable SUNNÎ collections of tradition.

saḥûr (Arabic)

The last meal eaten before starting fasting at daybreak during the days of RAMAḌÂN. This is often a time for inviting close friends as guests, and the preparations can be extensive and time-consuming.

saint, sainthood

See WALÎ.

sa'îr (Arabic)

The name used in the QUR'ÂN for one of the ranks of Hell or for Hell itself (Q. 22:4 *et passim*).

sajjâdah (Arabic)

Prayer rug or carpet, often elaborately decorated with a mosque scene in a one-way design and placed with the head of the design toward the QIBLAH, the direction of prayer toward MECCA.

sakînah (Arabic from Hebrew/Aramaic: spirit of God)

This word is used with various meanings in the QUR'ÂN. In one meaning, it has the sense of abiding or dwelling in a place. This is the ordinary Arabic use of the root. In another sense, also in the Qur'ân, it refers to the spirit of God. This meaning is found in TAFSÎR and ISRÂ'ÎLIYYÂT literature, as, for example, when IBRÂHÎM and ISMÂ'ÎL are looking for the place to build the KA'BAH, the *sakînah* circles around the right spot, saying, "Build over me; build over me." It is supposed to be like a wind, but with a face that can talk. In Islamic mysticism (Ṣûfism), it becomes an inner light that guides the mystic on the path.

salafiyyah (Arabic: forebear, ancestor)

In Islamic religious parlance, the term covers several different concepts. In the first instance, it refers to the earliest three generations of Muslims, the ṢAḤÂBAH, the TÂBI'ÛN, and the *tâbi'û at-tâbi'în*, whose proximity to the model of the Prophet and whose interpretive role in forming Islam set them apart as exemplars for future Muslim behavior. In this sense, it was used by JAMÂL AD-DÎN AL-AFGHÂNÎ and MUḤAMMAD 'ABDUH as the name of their reform movement that sought to mediate between the social conditions of the early twentieth century and strict requirements of the fundamentals of Islam. The term is now used in two opposite senses. It is used in the sense of "renewal" or "reform," usually involving a reassessment of the foundational sources of Islam. In the opposite sense, it is used as an attempt to translate the Western term "fundamentalism" into a meaningful Islamic term. In this sense, it is used as a synonym of *uṣûliyyah*.

salâm (Arabic: peace)

The noun is related to the verb meaning "to be safe and free from harm." It is used to mean the range of "safety, unharmed, peace, and quiet." It is used in various forms as a greeting throughout the Islamic world. (*See also* ISLAM; MUSLIM.)

ṣalât (Arabic: prayer)

Ritual prayer or prayer service as opposed to a supplicatory prayer, DU'Â'. Participation in *ṣalât* is generally regarded as the second of the five major duties or PILLARS OF ISLAM, ranking immediately after the declaration of faith. Many commentators remark that this ranking is because direct ritual communication between the individual believer and God is central to being a Muslim. No priest performs this function for the believer. Ritual prayer in Islam is characterized by constraints of time, ritual purity, intention, and physical location, and consists of a series of recitations and prostrations. There are

Muslim praying, Dar-al-Islam mosque, New Mexico, U.S.A.

five *ṣalawât* per day, consisting of a total of seventeen RAKʿAH, or prostration units. These are the morning prayer, *ṣalât al-fajr* or *aṣ-ṣubḥ*, said just before sunrise; the midday prayer, *ṣalât aẓ-ẓuhr*, said between noon and mid-afternoon, the afternoon prayer, *ṣalât al-ʿaṣr*, said between mid-afternoon; and before sunset; the sunset prayer, *ṣalât al-maghrib*, said between sunset and darkness; and the nighttime prayer, *ṣalât al-ʿishâʾ*, said at night. The *ṣalât al-maghrib* is the first prayer of the day, since the beginning of the day is counted from sunset. Each believer, male or female, of sound mind and body is obligated to perform the five prayers. If one is ill and misses a prayer, it is often recommended that the prayers be made up at a later date. It is recommended to pray in congregation, following the lead of an IMÂM, but the prayer is still individual and the believer can pray alone as well.

Responding to the call to prayer, the ʾADHÂN, the believer must make ABLUTION, (WUḌÛʾ, GHUSL), which is a physical cleansing and a spiritual purification, in which one focuses on the act and spiritual purpose of the prayer. Next, the believer must declare the intent (NIYYAH) to perform the particular prayer, and determine the direction of the prayer, QIBLAH, in which the worshiper faces MECCA. The believer can pray in any place that is ritually pure, with the prostrations performed on a SAJJÂDAH, or prayer mat. After meeting the above requirements, the worshipper performs the required *rakʿah*s by reciting the TAKBÎR, saying "*Allâhu ʾAkbar*" ("God is the Greatest"). Then the opening chapter of the QURʾÂN is recited. After this, the worshiper bows, remains still for a moment, raises back up, remains still for a moment, prostrates with the forehead touching the ground and the hands outstretched, sits back, prostrates again, sits back, recites the SHAHÂDAH, or declaration of faith, the blessings on the Prophet, and the *taslîm* (the uttering of *as-salâmu ʿalaykum*). This is done twice. During the bowings and prostrations, formulaic utterances praising God are recited.

Mystical interpretations of *ṣalât* stress the direct, unmediated spiritual connection between the worshiper and God during the time of prayer. This is seen to have both spiritual values and healing and restorative powers on the body. Historians and modern Muslim revivalists have noted the role *ṣalât* has played in building communal discipline and a sense of group solidarity.

In addition to the five required prayers each day, certain congregational prayers are associated with particular festivals and times of community need. There are, for example, communal *ṣalawât* for rain. The Friday noon prayer, *ṣalât al-jumʿah*, is the most common communal prayer, and regularly includes a "sermon," or KHUṬBAH. The Friday noon prayer is normally held in a congregational mosque. (*See also* PURIFICATION.)

ṣalât al-janâzah

The funeral prayer in Islam consisting of the FÂTIḤAH, the recitation of *Allâhu ʾakbar*, prayer for the Prophet, *Allâhu ʾakbar*, supplication for the deceased, *Allâhu ʾakbar*, supplication for all deceased Muslims, and the recitation of *as-salâmu ʿalaykum*, to finish the prayer.

ṣalât al-jumʿah

See ṢALÂT.

Ṣâliḥ

The prophet mentioned in the QURʾÂN as having been sent to the THAMÛD. The Thamûd hamstrung the she-camel sent from God as proof of the prophetic warning, so they were destroyed by an earthquake.

Saljûqs, also Seljuks

A Turkish dynasty that established itself in Persia in the fifth/eleventh century and moved westward through Iraq toward Anatolia. They were SUNNÎ and adherents of GHÂZÎ JIHÂD ideals. They controlled Persia and Iraq until the end of the sixth/twelfth century.

Salmân al-Fârisî

A Persian convert to Islam during the lifetime of MUḤAMMAD, Salmân is credited with engineering the ditch in the battle of KHANDAQ that thwarted the attack by the people of MECCA on Muḥammad's nascent community in MADÎNAH. He is said to have been one of the founders of Ṣufism, and some SHÎʿÎ regard him as an early supporter of the caliphate of ʿALÎ. He is the subject of a considerable body of Islamic legend and lore. (*See also* ṢÛFÎ.)

samâʿ (Arabic: hearing)

A ṢÛFÎ mystical or spiritual performance or concert. *See also* DHIKR; ḤAḌRAH.

as-sâmirî

The "Samaritan" mentioned in the QUR'ÂN as having instigated the worship of the golden calf among the Israelites. His punishment was to be condemned to ward off all human touch.

Santri

Indonesian Muslims claiming to follow a pure form of Islam.

Sanûsiyyah

A revivalist ṢÛFÎ order founded in North Africa and named after Sayyid Muḥammad b. ʿAlî as-Sanûsî (*c.* 1202/1787–1276/1859). It seeks to return its adherents to the puritanical principles it sees in early Islam. While the DHIKR does not have the aim of inducing an ecstatic trance-state, it does promote a union between the worshiper and the Prophet MUḤAMMAD.

saqar (Arabic)

One of the seven ranks of Hell, characterized by scorching fire.

saqîm (Arabic: ill, infirm)

A technical term used in ḤADÎTH criticism indicating that the tradition is at the lowest level of reliability.

Sârah, or Sârâ

The biblical Sarah, she is not named in the QUR'ÂN. In TAFSÎR literature, her role is significant. She is the mother of ISḤÂQ and the wife of IBRÂHÎM. When she was with Ibrâhîm in Egypt, he is supposed to have referred to her as his sister. The commentators, holding that a prophet cannot lie, go to great lengths to explain this. She is the one who instigated the expulsion of HÂJAR and ISMÂʿÎL and who grieved to death over the sacrifice of the son of Ibrâhîm.

Satan

See IBLÎS; SHAYṬÂN.

Satpanthî

A group of NIZÂRÎ ISMÂʿÎLÎ SHÎʿÎ formed in the tenth/sixteenth century in India. They claim to follow the "true way," *satpanth*. They have developed their own tradition of GINÂNS and other religious traditions and do not acknowledge the Nizârî IMÂMS.

Saudi Arabia

The Kingdom of Saudi Arabia was formed in 1932 as a hereditary monarchy. The kingdom occupies over eighty percent of the Arabian Peninsula and has a population estimated to be between ten and fifteen million people. The eastern part of the kingdom is the location of agricultural lands, oil fields and the kingdom's largest SHÎ'Î population, numbering over a half million. Its capital is Riyadh, and the kingdom includes the holy cities of MECCA and MADÎNAH. The laws of the kingdom are based on an interpretation of Islamic law (SHARÎ'AH), as understood through the WAHHÂBÎ movement, which is a revivalist, puritanical SUNNÎ movement that advocates a strong link between political power and religious authority. In the last half century, there has been considerable tension between the Saudi Arabian government and the Shî'î minority, which has begun protest movements to eliminate discrimination.

Sawdah bt. Zam'ah

One of the wives of the Prophet MUḤAMMAD. She was his second wife, and one of the first women to convert to Islam.

ṣawm (Arabic: fasting)

Fasting during the month of RAMAḌÂN is one of the requirements, or PILLARS OF ISLAM. It is incumbent on all Muslims over the age of majority, who are of sound body and are able to fast without harm to their health, to observe a total abstinence fast during the daylight hours. During that period, no ingestion of foods or liquids is permitted, nor is sexual intercourse. These rules include smoking tobacco. There are complex exemptions from the strictures of fasting, which can include the aged, the infirm, pregnant women and nursing mothers, travelers, and those engaged in heavy manual labor. It is customary to make up missed fast days as soon as possible, and, if circumstances change during a fast day such as to permit fasting, it is customary to spend the rest of the day fasting. The Ramaḍân daily fast is broken by an evening meal each day and at the end by the great feast of the 'ÎD AL-FIṬR. There are numerous traditions of voluntary fasting in Islam to seek forgiveness of sins, satisfy vows, and for general reasons of piety, but Islamic tradition forbids successive days of fasting that would harm the body. As with the other "Pillars" of Islam, the FIQH treatises detail the permissible and impermissible conditions of fasting for each school of Islamic law.

sa'y (Arabic: running)

The ceremony of running between the hills of ṢAFÂ and al-Marwah during the ḤAJJ.

sayyid (Arabic: lord, master)

A title of respect used to indicate descendants of the Prophet, Muḥammad. It is also used as a title for Muslim saints. (*See also* WALÎ.)

Sayyid 'Alî Muḥammad Shîrâzî

See BÂB.

Sayyid Quṭb

See QUṬB, SAYYID.

school

See MADRASAH.

school of law

See MADHHAB.

Seal of the Prophets

See KHÂTAM AN-NABIYYÎN.

Seljuks

See SALJÛQS.

sermon

See KHUṬBAH.

Seveners

See ISMÂ'ÎLÎ.

Shabazz, El-Hajj Malik El-

See MALCOLM X.

Shâdhiliyyah

A ṢÛFÎ ṬARÎQAH named after Abû al-Ḥasan ʿAlî ash-Shâdhilî (593/1196–656/1258), it spread through North Africa and the Middle East. Its adherents regard themselves as fully compliant with the tenets of Islam and as the source for the QUṬB of the universe.

shafâʿah (Arabic: intercession)

The possibility of intercession or mediation with God has been the subject of debate in Islam, with most theologians holding that there is no mediator between the believer and God. There are traditions, however, that MUḤAMMAD will intercede for the believers on the YAWM AD-DÎN. In the practice of the veneration of saints, many hold that the saint (WALÎ) has the power to invoke God's help with earthly problems.

ash-Shâfiʿî, Muḥammad b. Idrîs (150/767–205/820)

The founder and eponym of the Shâfiʿî MADHHAB, he is credited with being the founder of ʾUṢÛL AL-FIQH. In his major work, *ar-Risâlah*, he established Islamic jurisprudence on the principles of QUR'ÂN, SUNNAH, IJMÂʿ, and QIYÂS. Because of his central role in founding Islamic jurisprudence, his biography has attracted numerous legends. His tomb in Cairo is the object of veneration and petitions for intercession. (*See also* QUBBAH.)

shâh (Persian: king, ruler)

This term, derived from pre-Islamic usage, has been used to indicate an Islamic religious ruler in PERSIAN-speaking areas.

shahâdah (Arabic)

From an Arabic root meaning to testify or bear witness, this term refers to the first of the PILLARS OF ISLAM, the declaration of faith: "I declare that there is no deity but Allâh and that Muḥammad is the Prophet of Allâh."

shahîd (Arabic: witness)

A martyr; one who bears witness.

shaikh

See SHAYKH.

Shaltût, Maḥmûd (1893–1963)

A reformist Islamic jurist who led the modernization of AL-AZHAR. During his tenure, the institution expanded its curriculum to include the modern sciences as well as training for women.

Shams ad-Dîn Muḥammad (*c.* 640/1240–710/1311)

The first of the NIZÂRÎ ISMÂʿÎLÎ SHÎʿÎ IMÂMS after the fall of ALAMUT. He lived his life in hiding, working as an embroiderer. He presided over a problematic period in Nizârî history, and after his death, dispute over succession led to factions within the community.

sharîʿah (Arabic: a path to the watering hole; the spring itself)

The term refers to God's law in its divine and revealed sense. This is related to FIQH, which is the human process of understanding and implementing the law. Commentators have argued that the aggregate of all the sources by which we know God's law is but a small part of *sharîʿah*, which, like God, is unknowable and must be accepted. When the word is used as synonymous with *fiqh*, it refers to the entirety of Islamic law, often in its actual, historical, and potential senses. Following the original meaning of the Arabic word, it is said to be the source from which all properly Islamic behaviors derive.

Sharîf, Sharîfî (Arabic: honored, highborn)

A term applied to a person who claims descent from the Prophet MUḤAMMAD.

shaykh (Arabic: old man)

An appellation of respect for an Islamic religious leader, a scholar, or the head of a ṢÛFÎ MADHHAB.

Shaykh al-Islâm (Arabic)

In the OTTOMAN EMPIRE, the title was used to designate the chief legal figure and head of the ʿULAMÂʾ.

Shaykhiyyah

A division of the ITHNÂ ʿASHARIYYAH SHÎʿÎ, who derive their name from Shaykh Aḥmad Aḥsâʾî (1753–1826). They hold that everyone is obligated to be a MUJTAHID and understand Islam and the will of the HIDDEN IMÂM. They are opposed by the ʾUṢÛLÎ Shîʿî.

Shayṭân (Arabic)

The devil, Satan. When used in the plural, *shayâṭîn*, it refers to the demonic creatures that form the army of IBLÎS, the chief ruler of Hell.

Sheba

See BILQÎS; SABAEANS; SULAYMÂN.

Shîʿî (Arabic: party, sect)

The name Shîʿî applies generally to a number of groups or divisions in Islam, all of whom hold that temporal and spiritual authority was passed on from MUḤAMMAD through his immediate descendants, the AHL AL-BAYT. All groups of Shîʿî Muslims differ from other Muslims on two general points, the line of successorship from Muḥammad and the elements of foundation for Islamic law. Shîʿî Muslims contend that ʿALÎ B. ABÎ ṬÂLIB should have been the first caliph, since he was the rightful IMÂM, appointed by Muḥammad at GHADÎR KHUMM. This view of governance is at odds with the later-formed SUNNÎ perspective that authority rested more broadly with the Companions (the ṢAḤÂBAH) and their successors. They also differed from the KHAWÂRIJ, who held that any Muslim of good standing could assume community leadership. The second point of divergence from other Muslims can be traced to ʿAlî's refusal to swear that he would follow the precedents of ABÛ BAKR and ʿUMAR when the caliphate was offered to him after ʿUmar's death. For the Shîʿî, precedent, and its concommitant transmission through ḤADÎTH, also had to pass through the *ahl al-bayt*. The result has been the elevation of the *Imâm* to a position of greater importance than the caliph in Sunnî Islam, since the *Imâm* embodies divine spiritual authority in addition to temporal power to rule.

Shîʿî have divided into various groups, mostly over issues surrounding the imâmate. For the ISMÂʿÎLIYYAH (the Seveners), and the ITHNÂ ʿASHARIYYAH (the Twelvers), the separation involved the belief that the seventh or the twelfth *Imâm* went into GHAYBAH, or occultation. The GHULÂT, or extremists, because of their attribution of divinity to their *Imâm*s, were never accepted by the majority of either Shîʿî or Sunnî. At this point in history, Ithnâ ʿAsharî Shîʿî are the numerical majority of Shîʿî, found in Iran, Iraq, and southern Lebanon. Ismâʿîliyyah can be found throughout the world in India, Africa, and North America.

In the period after *ghaybah*, Shîʿî legal practice has appeared in many ways identical with Sunnî practice. In areas and times when intermingling is possible, Shîʿî and Sunnî jurists have exchanged legal and jurisprudential ideas, and attended each other's schools. Even so, Shî'î legal practice differs from Sunnî practice in areas of marriage, inheritance, and, often, a more restrictive code of ritual purity.

The veneration of the tombs and shrines of the *Imâms* is an important part of Shî'î Islam, with many shrines found in the area of QOM in Iran and in southern Iraq. The shrine at KARBALÂ' in particular is a site of veneration as the location of the martyrdom of *Imâm* AL-ḤUSAYN B. 'ALÎ. (*See also* ZAYDIYYAH.)

shirk (Arabic: association)

This is the sin of associating another deity with ALLÂH, the most severe sins mentioned in the QUR'ÂN. Polytheism is the one sin that cannot be forgiven, according to the Qur'ân.

shrine

See QUBBAH.

Shu'ayb

An Arabian prophet, sometimes identified with the biblical Jethro, who was sent to warn the people of Madyan. When they rejected the warning, God destroyed them by earthquake.

shûrâ (Arabic: consultation)

The term used for a consultative council. It was the name used for the small body that chose 'UTHMÂN to be caliph (KHALÎFAH). In Muslim Spain, the *shûrâ* was part of the career path of *'ulamâ'*, who were members of an advisory council of judges, before assuming judgeships themselves. In some modern Islamic countries, it is used to mean parliament or legislature. (*See also* QÂḌÎ.)

Shu'ûbiyyah (Arabic)

Derived from a term meaning "people," it is the name of a movement that promoted the equality of non-Arabs with Arabs in the early Islamic centuries. (*See also* DHIMMÎ.)

aṣ-Ṣiddîq (Arabic: righteous, just, truthful)

This is an epithet borne by the prophet YÛSUF and the caliph ABÛ BAKR.

ṣifah (Arabic: quality, property, attribute)

This term is used by theologians to refer to God's attributes. Often these are identified with some of the ninety-nine 'ASMÂ' AL-ḤUSNÂ.

Ṣiffîn, battle of

The battle in 37/657 between 'ALÎ B. ABÎ ṬÂLIB and the 'UMAYYAD governor of Syria, MU'ÂWIYAH, in which 'Alî agreed to arbitration. (*See also* SHÎ'Î.)

silsilah (Arabic: chain)

When used in ḤADÎTH criticism, it is synonymous with ISNÂD. Among the ṢÛFÎ it refers to the chain of spiritual authorities or teachers connecting the current leader with the founder.

sin

See DHANB; ḤADD; SHIRK.

sîrah (Arabic: course, road, way)

The biography of MUḤAMMAD. The first and most famous was composed by IBN ISḤÂQ under the title *Sîrat rasûl Allâh*. It established the genre, and, starting with creation, included all of world religious history up to the Prophet. This genre of sacred biography is opposed to SUNNAH, since it is narrative rather than normative. Ibn Isḥâq's work was abridged by a later editor, IBN HISHÂM. The shortened version is the most popular biography of the Prophet.

aṣ-ṣirâṭ al-mustaqîm (Arabic: straight path)

This is mentioned in Q. 1:6 as leading over Hell to Heaven. It is used also to mean the strict adherence to the principles of Islam.

Sirhindî, Ahmad (971/1564 – 1034/1624)

A SUNNÎ reformer and mystic in INDIA, and a member of the NAQSHBANDIYYAH ṬARÎQAH. He was a strong polemicist against SHÎʿÎ Islam and against the innovations introduced into the community by the emperor Akbar (1556–1605). His preaching earned him a period of time in prison, but he was reconciled to the emperor and received a grant of money and honors. His letters had great influence, helping spread his reputation outside India into Afghanistan and Central Asia. His disciples, known as *mujaddidîs* (Arabic: reformers), did much to spread his beliefs in reform. In the field of mysticism, he advocated replacing pantheism with a notion of the "unity of worship," which did not rely on viewing all objects in the world as divine.

slaughter

See DHABḤ.

Sokoto caliphate

The Islamic rule in Nigeria founded by Usuman DAN FODIO.

Somalia

The East African nation with a coastline along the Red Sea and the Indian Ocean, it is almost entirely SUNNÎ Muslim. Its capital is Mogadishu. Known as the Land of Punt to the ancients, who sought it out for frankincense and myrrh, it became Islamized starting in the third/tenth century. In modern times, the country has been plagued by civil strife and famine.

soul

See NAFS.

South Africa

Islam came to South Africa in the mid-seventeenth century, when the Dutch brought Muslim slaves from elsewhere in Africa and Southeast Asia. These were known as "Cape Malays," because many of them came from the Malay archipelago. In the nineteenth century, the British colonial powers brought Indian Muslims as indentured servants and free laborers. By the first half of the twentieth century, many of these Muslims had entered widely into commerce and the professions. In the second half of the century, many South African Muslims had established intellectual and physical contact with Muslims in the Middle East and in the rest of the Islamic world with the result that the community, though comprising only about two percent of the total population, exerts a dynamic influence on South African society.

subḥah (Arabic: praise)

The Islamic "rosary" consisting of sets of beads in groups of three used to contemplate the ninety-nine names of God, ʾASMÂʾ AL-ḤUSNÂ, in supererogatory prayer.

Ṣûfî (Arabic: wearer of wool?)

The origin of the term Ṣûfî is disputed, as is the exact meaning of who is a Ṣûfî. In the West, it is generally referred to as Islamic mysticism. As with mysticism in other religious traditions, Ṣûfism transcends many of the usual categories, so cannot be used as a sectarian term in opposition to either SUNNÎ or SHÎʿÎ. Ṣûfî orders, TARÎQAHS, are an important expression of personal piety and social organization. They began to develop around certain central organizing figures in the fifth/twelfth century, while claim-

A Ṣûfî whirling dervish.

ing earlier foundation. Some of the founders would claim authority from AL-KHAḌIR or from MUḤAMMAD himself. Other orders centered on shrines of holy figures, WALÎs, whose tombs were reputed to be centers of *barakât*. In the age of the great Muslim empires, many *ṭarîqah*s became trans-regional and contributed to the spread of reformist ideas. An important aspect of Ṣûfî orders is their role in spreading Islam into new areas. In many places in Africa and Southeast Asia, Ṣûfism was a major organizing force in new Muslim communities. The term Ṣûfî has been adopted in Western Europe and North America by some New Age practitioners who have little relationship to Islam or the traditions of Ṣûfism.

Suhrawardiyyah

A ṢÛFÎ ṬARÎQAH named after ʿAbd al-Qâhir Abû Nâjib as-Suhrawardî (died 564/1168), it became a major order in South Asia.

suicide

While the QUR'ÂN is ambiguous about prohibiting suicide, the ḤADÎTH clearly indicate that suicide is prohibited in Islam and regarded as a sin. One's life is regarded as a gift from God, and God has absolute and final authority over it.

sujûd (Arabic: prostration)

Ritual prostration during ṢALÂT.

Sulaymân

Identified with the biblical Solomon, the son of David, he is portrayed in the QUR'ÂN as the wise possessor of much of God's knowledge about the world, including the languages of birds and beasts. He dealt wisely with BILQÎS, the Queen of Sheba, and ruled over the JINN. Islamic legend elaborates these and other stories, making him a practitioner of magic as well as a prophet.

sulṭân (Arabic: authorized power)

The title of a Muslim ruler over the secular sphere, it first was used for the ruler of BAGHDÂD in the fourth/eleventh century, as opposed to the caliph (KHALÎFAH). Rulers of the various Muslim empires, such as the OTTOMAN and MUGHAL empires, held the title *sulṭân*. The duties of the sulṭân are to uphold and implement the SHARÎʿAH. Oman remains as one of the last Islamic states governed by a *sulṭân*.

sunnah (Arabic: customary procedure; well-followed path; pl. *sunan*)

Sunnah is similar in meaning to the English word "precedent," in that it indicates those actions performed in the past that establish a pattern to be followed, or avoided, in the future. In Islamic religious discourse, one usually refers to the *sunnah* of the Prophet MUḤAMMAD. This encompasses all that

Muḥammad ever did and all that he did not do, all that he ever said, and all that he did not say. Individual instances of this are reported as ḤADÎTHS. The *sunnah* of the Prophet is one of the roots (*ʾuṣûl*) of Islamic law.

Sunnî (Arabic: follower of *sunnah*)

The practice of the majority of the world's Muslims. The name is derived from the word SUNNAH and is meant to indicate adherence to the customary practice of the Prophet MUḤAMMAD. In this regard, it can be seen as a reaction to the development of SHÎʿÎ Islam. Sunnî Muslims are subdivided into numerous groups based on different legal schools (MADHHABS), different theological views, different social and historical locations, and different cultures. They share a common view that religious authority descends from the Prophet and from his companions, (ṢAḤÂBAH), as opposed to the view of the Shîʿî, that authority derives only from the AHL AL-BAYT. They also hold that the rule of the caliph (KHALÎFAH) is open to any male Muslim descendant of Muḥammad's tribe of QURAYSH, as opposed to the KHAWÂRIJ, who hold that authority over the community (ʾUMMAH) can be held by any male Muslim over the age of majority in good standing. For the Sunnî, the role of the caliph is less central to individual religious conduct than the role of the IMÂM is in Shîʿî Islam.

Historically, both the term and the practice of Sunnî Islam arise as a middle way out of the conflicts and controversies that beset the early community. In this way, it can be seen as built on a foundation of Murjiʾism. It is both a religious and a socio-political system. Early theologians had to reconcile such questions as who is a true Muslim, what constitutes proper Muslim practice, what is the balance between individual and group responsibility, and what is Islam's relationship to other religions, questions that still remain today. (*See also* MURJIʾAH.)

sûrah (Arabic: chapter; pl. *suwar*)

A chapter of the QURʾÂN. There are one hundred fourteen chapters of the Qurʾân, each divided into verses (ʾÂYAH.)

Suriname

A former Dutch colony, this country has the highest percentage of Muslims of any country in the Western hemisphere, constituting an estimated twenty-five percent of the population. Muslims were first brought by the Dutch as indentured servants from Southeast Asia and from South Asia. Indian and Indonesian Muslim communities form two distinct groups, each with separate mosques based on language. ʿÎD AL-FIṬR is celebrated as a national holiday.

as-Suyûṭî, Jalâl ad-Dîn (849/1445–911/1505)

Prolific jurist, historian, grammarian, and commentator on the QURʾÂN, his *Tafsîr jalâlayn* is one of the standard SUNNÎ works of TAFSÎR.

Syria (Arabic *ash-Shâm*; *Sûriyâ*)

Syria was one of the first areas outside Arabia to come under Muslim control in the conquest. The ancient capital, DIMASHQ (Damascus), became the headquarters of the ʾUMAYYAD dynasty. Syria retained large Christian and Jewish populations until after the period of the Crusades. Modern Syria is Arabic speaking, and about seventy percent Sunnî Muslim, with minorities from the ʿALAWIYYAH, DRUZE, ISMÂʿÎLÎ, and ITHNÂ ʿASHARIYYAH.

T

ṭabaqât (Arabic: class, generation)

A genre of biographical literature arranged by generations, this sort of biographical encyclopedia developed as a tool for the analysis of ḤADÎTHs. In particular, such biographical works were designed to scrutinize the ISNÂDs to determine if each member was truthful, could have possibly met the other members of the chain, and so on. (*See also* AL-JARḤ WA-T-TAʿDÎL.)

aṭ-Ṭabarî, Abû Jaʿfar Muḥammad b. Jarîr (225/839–310/923)

He was one of the most influential Muslim historians and commentators on the QUR'ÂN. His history of the world, *Ta'rîkh ar-rusul wa-l-mulûk*, (The history of prophets and kings), started with creation, continuing to his own time, and presented an integrated model of world history that supported his views of a universal Islam. His monumental TAFSÎR, still a standard reference, was comprehensive in presenting all the major views about the Qur'ân known at his time. He wrote a biographical dictionary, *Ta'rîkh ar-rijâl*, of the ṬABAQÂT style, which was meant to accompany his other works and give the necessary facts about the individuals he used as authorities. He also founded a legal MADHHAB that adhered closely to the Shâfiʿî school.

Ṭabâṭabâ'î, Muḥammad Ḥusayn (1903–1981)

A well-known SHÎʿÎ philosopher and commentator on the QUR'ÂN, his monumental TAFSÎR, *Tafsîr al-mîzân*, analyzes the Qur'ân verse by verse using other verses as support for the arguments. Since his death, many of his works have been translated into English.

tabdîl

See TAḤRÎF.

tâbiʿûn (Arabic: followers; sing. *tâbiʿ*)

The next generation after the ṢAḤÂBAH, or the Companions of the Prophet. In SUNNÎ Islam, they are looked to as part of the formative founding generations to be used as models on which to construct modern interpretations.

tablîgh (Arabic: announcement)

The delivery of the message of Islam to non-Muslims. (*See also* DAʿWAH.)

Tablîghî Jamâʿat

A grassroots movement from South Asia for promotiong the development of faith and Muslim identity and for promoting DAʿWAH, it has a worldwide following with large numbers in North America.

tafsîr (Arabic: to explain)

In Islam, exegesis of the QUR'ÂN has concentrated on explaining the text from a wide variety of perspectives, such as grammatical, historical, lexigraphic, theological, psychological, etc. The intention is to understand the Qur'ân as fully as humanly possible. Most commentators assume that there are clear, understandable portions of the Qur'ân, referred to as ẒÂHIR, and portions that are obscure or hidden from human understanding, which are called BÂṬIN. SHÎ'Î commentaries resemble SUNNÎ *tafsîr* in scope and method, but also tend to concentrate on those verses that support Shî'î theology. Some modernist commentaries have sought to prove that the Qur'ân contains the roots of the modern sciences, thus trying to harmonize science and religion. The writing of *tafsîr* is an active religious genre today in all Islamic areas of the world. (*See also* TA'WÎL.)

ṭâghût (Arabic: idol)

This word has come to mean a human tyrant or oppressor. This was the term used in IRAN the 1979 revolution to describe the SHÂH.

ṭahârah (Arabic: purity)

Purity and PURIFICATION achieved by ABLUTION and spiritual cleansing. The rules for purity differ between SUNNÎ and SHÎ'Î and among the several groups within each tradition. (*See also* GHUSL; WUḌÛ'.)

taḥrîf (Arabic: letter substitution)

The practice, mentioned in the QUR'ÂN, of substituting letters and otherwise changing the text to alter the meaning of the original. This practice is also called *tabdîl*. One of the techniques of interpreting scripture found among Jews and Christians in the late ancient world was the notion that letters and numbers could be substituted according to set rules that would bring out the hidden meaning of a text. The most common of these techniques derived from Neopythagorean and Neoplatonic number–letter codes, in which each letter had a numerical value. The sum of the letters in any word could then be deemed to be equivalent to any other word with that same sum, and that word could be read in the place of the first word. The most famous example is the association of the number 666 with various personalities, historical and otherwise. Such techniques as well as forms of punning were also common among Arabian poets. The Qur'ân rejects such techniques and favors more plain readings.

tajdîd (Arabic: renewal)

According to some ḤADÎTHS, someone would come at the beginning of each century to renew Islam and bring the faithful back to correct practice. Such a person is termed a *mujaddid*, a person who brings *tajdîd*. While always a feature of Islamic thought, the reformation or renewal of Islam has become more prominent in modern times. As early as the eighteenth century, thinkers such as IBN 'ABD AL-WAHHÂB opposed the innovations (BID'AH) they saw as having been introduced into Islam by TAQLÎD, blind adherence to customary authority. For him, this included ṢÛFÎ veneration of saints (WALÎS) and anything that was not explicitly practiced by the Prophet MUḤAMMAD and the first three generations after him. In modern times, *tajdîd* has been invoked in nationalist as well as religious senses with a call to remove all Western influences from Islamic countries.

Tajikistan

This Central Asian country with its capital at Dushanbe is predominantly SUNNÎ. Its official language is Tajik, a language related to PERSIAN, although Russian is still used as a holdover from the days of the Soviet empire. Since independence from Soviet influence, the Muslim population has been engaged in revitalizing Islamic institutions, which has included the construction of a new MADRASAH in Dushanbe.

tajwîd (Arabic: to make things better)

The art of QUR'ÂN recitation. This is a complex and highly developed art form in Islamic countries, and reciters are generally present at major ceremonies and life-cycle events. International competitions attract Muslims worldwide, and the modern technology of sound recording has enabled some reciters to achieve worldwide popularity.

takbîr (Arabic)

To pronounce the Arabic phrase *Allâhu 'akbar*, "God is great."

takfîr (Arabic: to declare someone an unbeliever)

Modern militant Islamic groups have adopted the technique of pronouncing people whom they consider to be enemies of Islam as KÂFIR. Under their interpretation of Islamic law, this removes any prohibition from killing them, forces their spouses to divorce them or face the same penalties, and forces other Muslims to dissociate from them, again with the same penalties. Medieval jurists and some modern groups, such as the IKHWÂN AL-MUSLIMÛN, have denounced the practice as un-Islamic and as promoting FITNAH (strife) among Muslims that endangers the community.

ṭalab al-'ilm (Arabic: seeking knowledge)

Muslims are enjoined to seek God's knowledge wherever it can be found. In the classical period, it was part of the credentials of any scholar to have traveled to another place to study, and

Muslim scholar, Mazar-i Sharif, Afghanistan.

the number and location of the RIḤLAHS, or educational trips, would be listed in a scholar's biography.

ṭalâq

See DIVORCE.

Ṭâlibân

The militant fundamentalist leaders of AFGHANISTAN, who came to power after the expulsion of Soviet troops and were ousted from power in 1423/2002. Their name derives from an Arabic word meaning "seeker" or "student," and they characterize themselves as seekers after true Islamic knowledge. Led by Mullah Muḥammad 'Umar, they have sought to unify the Afghan population under their own fundamentalist interpretation of Islamic law. Their supporters praise them for establishing order and the rule of Islamic law in Afghanistan, while their detractors criticize them for exporting terror, supporting terrorist groups, slaughtering their opposition, and abolishing the rights of women.

ta'lîm (Arabic: instruction)

In the ISMÂ'ÎLÎ SHÎ'Î tradition, it is the authoritative teaching of an IMÂM that makes the esoteric meaning of revelation accessible to the believer.

Ṭâlût

The biblical Saul, mentioned in Q. 2:247–249. We are told that the BANÛ ISRÂ'ÎL demanded a king, and Ṭâlût was given them by God, but they found him to be unworthy. He is said to have had great knowledge and fine physical stature. When he went out against JÂLÛT (Goliath), it was DÂ'ÛD (David) who killed the giant and became king.

tanzîl (Arabic: that which comes down)

Revelation; the message of the QUR'ÂN. (*See also* WAḤY.)

Tanẓîmât (Turkish: reorganization)

The modernist reforms in the OTTOMAN EMPIRE in the thirteenth/nineteenth century aimed at guaranteeing rights to all members of the empire, regardless of their religion.

taqdîr (Arabic: predestination)

Verses in the QUR'ÂN have been interpreted as meaning that God's absolute power and all-knowing mean that human actions are predetermined. Other verses indicate that humans have free will to choose good or evil. (*See also* QADAR; QADARIYYAH.)

taqiyyah (Arabic: guard or preserve)

The practice, found chiefly among SHÎ'Î and the DRUZE, of using dissimulation to preserve oneself in a time of danger or persecution. According to this doctrine, the preservation of life overrides a duty to bear witness to one's faith and be a martyr (*shahîd*).

taqlîd (Arabic: imitation)

Often interpreted polemically as "blind" adherence to the precedents of a master or school (MADHHAB), it means the unchallenging acceptance of past patterns of behavior. (*See also* IJTIHÂD; TAJDÎD.)

taqwâ (Arabic: piety)

Piety, faith, fear of God.

tarâwîḥ (Arabic: diversions)

The *ṣalât at-tarâwîḥ* are prayers performed during the night in the month of RAMAḌÂN.

ṭarîqah (Arabic: road, way)

A term used among the ṢÛFÎ to designate both an order within the movement and the mystic path to the ultimate goal.

taṣawwuf

Ṣûfism, or Islamic mysticism. (*See also* ṢÛFÎ.)

tasbîḥ (Arabic)

Uttering the phrase *subḥân Allâh*, "Praise be to God."

tashbîh (Arabic)

Anthropomorphism or the ascription to God of human elements. There has been considerable debate among theologians about whether to interpret statements in the QUR'ÂN about God having hands or being able to see or hear as meaning that He has human-like features. One of the features of the MIḤNAH, or inquisition, of the early 'ABBÂSIDS was the attempt to counter rampant anthropomorphism.

ṭawâf (Arabic: circumambulation)

One of the rites of the ḤAJJ is to walk around the KA'BAH at the beginning and end of the pilgrimage. This appears to have been a pre-Islamic practice, and MUḤAMMAD is said to have done it in his youth. In Islamic stories about ADAM and IBRÂHÎM, we are told that they both performed *ṭawâf* at the Ka'bah, as, apparently, did the SAKÎNAH. In the rites of the veneration of saints, *ṭawâf* is sometimes performed around the tomb of the WALÎ. (*See also* QUBBAH.)

tawbah (Arabic: repent, forgive)

Repentance, turning away from sin. Repentance in Islam can come at any time, and the QUR'ÂN invites sinners to repent and turn away from sin constantly.

tawḥîd (Arabic)

The declaration that ALLÂH is One. This constitutes one of the most fundamental beliefs in Islam, but the details of God's unity have been debated extensively by theologians. Many saw AL-'ASMÂ' AL-ḤUSNÂ as attributes of God and indicating great complexity in His unity. The recitation of Q. 112 is held to be the starting point for understanding the unity of God.

ta'wîl (Arabic: important, fundamental, first)

The allegorical interpretation of the QUR'ÂN or the quest for its hidden, inner meanings. It was a synonym of TAFSÎR in its earliest use, but came to mean a process of getting to the most fundamental understandings of the Qur'ân. A number of groups, such as the SHÎ'Î, used *ta'wîl* as the means to harmonize Qur'anic meaning with their own doctrines, contending that a fundamental understanding of the text would prove them to be correct.

tawrât

The Torah, along with the ZABÛR, the Psalms, are the two portions of Jewish scripture mentioned in the QUR'ÂN. This is the Scripture acquired by MÛSÂ. The relationship between the Qur'ân and the *Tawrât* is similar to the relationship between the INJÎL, the Gospels, and the *Tawrât*. The Qur'ân both confirms it and corrects the errors that have been introduced into it over time. Post-Qur'ânic tradition builds on the extensive passages in the Qur'ân and elaborates the narrative histories of the patriarchs and heroes of the Torah, primarily in the body of literature known as ISRÂ'ÎLIYYÂT. For Muslims, the *Tawrât* contains passages that are understood as predicting the coming of MUḤAMMAD. (*See also* TAḤRÎF.)

taxation

See JIZYAH; ZAKÂT.

tayammum (Arabic: dust)

The substitution of sand or stones for water during the ABLUTIONS for prayer when necessity requires it. The various schools (MADHHABS), of Islamic law, while generally acknowledging the permissibility of this practice, seek to limit it both to emergencies and to the cleansing of the hands and feet only. The Babylonian Talmud allows the use of sand for ablutions, and some Christian writings recognize the validity of baptism done with sand when water was unavailable. (*See also* GHUSL; ṢALÂT.)

Ṭayyibiyyah

A branch of the ISMÂ'ÎLÎ SHÎ'Î found in Yemen and India. They preserved a large part of the extensive FÂṬIMID religious literature and beliefs.

Ta'ziyah (Persian and Arabic: expression of condolence)

The dramatic reenactment among the SHÎ'Î of the martyrdom of ḤUSAYN B. 'ALÎ in 61/680 at KARBALÂ'. This tradition of passion plays is the only serious religious drama to have developed in Islam. In their most elaborate forms, these plays are made up of many characters from the QUR'ÂN and from Islamic history. Prophets, including MUḤAMMAD, appear, foretelling the martyrdom. MARYAM exemplifies FÂṬIMAH's anguish, and 'ÎSÂ (JESUS) is both the warner and the martyr. All of the non-Shî'î are portrayed as the enemy without distinction, so IBN MULJAM, the Khârijî slayer of 'ALÎ, is presented as a SUNNÎ. The anguish, deprivation, and death on the stage is contrasted with the comfort and pleasure of the audience, who consume refreshments while watching the drama unfold. All in the audience, however, have token signs of grief, such as pieces of earth, with which to express themselves.

tekke (Turkish: shrine, meeting hall)

A ṢÛFÎ teaching mosque or place of worship. (*See also* ZÂWIYAH.)

temporary marriage

See MUT'AH.

Thailand

This predominantly Buddhist country has a small Muslim population, which is, nevertheless, the second largest religious group in the country. The Muslims are divided into two ethnic groups, the Malay-speaking Muslims in the southern part of the country and the Thai-speaking Muslims of the central and northern part. The traditional practices among both groups have included elements from Buddhism, animism, and other traditions. Reformist movements from the Middle East have introduced Thai Muslims to *dakwah* (Arabic DA'WAH) movements like those in Malaysia and Indonesia.

Thamûd

A pre-Islamic Arabian tribe mentioned by ancient geographers and historians as well as in the QUR'ÂN, to whom God sent the prophet ṢÂLIḤ. As proof of God's existence, they were given a she-camel and a foal, the tendons of which were sacred. The people hamstrung the animals, however, which earned them God's anger. Their refusal to heed the warnings of God's prophet, in spite of clear proofs, resulted in their destruction by earthquake.

theology

See KALÂM.

Tijâniyyah

The ṢÛFÎ ṬARÎQAH founded by Aḥmad at-Tîjânî (1150/1738–1230/1815), who was inspired to found the order after seeing a vision of the Prophet MUḤAMMAD. As a reformist order, it stressed the adherence to the "way of Muḥammad" (Arabic *aṭ-ṭarîqah al-Muḥammadiyyah*), a simplified practice that gained rapid popularity in North Africa. Recent independence movements have driven underground the influence and practice of the order and Ṣûfism in general.

at-Tirmidhî, Abû 'Îsâ Muḥammad (209/824 – *c.* 275/888)

One of the six revered collectors of ḤADÎTH in SUNNÎ Islam. Little is known of his biography. His works are characterized by a careful analysis of the ISNÂD of each tradition. (*See also* 'ILM AR-RIJÂL.)

tradition

See ḤADÎTH; SUNNAH.

tribe

From the beginning of Islam there has been a tension between the universalist tendencies of Islam and particularist social groupings, often subsumed under the term "tribe." In the practice of the Prophet, all Muslims by virtue of their faith are to be regarded as one family group. This is the very meaning of the word ʾUMMAH, which has, at its root, the concept of *ʾumm,* mother. While Islamic legal practice does not forbid tribal affiliations and the history of Muslim peoples has shown some support for tribalism, the message of Islam shows those human distinctions to be trivial.

Trinidad and Tobago

Muslims comprise slightly less than ten percent of these two Caribbean islands. The community started originally from West African slaves. The British then introduced South Asian Muslims into the population. While independence has not eliminated social and economic problems that keep many Muslims at the bottom of the society, the government recognizes ʿÎD AL-FIṬR as a national holiday.

Tunisia (Arabic: al-Jumhûriyyah at-Tûnisiyyah)

This predominantly SUNNÎ North African republic has been an influential intellectual and religious center. It became a French Protectorate in 1883 and gained independence in 1956. At that time, SHARÎʿAH codes were replaced by a Personal Status Code by the ruler, Ḥabîb Bourguiba, who even attacked the practice of fasting (ṢAWM) during RAMAḌÂN. Recently, there has been a resurgence of Islamic practices and institutions.

aṭ-Ṭûr (Arabic: mountain)

Mount Sinai.

Turkey

The modern state of Turkey, founded in 1923 by Mustafa Kemal ATATÜRK, occupies the region of Anatolia that was first Islamized by Turkic-speaking peoples in the fifth/eleventh century after the defeat of the Byzantine Greeks. The area, known as Rûm, ("Rome") became the home of a succession of Perso-Turkic SUNNÎ kingdoms. In the tenth/sixteenth century, the OTTOMAN EMPIRE expanded into much of the east Mediterranean and North Africa. After World War I, and the declaration of the modern state of Turkey, many Islamic practices were abolished by the secularist state, including the use of the Arabic script. Despite attempts to remove Islam from public discourse, Turkey has seen a reassertion of Islamic institutions and interests.

Turkmenistan

Bordering the Caspian Sea, this Central Asian country is estimated to be ninety percent SUNNÎ Muslim. It was Islamized during the period of the SALJÛQS and was important in the overland trade between the Mediterranean and the Far East. Its recent history as a member of the Soviet empire and as an independent socialist republic since 1991 has seen a suppression of Islamic participation in the civil life of the people.

Twelvers

See ITHNÂ ʿASHARIYYAH.

U

Uganda

The Central African Republic of Uganda has an estimated sixteen percent of Muslims in its population of 24 million. Islam arrived in the nineteenth century, and the country, only partially Arabized, is predominantly SUNNÎ. During the dictatorship of Idi Amin, the influence of Islam increased, but with his fall in 1979, the state has been more secular. Still, many Muslims observe Friday prayers, and ʿÎD AL-FIṬR and ʿÎd al-Ḥajj are national holidays.

ʿulamâʾ (Arabic: persons of knowledge; sg. *ʿâlim*)

One of the significant features of Islam is the role of the religious scholar in determining the religious and public lives of Muslims. From the period shortly after the death of MUḤAMMAD, men knowledgeable about the QURʾÂN and SUNNAH have occupied positions of religious and political authority as QÂḌÎs, MUFTÎs, IMÂMS, MULLÂs, and other figures of leadership. They have been the teachers, preachers, authors of TAFSÎR, social critics, and members of the conservative establishment. While they are often referred to as a class or cohesive group, such a classification reflects only a small aspect of the position of such individuals in Islamic history. Nor should one assume that an *ʿâlim* or group of *ʿulamâʾ* will always be defenders of the status quo, since many have been at the forefront of Islamic change and revolution. *ʿUlamâʾ* are found in all branches of Islam. While they are not clergy as such, most, to be designated as *ʿulamâʾ* must attend special schools and receive recognized diplomas attesting to the competence of their religious knowledge. (*See also* ÂYATOLLÂH; IJÂZAH.)

ʿUmar b. ʿAbd al-ʿAzîz (died 101/720)

Known as ʿUmar II, he was revered alone among the ʾUMAYYAD caliphs as a righteous and true Muslim by later Islamic historians and ranked by some among the RÂSHIDÛN, or "Rightly Guided." He is known for working to assure equity between Arab and non-Arab Muslims.

ʿUmar b. al-Khaṭṭâb (died 23/644)

The second caliph in Islam after ABÛ BAKR, he is known for his organizational skills and for expanding the Islamic conquest. He was a strong opponent of Islam before his conversion, usually placed about four years before the HIJRAH, and he became its most strong-willed supporter thereafter. In MADÎNAH, he served as one of MUḤAMMAD's closest advisors. He had exceptional organizational skill and determination to see tasks completed. While this earned him some enemies, he was able to create the structure of a religious empire that made Islam a world religion. There is considerable debate about whether he was appointed caliph by the dying Abû Bakr in 12/634, but this represents after-the-fact speculation. He is noted for assuming the title of ʾAMÎR AL-MUʾMINÎN, the Commander of the Faithful, and of instituting the *dîwân*, the distribution bureaucracy that dispersed the booty from the conquests. He also divided the rule of the conquered territories between a military commander, ʾAMÎR, and a fiscal officer, *ʿâmil*, thereby dividing the power and making the caliph the center of it all. He was assassinated by a Persian slave, Abû Luʾluʾah, angry at the caliph's tyranny.

ʾUmayyads

The quasi-hereditary dynasty that followed the death of ʿALÎ B. ABÎ ṬÂLIB in 41/661. They ruled until their overthrow by the ʿABBÂSIDS in 132/750, and longer in the Iberian peninsula. Some later histories have condemned them for secularism and failure to implement fully the rule of Islam, yet many later Islamic institutions saw their first development under ʾUmayyad rule.

ʾummah (Arabic: community)

Derived from the Arabic word for mother, *ʾumm*, the earliest Islamic concept of the *ʾummah* can be found in the so-called CONSTITUTION OF MADÎNAH, in which MUḤAMMAD agreed with the Muslims and Jews on their mutual rights and obligations in the one community. This formed the pattern for the inclusion of the AHL AL-KITÂB as DHIMMÎ in later Islamic societies. This term has been used in many different senses throughout history, but, generally, Muslims, regardless of differences, regard themselves as one *ʾummah*.

ʾUmm Ḥabîbah

A widowed daughter of ABÛ SUFYÂN, who became one of the wives of MUḤAMMAD.

ʾummî (Arabic: of the people)

This word has come to mean "illiterate" in those polemics that hold that MUḤAMMAD was unable to read. This notion developed to counter charges that Muḥammad had stolen the ideas for the QURʾÂN from Jewish and Christian scripture.

ʾumm al-kitâb

See AL-LAWḤ AL-MAḤFÛẒ.

ʾUmm Kulthûm (died 9/630)

A daughter of MUḤAMMAD and KHADÎJAH, she married ʿUTHMÂN B. ʿAFFÂN.

ʾUmm Salamah

The widow of Abû Salamah, she married MUḤAMMAD in about 4/626.

ʿumrah

See ḤAJJ.

Union des Organisations Islamiques de France

Founded in 1983, this umbrella organization seeks to promote the welfare and education of Muslims in France. It has been regarded as a fundamentalist organization, but has not exhibited any radical political activity.

United Kingdom Islamic Mission

Founded in 1962, the mission functions as an important DAʿWAH organization in Britain, providing centers for the instruction of children and for worship.

United States of America

Islam in the United States of America began with the arrival of the earliest colonialists in the New World, and, with the importation of slaves from Africa, a steady growth of Muslims started, reaching just under two percent of the population at the end of the twentieth century. Regular immigration of Muslims to America began in the last half of the nineteenth century with Muslims from Syria, Lebanon, Jordan, and Palestine. By the second half of the twentieth century, Muslims from South Asia, Iran, and other areas of the Middle East began to arrive. The current Muslim population is increasing by immigration, procreation, and conversion, so that some scholars estimate that it is the fastest-growing religion in North America. Most Muslims are located in major urban centers, but some small towns have actively welcomed Muslims, particularly when they have brought professional or mercantile skills. While the majority are SUNNÎ, the other branches are also represented. ISMÂʿÎLÎ and ITHNÂ ʿASHARIYYAH SHÎʿÎ are found in many major centers, such as Atlanta and Los Angeles. Among American blacks, the NATION OF ISLAM has had considerable influence, but most Muslims who are Black are not members of the Nation of Islam. Islam has become sufficiently integrated into the American religious fabric that Muslims regularly hold positions on community religious councils, and Muslim religious food emporia are found in most large urban centers.

Urdu

One of the world's major Islamic languages, it is related to Hindi. It is written in a modified Persian script and has much Persian and Arabic vocabulary, particularly for religious terms and conventional greeting. It is the official language of PAKISTAN.

ʿurf (Arabic: knowledge)

In many Islamic countries this is the term for customary law, in contrast with SHARÎʿAH), or written holy law. Histori-

Grand Mosque, Cleveland, Ohio, U.S.A.

cally, it has existed side by side with *sharî'ah*, and often in conflict with it. In some courts in Muslim Spain, rulers used *'urf* to justify the use of police courts to circumvent the strictures of evidence. In a positive sense, it designates the inclusion of local practices under the umbrella of Islamic law: Islamic reformers have often attempted to purge their societies of what they see as man-made customs, as opposed to divine law. (*See also* ADAT.)

'uṣûl al-fiqh (Arabic: roots of law)

The sources or "roots" of Islamic jurisprudence, which, after ASH-SHÂFI'Î, are identified as QUR'ÂN, SUNNAH, IJMÂ' and QIYÂS.

'Uṣûlî, or 'Uṣûliyyah

Based on the concept of the 'UṢÛL AL-FIQH, this rationalist school of law became the basis for jurisprudence among the ITHNÂ 'ASHARIYYAH SHÎ'Î.

usury

See BANKS AND BANKING; RIBÂ.

'Uthmân b. 'Affân (23/644–35/655)

He was a member of the Meccan family, the 'UMAYYADS. He converted early in the Prophet's mission, well before the HIJRAH. Not only did he come from well-to-do stock, he was a wealthy merchant in his own right. He married two of MUḤAMMAD's daughters, RUQAYYAH, who died, and then 'UMM KULTHÛM. He did not take part in the battle of BADR, and the role that he played in the community while the Prophet was alive was a minor one. When the caliph 'UMAR died, the council (SHÛRÂ) chose him to be the new caliph. The reasons for their choice are still the subject of scholarly speculation, some asserting, following his critics, that he was not a particularly good administrator. He did have a religious vision, however, and it was under him that the commission was formed to collect the pieces of the QUR'ÂN and make an official recension. This commission was under the direction of ZAYD B. THÂBIT, and produced a copy of the Qur'ân that still bears the caliph's name. He was killed over issues of nepotism and inept governance, and the ensuing battle over succession between 'ALÎ B. ABÎ ṬÂLIB and Mu'âwiyah of the 'Umayyads was the first civil war in Islam.

'Uthmân (Usuman) dan Fodio

See DAN FODIO.

'Uzayr

Identified with the biblical Ezra, he is mentioned once in the QUR'ÂN, in a passage that has caused considerable discussion. In Q. 9:30, we read, "The Jews say 'Uzayr is the son of ALLÂH, and the Christians say AL-MASÎḤ is the son of Allâh . . ." While this view does not represent mainstream Rabbinic Judaism in any period, there seem to have been some Jews in pre-Islamic Arabia that equated Ezra with Enoch and said that Enoch was assumed into Heaven, stripped of his humanity and transformed into Meṭaṭron, who, in some cosmologies, was the head of the heavenly creatures known as the *b'nê 'elôhîm*, a literal translation of which would be "sons of God." Post-Qur'ânic polemics between Muslims and Jews have been colored by this passage.

Uzbekistan

One of the most important Central Asian Islamic countries, it was Islamized in the second/seventh century. The major cities of BUKHÂRÂ and Samarqand were centers of Islamic material and spiritual culture for centuries. Under the domination of the Soviet Union, Islam was suppressed, but with independence in 1991, it

Poi Kalyan minaret, Bukhârâ old city, Uzbekistan.

reasserted itself in the form of an Islamic republic that has proved to be as totalitarian as the previous Soviet regime.

al-ʿUzzâ (Arabic: the strong one)

She was the pre-Islamic Arabian goddess, sometimes identified with Venus, that was joined with AL-LÂT and MANÂT as the so-called "daughters of ALLÂH." Her worship seems to have extended throughout the northern part of Arabia and into southern Syria, particularly in her astral form. After MUḤAMMAD's capture of MECCA and the destruction of her idol, the cult seems to have quickly faded in the face of the expansion of Islam.

V

veil

See BURQUʿ; CHÂDÔR; ḤIJÂB.

verse (of the Qur'ân)

See 'ÂYAH.

vicegerent

See KHALÎFAH.

vizier

See WAZÎR.

W

waḥy (Arabic: inspiration)

This term is used extensively in the QUR'ÂN to mean revelation. It is usually understood as meaning some process of inspiration, as opposed to TANZÎL, which means to "come down, descend." Commentators have speculated about the actual process of revelation, and the evidence of the Qur'ân and the SÎRAH shows that MUḤAMMAD received revelation both through direct inspiration from God and through the intermediation of the archangel JIBRÎL. It is not only prophets who receive *waḥy*, but also the earth, as is seen in Q. 99:5. IBLÎS inspires, or tempts, humans and JINN through the process of WASWÂS (whispering).

al-wakâlah al-'âmmah (Arabic: deputyship of the people)

The concept in ITHNÂ 'ASHARIYYAH SHÎ'Î Islam that the 'ULAMÂ' are to assume the deputyship and prerogatives of the IMÂM, who is in GHAYBAH. This concept has given greater power to the Shî'î *'ulamâ'* than that generally held by the SUNNÎ to assume governmental leadership roles based on religious principles.

walâyah, or wilâyah (Arabic: guardianship, succession)

GUARDIANSHIP of minors, orphans, and wives is an important obligation in Islam. Islamic legal practice expounds many rules that assure that the weaker members of society are protected by a guardianship structure. *Walâyah* is also used as a political term. One of the fundamental tenets of SHÎ'Î Islam is that before his death MUḤAMMAD appointed as his successor 'ALÎ B. ABÎ ṬÂLIB. From 'Alî, the line of succession progresses through the line of the AHL AL-BAYT through the principle of *walâyah*.

walî (Arabic: to be near)

Often translated as "saint," this term refers to the holy person in Islam who is the conduit through which the *barakât* of ALLÂH is transmitted. Unlike Christian saints, there is not a formal process for determining who becomes a saint and who does not, nor is there a regular way of including Islamic saints into a regular rotation of the liturgy. In popular practice, the *walî* has the power to intercede for the worshiper, to bring about fertility, healing, and wealth. Critics of this practice sometimes assert, as have the Wahhâbîs, that this practice is un-Islamic. (*See also* BARAKAH; IBN 'ABD AL-WAHHÂB; QUBBAH.)

Walî Allâh, Shâh (1703–1762)

A prolific and prominent Indian Muslim thinker and a member of the NAQSHBANDIYYAH ṢÛFÎ ṬARÎQAH, he traveled to MECCA and MADÎNAH for education in ḤADÎTH and FIQH. His most important work, *Ḥujjat Allâh al-bâlighah*, sought to reform Islamic sciences through revitalized *ḥadîth* studies. His life and work have been so influential that nearly every Islamic reform group in India has claimed him as a forebear.

waqf (Arabic: religious endowment; pl. *'awqâf*)

A religious foundation made in perpetuity in which the owner has limited access to the usufruct but no ability to dispose of the principle. Such pious foundations have been an important means of endowing such Islamic institutions as schools, mosques, hospitals, and so on. Many Islamic countries have special divisions of government to assist in managing the assets of the endowments. In North Africa, the preferred word is *ḥubs* (pl. *'aḥbâs*).

al-Wâqidî, Abû 'Abd Allâh Muḥammad (130/747–207/823)

Prominent Muslim historian and biographer of the Prophet, his *Kitâb al-maghâzî* (The book of conquests) is an important source for the life of MUḤAMMAD and the history of early Islam.

Waraqah b. Nawfal

A cousin of MUḤAMMAD's first wife, KHADÎJAH, he is said to have been a ḤANÎF, who had studied Christian scripture. It is reported that when Khadîjah asked him about the veracity of Muḥammad's first revelation, he affirmed that it fitted the expectations of previous scripture. He did not convert to Islam because he died before Muḥammad's command to preach publicly.

Wâṣil b. 'Aṭâ' (80/699–131/749)

A student of AL-ḤASAN AL-BAṢRÎ, he is reported to have broken with his master to become one of the founders of the MU'TAZILAH movement. Few facts are known about his life other than his association with al-Ḥasan al-Baṣrî. He is said to have believed in human free will and that a sinner who commits a grave sin is in an in-between state, being neither a believer or an unbeliever, a position in opposition to the KHAWÂRIJ and those who held that sin has no relationship to belief. (*See also* MURJI'AH.)

waswâs (Arabic: whisper)

This is the means by which the devil, IBLÎS, insinuates temptation and evil thoughts into humans and JINN. The recitation of Q. 114 is thought to be a prophylactic against such temptations.

waẓîfah (Arabic: portion)

The assigning of sections to the QUR'ÂN for orderly recitation. For the weekly reading, the Qur'ân is divided into seven MANÂZIL (sg. *manzilah*) to facilitate the complete reading of the text in a week. Another common division is into thirty parts, *ajzâ'* (sg. *juz'*), one for each day of the month of RAMAḌÂN. The divisions do not correspond to the division of the Qur'ân into chapters.

wazîr (Arabic: vizier)

Originally an assistant to a caliph, the term came to have the sense of an important governmental minister in charge of a major department of the bureaucracy.

wine

See KHAMR.

witr (Arabic: uneven)

A voluntary prayer said in the night, comprising of an odd number of RAK'AHS.

wuḍû' (Arabic: ablution)

The minor ritual ABLUTION before prayer, consisting of the washing of the face, hands and forearms, the head and the feet, using ritually pure water, or, if unavailable, sand or stones. Most commentators also include the notion of spiritual purification in this concept. (*See also* GHUSL; PURIFICATION; ṢALÂT; TAYAMMUM.)

wuqûf (Arabic: pause)

The stopping or standing as part of the performance of the ḤAJJ.

Y

al-yahûd (Arabic: the Jews)

Along with the term BANÛ ISRÂ'ÎL, this term is used in the QUR'ÂN to refer both to the biblical Jews and to those contemporary with MUḤAMMAD. During Muḥammad's lifetime, he was opposed by some of the Jewish tribes of MADÎNAH, but was also helped by others. In the CONSTITUTION OF MADÎNAH, which was drawn up shortly after Muḥammad's arrival in the city, Jews were included in the community as long as they contributed to the welfare of the community. This and similar treaties form some of the basis for the inclusion of Jews, Christians, and Zoroastrians as legal members of Islamic societies. (*See also* DHIMMÎ.)

Yaḥyâ (Arabic)

A prophet mentioned in the QUR'ÂN, often identified with John the Baptist. In extra-Qur'ânic traditions, he is said to have been born miraculously to parents of advanced years after an annunciation about his birth and his name. He was able to speak from the cradle and had immense wisdom as a child. His mission was to confirm the TAWRÂT. He is said to have baptized 'Îsâ (JESUS), and to have been killed by the wife of Herod, who had him decapitated and his head sent to the king, whereupon, according to some stories, the blood boiled and the head spoke against the crime.

Ya'jûj wa-Ma'jûj

Identified with the biblical Gog and Magog, these are the eschatological armies that will overrun the earth as one of the signs of the YAWM AD-DÎN. According to Islamic legend, they will be led by AD-DAJJÂL. According to the QUR'ÂN and elaborated on in the TAFSÎR traditions, DHÛ-L-QARNAYN (Alexander the Great) walled Gog and Magog behind a barrier that will only be breached at the end of time.

Ya'qûb (Arabic)

Jacob, the father of YÛSUF (Joseph), named in the QUR'ÂN as a prophet. In the TAFSÎR to Q. 12, which contains the story of Yûsuf, we read more details about his life than are found in the Qur'ân. In one story, Yûsuf's brothers are asked to produce the wolf that they claim ate Yûsuf. When they bring a wolf, it suddenly is given the power of speech and reveals their deceit.

Yathrib

The original name of the city of MADÎNAH in Arabia. It appears to be an ancient name, indicating the antiquity of the city.

yawm ad-Dîn (Arabic: day of judgment)

The eschatological day on which all souls will be judged and this temporal order of the world will end. The QUR'ÂN describes in vivid detail some of the events associated with that day.

yawm al-jum'ah (Arabic: the day of congregation)

Friday, on which Muslims traditionally observe a congregational prayer at the noon prayer. The story is told that the day is so called because God gathered together all of the works of creation on that day. (*See also* KHUṬBAH; ṢALÂT.)

yawm al qiyâmah (Arabic: the day of resurrection)

A synonym for YAWM AD-DÎN.

Yûnus

See DHÛ-N-NÛN.

Yûsuf

Identified with the biblical Joseph, Yûsuf is the subject of the twelfth chapter of the QUR'ÂN, described as the most beautiful story in the Qur'ân. He is a prophet, interpreter of dreams, and model of how to deal with temptation. His recommendation that grain be saved against the threat of famine has served Muslim governments as a model for social planning.

Z

al-zabâniyah

The nineteen guardians of Hell.

zabûr (Arabic)

The biblical book of Psalms. This is coupled with the word TAWRÂT (Torah), as the two portions of scripture revealed by God to the Jews.

ẓâhir (Arabic: exoteric)

The term is used in TAFSÎR to refer to the easily understood, non-problematic portions of the QUR'ÂN. Commentators differ over which portions fall into this category. (*See also* BÂṬIN.)

Ẓâhiriyyah

A school (MADHHAB) of Islamic law that relied on the literal interpretation of the QUR'ÂN and SUNNAH.

Zakariyyah

The biblical Zachariah.

zakât (Arabic: alms)

One of the obligations placed on Muslims is the giving of charity as alms from the surplus of their wealth at the rate of about two-and-a-half percent. The proceeds from this charity are to be used only for the welfare of the needy in the Islamic state. Among some, particularly the SHÎ'Î, the rate of charity on some types of wealth is one-fifth, KHUMS. (*See also* PILLARS OF ISLAM; ṢADAQAH.)

az-Zamakhsharî, Abû al-Qâsim Maḥmûd b. 'Umar (467/1075–538/1144)

He is best known for his TAFSÎR, entitled *al-Kashshâf 'an haqâ'iq at-tanzîl*, in which he declares the QUR'ÂN to be created, placing him in the MU'TAZILAH school of thought. The work, however, is widely circulated among non-Mu'tazilite SUNNÎ. He devoted considerable attention in his work to the rhetorical nature of the Qur'ân and to dogmatic exegesis. His grammatical work, *al-Mufaṣṣal*, is also widely used for its clarity and brevity.

Zamzam

The well near the KA'BAH in MECCA. Its origin is said to have been to provide water for ISMÂ'ÎL when he and his mother, HÂJAR, were sent to the desert by IBRÂHÎM. The water of this well is held by pilgrims to have special spiritual powers.

az-zaqqûm

A terrible-smelling and foul-tasting tree in Hell, the fruit of which sinners will be obliged to eat as punishment.

zâwiyah (Arabic: corner)

Associated with Ṣûfism, the term can refer to a corner of a mosque, a small room for devotion, or, more usually, a small mosque built over or in association with the tomb of a WALÎ. The *zâwiyah* is usually associated with a particular ṬARÎQAH. (*See also* ṢÛFÎ.)

Zayd b. Thâbit (died *c.* 35/655)

He was the secretary of the Prophet MUḤAMMAD, and is reputed to have been able to learn languages quickly. After the Prophet's death, he was given the charge of heading the commission that prepared the ʿUthmânic recension of the QUR'ÂN from all the available written and oral sources. (*See also* ʿUTHMÂN B. ʿAFFÂN.)

Zaydiyyah

The so-called "Fiver" branch of the SHÎʿÎ, they chose Zayd b. ʿAlî b. Abî Ṭâlib as the fifth IMÂM, hence their name. This branch is known to have existed in a number of forms in such areas as Iran, Tabaristan, and the southern Caspian Sea area, but their most enduring location has been in the Yemen, where they have been dominant since the fourth/ninth century. Unlike the ISMÂʿÎLÎ and the ITHNÂ ʿASHARIYYAH branches, the Zaydiyyah accept the legitimacy of the caliphates of ABÛ BAKR, ʿUMAR, and ʿUTHMÂN. They do not attribute any supernatural powers to the *Imâm* in GHAYBAH, and hold that there can be more than one *Imâm* at any one time.

Zaynab bt. Jaḥsh

A cousin of MUḤAMMAD and, after her divorce from Zayd b. Ḥârithah, the adopted son of the Prophet, was one of his wives.

Zaynab bt. Khuzaymah

A widow who married MUḤAMMAD.

az-Zaytûnah (Arabic: olive tree)

The "Mosque of the Olive Tree," in Tunis. Founded in 114/732 as a mosque-university, it rivaled the mosque of AL-AZHAR as a center for Islamic learning. It now continues as a constituent part of the University of Tunis.

zikr

See DHIKR.

zinâ' (Arabic: adultery, fornication)

Both of these are considered sins in Islam.

zindîq (Arabic from Persian: heretic, unbeliever)

The term originally referred to the dualist worldview of Zoroastrians, but became used generally for any heretic or skeptic.

ziyârah (Arabic: visit)

The practice of visiting or making pilgrimage to the tombs of saints. (*See also* QUBBAH; WALÎ.)

zuhd (Arabic: asceticism)

This term is often associated with ṢÛFÎ renunciationism, a feature of some but not all ṬARÎQAHS. Extreme renunciation is, however, frowned on in Islam, and there is often-cited ḤADÎTH from the Prophet MUḤAMMAD that "there is no monkhood in Islam."

aẓ-ẓuhr (Arabic: noon)

The midday prayer.

Zulaykhâ

Potiphar's wife, who attempted to seduce YÛSUF. Her name is only found in the TAFSÎR and ISRÂ'ÎLIYYÂT traditions. (*See also* QIṬFÎR.)

ẓulm (Arabic: wrongdoing)

This Arabic word means iniquity or injustice. It is used in the QUR'ÂN as the opposite of light (NÛR), as well as in the sense of wrong and evil, and is condemned. See, for example, the story of Adam and Eve in Q. 2:35. Wrongdoing can be either in the form of words or deeds. Following from the general Qur'ânic and Islamic use, the word has the special sense of tyranny in the SHÎ'Î tradition, referring chiefly to the wrong actions and tyranny imposed on the followers of 'ALÎ B. ABÎ ṬÂLIB by the 'UMAYYADS. This highly charged term was used against the rule of the *shâh* in IRAN around the time of the 1979 revolution. (*See also* PAHLAVI.)

God's Ninety-Nine Names[1] *al-'Asmâ' al-Ḥusnâ*

1. *Allâh*
2. *ar-Raḥmân* the Merciful
3. *ar-Raḥîm* the Compassionate
4. *al-Malik* the King
5. *al-Quddûs* the Holy
6. *as-Salâm* Peace
7. *al-Mu'min* the Bringer of Safety
8. *al-Muhaymin* the Watchful Guardian
9. *al-ʿAzîz* the Powerful
10. *al-Jabbâr* the Strong
11. *al-Mutakabbir* the Proud
12. *al-Khâliq* the Creator
13. *al-Bâri'* the Creator
14. *al-Muṣawwir* the Former
15. *al-Ghaffâr* the Pardoner
16. *al-Qahhâr* the Subduer
17. *al-Wahhâb* the Giver
18. *ar-Razzâq* the Nourisher
19. *al-Fattâḥ* the Victorious
20. *al-ʿAlîm* the Knower
21. *al-Qabîd* the Restrainer
22. *al-Khafîḍ* the Humiliator
23. *al-Bâsiṭ* the Expander
24. *ar-Râfiʿ* the Elevator
25. *al-Muʿizz* the Strength-Giver
26. *al-Mudhill* the Debaser
27. *as-Sâmiʿ* the Hearer
28. *al-Baṣîr* the Seer
29. *al-Ḥakam* the Judge
30. *al-ʿAdl* the Just
31. *al-Laṭîf* the Kind
32. *al-Khabîr* the Knowing
33. *al-Ḥalîm* the Gentle
34. *al-ʿAẓîm* the Majestic
35. *al-Ghafûr* the Indulgent
36. *ash-Shakûr* the Thankful
37. *al-ʿAlî* the Exalted
38. *al-Kabîr* the Great
39. *al-Ḥâfiẓ* the Preserver
40. *al-Muqît* the Nourisher
41. *al-Ḥasîb* the Calculator
42. *al-Jalîl* the Majestic
43. *al-Karîm* the Generous
44. *ar-Raqîb* the Watchful
45. *al-Mujîb* the Answerer
46. *al-Wâsiʿ* the Omnipresent
47. *al-Ḥakîm* the Wise
48. *al-Wadûd* the Loving
49. *al-Majîd* the Glorious
50. *al-Bâʿith* the Reviver
51. *ash-Shahîd* the Witness
52. *al-Ḥaqq* the Truth
53. *al-Wakîl* the Trustee
54. *al-Qawî* the Strong
55. *al-Matîn* the Unshakeable
56. *al-Walî* the Friend
57. *al-Ḥamîd* the Praiseworthy
58. *al-Muḥṣî* the Enumerator
59. *al-Mubdiʿ* the Innovator
60. *al-Muʿîd* the Resuscitator

1 This is one of many possible lists of names of Allâh. Both the order and the actual names themselves vary from community to community and from commentator to commentator. The list of names is used for private devotion, often with a *ṣubḥah*, or rosary, for counting and keeping track. It is also used among the Ṣûfî in their *dhikr* or worship.

61. *al-Muḥyî* the Lifegiver
62. *al-Mumît* the Deathgiver
63. *al-Ḥayy* the Living
64. *al-Qayyûm* the Self-Sufficient
65. *al-Wâjid* the Perfect
66. *al-Majîd* the Noble
67. *al-Aḥad* the One
68. *aṣ-Ṣamad* the Sought
69. *al-Qâdir* the Powerful
70. *al-Muqtadir* the All-Powerful
71. *al-Muqqadim* the One Who Brings Near
72. *al-Mu'akhkhir* the One Who Sends Away
73. *al-Awwal* the First
74. *al-'Âkhir* the Last
75. *aẓ-Ẓâhir* the Manifest
76. *al-Bâṭin* the Hidden
77. *al-Wâlî* the Sovereign
78. *al-Muta'âlî* the Very High
79. *al-Bârr* the Source of Piety
80. *at-Tawwâb* the Cause of Repentance
81. *al-Muntaqim* the Avenger
82. *al-'Afû* the Effacer of Faults
83. *ar-Ra'ûf* the Merciful
84. *Mâlik al-Mulk* King of the Kingdom
85. *Dhû-l-Jalâl wa-l-Ikrâm* Lord of Majesty and Generosity
86. *al-Muqṣiṭ* the Just
87. *al-Jâmi'* the Assembler
88. *al-Ghanî* the Rich
89. *al-Mughnî* the Enricher
90. *al-Mâni'* the Defender
91. *aḍ-Ḍârr* the Afflicter
92. *an-Nâfi'* the Benefactor
93. *an-Nûr* the Light
94. *al-Hâdî* the Guide
95. *al-Badî'* the Creator
96. *al-Bâqî* the Eternal
97. *al-Wârith* the Inheritor
98. *ar-Rashîd* the Leader
99. *aṣ-Ṣabûr* the Patient

Chronology

570	Birth of Muḥammad. Year of the Elephant and the unsuccessful invasion of Mecca by Abraha the Viceroy of Yemen; death of Muḥammad's father, ʿAbdullâh b. ʿAbd al-Muṭṭalib.
576	Death of Âminah bt. Wahb, Muḥammad's mother.
580	Death of ʿAbd al-Muṭṭalib, Muḥammad's grandfather.
583	Muḥammad's journey to Syria in the company of his uncle Abû Ṭâlib and encounter with the monk Baḥîrâ.
595	Muḥammad marries Khadîjah.
605	Muḥammad adjudicates a dispute among the Quraysh about replacing the Black Stone in the Kaʿbah.
610	The first revelation in the cave at Mt. Ḥirâʾ, during which Muḥammad is declared by God to be His Prophet.
613	First public declaration of Islam.
615	Persecution of Muslims by the Quraysh resulting in the first *hijrah* to Abyssinia.
616	Second *hijrah* to Abyssinia.
617	Social boycott of the Banû Hâshim and Muḥammad by the Quraysh.
619	Lifting of the boycott; deaths of Abû Ṭâlib and Khadîjah.
620	Night journey to Jerusalem and *miʿrâj*.
622	*Hijrah*: Muḥammad and the Muslims migrate to Yathrib/Madînah; foundation of Islamic state and Constitution of Madînah.
3/624	Battle of Badr. Expulsion of the Jewish Banû Qaynuqâʿ from Madînah.
4/625	Battle of Uḥud; expulsion of the Jewish Banû an-Naḍîr from Madînah.
6/627	Battle of the Trench; expulsion of the Jewish Banû Qurayẓah.
7/628	Truce of Ḥudaybiyyah; expedition to Khaybar.
9/630	Conquest of Mecca; death of ʾUmm Kulthûm.
10/632	Farewell Pilgrimage.
11/632	Death of Muḥammad; death of Fâṭimah; election of Abû Bakr as caliph; death of Rayḥânah bt. Zayd.
13/634	Death of Abû Bakr; ʿUmar becomes caliph.
14/635	Conquest of Damascus.
16/637	Conquest of Syria and the fall of Jerusalem.
20/640	Conquest of Persia.
22/642	Conquest of Egypt; foundation of Fusṭâṭ.

24/644	Death of ʿUmar; ʿUthmân becomes the caliph; promulgation of recension of the Qur'ân.
33/653	Death of Ibn Masʿûd.
35/655	Death of Zayd b. Thâbit.
36/656	Death of ʿUthmân; ʿAlî becomes caliph and fights the battle of the Camel.
37/657	ʿAlî shifts the capital from Madînah to Kûfah; battle of Ṣiffîn; arbitration between ʿAlî and the 'Umayyads.
39/659	Conquest of Egypt by Muʿâwiyah.
40/660	ʿAlî recaptures Ḥijâz and Yemen from Muʿâwiyah. Muʿâwiyah declares himself caliph at Damascus.
41/661	Martyrdom of ʿAlî. Accession of Ḥasan and his abdication. Muʿâwiyah becomes the sole caliph.
42/662	Khawârij revolt.
49/669	Death of al-Ḥasan b. ʿAlî.
59/678	Death of ʿÂ'ishah; death of Abû Hurayrah.
61/680	Martyrdom of Ḥusayn.
64/683	ʿAbd Allâh b. az-Zubayr rules Mecca as self-proclaimed caliph until 692.
73/692	Defeat and death of ʿAbd Allâh b. az-Zubayr; end of dual caliphate.
81/700	Conquest and conversion of Berber tribes in North Africa.
91/709	Death of 'Anas b. Mâlik.
92/711	Conquest of Spain, Sind and Transoxania.
102/720	Death of ʿUmar II.
114/732	The battle of Tours in France.
123/740	Shîʿî revolt under Zayd b. ʿAlî. Capture of Kûfah by the ʿAbbâsids. As-Saffâh becomes the ʿAbbâsid caliph at Kûfah.
126/743	Death of Muḥammad al-Bâqir, the fifth *Imâm*.
129/746	Death of Jahm b. Ṣafwân.
132/749	Persia captured by the ʿAbbâsids; death of Wâṣil b. ʿAṭâ'.
133/750	Fall of Damascus. End of the 'Umayyads in the east.
139/756	Establishment of 'Umayyads in Spain.
145/762	Shîʿî rebellions against ʿAbbâsids.
146/763	Foundation of Baghdâd; defeat of the ʿAbbâsids in Spain.
150/767	Khârijî state set up by Ibn Madrar at Sijilmasa; death of Abû Ḥanîfah; death of Ibn Isḥâq.
179/795	Death of Mâlik b. 'Anas.
183/799	Death of Mûsâ al-Kâẓim.
185/801	Death of Râbiʿah al-ʿAdawiyyah.
201/816	Shîʿî revolt in Mecca.
205/820	Death of ash-Shâfiʿî.
208/823	Death of al-Wâqidî.
212/827	ʿAbbâsid caliph al-Maʿmûn declares the Muʿtazilah creed as the state religion; the beginning of the *miḥnah*.
218/833	Death of Ibn Hishâm.
221/835	Death of Muḥammad at-Taqî, ninth *Imâm*.
225/839	Muslims capture Sicily and southern Italy.
236/850	ʿAbbasid caliph al-Mutawakkil ends the *miḥnah*.
241/855	Death of Aḥmad b. Ḥanbal.
243/857	Death of al-Muḥâsibî.

252/866	Death of al-Kindî.
254/868	Aḥmad b. Ṭûlûn founds the Ṭûlûnid rule in Egypt.
255/868	Death of al-Jâḥiẓ
257/870	Death of al-Bukhârî.
260/874	*Ghaybah* of Muḥammad al-Qâ'im.
262/875	Death of Muslim b. al-Ḥajjâj.
274/887	Death of Ibn Mâjah.
275/888	Death of at-Tirmidhî.
276/889	Death of Abû Dâ'ûd.
278/891	The Qarmâṭî state established in Baḥrain.
285/898	Qarmâṭî sack Baṣrah.
297/909	Foundation of Fâṭimid Ismâ'îlî Shî'î dynasty in North Africa.
303/915	Death of an-Nasâ'î.
311/923	Death of aṭ-Ṭabarî.
317/929	Qarmâṭî sack Mecca and carry away the Black Stone from the Ka'bah.
319/931	Death of the Qarmâṭî ruler Abû Ṭâhir.
323/934	Death of Abû Ḥâtim ar-Râzî; death of Muḥammad 'Ubayd Allâh.
324/935	Death of Abû-l-Ḥasan 'Alî al-'Ash'arî.
340/951	The Qarmâṭî restore the Black Stone to the Ka'bah.
359/969	The beginning of Fâṭimid Ismâ'îlî rule in Egypt; Cairo founded.
371/981	End of Qarmâṭî rule in Bahrain.
392/1001	Maḥmûd al-Ghaznavî defeats the Hindus; beginning of Islamic rule in South Asia.
412/1021	The Fâṭimid caliph al-Ḥâkim disappears/dies; Druze religion founded.
412/1021	Death of al-Kirmânî.
421/1030	Death of Maḥmud Ghaznavî.
429/1037	Death of Ibn Sînâ.
432/1040	Battle of Dandanqân; Saljûqs defeat the Ghaznavids.
457/1064	Death of Ibn Ḥazm.
464/1071	Battle of Manzikert, the Byzantine emperor taken captive by the Saljûqs.
468/1075	Death of al-Hujwîrî.
484/1091	Normans recapture Sicily and end Muslim rule.
488/1095	The first Crusade called.
492/1099	The Crusaders capture Jerusalem.
505/1111	Death of Abû Ḥâmid al-Ghâzalî.
518/1124	Death of Ḥasan-i Ṣabbâḥ.
533/1138	Death of Kiyâ Buzurg-Umîd; death of Ibn Bâjjah.
539/1144	Second Crusade.
562/1166	Death of al-Jîlânî.
567/1171	End of the Fâṭimids; Ṣalâḥ ad-Dîn b. Ayyûb founds the Ayyûbid dynasty in Egypt.
570/1174	Ṣalâḥ ad-Dîn annexes Syria.
582/1186	End of Ghaznavid rule in Punjab.
583/1187	Jerusalem retaken from Crusaders.
590/1193	Death of Ṣalâḥ ad-Dîn.
591/1194	Occupation of Delhi by Muslims.
595/1198	Death of Ibn Rushd.

596/1199	Conquest of northern India and Bengal by Ghûrids.
600/1203	Founding of Mongol Empire by Chingiz Khân.
608/1211	End of Ghûrid rule.
638/1240	Death of Ibn al-ʿArabî.
643/1245	Muslims reconquer Jerusalem.
657/1258	The Mongols sack Baghdâd. Death of the ʿAbbâsid caliph al-Muʿtasim. End of the ʿAbbâsid rule. Fall of Baghdâd, end of the ʿAbbâsid caliphate. The Mongol Il-Khâns under Hulagu establish their rule in Iran and Iraq.
659/1260	Battle of ʿAyn Jâlût in Syria. The Mongols are defeated by the Mamlûks of Egypt.
672/1273	Death of Jalâl ad-Dîn Rûmî.
711/1311	Death of Shams ad-Dîn Muḥammad.
726/1325	Death of al-Ḥillî.
727/1326	Death of ʿUthmân, founder of the Ottomans.
729/1328	Death of Ibn Taymiyyah.
771/1369	Death of Ibn Baṭṭûṭah.
809/1406	Death of Ibn Khaldûn.
857/1453	Muslims capture Constantinople, renamed Istanbul.
898/1492	Fall of Granada and end of Moorish (Islamic) rule in Spain.
905/1499	The Turks defeated the Venetian fleet in the battle of Lepanto.
907/1501	Ismâʿîl I establishes the Ṣafavid dynasty in Persia, and Ithnâ ʿAsharî Shîʿism becomes the state religion.
911/1505	Death of as-Suyûṭî.
923/1517	The Ottomans conquer Egypt.
927/1520	The reign of the Ottoman *ṣulṭân* Sulaymân the Magnificent begins.
933/1526	The Mughal conquest of India with Delhi as the capital.
935/1528	The Ottomans take Buda in Hungary.
936/1529	Unsuccessful Ottoman siege of Vienna.
957/1550	The rise of the Muslim kingdom in Sumatra.
957/1550	Islam spreads to Java, the Moluccas, and Borneo.
964/1556	The death of Sulaymân the Magnificent.
976/1568	Uprising of the Moriscos (Muslims forcibly converted to Catholicism) in Spain.
979/1571	The Ottomans are defeated at the naval battle of Lepanto, and their dominance in the Mediterranean is brought to a close.
1000/1591	Mustaʿlî Ismâʿîlî Shîʿî split into Sulaymânî and Dâʾûdî branches.
1012/1603	Ottomans defeated; Persia occupies Tabrîz, Mesopotamia, Mosul and Diyarbekr.
1014/1605	Death of the Mughal emperor Akbar.
1051/1641	Accession of Queen Tâj al-ʿÂlam in Indonesia.
1069/1658	Deposition of the Mughal emperor Shâh Jahân, accession of Aurangzeb.
1086/1675	Death of Queen Tâj al-ʿÂlam; accession of Queen Nûr al-ʿÂlam in Indonesia.
1089/1678	Death of Queen Nûr al-ʿÂlam, accession of Queen Inâyat Zakiyyah in Indonesia.
1095/1683	The Turks lift the siege of Vienna and retreat.
1100/1688	Death of Queen Inâyat Zakiyyah, accession of Queen Kamâlah in Indonesia.

1111/1699	Death of Queen Kamâlah in Indonesia.
1112/1700	Murshid Quli Khan declares the independence of Bengal and establishes his capital at Murshidabad.
1115/1703	Birth of Shâh Wâlî Allâh; birth of Muḥammad b. ʿAbd al-Wahhâb.
1119/1707	Death of the Mughal emperor Aurangzeb.
1131/1718	Austrians defeat the Ottomans and, by the treaty of Passarowich, Turkey loses Hungary.
1176/1762	Death of Shâh Walî Allâh.
1178/1764	Conversion to Islam of Areadi Gaya, ruler of Futa Bandu state in West Sudan.
1204/1789	Napoleon captures Egypt.
1207/1792	Death of Ibn ʿAbd al-Wahhâb.
1219/1804	Usuman dan Fodio establishes Islamic state of Sokoto in Central Sudan.
1226/1811	Birth of Sayyid ʿAlî Muḥammad Shîrâzî, founder of Bâb movement; British occupy Indonesia.
1227/1812	Madînah captured by the Egyptians.
1228/1813	Mecca and Ṭâʾif captured by Egyptian forces and Saʿûdis expelled from Ḥijâz.
1232/1816	British withdraw from Indonesia, restoring it to the Dutch.
1233/1817	Death of Usuman dan Fodio.
1243/1827	Malaya becomes a preserve of the British according to Anglo-Netherland treaty in 1824.
1244/1828	Russia declares war against Turkey.
1245/1829	Treaty of Adrianople.
1246/1830	French forces land near Algiers and occupy Algeria, ending 313 years of Turkish rule.
1253/1837	Death of Ibn Idrîs.
1255/1839	Defeat of Turkey by the Egyptians in the battle of Nisibîn.
1256/1840	Quadruple alliance by the European powers forces Egypt to relinquish Syria.
1274/1857	British capture Delhi and eliminate Mughal rule in India after 332 years. This was also the end of 1,000 years of Muslim rule over India.
1293/1876	Britain purchases shares of the Suez Canal and becomes involved in Egyptian affairs.
1296/1878	Turkey relinquishes Cyprus to Britain.
1297/1879	Treaty of Berlin. Turkey loses four-fifths of its territory in Europe.
1299/1881	France invades Tunisia and the Bey acknowledges supremacy of France as a result of the treaty of Bardo.
1299/1881	Muḥammad Aḥmad declares himself Mahdî in northern Sudan.
1300/1882	Egypt comes under British military occupation.
1303/1885	Death of the Mahdî in Sudan five months after the occupation of Khartoum.
1313/1895	Death of Chirâgh ʿAlî.
1315/1897	Death of Jamâl ad-Dîn al-Afghânî.
1316/1898	Death of Sayyid Aḥmad Khân.
1317/1899	Fall of Mahdist state in the Sudan and its occupation by the British and Egyptians jointly.
1319/1901	ʿAbd al-ʿAzîz b. Saʿûd captures Riyadh.

1319/1901	French forces occupy Morocco.
1322/1904	Morocco becomes a French Protectorate under the Conference of Algeciras; the Persian constitution is promulgated.
1323/1905	The beginning of the Salafiyyah movement in Paris with its main sphere of influence in Egypt; death of Muḥammad ʿAbduh.
1325/1907	The beginning of the Young Turks movement in Turkey; Persia divided into Russian and British spheres of influence.
1326/1908	Revolution of Young Turks.
1331/1912	The beginning of the Muḥammadiyyah reform movement in Indonesia.
1333/1914	World War I begins.
1335/1916	Arab revolt against Ottoman (Turkish) rule. Lawrence of Arabia leads attacks on the Ḥijâz Railway.
1337/1918	Syria and Damascus become a French Protectorate; death of Malak Ḥifnî Nâṣif.
1337/1918	World War I ends on November 11.
1340/1921	ʿAbd Allâh b. Ḥusayn made King of Transjordan.
1340/1921	Fayṣal b. Ḥusayn is made King of Iraq.
1341/1922	Mustafa Kemal Atatürk abolishes the Ottoman Turkish sultanate.
1343/1924	The Turkish caliphate is abolished.
1343/1924	King ʿAbd al-ʿAzîz conquers Mecca and Madînah, which leads to the unification of the kingdoms of Najd and Ḥijâz.
1344/1925	Rezâ Khân seizes power in Persia and establishes the Pahlavi dynasty.
1345/1926	ʿAbd al-ʿAzîz b. Saʿûd assumes title of King of Najd and Ḥijâz.
1347/1928	Turkey is declared a secular state, adopts Latin alphabet.
1347/1928	Ḥasan al-Bannâʾ founds the Muslim Brotherhood.
1351/1932	Iraq granted independence by League of Nations.
1354/1935	Iran becomes the official name of Persia; death of Rashîd Riḍâ.
1355/1936	Death of Riẓâeddîn Fakhreddîn; increased Jewish immigration provokes widespread Arab–Jewish fighting in Palestine.
1357/1938	Death of Mustafa Kemal Atatürk.
1357/1938	Death of Muḥammad Iqbal.
1359/1939	World War II begins.
1359/1940	Death of Ibn Bâdîs.
1360/1941	British and Russian forces invade Iran and Rezâ Khân is forced to abdicate in favor of his son Muḥammad Rezâ Shâh in Iran.
1362/1943	Beginning of Zionist fighting in Palestine.
1364/1944	Death of Mawlânâ Muḥammad Ilyâs.
1364/1945	End of World War II; death of al-Marâghî.
1366/1946	Jordan, Lebanon, and Syria are granted independence from Britain and France.
1367/1947	Creation of Pakistan from Muslim majority area in India.
1368/1948	Creation of state of Israel. Arab armies suffer defeat in war with Israel.
1368/1948	Death of Muḥammad ʿAlî Jinnah.
1369/1949	Ḥasan al-Bannâʾ, leader of the Muslim Brotherhood, is assassinated.
1371/1951	Libya becomes independent.
1372/1952	King Fârûq of Egypt forced to abdicate.
1376/1956	Morocco becomes independent.

1376/1956	Tunisia becomes independent.
1377/1957	The Bey of Tunisia is deposed, and Bourguiba becomes president.
1377/1957	Enlargement of the *Ḥaram* in Mecca begins.
1382/1962	Algeria becomes independent.
1383/1963	Death of Shaykh Shaltût.
1385/1965	Malcolm X is assassinated.
1386/1966	Death of ʿAlî ʿAbd ar-Râziq; death of Sayyid Quṭb.
1388/1968	The enlargement of the *Ḥaram* in Mecca is completed.
1389/1969	King Idris of Libya is ousted by a coup led by Colonel Qadhdhâfî.
1395/1975	Death of Elijah Muḥammad, leader of Nation of Islam among African Americans in North America.
1395/1975	Wallace Warith Deen Mohammed assumes leadership of Nation of Islam and shifts movement toward Islamic orthodoxy, renaming it American Muslim Mission.
1399/1978	Mûsâ aṣ-Ṣadr is apparently assassinated after he disappears on a trip to Libya. He was the religious leader of the Lebanese Ithnâ ʿAshariyyah Shîʿî and promoted the resurgence of Shîʿî in Lebanon and set the foundation of Amal.
1399/1979	The *shâh* leaves Iran on January 15, thus bringing the Pahlavi dynasty to an end; beginning of Islamic Republic in Iran; on 1 Muḥarram AH 1400/November 21, the first day of the fifteenth Islamic century, students of the Theological University of Medina unsuccessfully attempt to promote one of their group as Mahdî; death of Mawdûdî.
1400/1980	Beginning of the Iran–Iraq war; death of Muḥammad Rezâ Shâh Pahlavi; death of Muḥammad Bâqir aṣ-Ṣadr.
1402/1981	Death of Asaf ʿAli Asghar Fyzee; death of Ṭabâṭabâʾî.
1407/1986	Death of Ismâʿîl and Lois Fârûqî
1410/1989	Iran–Iraq war ends; death of Khomeinî; death of Fazlur Rahman.
1411/1990	Military annexation of Kuwait by Iraq, under Iraqî Saddâm Ḥusayn, is reversed in 1991 by a coalition of United States-led forces.
1413/1992	Death of Abol-Qâsem Khoʾi.

Bibliography

Encyclopaedia of Islam, 2nd edn. Edited by H.A.R. Gibb et al. Leiden, E.J. Brill, 1960–

Shorter Encyclopaedia of Islam. Edited by H.A.R. Gibb and J.H. Kramers. Ithaca, N.Y., Cornell University Press, 1953

Index Islamicus 1906–1955. J.D. Pearson and J.F. Ashton. Cambridge, Cambridge University Press, 1958. Subsequent volumes cover the years 1956–1960, 1961–1965, 1966–1970, 1971–1975, 1976–1980, and then quarterly from 1977 to date. See also 1998 *Index Islamicus on CD-ROM*. London; New Providence, N.J., Bowker-Saur

Islamic Foundation (Great Britain) and International Institute of Islamic Thought. *Index of Islamic literature*. [Leicester, U.K.] Islamic Foundation, 1996

Adamec, L.W. *Historical Dictionary of Islam*. Lanham, Md., Scarecrow Press, 2001

Anees, M.A. and A.N. Athar *Guide to Sira and Hadith Literature in Western Languages*. London; New York, Mansell, 1986

Esposito, J.L. (ed.) *The Oxford Encyclopedia of the Modern Islamic World*, 4 vols. Oxford, Oxford University Press, 1995

Federspiel, H.M. *A Dictionary of Indonesian Islam*. Athens, OH, Ohio University Center for International Studies, 1955

Haron, M., South African Library, *et al. Muslims in South Africa, an Annotated Bibliography*. Cape Town, South African Library in association with Centre for Contemporary Islam, UCT, 1997

Nanji, A.A. *The Muslim Almanac: A Reference Work on the History, Faith, Culture and Peoples of Islam*. Detroit, Gale Research, 1996

Robinson, F. *Atlas of the Islamic World Since 1500*. New York, Facts on File, 1982

Roolvink, R. *Historical Atlas of the Muslim Peoples*. Amsterdam, Djambatan, 1957

Islamic Religion

Ahmed, K. *The Sacred Journey Being Pilgrimage to Makkah*. New York, Duell, Sloan, & Pearce, 1961

Ahmad, I. *Ritual and Religion Among Muslims in India*. New Delhi, Manohar, 1981

Arberry, A.J. *The Koran Interpreted: A Translation*. New York, Macmillan, 1955

—— *Religion in the Middle East: The Religions in Concord and Conflict*, 2 vols. London, Cambridge University Press, 1969

—— *Sufism: An Account of the Mystics of Islam*. London, George Allen & Unwin, 1950

Baldick, J. *Mystical Islam: An Introduction to Sufism*. New York, New York University Press, 1989
Bowker, J.W. *What Muslims Believe*. Oxford, Oneworld, 1998
Bulliet, R.W. *Islam: The View from the Edge*. New York, Columbia University Press, 1994
Cragg, K. *The Call of the Minaret*. Oxford, Oneworld, 2000
—— *The Event of the Qur'ân: Islam in its Scripture*. Oxford, Oneworld, 1994
Cragg, K. and R.M. Speight *The House of Islam*. Belmont, Calif., Wadsworth Publishing Co., 1998
Denny, F.M. *An Introduction to Islam*. New York, Macmillan Publishing Co., 1994
Denny, F.M., A.A. Sachedina, *et al. Islamic Ritual Practices*. [New York], American Council of Learned Societies, 1983
Farah, C.E. *Islam: Beliefs and Observances*. Woodbury, N.Y., Barron's Educational Series, 1970
Gätje, H. *The Qur'an and its Exegesis: Selected Texts with Classical and Modern Interpretation*, trans. A.T. Welch. Oxford, Oneworld, 1996
Gaudefroy-Demombynes, M. *Muslim Institutions*. Westport, Conn., Greenwood Press, 1984
Geertz, C. *Islam Observed: Religious Development in Morocco and Indonesia*. Chicago, University of Chicago Press, 1971
Graham, W.A. *Beyond the Written Word: Oral Aspects of Scripture in the History of Religion*. Cambridge, Cambridge University Press, 1987
Izutsu, T. *The Concept of Belief in Islamic Theology*. New York, Books for Libraries, 1980
Jomier, J. *How to Understand Islam*. New York, Crossroad, 1989
Khan, M.Z. *Muhammad, Seal of the Prophets*. London, Routledge & Kegan Paul, 1980
Knight, K. *Islamic Festivals*. Crystal Lake, Ill., Heinemann Library, 1997
Kurzman, C. *Liberal Islam: A Sourcebook*. New York, Oxford University Press, 1998
Lawrence, B. *Defenders of God*. San Francisco, Harper & Row, 1989
Levtzion, N. *Conversion to Islam*. New York, Holmes & Meier, 1979
Martin, R.C. *Islam, a Cultural Perspective*. Englewood Cliffs, N.J., Prentice-Hall, 1982
—— *Islam in Local Contexts*. Leiden, E.J. Brill, 1982
Martin, R.C. *Islamic Studies, A History of Religious Approach*, 2nd edn. Upper Saddle River, N.J., Prentice-Hall, 1982
Martin, R.C. and Arizona State University. Dept. of Humanities and Religious Studies *Approaches to Islam in Religious Studies*. Oxford, Oneworld, 2001
Maudoodi, S.A.A. *Islam Today*. Karachi, Islami Jamiat-e-Talaba, 1963
Maudoodi, S.A.A. and K. Ahmad *Towards Understanding Islam*. London, Islamic Foundation, 1980
Maudoodi, S.A.A., K. Murad, *et al. The Islamic Way of Life*. Leicester, Islamic Foundation, 1986
Nasr, S.H. *Ideals and Realities of Islam*. Boston, Beacon Press, 1972
—— *Islamic Spirituality: Foundations*. New York, Crossroad, 1987
Nicholson, R.A. *The Mystics of Islam*. London; Boston, Routledge & Kegan Paul, 1979
Pickthall, M.M. *The Meaning of the Glorious Koran: A Bilingual Edition with English Translation, Introduction and Notes*. Albany, N.Y., State University of New York Press, 1976

Rahman, F. *Islam*, 2nd edn. Chicago, University of Chicago Press, 1979
Robinson, N. *Islam: A Concise Introduction*. Richmond, Curzon, 1999
Rodinson, M. *Islam and Capitalism*. New York, Pantheon, 1974
Schimmel, A. *Islam: an Introduction*. Albany, State University of New York Press, 1992
—— *Mystical Dimensions of Islam*. Chapel Hill, University of North Carolina Press, 1975
Tayob, A. *Islam: a Short Introduction: Signs, Symbols and Values*. Oxford, Oneworld, 1999
Trimingham, J.S. *The Sufi Orders in Islam*. Oxford, Clarendon Press, 1971
Watt, W.M. *Bell's Introduction to the Qur'an*. Edinburgh, Edinburgh University Press, 1970
—— *Muhammad, Prophet and Statesman*. London, Oxford University Press, 1964
Zia Ullah, M. *Islamic Concept of God*. London; Boston, Kegan Paul International, 1999

Historical Studies

The Cambridge History of Islam. Cambridge, Cambridge University Press, 1977
Adeleye, M.I.O. *A Handbook of Islam for Schools and Colleges*. [Lagos], Macmillan Nigeria Publishers Ltd., 1985
Ahmed, A.S. *Islam Today: A Short Introduction to the Muslim World*. London, New York, I.B. Tauris Publishers, 1999
Arberry, A.J. and R. Landau *Islam To-day*. London, Faber & Faber Ltd., 1943
Arnold, T.W. and A. Guillaume *The Legacy of Islam*. London, Oxford University Press, 1931
Bravmann, R.A. *African Islam*. Washington, D.C., Smithsonian Institution Press; London, Ethnographica, 1985
Brelvi, M. *Islam in Africa*. Lahore, Institute of Islamic Culture, 1964
Clarke, P.B. *West Africa and Islam: A Study of Religious Development from the 8th to the 20th Century*. London, E. Arnold, 1985
Cook, M.A. *Muhammad*. New York; Oxford, Oxford University Press, 1983
Corbin, H. *History of Islamic Philosophy*. London; New York, Kegan Paul International, 1993
Daniel, N. *Islam and the West: The Making of an Image*. Oxford, Oneworld, 1993
Dozy, R.P.A. *Spanish Islam: A History of the Moslems in Spain*. London, Frank Cass, 1972
Esposito, J.L. *Islam in Asia: Religion, Politics, and Society*. New York, Oxford University Press, 1987
—— *Islam and Politics*. [Syracuse, N.Y.], Syracuse University Press, 1991
—— *Islam: The Straight Path*. New York, Oxford University Press, 1991
—— *Voices of Resurgent Islam*. New York, Oxford University Press, 1983
Al-Faruqi, I. and L.I. Al-Faruqi. *Cultural Atlas of Islam*. New York, Macmillan, 1986
Firestone, R. *Jihâd: The Origin of Holy War in Islam*. New York, Oxford University Press, 1999
Friedmann, Y., R. Israeli, *et al. Islam in Asia*. Jerusalem, Magnes Press Jerusalem University; Boulder, Colo., Westview Press, 1984
Haddad, Y.Y. *Contemporary Islam and the Challenge of History*. Albany, State University of New York Press, 1982

Haddad, Y.Y., University of Massachusetts at Amherst Dept. of History, *et al. The Muslims of America*. New York, Oxford University Press, 1991

Haleem, H.A. *Islam and the Environment*. London, Ta-Ha Publishers, 1998

Harries, L. *Islam in East Africa*. London, Universities' Mission to Central Africa, 1954

Hasan, A.G. *American Muslims: The New Generation*. New York, Continuum, 2000

Hiskett, M. *The Development of Islam in West Africa*. New York, Longman, 1984

Hodgson, M.G.S. The Classical Age of Islam. In *The Venture of Islam: Conscience and History in World Civilization*. Chicago, University of Chicago Press, 1974

—— The Expansion of Islam in the Middle Periods. In *The Venture of Islam: Conscience and History in World Civilization*. Chicago, University of Chicago Press, 1974

—— The Gunpowder Empires and Modern Times. In *The Venture of Islam: Conscience and History in World Civilization*. Chicago, University of Chicago Press, 1974

Hooker, M.B. and University of Kent at Canterbury. *Islam in South-East Asia*. Leiden, E.J. Brill, 1983

Insoll, T. *Archaeology of Islam*. Oxford, Blackwell, 1999

Lapidus, I.M. *A History of Islamic Societies*. Cambridge; New York, Cambridge University Press, 1988

Lewis, I.M. *Islam in Tropical Africa*. Bloomington, International African Institute in association with Indiana University Press, 1980

Mahmud, S.F. *A Short History of Islam*. Karachi, Pakistan Branch Oxford University Press, 1960

Makdisi, G. *The Rise of Colleges: Institutions of Learning in Islam and the West*. Edinburgh, Edinburgh University Press, 1981

—— *The Rise of Humanism in Classical Islam and the Christian West With Special Reference to Scholasticism*. Edinburgh, Edinburgh University Press, 1990

Mez, A. *The Renaissance of Islam*. New York, AMS Press, 1975

Momen, M. *An Introduction to Shi'i Islam: the History and Doctrines of Twelver Shi'ism*. New Haven; London, Yale University Press, 1985

Mortimer, E. *Faith and Power: the Politics of Islam*. New York, Vintage Books, 1982

Mottahedeh, R.P. *The Mantle of the Prophet: Religion and Politics in Iran*. Oxford, Oneworld, 2000

Nasr, S.H. *Science and Civilization in Islam*. Cambridge, Mass., Harvard University Press, 1968

Newby, G.D. *The Making of the Last Prophet*. Columbia, University of South Carolina Press, 1989

Nonneman, G., T. Niblock, *et al. Muslim Communities in the New Europe*. Reading (UK), Ithaca Press, 1996

Peters, F.E. *Children of Abraham: Judaism, Christianity, Islam*. Princeton, N.J., Princeton University Press, 1982

Peters, R. *Jihad in Classical and Modern Islam: A Reader*. Princeton, Markus Wiener, 1996

Raitt, J. *Islam in the Modern World*. Columbia, Mo., University of Missouri, 1984.

Roy, A. *Islam in South Asia: A Regional Perspective*. New Delhi, South Asian Publishers, 1996

Ruthven, M. *Islam in the World*. Harmondsworth, Penguin, 1984

Said, E.W. *Covering Islam: How the Media and the Experts Determine how we See the Rest of the World*. New York, Pantheon, 1981

Schacht, J., C.E. Bosworth, *et al. The Legacy of Islam*. Oxford, Clarendon Press, 1974

Schimmel, A. *Islam in the Indian Subcontinent*. Leiden; Köln, E.J. Brill, 1980

—— *Islam in India and Pakistan*. Leiden, E.J. Brill, 1982

Smith, J.I. *Islam in America*. New York, Columbia University Press, 1999

Smith, W.C. *On Understanding Islam: Selected Studies*. The Hague; New York, Mouton, 1981

Trimingham, J.S. *A History of Islam in West Africa*. London; New York, published for the University of Glasgow by the Oxford University Press, 1970

—— *The Influence of Islam upon Africa*. New York, Praeger, 1968

—— *Islam in East Africa*. Oxford, Clarendon Press, 1964

—— *Islam in West Africa*. Oxford; New York, Clarendon Press, 1961

—— *The Sufi Orders in Islam*. Oxford, Clarendon Press, 1971

Watt, W.M. *Islamic Philosophy and Theology*. Edinburgh, Edinburgh University Press, 1967

Islamic Art

Dodds, J.D., Metropolitan Museum of Art New York, *et al. al-Andalus: The Art of Islamic Spain*. New York, Metropolitan Museum of Art, distributed by H.N. Abrams, 1992

Ettinghausen, R. and O. Grabar *The Art and Architecture of Islam, 650–1250*. Harmondsworth, Penguin; New York, Viking Penguin, 1987

Grabar, O. *The Formation of Islamic Art*. New Haven, Yale University Press, 1973

Hillenbrand, R. *Islamic Art and Architecture*. London, Thames & Hudson, 1999

Kuhnel, E. *Islamic Art and Architecture*, trans. K. Watson, London, G. Bell & Sons, 1966

—— *The Minor Arts of Islam*, trans. K. Watson, Ithaca, Cornell University Press, 1970

Rice, D.T. *Islamic Art*. London, Thames & Hudson, 1965

Ry van Beest Holle, C.J. *Art of Islam*. New York, H.N. Abrams, 1970

Islamic Internet Resources

www.understanding-islam.com/
www.al-islam.org/
www.ummah.net/
www.unn.ac.uk/societies/islamic/
www.discoverislam.com/
www.emuslim.com/
www.msa-natl.org/
www.iad.org/
www.hti.umich.edu/k/koran/
www.stg.brown.edu/webs/quran_browser/pqeasy.shtml
etext.virginia.edu/koran.html
www.unn.ac.uk/societies/islamic/quran/naeindex.htm
www.audiokoran.com/
www.efarsi.org/arabic/a_quran.html
www.kuwait.net/~akar/html/koran.html
www.iiu.edu.my/deed/quran/index.html
www.quran.org.uk/
www.the-webplaza.com/hajj/
hajj.al-islam.com/
www.hajj.org/
www.ummah.net/hajj/
www.prophetmuhammed.org/

Thematic Index

Books and writings

Alf laylah wa-laylah
injîl
al-Manâr
Nahj al-balâgha
Pandiyât-i jawânmardî
Qur'ân
ṣaḥîfah
sîrah
sûrah
tawrât
zabûr

Languages

Aljamia
Arabic
khojkî
Persian
Turkish
Urdu

Beliefs

Allâh
Allâhummah
angels
'ankabût
'aqîdah
'aqrab
al-'asharah al-mubashsharah
'ayn
al-burhân
clitoridectomy
ad-Dajjâl
dunyâ
fanâ'
ghaybah
'iṣmah
muḥâsabah
Munkar wa-Nakîr
nafs
Pillars of Islam

Terms and concepts

'abd, 'Abd
abortion
adab
adoption
afterlife
'aha
ahl al-ahwâ'
ahl al-bayt
ajal
al-âkhirah
âkhûnd
'âlam
'Alî ilâhî
'âlimah
amîn
âmîn
amîr
Amîr al-Mu'minîn
amr
'aql
architecture
'aṣabiyyah
'askarî
astrology
'âyah

Tanẓîmât
tanzîl
taqdîr
taqiyyah
taqwâ
taṣawwuf
tashbîh
tawbah
tawḥîd
ta'wîl
tribe
'ulamâ'
'ummah
'ummî
waḥy
al-wakâlah al-'âmmah
walî
waswâs
wazîr
yawm ad-dîn
yawm al qiyâmah
yawm al-jum'ah
ẓâhir
az-zaqqûm
zindîq
zuhd
'ẓulm

Festivals

Bairam, or Bayram
Ramaḍân

Groups and organizations

'Abbâsids
ABIM
'Âd
Afsharids
ahl al-kitâb
ahl al-ṣuffa
ahl-i ḥadîth
ahl-i ḥaqq
Ahmadiyah, or Aḥmadiyyah
'Alawids
'Alawiyyah
All-India Muslim League
Amal
'ânâniyyah
anṣâr
'Arab
ar-râfîdah
aṣḥâb al-kahf
aṣḥâb al-ukhdûd
aṣḥâb ar-rass
Assassins
Avrupa Milli Görüş Teşkilati
Awami League
al-'Aws
Ayyûbids
Ba'th Parties
Bâbî, Bâbism
Bahâ'î
Bairamiyya
Banû Isrâ'îl
Baqliyyah
Barelwis
Bektâshî, or Bektâshiyyah
bohra, or *bohorâ*
Burhâniyya
Chishtiyyah
Conseil National des Français Musulmans
Dar Ul Arqam
Darul Islam
Deobandis
dhimmî
Druze
Durrânîs
Fâṭimids
Fédération Nationale des Musulmans de France
Fidâ'iyyân-i Islâm
futuwwah
Ghassânids
ghâzî
ghûlât
Ḥâfiẓiyyah
Ḥamâs
Hâshimites
Hâshimiyyah
Ḥizb ad-Da'wah al-Islâmiyyah
ḥizb Allâh
Ḥizb al-Nahḍah
Ḥizb at-Tahrîr al-Islâmî
Ḥizbullâh
Ḥujjatiyyah
Ibâḍiyyah, also Abâḍiyyah
Idrîsiyyah
ifranj

Cultural items

Legal terms and concepts

Places and geographic locations

Persons

al-Qushayrî, Abû al-Qâsim 'Abd al-Karîm b. Hawâzin
Quṭb, Sayyid
Râbi'ah al-'Adawiyyah
Râḥîl
Rahman, Fazlur
Rashîd Riḍâ, Muḥammad
Rayḥânah bt. Zayd
Riḍwân
Rûmî, Jalâl ad-Dîn
Ruqayyah bt. Muḥammad
aṣ-Ṣadr, Muḥammad Bâqir
aṣ-Ṣadr, Mûsâ
Ṣafiyyah bt. Ḥuyayy
Ṣâliḥ
Salmân al-Fârisî
as-sâmirî
Sârah, or Sârâ
Sawdah bt. Zam'ah
ash-Shâfi'î, Muḥammad b. Idrîs
Shaltût, Maḥmûd
Shams ad-Dîn Muḥammad
Shayṭân
Shu'ayb
Sirhindî, Ahmad
Sulaymân
as-Suyûṭî, Jalâl ad-Dîn
aṭ-Ṭabarî, Abû Ja'far Muḥammad b. Jarîr
Ṭabâṭabâ'î, Muḥammad Ḥusayn
Ṭâlût
at-Tirmidhî, Abû 'Îsâ Muḥammad
'Umar b. 'Abd al-'Azîz
'Umar b. al-Khaṭṭâb
'Umm Ḥabîbah
'Umm Kulthûm
'Umm Salamah
'Uthmân b. 'Affân
'Uzayr
al-'Uzzâ
Walî Allâh, Shâh
al-Wâqidî, Abû 'Abd Allâh Muhammad
Waraqah b. Nawfal
Wâṣil b. 'Aṭâ'
Yaḥyâ
Ya'jûj wa-Ma'jûj
Ya'qûb
Yûsuf
al-zabâniyyah
Zakariyyah
az-Zamakhsharî, Abû al-Qâsim, Maḥmûd b. 'Umar
Zayd b. Thâbit
Zaynab bt. Jaḥsh
Zaynab bt. Khuzaymah
Zulaykhâ

Ritual terms and concepts

ablution
al-'asmâ' al-ḥusnâ
'aqîqah
'Âshûrâ'
'awrah
birth rites
dawsah
dhikr
Dhû-l-Ḥijjah
funerary rites
ghusl
ḥadath
ḥajj
ḥusayniyyah
'Îd al-Aḍḥâ
'Îd al-Fiṭr
i'tikâf
ifṭâr
iḥrâm
istinjâ'
istinshâq
janâbah
kaffârah
mîḍâ'ah, or *mîḍa'ah*
mîqât
miswâk
muṭawwif
Nawrûz
puberty rites
purification
rajm
Rawzah khvânî
ṣadaqah
ṣawm
sacrifice
sa'y
saḥûr
samâ'
shahâdah
ṭahârah
ṭawâf

Ta'ziyah
tajwîd
tasbîḥ
tayammum
waẓîfah
wuḍû'
wuqûf
ziyârah

Prayer terms and concepts

adhân
aẓ-ẓuhr
du'â'
istisqâ'
khuṭbah
miḥrâb
minaret
mu'adhdhin
namâzgâh
qiblah
rak'ah
ṣalât
ṣalât al-janâzah
sajjâdah
subḥah
sujûd
tarâwîḥ
witr